THE

SOCIAL

WORKER

AS

MANAGER

THEORY AND PRACTICE

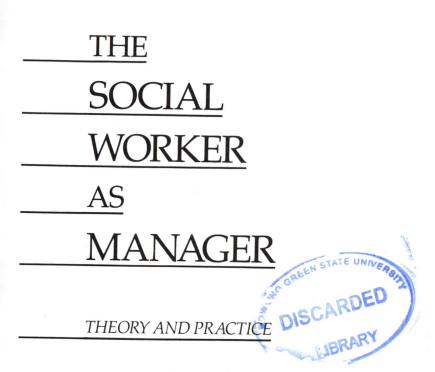

ROBERT W. WEINBACH

University of South Carolina

Longman

New York & London

The Social Worker as Manager: Theory and Practice

Copyright © 1990 by Longman, a division of Addison-Wesley Publishing Co., Inc.
All rights reserved.
No part of this publication may be reproduced, stored
in a retrieval system, or transmitted in any form
or by any means, eletronic, mechanical, photocopying,
recording, or otherwise, without the prior permission
of the publisher.

Longman, 95 Church Street, White Plains, N.Y. 10601
A division of Addison-Wesley Publishing Co., Inc.

Associated companies:
Longman Group Ltd., London
Longman Cheshire Pty., Melbourne
Longman Paul Pty., Auckland
Copp Clark Pitman, Toronto
Pitman Publishing Inc., New York

This book is dedicated with appreciation to two people who demonstrated both sensitivity and innate management skill while working within their chosen vocations—Lydia M. Weinbach and William J. Weinbach, DDS.

Senior Editor: David J. Estrin
Production Editor: Camilla T.K. Palmer
Cover Design: Susan J. Moore
Text Art: K + S Graphics
Production Supervisor: Kathleen Ryan

Library of Congress Cataloging-in-Publication Data

Weinbach, Robert W.
 The social worker as manager: theory and practice/by Robert W. Weinbach
  p.   cm.
 Includes bibliograhies and index.
 ISBN 0-8013-0042-8
 1. Social work administration—United States. I. Title.
HV95.W43   1990
361.3′068—dc 19   88-27132
                                                                    CIP

ISBN 0-8013-0042-8

ABCDEFGHIJ-AL-99   98   97   96   95   94   93   92   91   90

Contents

Preface

The teacher and student of management theory can choose from a wide assortment of writings. Many good books exist on the subject. Most have been written either by theorists in the field of business or by managers and academicians in the human service professions. They offer valuable insights, particularly for the administrator of large public and private social agencies. The obvious question is, What makes this book unique and how does its perspective differ from others?

The text has been written with certain assumptions that I have found useful over the years in demystifying management for students. These include:

1. Management is most readily understood and appreciated if perceived as a group of activities that all social workers perform daily. It is not the exclusive domain of those who occupy the highest levels on the organizational chart. Some practitioners who carry the title of manager, director, or administrator may spend the majority of their workday managing. But others who carry the titles of coordinator or supervisor are also required to manage. They may divide their day more evenly between managing activities and other activities. Still others who may be called caseworkers, therapists, or, simply, social workers will spend most of their day in offering direct services to individual clients, families, or groups, but they still will be required to perform management functions many different times throughout the day. Whether a social worker ultimately assumes a position as a manager or not in the course of his or her professional career (and most will), this person will need to understand and to become competent in the management tasks of planning, staffing, organizing, controlling, and leading.

2. The activities of management are a natural extension of the knowledge, values, and skills possessed by the social worker. An understanding of the dynamics of human behavior, an appreciation of all people as unique individuals, a recognition of the importance of fairness and objectivity in human interaction—these are only a few examples of characteristics possessed by social workers that greatly facilitate the performing of management functions. Although, on rare occasions, being a social worker in the role of manager may result in a problem or conflict, the attributes of a social worker are more likely to be an asset in meeting the requirements of the role. Management is much more a people skill than a technical one. It is much more similar to social work practice than it is dissimilar to it.

3. Knowledge derived from research on management that has been conducted in the corporate world is not always applicable to the needs of the social worker as manager. But a good amount of it, with a little translation, has much to teach us. Many useful insights are to be found in today's literature of business and organization theory, but also in the literature of 20, 30, or even 40 years ago.

4. There is a wide variety of approaches to management tasks that can be effective. The human characteristics and personality of the manager and of other staff as well as the specific requirements of the situation will suggest a decision or behavior that may be successful in one instance but is likely to result in failure in another. Social work students beginning their study of management require broad insights into management activities and an understanding of issues and variables that impact on their role. The technical skills such as budgeting, policy development, and grant writing are more appropriate for advanced courses on management or for specialized seminars on these topics.

Which students would be most likely to find this book useful and appropriate for their learning needs? It has been written so that it is ideally suited for a generic, one-term course in management in BSW or MSW programs. It provides a broad base of knowledge that is equally appropriate for use by the future clinician, for the group-treatment specialist, or for students preparing for work in any other practice specialization. It also is suitable for use as a first course introduction to management for students anticipating a career in mid-level management or as social agency administrators.

The text is organized into 13 chapters, each appropriate as a course unit. The chapters are grouped into three sections but are designed to be studied in sequence. Later chapters occasionally refer to and build upon content presented in earlier ones.

Through the use of numerous case examples to illustrate management principles, I have tried to keep the study of management as it ought to be, interesting and intellectually stimulating. References have been kept to a minimum to avoid interrupting the flow of the text any more than is absolutely necessary. The student who wants to read more about the subject of a chapter should find the "Additional Readings" at the end of each chapter a useful place to begin.

The relatively small number of bibliographical references used is in no way meant to discount the contributions of others to this book. In many instances, it was a researcher/author, a student, or a colleague who was the inspiration for an idea or way of conceptualizing a management situation. A number of managers that I have known have also influenced the ideas about management that are reflected in the pages that follow. They are Ethel R. Brady, Mary Frances Danner, O. Norman Evans, Joseph I. Hungate Jr., Frank B. Raymond III, and Mario Urdaneta.

Three graduate assistants have contributed their library skills and their candid assessments of the book's content. They are June Beasley, Jo Coleman Hancock, and Jim Taylor. Sheryl Epperly typed the manuscript. Her knowledgeable assistance was absolutely essential to the book's timely completion. Colleagues John Poertner and John Tropman reviewed an earlier draft and made many valuable suggestion for revisions. I deeply appreciate the contributions of all of the above individuals.

Robert W. Weinbach
University of South Carolina
1988

PART I

Understanding Social Work Management

In order to develop a clear understanding of management and the forms that it takes in social work practice, we approach the topic from several different angles. In Chapter 1 we begin by clearing away some misperceptions about management that seem to characterize some of the thinking that exists among social work professionals. Having done so, we work toward a definition of management that accurately reflects its richness and its complexity.

Chapter 2 examines the similarities and differences that exist between business and human service organizations and how they affect the management functions of the social worker. The concepts of the task environment and of the prime beneficiary are introduced; they will be central to our discussion of management throughout this text. Another concept familiar to the social worker, namely values, is proposed as critical to an understanding of differences that exist between nonprofit and profit-oriented organizations. The values gap is beginning to close as businesses are discovering the importance of human factors and as human service agencies have had to become more businesslike. But important differences that make social work management unique continue to abound.

In Chapter 3 we review the legacy of management theory that continues to influence management behaviors today. Classical management theories are examined. Both their contributions to current thought and their areas of limited relevance are identified.

CHAPTER 1

The Need for Management

Human service organizations are multibillion dollar businesses. They are an integral part of the economy of all nations in the Western Hemisphere. This fact alone suggests the need for good management and for a study of relevant theory. But for the social worker, there is another and more compelling reason to study management. We are committed to providing the best possible services to clients. Good management, accomplished at all levels, contributes greatly to achieving this objective.

Students who are planning for a career as a higher-level administrator in a human service organization readily recognize the need for studying the topic of management. But others who have no immediate plans to become a "boss" or for whom direct client contact is a major source of gratification may have more difficulty in understanding why the study of management is relevant to their professional goals. This occurs primarily because management is so often misunderstood. Even the word *management* itself connotes several different images. It is sometimes used as a proper noun ("Management") in referring collectively to a few people who occupy the highest positions on the organizational chart within an organization. It is also frequently used as a verb to suggest a wide range of activities that, in human-service organizations, can be virtually anything that does not constitute treatment services to clients. As we will use the term, management consists of specific activities performed by social workers at all administrative levels within human service organizations. It is an important part of social work practice that deserves the careful attention of all present and future social practitioners. In this chapter we will begin by endeavoring to dispel some of the mistaken ideas that social workers have about management and that seem to get in the way of a productive relationship with it. Then we will look at what management really is and how it contributes to client service.

COMMON MYTHS ABOUT MANAGEMENT

It is our experience that social workers hold many mistaken ideas about management that lead to destructive attitudes and practices. Let us look at a few of the more common ones.

Myth No. 1: Management Is the Work of Managers

If we believe this myth, we are inevitably led to several erroneous conclusions. First, it implies that management is the sole responsibility of a certain elite group of "senior" individuals within an organization. They may be called directors, administrators, or (unfortunately, for our purposes) managers. The myth leads to the conclusion that there is a distinct division of labor—managers manage, supervisors supervise, direct-service practitioners deliver services, etc. For example, if we are a caseworker, it suggests that we should want little more than to be left alone to see our clients. Let *them* handle the management, and *we'll* do the service delivery. A "we-they" dichotomy can readily occur.

As problems and frustrations arise on the job, as they inevitably will, a logical response is to blame those high up in the administrative hierarchy. An adversarial relationship, rather than a cooperative one, quickly develops. People who don't perceive themselves as managers don't understand what *they* (managers) do, and they generally don't want to know until it somehow impinges on their ability to do *their* jobs. Then these individuals blame *them* (managers) and make all kinds of accusations that *they* are insensitive to client needs, obsessed with efficiency, out of touch with social work practice, etc. Not surprisingly, staff ignorance of that mysterious activity called management leads to suspicion and assumptions that *they* must possess a different set of values and priorities.

Viewing management as the work of managers does more than allow us to blame any misfortune or unhappy circumstance on the mismanagement of a few higher-level individuals. (Our hostility is further fueled by the fact that they probably make more money, have a more glamorous title, and enjoy more status in the community than most other employees.) The myth also relieves anyone except those bearing management titles of any responsibility for performing management functions. Actually, as we will discuss a little later, no one can relinquish this responsibility, even if one chooses. But there exists the dangerous perception that a nonmanager's tasks are limited to nonmanagement functions and that they cannot be held accountable for any mismanagement within the agency or organization.

Another dangerous conclusion that follows from Myth No. 1 is that all activities of those called managers or administrators or directors are, by definition, management. Clearly, eating lunch, talking to a friend on the phone, or scratching a part of one's anatomy are common to employees in all job titles—no one would suggest that they constitute management activities despite the fact that they occur during the workday and are performed by individuals who hold management titles. No problem here. But there is a dangerous spin-off from the conclusion that the role of management is synonymous with the function of management. It relates to the "grayer" areas of activity that are neither shared by all persons nor clearly those performed as management. They *might* be management activities evolving from the role of manager. But they also *might not* be. Influencing the work of others, as we shall discuss, is the primary business of management. If other staff members mistakenly perceive a higher-level employee to be giving an order based on his or her occupation of the role of manager, they will be inclined to follow, even though it may not have been the superior's intention. For example, the manager will be assumed to be performing management in other situations when he or she was merely expressing a personal preference, responding subjectively to a situation, emoting as a human being, or simply meeting an individual need. Like any other employee, higher-level managers are entitled to and will inevitably spend a sizable portion of their day in behaviors that are not, strictly speaking, their primary function. But it is easy to see the potential danger that develops when *all* of a person's activities are assumed to be management. Communication can be seriously impaired as others tend to respond to the role without regard to the person occupying it.

Myth No. 2: Management Has Little Effect on Services

There exists the mistaken idea among many social workers (short of gross mismanagement, usually within the fiscal area) that the quality of client services is little affected by management decisions and practices. The belief is that competent direct-service workers can insulate themselves from management and go about their business. A corollary idea would be that services are good, bad, or somewhere in-between, based totally on the skill level of those who deliver them. Management should consist of little more than hiring good people and leaving them alone.

This myth perpetuates the idea among both students of social work and direct practitioners that management is not *really* social work practice; that, as an activity not requiring face-to-face contact with clients or client groups, it cannot contribute to achievement of the profession's goals. This leads to statements such as, "I want to be a social worker, not a manager." Obviously, if we view an activity as outside the mainstream of professional practice (research is often thought of in the same way), we value it less and tend to distance ourselves from it. We begin to believe that management functions derive from a different set of values and ethics that are sometimes in opposition to those of the social work profession. We tend to make certain assumptions about the motivation of those who make management decisions. This can result in antagonism and unnecessary conflict among those who are really working toward the same goals.

Myth No. 3: Management Is Just a Technical Skill

This myth is really somewhat similar to Myth No. 2, which tended to make some false assumptions about the values and professional identification of people involved in management. But Myth No. 3 suggests that the real business of management involves activities that place a high premium on certain sterile activities that appeal to those with characteristics not often seen among social work practitioners. It contends that management is "anti-people." It is basically a function that could be performed by a computer. It involves tasks like number crunching, flowcharting, formula plugging, and application of the laws of probability to empirical data. Technology, not human interaction, is valued above all else. This leads to the belief that management decision making is enhanced when managers remain isolated in their own mysterious world and relate to other personnel only as interchangeable parts. The interaction of roles, not persons, is central to this myth. Skills are learned; personality, art, and style find little place in the business of management. Management is a necessary evil performed by those who "sort of like that kind of thing." The implication is that it helps to be a little weird and removed from the rest of the world. An identification with social work and skill in professional practice are obstacles rather than assets to performing management tasks. After all, so the myth goes, social work practice and management have little or nothing in common.

Myth No. 4: Management Is Really Just the Application of Practice Skills

This myth is almost the opposite of the last one. It is also a very dangerous and prevalent one that has resulted in many of the problems that exist within social agencies. It assumes that management is only a "people skill." It leaps easily to viewing fellow employees as clients and encourages persons functioning as managers to treat them accordingly. It promotes the ignoring of a wealth of empirical knowledge that exists within fields like organizational theory and business because "what do *they* know about working with people?" A high premium is placed on relationships and interpersonal skills, not really a problem in itself. But this emphasis is accompanied by an anti-intellectual attitude toward the technical and theoretical contributions of those outside the profession.

Besides the fact that a belief in Myth No. 4 results in demeaning and annoying behavior (who wants to be "social worked" by a colleague?), it results in some very destructive personnel practices. It tends to promote a common practice within our field whereby good direct practitioners are rewarded by being granted more responsibility for management functions. If after some time they are judged as having performed well, they may assume yet another position in the organization where most of their time is spent in management and where they have little or no client contact. The assumption is that their practitioner skills are evidence of their capacity to do more management; a good practitioner will necessarily be good at management tasks *and vice versa*. Good practitioners should be "moved up" to where they can exert greater influence on what goes on within the organization. Their one-to-one, group, community organization and other skills will certainly serve them well in their role as manager. If a social worker is not chosen to move up or elects not to, it may be erroneously assumed that he or she must lack the interpersonal skills required of a competent practitioner.

DISPELLING THE MYTHS

The four myths noted above are by no means an exhaustive list. They also clearly overlap. But they are some of the most common and most destructive ones for the study and practice of management. They also help to explain why students sometimes fail to approach the study of management with much enthusiasm. If any of the myths were true, management understandably would be avoided by the kind of people who enter social work as a life's work.

The process of dispelling the myths should prove helpful in understanding our definition of management, one that we think is "user friendly" and unintimidating to the social worker. We will refute each myth and attempt to move toward some common understandings.

Correction: Management Is Everyone's Work

Certainly, people who carry the title of director, administrator, or manager are involved in management, but they have no monopoly on it. Supervisors and other middle-level employees manage too, primarily in their tasks of administrative supervision[1] but in other ways as well. Social workers who offer direct services manage their workday (time management), manage individual cases (case management), and engage in other management functions every hour of the day while on the job.

Management is neither a group of high-level staff *nor* activities that are the exclusive province of these elite individuals. Management, as we shall use the term in this text, is a word used to describe a specific group of important functions that are performed by *all* persons within a work setting. There appears to be no other term that is so widely accepted and appropriate for describing them, even though the word *management* carries with it a heavy baggage of misconception and misunderstanding. Complicating matters even further, it is frequently used arbitrarily and interchangeably with another term, *administration*, within the social work literature (see, for example, the content of any recent issue of the journal *Administration in Social Work*). All these problems aside, we will use the term *management* to describe certain functions performed at all levels and by all persons within human-service organizations.

The contention that, like it or not, all staff members "manage" within social work organizations, private practice, or the private sector does not suggest that all persons in these settings devote as much time to management or that their management activities all take the same specific form. In fact, those who carry titles such as director, administrator, or manager spend a large percentage of their time performing management functions, a much larger percentage than most people with the job title of supervisor. In turn, supervisors generally spend more of their time in management functions than do those with titles such as caseworker, therapist, or group worker. The basic functions, when they are performed at each level, are the same and can be categorized into four or five principal groupings. The specific tasks or activities that fall within these management functions, however, will often tend to look different when performed at the various staff levels. For example, organizing is a management function performed by all staff members within an organization. However, it might involve (among other things) the task of designing a system of client flow, from intake to discharge, for the person called *director*. The supervisor would need to organize his or her time to accommodate the supervisory needs of staff. Organizing for the casework counselor might include scheduling of home visits to minimize the amount of road travel required. All these individuals need to know how to organize and perform the managerial function of organizing, but their managerial tasks are obviously different.

The assertion that all staff members manage (or "do management") precludes the notion that only certain persons are held accountable for management within an organization. Individuals within an agency suffering from mismanagement—whatever that is—cannot simply blame the administration for their problems. They must all go through a period of self-examination and share the responsibility for management difficulties that exist.

Because everyone manages, a "we-they" dichotomy is not likely to occur. Although a caseworker may lack skills and insight into the long-range planning tasks of the director, there is no reason why that person cannot understand and experience the generic functions of planning. Both the mystery and some of the suspicion are less likely when we are all perceived as performing similar functions and understand, at least in a general sense, what each other is doing.

By acknowledging that some individuals do more managing than others —based in part on the role they occupy—and by observing that no one manages all the time, we can avoid the trap of concluding that whatever a person bearing a manager-sounding title does is, necessarily, a function of that person's role as manager. This leaves open the possibility that perhaps these people are acting as Mary Smith or Bill Jones, not Ms. Smith or Mr. Jones the Director. Suggestions are likely to be viewed as suggestions rather than directives from one "in charge." Of course, it is incumbent on those within higher levels of the organization to communicate clearly the difference between suggestions and directives. Our perception of management brings new communication responsibilities for the manager who intends to direct rather than suggest and vice versa.

Correction: Management Affects Services

Management is an integral part of social work practice. Management decision making at all levels can serve either to support or jeopardize the delivery of effective services. This occurs in both direct and subtle ways. Those decisions that determine how services will be delivered exert a direct effect. For example, policy decisions regarding the appropriate use of group services *vis-à-vis* individual counseling have clear implications for the treatment-success potential for a given client of the agency.

Research over the past few decades has also highlighted the importance of management style and management culture to service delivery. The climate within an organization and the attitudes of higher-level personnel toward lower-level staff, as reflected in management practices and decisions, may get played out again in the attitudes of direct-service workers toward their clients. Both flexibility and tolerance toward clients occur more frequently in organizations where higher-level management decision making also reflects flexibility than in settings where managers reflect a need for routinization in decision affecting staff.[2]

The best management practice in social agencies is probably carried out by those who possess not only a clear identification as social workers but also a clear understanding of the functions of management. Sound management decisions may sometimes appear to be in conflict with practice values. For example, the decision to refer rather than to treat clients diagnosed as alcoholic may appear on the surface to be in conflict with the "right to help" value of the profession, at least as it affects a given client. This decision may, however, be quite consistent with practice values emphasizing that the client is entitled to the best assistance available. It may also be reflective of the economic necessities for survival of the agency that are unknown to staff at all levels. If we can assume that all of us are both social workers *and* managers, we are less likely to conclude that we operate out of a different value base. Management is *a part of* social work practice, and, as such, it *cannot* be separated from services. It is illogical to say that decisions and activities that effect service delivery are somehow distinct from it.

Correction: Management Is More than Application of Technical Skills

If management were nothing more than the application of technical skills, we could easily train people to be managers. Once having learned the standard skills, people could be employed interchangeably to perform required management functions. Admittedly, there are management skills to be learned. For example, constructing a budget, writing a grant proposal, and developing a flowchart require specific, detailed instruction. Once the skills are acquired, they can be applied in a variety of situations with very few modifications needed. But while everyone can benefit from the acquisition of these skills, they are not in themselves a guarantee of success in management.

Within most work settings, an overreliance on technical skills is almost certain to result in problems for a manager. Unlike most people in business enterprises, we frequently work among a group of professional peers. There is no reason to assume that the expertise, insight, and judgment needed for any given decision are concentrated at the top. In fact, those most knowledgeable about a specific area of practice can exist among staff members anywhere in the hierarchy, and the manager needs to be able to tap their knowledge. This requires the use of interpersonal skills. Sensitivity to the behavior and attitudes of one's colleagues is probably far more critical to successful management than is the use of technical skills. We will place greater emphasis on the former in our study of management, acknowledging that, although technical skills are useful, they are better acquired in a hands-on training environment than through the reading of a textbook. Moreover, the person doing the managing and those with whom one must interact will be emphasized repeatedly as important considerations in management decision making and in the creation of an individualized management style.

Social workers who choose a position that requires that much of their day is spent in management will find that they use many of the same principles, insights, and knowledge as do social workers who devote much of their time to service delivery. What's more, many (but not all) of their practice skills will serve them well in their roles as managers. Social workers who take positions where much of their time is spent in management will look and act strikingly like other social workers and will share their values, ethics, and identity as professionals. However, there may be two notable differences. First, they might simply enjoy the tasks of management performed at the administrative level more than those management tasks required of the direct-service worker. Second, they may be less hesitant to give up direct contact with clients than are some of their colleagues.

Correction: Management Is More than Application of Practice Skills

If we were to approach the functions of management from the perspective that it requires interaction skills no different from those that are successful in work with clients, we would also be unsuccessful in management. Principles, not technological skills, should be adapted from direct practice.[3] *Too much* emphasis on the interpersonal can quickly antagonize staff members who can feel manipulated, treated as clients, or demeaned in some other way.

We also cheat ourselves as managers when we fail to take advantage of the wealth of relevant knowledge that has been generated by those outside of social work. This text relies heavily on the work of many people who may never have studied human-service organizations and who certainly would not identify themselves as social workers. Yet some of what they have learned has universal application to management within situations that exist within all work settings. The knowledge and theory of other fields, with a little translation and adaptation here and there, can provide us with valuable insights to assist in our management practices. While knowledge derived from empirical research conducted within the business sector is not inherently applicable to social agencies or social work private practice, neither is it inherently *inapplicable*. Contemporary business literature is often on the cutting edge of management theory. It is both controversial and exciting, and it provides the social worker with interesting reading while offering valuable assistance in performing the functions of the manager. We will examine some of the many theories and conceptualizations that seem to have something relevant to say to social workers in their roles as managers.

If we acknowledge that management is more than the application of social work intervention skills to management activities, it follows that a first-rate direct-service social worker may or may not be a good choice for another position that requires that a larger percentage of one's time be spent in management activities. First, the organization may not be able consistently to take its best direct practitioners and remove them from client contact where their services are needed and valued. Second, success as a treatment person is no guarantee of success as a supervisor, and success as a supervisor is no guarantee of success at a higher administrative level. As we have discussed earlier, the functions of management are the same at all administrative levels, but the tasks and activities required to manage well are not. Repeated misunderstanding of this concept often has led to the perpetuation of a vertical career ladder within social agencies. The best treatment workers have been picked to be supervisors; the best supervisors become higher-level supervisors, and the best of these may be chosen to be agency directors someday if they don't die or retire before the incumbent occupying the position. While this can work well, it also can cause real problems. By the time a worker "survives" to become director, this individual may have lost touch with direct practice, if not some of his or her faculties. In addition, some would argue, the Peter Principle[4] is likely to occur; that is, most employees will simply leave positions where they function well and continue to be promoted until they reach their level of incompetence, where they will remain at great cost to the agency. The understanding that good management is much more than social work practice with staff can help us to avoid situations where people leave jobs where they are performing well in order to take positions for which they lack the necessary interest, aptitude, and/or skills.

WHAT IS MANAGEMENT?

In some ways, it is easier to dispel myths about management, to say what it is not, rather than what it is. The literature in business and elsewhere is replete with attempts to define it, but unfortunately, there is only limited consensus. Based upon an extensive review of the work of others and our own biases as expressed in this book, we will provide a working definition that should simplify our study.

Management can be thought of as those specific functions performed by persons within the work setting that are intended to promote productivity and organizational goal attainment. Social workers functioning as managers are attempting to build and to maintain an optimal internal work environment conducive to the efficient delivery of effective services to clients. Management implies shaping and exerting an influence over the work environment. It is a proactive rather than a reactive activity. There is the implicit assumption that the work environment can range from highly supportive, efficient delivery of effective services at one extreme to the opposite extreme where the environment is destructive and actually seems to sabotage delivery of services. Of course, both extremes are rare; the work environment usually falls somewhere closer to the middle of the continuum. Management seeks to exert positive influence over the environment, to build in more sources of support for good service delivery, and to remove or minimize the effects of those conditions that tend to make the delivery of effective services difficult.

Social-work–management functions are accomplished with conscious awareness of the need for better services to clients. But in a work environment with limited resources and many internal and external political realities that constrain what can and should be done, management functions often require a difficult balancing act. The best interests of the individual client and all of the support needs of professional staff cannot always be accommodated within available resources. This is when management becomes difficult and when the ideal definitions of management that we have proposed must be tempered by reality. "Clients" and "services" as we have used the terms refer to composite groups. The individual direct practitioner, functioning in a role as caseworker or therapist, can afford the luxury of making all decisions with the best interest of a given client in mind. The same professional, functioning as a manager or a supervisor, may have to make a decision that subordinates the individual client's best interest to that of the agency's present and future clientele; that is, *all* clients as a group who are being served as well as those who might be served in the future. Management requires the use of one or more additional perspectives not usually required for the treatment functions of practice. Consequently, it often involves decisions that are unpopular and that represent trade-offs or compromises rather than ideal solutions applauded by all. Managers may be accused of having "sold out" or having lost sight of the needs of clients. This can be one of the most difficult aspects of managing.

Some business-oriented definitions of management focus heavily on management's role in promoting efficiency. A manager's function is sometimes described as the creation of surplus.[5] The idea is that the output of an organization should exceed its input; it should generate more than the resources required to produce its products or services. The difference is called the *surplus*. In the corporate sphere, surplus is easily understood—it is profit. The money derived from the sale of a product is expected to exceed the cost in personnel, raw materials, advertising, etc., required to produce and market the product. Management is used to make the organization function more efficiently, thereby increasing the likelihood that surplus will be great.

The "surplus" concept of understanding management is not without applicability for social work management practice. Clinical practice is often based on the assumption that well-managed treatment can and will produce a surplus. For example, social workers offering weekly counseling to unemployed clients to help them again become financially self-sufficient are hoping to generate a surplus. Specifically, they hope that their services will result in financial gain to clients (namely wages from employment) that will exceed the cost of counseling offered. If most social agencies did not believe that well-managed counseling is effective in generating surplus, it would make more sense simply to calculate the cost of services, stop offering them, and give the money saved directly to clients to help them pay their bills or otherwise alleviate their problems. In fact, in those social agency settings where counseling services have not been able to document the production of a surplus (for example, the public welfare sector), some social workers and members of the general public have concluded that this latter approach is preferable to treatment strategies.

In human service agencies, even the best of management cannot always generate a surplus in dollars and cents. By its very nature, social work intervention is often a very expensive, inefficient enterprise. Furthermore, documenting the value of intervention in fiscal terms can be extremely difficult. It is usually not possible to compute how much our efforts are worth. Sometimes we can't even prove that we have been instrumental in changes that occurred. Sometimes we cannot even document that they occurred at all.

The constraints on producing and documenting the existence of surplus in social work settings do not preclude our viewing its production as a way of conceptualizing the work of management. The practice of good management at any level will increase the likelihood that a surplus will be generated. The counselor in some situations may be able to produce a surplus in human benefits if not in dollars and cents (increased self-esteem, improved family communication, etc.). In others, maintenance of the status quo may be a treatment goal, and it would be unreasonable to expect to be able to document the production of surplus. Staff members performing management at all levels use the differing tasks of management to contribute to the goal of surplus. For example, the training director may produce surplus by designing and implementing an orientation program for new workers that, over time, will more than pay for itself in reduced supervisory demands.

ELEMENTS OF MANAGEMENT

Management, not unlike other aspects of social work practice, is both a science and an art. It is a science in that there exists a body of knowledge relevant to the practice of management. Some of this knowledge, particularly that related to such phenomena as motivation, group dynamics, morale, etc., has been derived from the work of researchers in fields such as psychology, education, sociology, and social work. Another sizable body of relevant knowledge has been accumulated in the business field. Certain fields of study such as organizational theory or social psychology bridge two or more disciplines. A relatively new phenomenon is the accumulation of a variety of relevant material into a category loosely identified as management theory or some similar term. Social work has recently attempted to define a body of knowledge for the practice of management as evidenced by the emergence of books and a professional journal with this specific focus.

Who stakes a claim on the knowledge useful to the functions of management may be important to those academicians who have some investment in turf protection. It is of less importance to us. We will take and use helpful knowledge wherever we can find it. This is consistent with what social workers have done in acquiring needed knowledge for other areas of social work practice.

What *is* important to understanding the knowledge component of management is a recognition of both the nature and the limitations of the knowledge that is available. Knowledge can be thought of as existing in three forms: descriptive, predictive, and prescriptive.[6] The mix of management knowledge is very similar to that available for other areas of practice. Because of the complexity of the problems that social workers encounter and the phenomena involved (that is, human behavior) and because, for ethical and other reasons, our research is often limited to the use of certain designs, the preponderance of the available knowledge is descriptive. Specifically, it consists of observations of patterns that have been observed in the natural setting or in some setting where minimal control was exerted.

When descriptive knowledge begins to accumulate from a variety of empirical observations and there is general consensus among these observations, we feel sufficiently bold to begin to make predictions. Predictive knowledge is knowledge that provides an educated guess regarding what will occur in the future in a given situation. It is based upon patterns of what has been observed to occur in the past when similar conditions were present. Predictive knowledge is an extension of descriptive knowledge. It is based on the assumption of subjective probability that states that the patterns of what occurred in the past are generally pretty good indicators of what will occur in the future. However, there arc no guarantees. Weather forecasters employ predictive knowledge. They base their prediction that there is a 30 percent chance of rain on the knowledge that 30 percent of the times in the past when similar conditions were present, it rained. Their predictive knowledge allows them to be right more often than they are wrong.

Persons who play the stock market also depend on past trends in predicting the direction of the price of a stock. Subjective probability and predictive knowledge are based on studies of the past, not on laws of mathematics that form the basis of objective probability. Frequently, we use subjective probability in making decisions and in anticipating the future without even realizing it. Subjective probability is a "best guess" based on the past and its similarity to the present situation, but it cannot consider all of the variables that exist in the present. These "unknowns" will have the effect of adjusting the "real" probability either up or down (see Figure 1.1).

In the same way that we sometimes predict a legislator's reaction to community action tactics or assess the likelihood of further abuse if an abused child is returned to the home and feel reasonably comfortable with our decisions based on past actions, we can sometimes make a management decision and feel relatively confident that we are right, based on available predictive knowledge. But we are always well aware that past observations do not guarantee future events. Furthermore, in management as well as other areas of practice, there are many problem areas where our descriptive knowledge is so incomplete or so conflicting that predictive knowledge simply doesn't exist to help us.

While there is a limited amount of predictive knowledge available for management, there is even less prescriptive knowledge. Again, the parallel to other areas of practice is strong. Prescriptive knowledge is knowledge about how to intervene, to act so that what can be predicted can be changed or avoided. Total prescriptive knowledge for child-protection workers (which, of course, does not exist) would tell them exactly what to say to and do with the perpetrator and the child to guarantee that the next instance of abuse will never occur. Prescriptive knowledge for the supervisor functioning as a manager would guide the supervisor to write the perfect evaluation form for each supervisee that will guarantee that individual's maximum productivity through useful feedback and constructive criticism. Obviously, any claim that we have very much prescriptive knowledge to assist the social worker would be extremely presumptuous.

The knowledge presented in this text will be representative of the knowledge levels most frequently found in management. There will be much more description than prediction and even less prescription in the form of specific "how to do it" suggestions. Rarely will we cross the line and offer what comes close to prescription. Because management involves human behavior on at least one side (the manager) and usually more than one (the manager and other staff), we can't really claim to have knowledge that is truly prescriptive. There is no telling just what one or more human beings can do to undermine a management activity that *should* work!

We said that management is both a science and an art. The art enters when we try to apply the knowledge. Knowledge may be the basis for management behaviors, but whether they can be successfully applied or not is a function of art factors. These are such factors as personality, intuition, experience, personal loyalties, group confidence, and self-confidence. All of these art factors, which we will be coming back to again and again, can be viewed as variables that change in degree and form from one manager to another over time. It is the combination of these that allows any given manager to succeed in the application of a management principle while another may fail. They explain why one manager can make a management decision and gain widespread support while another manager can make the same decision in a similar situation and provoke only resentment and suspicion.

A management behavior is often not inherently right or wrong; its success is dependent on the knowledge and skills of the manager, the human being through which it is "processed," and the unique situation in which it occurs. Where predictive knowledge exists, it is the human element that can either increase or decrease the likelihood of occurrence of the predictable

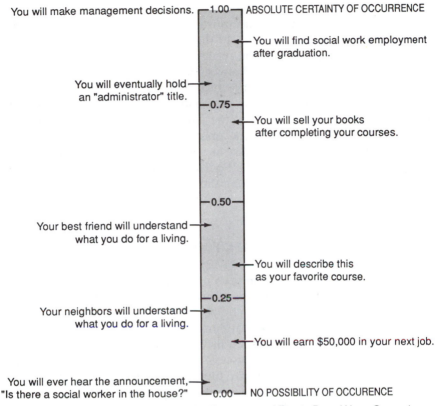

Figure 1.1. Subjective Probability of the Occurrence of Events Based Upon General Observations of the Past

event. (This is why the hypothetical probabilities in Figure 1.1 may be reasonably accurate in a collective sense but seem a little "off" from any one individual's perspective.) As an extreme example, an especially adept manager with the right combination of the art elements for a situation could gain support for a necessary pay cut without losing respect or causing resentment. A particularly inept manager with the sensitivity of a stone and a personality to go with it could propose a pay raise and cause a minor rebellion, even in an otherwise favorable environment.

The idea that art and knowledge interact to influence the likelihood of success in management should not be new or foreign to the social work practitioner. An insightful micro-practice social worker may know, for example, that confrontation may be indicated with a given client. But this person also may know that he or she could not "pull it off" successfully because it is so contradictory to that person's usual helping style. Similarly, a competent macro-level practitioner may not possess the "art" of working successfully with legislators for passage of a licensure bill, whereas a colleague might garner their support with ease. Some of the mystery and the intimidation of management will dissipate if we can recognize that management *is* practice and that there are many similarities between it and those other activities more commonly thought of as the province of the social worker. In all areas of practice certain innate abilities and personality characteristics can be supportive of or can present obstacles to the performance of a task. Of course, while some of us may have a "knack" in one area or another, we can also learn to perform any task better. Art in management, as in other areas of practice, is both innate and learned. We will be emphasizing the importance of recognizing the innate and acquiring the knowledge necessary to assist us to learn those skills necessary for successful management practice.

THE FUNCTIONS OF MANAGEMENT

The term *management* suggests the presence of several broad functions that are performed by persons functioning as managers. Unfortunately, there is a lack of consensus on what labels should be applied to these functions. Those authors and theoreticians who have attempted to compile a list of them have usually conceded that the items in their list tend to overlap anyway. In fact, in the chapters that follow, we will discuss some management activities that would seem to fall within several broad functions; others don't quite fit in any but are nevertheless critical to our study of management. Consistent with our purpose in this chapter, which is to better understand the meaning of the term management, we'll mention a few of the better-known lists of functions and their "common denominators."

The authors of one textbook commonly used in public administration and business and sometimes in social work courses, group its study of functions into five categories: planning, organizing, staffing, leading, and controlling.[7] (We have opted to organize this book around these five functions.) Another author uses only planning, organizing, and controlling.[8] A third cites the classical management functions as organizing, coordinating, planning, and controlling.[9] Another list contains planning, organizing, staffing, directing, and controlling.[10] All the lists suggest the efforts of a manager to take an active role in shaping various aspects of the work environment. They all reflect the manager's responsibility to do more than just let things happen naturally. They suggest attempting to improve on what might happen spontaneously if the manager did not take charge and did not manage.

The lists all contain words that are sometimes frustrating in their ambiguity and their vagueness. They hint at but do not tell us what a manager really *does*. While we will use these rather general terms in future chapters, we will focus more heavily on the specific activities, tasks, and behaviors of management.

THE IMPORTANCE OF MANAGEMENT

A world without management is almost unimaginable. Every human activity involves management. In fact, the human brain is sometimes used as an example of a full-time manager, managing our locomotion, our thought processes, our digestion, etc.; even our dreams and other activities while asleep. Unlike any person who manages, it never really takes a break or slips into another role. The point is, we couldn't get out of bed or do anything else without management, sometimes conscious, sometimes more automatic.

There is really no choice for social workers in their professional roles either. We can choose not to take a "management job" that demands that a high percentage of our time is spent in management activities, but we cannot choose to avoid management altogether. We must manage in order to function in our private lives; our professional work requires no less.

Persons generally enter into personal management activities with little preparation and formal instruction. They learn to manage their checkbooks, their social lives, or their budget through a combination of trial and error and informal tutorial from friends or relatives. Frequently, they become more active in managing because they have discovered the consequences of insufficient management or mismanagement of the activities. Unfortunately, many management activities in social agencies in the past have been conducted by those who have "backed into" management in a similar way. They have not seen the importance and inevitability of management and have, therefore, not prepared themselves to perform management activities. They have made management decisions without benefit of existing knowledge and, consequently, have engaged in some pretty unsuccessful management practices. When they fail, they frequently don't even know where to look to understand why they failed. We hope to assist the reader to avoid these errors.

Still not convinced of the importance of management in a social agency? Try to imagine an organization without such functions as planning, staffing, organizing, controlling, or leading. A few of its more dramatic features would be:

1. Clients and staff might show up (or they might not) as the mood hit them.
2. Staff would decide what they wanted to do each day when they got to work. Their work would be performed independently of any other staff member's activities.

3. No one would be held responsible for one's own work or anyone else's work.
4. No one would evaluate others' work or any programs or services.
5. No one would have any idea about the organization's current role in the community or would care about its future.
6. No one would share any information with anyone.
7. There would be no identifiable leader or clear role expectations for any staff member. All decisions would be unilateral.
8. There would be no goals or missions to guide behavior. All behavior would be random.
9. There would be no vehicle to help staff members upgrade their knowledge and skills.
10. There would be no task delegation.

What we have described is really a nonorganization. Without management, organizations do not exist. Management is inevitable and necessary, and it is what makes an organization different from just a building in which people rattle around in purposeless random activity.

SUMMARY

In this chapter we have attempted to present a picture of what social work management is. It is described as a group of functions performed by social workers at all levels. While the management, tasks, and activities will vary, all social workers will necessarily be involved in the basic management functions of planning, staffing, organizing, controlling, and leading.

We have presented and dispelled some common myths that exist about management and that result in resistance to a study of management theories. We have sought to identify what management is and to understand that management involves components of both science and art. We have emphasized the belief that management is both necessary and required for any kind of constructive activity to take place. It is an integral part of practice that is consistent with social work values and essential to the efficient delivery of effective services.

REFERENCES

1. Alfred Kadushin, *Supervision in Social Work* (New York: Columbia University Press, 1976), pp. 39–124.
2. Charles Glisson and Mark Durick, "Predictors of Job Satisfaction and Organizational Commitment in Human Service Organizations," *Administrative Science*

Quarterly, 33 (1988):61–81.

3. Aileen F. Hart, "Clinical Social Work and Social Administration: Bridging the Culture Gap," *Administration in Social Work*, 8, (1984); 71–88.

4. See, for example, Lawrence J. Peter and R. Hall, *The Peter Principle* (New York: Bantam Books, 1969).

5. Harold Koontz, Cyril O'Donnell, and Heinz Weihrich, *Essentials of Management* (New York: McGraw-Hill, 1986), pp. 5–6.

6. Eugene J. Meehan, *Economics and Policy Making* (Westport, CT: Greenwood Press, 1982), pp. 19–38.

7. Koontz, O'Donnell, and Weihrich, *op cit.*, p. 4.

8. Arthur G. Bedeian, *A Standardization of Selected Management Concepts* (New York: Garland Publishing, 1986).

9. Henry Mintzberg, *The Nature of Managerial Work* (Englewood Cliffs, NJ: Prentice-Hall, 1980), pp. 86–98.

10. Rex A. Skidmore, "Administration Content for All Social Work Graduate Studies," *Administration in Social Work*, 2(1) (1978):70–71.

ADDITIONAL READINGS

Donnelly, J. *Fundamental of Management*, 6th ed. Plano, TX: Business Publishing, 1987.

Foster, G. "Drucker on the Record." *Management Today*, September 1987, pp. 58–59.

Fulmer, R. *The New Management*, 4th ed. London: Macmillan, 1988.

Hasenfeld, Y. "The Administration of Human Services. *Annals of the American Academy of Political and Social Science*, 479 (1985):67–81.

Luthans, F.; Rosenkrontz, S.; and Hennessey, H. "What Do Successful Managers Really Do? An Observation Study of Managerial Activities." *The Journal of Applied Behavioral Science*, 21 (1985):255–270.

McLaughlin, C. *The Management of Non-Profit Organizations.* New York: Wiley, 1986.

Peters, T., and Austin, N. *A Passion for Excellence.* New York: Harper & Row, 1987.

CHAPTER 2

External Influences on Social Work Management

Although most management activities are designed to positively influence what takes place within an organization, our understanding of management cannot ignore the place of a human service organization within its external environment. In fact, the specific nature of required management activities and their potential for success are very much determined by the kind of interaction that exists between the organization and those persons and forces that exist outside its boundaries.

We will examine the external influences that must be addressed by the human service organization with particular emphasis on how they differ from those usually encountered by the corporate sector. By borrowing a few concepts from the business literature, we will identify some of the environmental factors that will tend to shape and direct the management activities of social workers in the 1990s and beyond.

THE TASK ENVIRONMENT

Over 30 years ago, a researcher who studied Norwegian manufacturing provided us with a concept that is still useful today in understanding the effect of external influences on social work management. It also is helpful in understanding how human service organizations differ from businesses. William Dill identified those parts of an organization's environment that are "relevant or potentially relevant to goal setting and goal attainment."[1] He referred to these as an agency's "task environment." No two organizations have the same task environment. An organization is successful or unsuccessful in goal achievement based largely on its capacity to interact successfully with its task environment. Many of the activities of management involve efforts to negotiate support from the task environment or at least to minimize the potential for resistance within it.

In the business world, the components of the task environment include its customers, suppliers of resources used by the organization, competitors, and regulatory groups. What is the task environment of a human service organization? It consists of any persons, organizations, or groups on whom it is dependent for goal achievement and who have the potential to support or to interfere with its efforts. For example, potential clients, other social agencies, funding organizations like United Way, professional organizations such as the National Association of Social Workers (NASW) and, of course, the general public would be part of the task environment. In business and manufacturing, the general public gets involved primarily as potential customers. Generally, if the product is a good one and is seen as fairly priced, the general public will be positively predisposed toward the organization. In contrast, the general public gets involved with human service agencies both as potential clients *and* as those who pay for services. Much of human service funding comes from tax revenues. The general public is not always terribly friendly toward human service organizations because the clients of our organizations are frequently those whom the general public see as a threat or somehow offensive to it. This is an important distinction between business and many human service organizations, one that ultimately shapes the role of the manager.

Different Types of Task Environments

Some organizations, based primarily on their functions and goals, operate in a task environment that is likely to be friendly. They find themselves wanted and supported. Many manufacturing concerns work within a friendly task environment. Unless they pollute the environment, exploit the labor force, or otherwise threaten the task environment, they receive support for their goal achievement. Producing a socially accepted and wanted product, providing employment within the community, and contributing to the tax base are other "pluses" for a manufacturing firm. Sometimes, special concessions are even made in the form of tax incentives, attractive leases, or relaxing of local codes to lure a given industry into an area. As a general rule, business and industry have much to give to the task environment and, therefore, find that it is likely to be friendly and supportive.

Human service agencies reflect wide variation in the attitudes of their task environment. Some are fortunate enough to work in a friendly one. A more common situation, particularly within the public sector, requires operating in a task environment that is downright hostile, one that is seeking to sabotage the organization's efforts at goal achievement. More favorable environments are found in those situations where the organization's services (1) cost the taxpayer nothing and (2) are seen as desirable, that is, consistent with the society's predominant values. A private adoption agency would be a good example. Costs are borne by those seeking the service; taxpayers contribute nothing. The placement of an unwanted child into a home where the child is wanted (and, incidentally, one that is more likely to be able to provide a higher level of financial support for the child) is viewed by the general public and other components of the task environment as a noble enterprise. The activities within the agency are open for public scrutiny. Management functions focus upon doing what is necessary to facilitate the flow of work and services. Financial clouds and threats from the task environment are infrequent; if expenses rise, the cost can be passed on to the consumer. Little management time need be spent on trying to placate and to buffer out the assaults of the task environment—they just don't occur very often. This is *not* to say that management is less important than in an agency where the task environment is less friendly. But it explains why a friendly task environment requires management activities that are closer to those seen in most of the corporate sector than those required in, for example, large public agencies. The trappings of bureaucracies (to be discussed in the next chapter) are less likely to exist because they are less *needed* in situations where the task environment is friendly.

For contrast, let us look at a hostile task environment, the kind more frequently seen and experienced by social workers. A county department of social services is a good example. Social workers (at whatever administrative level) involved with the Aid to Families with Dependent Children (AFDC) program almost certainly will encounter a hostile task environment. This is largely because of both the realities and public misperceptions of their work. The agency's employees are dispensing tax dollars collected from wage earners. That is reality. Generally, they are giving funds to persons who are not gainfully employed and who also are victims of public stereotyping that assumes that they are unwilling to work, sexually promiscuous, dishonest, etc. Toss in the general public's continuing racist and sexist attitudes, which can be applied to many welfare recipients, and the public's misinformation about the characteristics of welfare recipients who are neither women nor members of an ethnic group, and it is no surprise that the general public neither seems to value nor support the work of the AFDC social worker. Judging by the conservative attitudes that flourished during the Reagan administration, we can conclude that most Americans would probably vote to discontinue public assistance were a public referendum held.

Other components of the public welfare agency's task environment aren't much more friendly than the general public. Other social agencies and their personnel often seek to distance themselves, partly out of a need to create a more favorable task environment for themselves. They may also tend to blame public welfare bureaucracies for many of the client problems that they see. Professional organizations may push for licensure and other forms of credentialing that may have the ultimate effect of ostracizing many public welfare employees as "nonprofessionals." Even clients whom social workers seek to serve often bear great resentment toward the agencies and the systems that they feel are seeking to humiliate them. They are embarrassed and angry at having to request help and to have their privacy invaded as a prerequisite to receiving it. They may express their hostility directly to social workers or, for their own protection, find less dangerous outlets for it by denigrating the agency and its staff within the community. This only serves to make the general public more hostile. It feeds ideas that the agency is poorly managed and causes resentment by the general public at what is seen as clients' "ingratitude." The task environment only becomes more favorable when an effort to expose fraud is launched, eligibility is reduced, or the agency takes some other action consistent with generally held stereotypes and values.

Programs such as AFDC present the most readily seen examples of human services being delivered within a hostile task environment. Other social work enterprises, while receiving widespread social support on the surface, operate in a task environment that may not be much more friendly. Child-protection services often experience their share of hostility from the task environment. Their employees are engaged in investigating and exposing a problem that the general public prefers to believe "doesn't happen here." They create more work for overburdened county solicitors. They embarrass politicians, clergy, and educators who take pride in the well-being of citizens within "their" community. They find themselves working as advocates for children whose credibility and perceptions of events are constantly questioned. They are in an adversarial role, pitted against some of the community's leading citizens. Along with AFDC workers, they take tax dollars to perform a job that the general public may endorse in a general way, but resent as it is played out and as it impacts on them personally. Is it any wonder that they encounter the passive aggressiveness and, in some cases, the overt aggressiveness of a hostile task environment?

It is not surprising that many of the activities of management that occupy the time of social workers in public assistance and child protection are devoted to buffering out or in some way protecting the organization from the hostile task environment. The many bureaucratic controls in the form of policies, procedures, rules, etc., that exist are designed to defend the agency against charges of mismanagement, waste, uncontrolled staff activities, and other phenomena that could leave the organization vulnerable to withholding of funding or other tactics that could halt or curtail the achievement of objectives. Agencies find themselves pursuing elusive funding sources. They are left vulnerable to shifting service priorities and needs as perceived by legislators. A business or other organization with a more friendly task environment and more predictable funding sources (sales) worries less about protecting itself and can devote more of its management activities to production of goods or services. It knows that it has the support of the task environment.

Improving Relationships with the Task Environment

For those human service organizations that lack the good fortune of having a friendly task environment, a social worker's management tasks must be devoted in part to negotiating with the hostile environment in order to improve relationships. The goal is to decrease the vulnerability of the organization at the least possible cost in terms of compromise of professional values, autonomy, and service effectiveness. Because a task environment that is essentially hostile is not likely to reverse itself spontaneously to become more friendly, the only realistic way to negotiate successfully with it is to increase power over it. Several methods for accomplishing this are cited in the business literature.[2] Most have applicability to the functions of the social work manager. We will suggest how some of these might work and assess their relative costs.

Acquiring Prestige. The organization that can become recognized for its first-class products or services has an easier time dealing with its task environment. Develop a reputation as being the best and environmental resistance diminishes. Specialized treatment facilities such as The Menninger Foundation, The Mayo Clinic, or Roswell Park Memorial Institute meet far less hostility from their task environment than do other social agencies, in part because they are acknowleged as very good at what they do. Of course, what they do, namely psychiatric treatment and cancer research and treatment, makes a difference. These activities may be more valued than are public assistance and child protection. That's the problem with acquiring prestige—it is much easier for those organizations that *begin* with a relatively favorable task environment. It is far more difficult for those whose task environment is most naturally inclined to be hostile. Acquiring prestige, in the usual sense of the word, may be an unattainable goal for most public, tax-supported social agencies.

While a reputation for first-class services may be a less attainable goal for a public assistance agency than for a cancer research institute, there is one area where even a welfare agency can use its reputation to increase its power over a hostile task environment—management. The general public may not embrace the services or the clientele of the agency but may grudgingly acknowledge the inevitability and need for its existence. A well-managed, efficient organization that does a good job of demonstrating accountability will face less hostility from the task environment than will other similar organizations. A reputation for good management, which is especially difficult to attain while "giving away tax dollars," is a worthwhile goal for a human service agency. It will help to make the task environment less critical and more supportive, even if the services remain largely resented.

Acquiring prestige, particularly for those organizations offering services valued by the general public, is a relatively inexpensive way of negotiating with the task environment. First-rate, professional services are in the best interest of client and agency alike. They also result in increased prestige. In delivering services that are less popular with the general public, management that emphasizes efficiency and accountability can positively influence an organization's reputation and approach prestige as we have described it. But this way of acquiring a less hostile task environment can have its costs. There may come a time that demonstrating the kind of management that our society values and rewards hurts staff morale or results in staff turnover. Rigid adherence to eligibility requirements for AFDC or total compliance with laws relating to due process that results in leaving a child in a potentially dangerous home environment are just two examples of tight management that may appear to be in conflict with social work values. Professional staff may respond with anger and resentment. The manager must then assess whether the control gained over the task environment is worth the cost. They must weigh the human and organizational costs against benefits that might accrue to present and future clients from the existence of a more friendly task environment.

Contracting. Contracting can be thought of as cooperation with the task environment in such a way that interaction becomes more predictable and, therefore, less potentially threatening. It is most likely to be used to increase the power over those components of the task environment that provide the customers (in our case clients) or personnel needed for the organization to function. Contracting is a strategy that is well known to the profit sector and is also familiar to many organizations within the human service area. In business and manufacturing, a corporation will sign long-range leases for facilities or contracts for supply of raw materials needed to manufacture its products. By doing this, it not only assures the necessary input but also assures predictable manufacturing costs.

How do human service organizations contract to increase control over the task environment? Beginning in the mid-1970s, Title XX of the Federal Social Security Act provided reimbursement to state public welfare agencies that purchased services for their clients from other human service organizations. Services were bought by one agency from another. Costs were fixed and both agencies were able to operate with more certainty. One gained assurances regarding availability of services; the other, a fixed market for services.

A growing type of contracting used by social agencies in the 1990s involves the corporate sector. As more corporations develop Employee Assistance Programs (EAP), they are offering contracts to agencies in the community to provide services such as alcohol and marriage counseling to their employees. The corporation can project its costs, for it usually pays a negotiated fixed cost to the agency for services. The agency in turn is guaranteed a sizable number of pay-for-services clients, a source of both guaranteed client input and of funding. A major cost to the agency (and an issue yet to be resolved) is a frequent corporation demand that some social workers see as a violation of confidentiality. The company, paying for treatment, may feel that it has a right to know more about the nature of the client's problem than the social worker feels should be revealed.

In situations where an organization has difficulty hiring trained staff, it often contracts with potential employees (students). The organization may offer a stipend or paid field experience to a student nurse or social work student in exchange for a commitment to one or more years of employment. As in our other examples of contracting, the contract is mutually beneficial to the organization and to that part of the task environment that is not, by nature, supportive of it.

Contracting, like acquiring prestige, may be relatively inexpensive. As a reciprocal agreement, it often requires some loss of autonomy in decision making. For example, if an agency has a contract to provide services to a corporation in support of an EAP program, it cannot generally choose not to see a client, sometimes even if professional staff do not see the need for treatment. The corporation is buying more than just services. They buy rights to have input into decisions relating to the need for treatment, diagnosis, and the nature of treatment.

Agencies that have bought work commitments from students usually risk less in terms of loss of autonomy. They may not have to hire new graduates if they have decided they don't want them or need them. If they do, they can still fire them if they don't work out well during a probationary period. Of course, the up-front cost in dollars to provide the stipend of the student cannot be ignored in deciding whether this type of contracting is worth the cost. Guaranteeing the presence of an employee may be expensive, especially for one who may come to work "kicking and screaming" and seeking a way out of his or her commitment.

Contracting is likely to occupy an increasingly larger portion of time spent by social work managers as fiscal uncertainty increases for most human service organizations. It should be noted, however, that contracting is better for reducing uncertainty than for ameliorating the hostility of the general public. Like acquiring prestige, it can work best for those organizations (for example, family service agencies) that already enjoy a reasonably favorable task environment. It is not always an option for those (for example, public welfare) who work in the most hostile environment and for whom the attitudes of the general public are especially threatening to goal achievement.

Co-opting. Especially for those organizations that face a hostile task environment, *co-opting* is a useful activity. It provides a fresh perspective to the organization that may not be available among its natural "friends." It also increases control over the task environment. Basically, co-opting involves bringing a portion of the task environment into the organization. The idea is that if the boundary lines between the organization and its environment can become somewhat blurred, hostility will dissipate. How can the task environment want to oppose activities of which it is a part? Sometimes, co-opting really can be a kind of political ploy, but other times it is beneficial to the organization in several ways.

One common method of co-opting is to place a political opponent or otherwise outspoken critic on an advisory board or board of directors. Most boards consist of a mixture of people who have something to contribute in knowledge, those who contribute their names, and those whose goodwill has been courted by the offer of input into planning and decision making. The last group in particular represents the product of efforts to co-opt. For example, fundamentalist ministers *may* have valuable knowledge about the transmission of sexually transmitted diseases, but their knowledge is probably incidental to the belief that they will be less vocal in their opposition to certain prevention programs if they are allowed input into a health agency's policy-making. Conservative legislators on a county welfare agency board are also more likely to be there because of their perceived threat than because of their "real" contributions. The greater the individual legislator's following, the greater the portion of the task environment that has become less hostile.

The addition of a potential adversary to an agency board can be costly. Even one obstructive person, particularly if the individual is politically powerful and tends to command deference, can seriously jeopardize an organization's potential for goal achievement and/or divert its focus away from professionally sanctioned objectives. Co-opting of this type usually is used only in circumstances where it is absolutely necessary. Two or more such additions from a hostile task environment can paralyze the work of an organization. A shift away from professional values and ethics can even occur.

A less potentially costly method of co-opting a part of a hostile task environment is used when an organization makes use of volunteers drawn from families and groups that represent obstacles to goal achievement. Because volunteers can make a real and valued contribution and because they are not generally in a position to influence policy seriously, the approach is often desirable. But, as we shall discuss in Chapter 5, there are dangers inherent in use of volunteers. The practice of co-opting in this way generally should be used with caution.

Overall, co-opting can help to make a hostile task environment more supportive. It involves management decision making at the highest levels, but like most higher-level management practices, co-opting has implications for management functions of the social worker at all levels. For example, the task of case management becomes more complex when volunteers are involved. As with gaining prestige and contracting, some cost-benefit analysis is indicated to assess the advisability of co-opting.

Other Ways to Increase Control over the Task Environment. The business literature suggests other approaches that also would seem to have some utility for the social work manager seeking a more friendly task environment. These include expanding alternatives, diversification, and coalescing.[3]

Expanding alternatives, in business, includes using many different suppliers for raw materials. In human service organizations, this might translate as development of different client referral sources and networks, development of working relationships with universities to create sources for new staff, etc. *Diversification*, if you are a manufacturer, means manufacturing different products so that profits from one can balance off losses from low sales of another product during a given time period. In human services, we might similarly create more certainty and leave ourselves less vulnerable to a reduced need for services if we were to offer a variety of programs. It is hoped that some of these would generate wide public acceptance and could also "carry" the agency if support for the other, less popular services erodes even further and they must be discontinued.

Coalescing is an extremely costly method of increasing control over a hostile task environment. It is often a "last resort" tactic of survival. In business, the environment (often the competition) is brought in and shares in the profit, often through a "friendly takeover" or merger. Autonomy, jobs, and influence suffer great losses. While relatively rare in human services, we know of one merger of two state adoption agencies that recently occurred because state legislators concluded that wasteful duplication of services existed. While competition was eliminated and jobs were offered to all, some very knowledgeable and competent social workers could not live with conditions of the merger and chose to resign. Most importantly, in the opinion of some persons at least, client services suffered. Other coalescing arrangements, those that are not a result of legislative coercion, may have a better chance for success and may result in less cost. The creation of certain "umbrella" agencies is a type of coalescing that results in some loss of autonomy but one that can reduce a considerable amount of uncertainty and hostility in the task environment. This tactic, which sometimes takes the form of incorporating— as per business tradition—can result in a new agency with considerably more clout for negotiating with the task environment.

HUMAN SERVICE AGENCIES ARE
NOT BUSINESSES

We have pointed out the fact that businesses are far more likely to operate in a favorable task environment than are human service agencies, particularly publicly supported ones. We have chosen to explore this concept in depth because it goes a long way toward explaining why many of the activities of social workers, when they are managing, must be devoted to buffering out hostility from outside the organization. In Chapter 3 we will see how the task environment faced by most social agencies contributes to the proliferation of bureaucratic activities.

Other differences between businesses and human service organizations also help to explain the role and functions of social work management. As we look at some of these, it should be remembered that it is becoming increasingly more difficult to make many generalizations about either human service organizations or about businesses that will apply across the board. Large public agencies such as departments of social services, for example, are less similar to private psychiatric agencies or hospitals (some of which are really corporations) than they are to many businesses. Many for-profit treatment agencies and private practices bear close resemblance to businesses in their goals, indicators of success, etc. Many so-called nonprofit organizations seem really to have "profits," which they hide in salary increments and other expenditures. Generally, fiscal concerns *should be* less a driving force in a social agency than the need for high-quality client services. But as businesses become more sensitized to the need to recognize human factors and as social agencies operate in times of fiscal austerity, even this difference tends to blur somewhat. For our discussion that follows, we will be comparing the traditional profit-seeking business with the more traditional nonprofit service organizations in which large numbers of social workers continue to find employment. Many exceptions could be noted in our descriptions of both business and human service agencies.

Equity and Efficiency

A business or corporation exists to make a profit. Consequently, it is "efficiency driven." Any activity that will reduce the cost of production of a product has the potential to increase profit ("surplus" as we described it in Chapter 1). If, after a reasonable time, efficiency methods cannot generate a profit, the product will be dropped from the manufacturer's line, or, in the case of a large conglomerate, the manufacturing division may be sold, usually at some tax advantage to the corporation. The decision is purely an economic one; there is no place for a product or division that over time cannot contribute to profit and that affects the profitability of the company's other products by consuming valuable resources of the organization that are needed elsewhere. Sentiment and concerns over fairness rarely enter into the decision to drop a product or division. They may play a role only in treatment of employees who are displaced, require retraining, or are otherwise negatively affected by the decision.

In contrast, a social agency and the managers who must make decisions within it must attempt to balance efficiency and equity. A social agency cannot ignore efficiency. It must pay utility bills, salaries, and address the other expenses incurred. But it must also meet professional obligations to client service and cannot afford to develop a reputation for being overly preoccupied with efficiency. The decision to discontinue a service that is costly and represents a financial drain on resources will sometimes have to be made, but not without a good deal of soul-searching not usually required in a business enterprise. For example, the decision to refer out rather than to treat clients diagnosed as child molesters would be a simple one for a business. Treatment is unpopular, expensive, and the success rate does not justify the drain on resources required. A social work manager may have to make the decision and implement a policy consistent with it, but only *after* weighing ethical and value obligations to the client. Having made it, the manager can anticipate some criticism both within and outside the organization.

Sometimes, for professional and ethical reasons, a social agency will do what a business usually would choose not to do—operate at a loss. If, for example, the more efficient use of group services for treatment of victims of sexual abuse is not viewed as professionally sound, individual treatment may continue to be offered despite the fact that client fees in no way pay for all of the cost of treatment. In fact, many social agencies, by their very nature, regularly operate at a loss, at least in the purest sense. Social welfare services are very costly and, frequently, very inefficient. They give out more in ser- vices than what the client is willing or able to pay. Of course, as their defenders have often pointed out, failure to provide services may result in even greater financial and human costs to society.

Client needs, social responsibility, and professional ethics often dictate more loudly to social work managers than do demands for efficiency. And they should. We tend to compromise by making some abolutely necessary concessions to efficiency when the survival of the organization is at stake. Simultaneously, we listen to our professional conscience and "stonewall" many demands for efficiency that we see as ethically unacceptable. This is one of the most difficult tasks of the manager in a social agency. It occurs at every level in some form or other and often leaves the manager feeling that he or she is in a no-win situation. Managers are vulnerable to criticism whether they opt for efficiency or for equity. Business managers, possessing a much clearer set of priorities, usually have a much easier job of decision making—they *know* that opting for efficiency is the defensible and popular decision to make, at least among their stockholders.

Consumer Dependency

A business or manufacturing firm actively courts the dependency and trust of its customers. A company that produces a product that has a large share of the market is the envy of its competitors. Ideally, the customer will buy the product or service again and again and will "accept no substitutes." Nothing makes a business person happier than hearing a comment such as "my family has always bought Chevrolets and I wouldn't have any other car." Advertising dollars are often devoted to promoting the idea of repeat sales.

The reason why both customer dependency and customer trust in business are so desirable is pretty obvious. Having a customer "locked in" to a product has real advantage to the corporation. Knowing that they can count on repeat sales allows manufacturers to predict accurately the sales cycles and market for a product. Costly inventories will never get too large. A challenge for management sometimes entails determining how a product can be improved to attract new customers while sufficiently retaining its identity so as not to lose those whose dependency provides a cushion of certainty for the organization. But long-term dependency of customers is much more a blessing than a management burden; it can make a manager look good while others are more vulnerable to the ebb and flow of the fickle customer.

In contrast, social agencies do not generally seek to promote long-term client dependency; it would be contrary to social work values. In fact, while a business sees dependency as an indicator of success, a social agency sees it as a clear warning that services may be inefficient and that goal achievement is not being accomplished. What business would offer a product that its employees hope will soon not be needed? They wouldn't survive long if they did. Yet in social agencies, we value such treatment approaches as crisis intervention that are designed for brief client exposure to the agency. If successful, they will result in a client never having to return for more help. We often are skeptical of those social workers who seem to favor long-term treatment; we may wonder just who is dependent on whom. We seek to promote client self-sufficiency, beginning termination procedures sometimes when clients would prefer to continue to be seen, but when in our professional judgment we think that they are ready to function on their own. By not promoting dependency among our clients, we lack the relatively certain and predictable market for our "product" that often is present within businesses.

There would be more certainty and more predictability in long-term client dependency. For example, it might appear desirable to know that "Ms. Johnson has Tuesday at 10:00," is always on time, and always pays for her counseling in cash. Her guaranteed presence would be preferable to that of a new client who feels ambivalent about coming, may not show up, and who resents the agency's fee structure. Social workers might rather see clients like Ms. Johnson; they know and like her and may receive ego gratification from the realization that Ms. Johnson has not made an important decision in her life since 1956 without first discussing it with them. But professional values regarding dependence must take precedence over the comforts of Ms. Johnson's weekly presence. Staff members at higher levels must adapt their management activities to the uncertainty of client ebb and flow and to the costs that may result. They must devote energies to outreach activities designed to seek new and "unknown" clients. This would not be necessary if client dependency were viewed as desirable. Lower-level staff—for example, Ms. Johnson's social worker—must place greater emphasis on case management aimed toward a goal of self-sufficiency and less on the management functions required for long-term treatment.

The professional value that argues against promoting client dependency costs the agency and its staff by creating uncertainty. Increased uncertainty results in more management activities at all levels that are designed to keep the uncertainty tolerable so that staff can comfortably go about the work of the organization. While businesses and industries face many forms of uncertainty every day, offering services that are designed to be unneeded by a given client after a short period of time presents unique management difficulties for the social worker as manager.

In proprietary agencies that are publicly owned and must be more concerned with profit, in private practices, and in an increasing number of other human service organizations, the differences between business and human services are becoming less obvious. Client long-term dependence is less clearly viewed as desirable or undesirable. Client satisfaction is a high priority. Clients who wish to remain (and who can pay for it) may get their wish. Unoccupied beds and/or open treatment time cost money. Professional values about client dependence may be in direct opposition to the fiscal needs of the organization. Social workers can quickly get caught in the middle in their role as manager. Any decision regarding client discharge or termination can leave someone unhappy. In such situations, managers can only sort out their allegiances and priorities and strive to make difficult decisions in a consistent and defensible manner.

Attitudes toward Competition

In business, the competition cannot be ignored. It is always waiting for a marketing error or a bad product decision to move in and take a larger portion of the market. In a real sense, it would like to put you out of business. What's more, competition is inevitable—part of the American free-enterprise system. If you produce goods or services that result in a profit, competition will quickly pop up to try to share your profit. Rarely in our nation's history has a monopoly been allowed to exist. Only when it was believed that a lack of competition was beneficial to all (e.g., the old AT&T prior to its forced breakup in the 1980s) did the government permit a monopoly to last for long. As soon as a monopoly starts to look too self-serving, competition is encouraged or even enforced.

The inevitable presence of competition in business and industry results in a variety of management activities designed to gain an advantage. Competition keeps an organization "on its toes." Stale, old approaches to situations and problems can cause an organization to lose ground quickly. Competition provides a driving force to business that requires it to be dynamic.

The specter of competition is less important for most social agencies (those in the profit sector are, again, a notable exception). Client waiting lists and service gaps, which no one agency can see itself clear to fill, are more typical than are the highly competitive outside environment known to the business sector. In nonprofit organizations we are frequently delighted if another organization opens up to take away a few of our clients—we are probably overloaded anyway. Who fears competition? We would welcome some help.

This happy or unhappy situation (depending on how we wish to view it) does not mean that management activities related to other organizations are unimportant. It just means they take a different form. In most social agencies, cooperation rather than competition (at least not for clients) is the focus. For example, developing efficient referral networks and implementing inter-agency coordination are management activities at several levels. Getting another agency to take a referral through some reciprocal agreement is desirable. The activity of a manager in a business might involve strategies to take customers away from a competitor, not to facilitate their contact with them. Overall, the relationship with other related agencies in the human services sector is likely to be cordial and congenial, if occasionally a little strained by the tensions of overwork and feeling that *they* aren't pulling their weight. In business or industry, hostility and chicanery are more likely to suggest the attitude that exists toward the competition.

Marketing Strategies

Both business and human services advertise and seek out potential customers/clients. Both have limited financial resources available for this activity, but they may employ them quite differently. In business, marketing research is used to identify large groups of people with sufficient money who are likely to purchase a product. Then and only then is the product manufactured. If the potential market is concluded to be small, the product is usually not produced. Similarly, human service organizations sometimes conduct needs assessments before they offer a service to be sure that there is a need and that potential clients will use the service if it is offered. But the resemblance to business may end at the point of evaluating the results of the research. Social agencies, seeing that a large number of potential clients exist, will likely offer the service if sufficient funding is available. But, and this is an important difference, they *may* offer the service even if only a relatively few potential clients indicate an interest in it. If they do, it will be offered at a fair price, or even free. This occurs when the need of the few is great. Once again, professional values (in this case, the necessity of helping those in need) take precedence over efficiency or marketing principles.

A business would be unlikely to produce a left-handed widget, no matter how badly needed it is by 12 potential purchasers. The cost of the "specialty" item would have to be very high to recoup the high cost of manufacturing the product. Drug companies have recently received sharp criticism from social workers and others because of their refusal to manufacture "orphan" drugs for persons afflicted with very rare diseases. From a business perspective, their manufacture makes no sense. It is probably unrealistic to expect people with a profit-driven orientation to make decisions based upon social consciousness. However, in some human service organizations, we devote management activity and time to seeking out and serving small numbers of clients, often at a great financial loss. Such marketing strategies would be considered irrational to those in the corporate sector.

Level of Available Technology

As we suggested earlier, although management decisions in any environment usually are made based upon only descriptive or, perhaps, predictive knowledge, technology levels may differ markedly between manufacturing organizations and human services. A manufacturing plant is likely to have many of its employees engaged in simple, repetitive tasks where there exists fairly complete knowledge. Add two ounces of blue dye to the plastic compound and a toy of the desired hue will ultimately result. Grind a metal replacement part to within a certain tolerance as measured by a micrometer and it will be acceptable.

No comparable level of technology exists for the social work practitioner. Cause-effect knowledge is simply not available for use in most social work practice interventions, primarily because of the complexity of human behavior. We cannot say with certainty that a response of "how do you feel about that?" to a client description of a difficult life experience has a 100 percent chance of resulting in new insights that will ultimately contribute to alleviation of a problem. It could result in a quizzical look, a fit of laughter, an obscene gesture directed at the social worker, or any one of an infinite number of other behaviors. Similarly, a social worker's professional judgment that an AIDS education program will reduce the rate of anonymous sex may be correct, but it also may not. Another practitioner's use of confrontational strategies may produce landlord responsiveness, but the response may take many different forms, some of which would be advantageous to the community and some of which would reflect a more repressive attitude.

Social workers must operate with technology that is often vague and imprecise. Services that lack cause-effect knowledge as a foundation require different management activities than do those that have access to such knowledge. A supervisor functioning as a manager in a human service organization will need to nurture a work climate conducive to exercise of professional judgment and discretion. A manufacturing supervisor, in contrast, would be more likely to enforce conformity through vehicles such as rules. This person will seek to create an environment in which it is clear that deviation from the "right" way of doing something will not be tolerated. In social work practice, we cannot always know what is the "right" (that is, effective) way to intervene.

Consumer Interaction with the Organization

A business or corporation that manufactures a product has one primary occasion to interact with its potential customers. It occurs if and when the customers face the decision to buy or not buy a product. They vote on the desirability of the product by their decision. It reflects their evaluation of the product itself, of how it is displayed, of how well it was advertised, and of anything else aimed at their purchase decision. They never see those within the organization who manufactured the product or who made management decisions relative to its manufacture. They may write a letter to complain if dissatisfied with a product or even bring suit if it causes them some harm, but generally their interaction with the organization that made it is minimal.

Consumer feedback in social agencies tends to be more direct and frequent. Face-to-face contact with the "producer" of services is inevitable. In a manner similar to others who offer a service (e.g., plumbers, painters, etc.), social workers come face to face with the critical consumer (client) who expects value in return for (in some cases) money or for time spent. However, while a plumber or a painter has a reasonably solid yardstick available to resolve criticisms and conflicts with the consumer (the sink drains or it doesn't; the window frames are painted along with the siding or they aren't), the human service provider frequently lacks agreed-upon indicators of satisfactory service. Clients may simply take a dislike to a competent social worker (transference?), not choose to invest sufficient energies in change objectives, or sabotage treatment in many other ways, all of which result in apparent lack of treatment progress and dissatisfaction with the agency.

Community members may react with hostility to a social worker seeking to organize them for change—who else can they safely get angry at?

Determining whether social work intervention is effective is very difficult. Seeing consumers face-to-face when they are unhappy with their state in life, and who sometimes tend to project the blame onto those who would try to help, is no easy task. In human service organizations, management tasks frequently involve sorting out the wealth of direct client contact feedback. The manager must work to receive and process this information and also to recognize and to diffuse anger and other negative consumer reactions that may be neither valid nor constructive.

Evaluation Activities

In addition to processing consumer feedback, management involves ongoing evaluation of many aspects of organizational functioning. A business that manufactures a product has available good, clear indicators of success, sales, and earnings. Managers can devote most of their evaluation time to identifying factors that either contributed to, had no influence on, or detracted from sales and earnings.

In social agencies, as we suggested in the previous discussion, success and failure in service delivery are not easily operationalized or documented. In business, success is assumed to have occurred if the customer buys a product, takes it home, and doesn't ask for a refund. If the customer buys it again, this is even greater indication of success.

In human service organizations, managers must spend an inordinate amount of time just documenting whether success occurred. Their findings are very tentative and are arrived at from a variety of evaluation criteria that are much "softer" than those available in business or industry. Sometimes, for example, it can't easily be determined if clients even "took home" the progress that we think they made. Direct practitioners may use single-subject research to evaluate their work with clients where some objective measurement of success is available. Frequently, where treatment goals involve less easily measured objectives such as improved family communication, better self-esteem, or development of community leadership, some very elusive indicators of success must be employed. Most of these would make a business person very uncomfortable. In their roles as manager, social workers evaluate agency programs and services by focusing on process (a kind of system analysis), context (whether services are delivered "properly"), outcome (treatment success or failure rate), structure (facilities and personnel), or impact (presence of long-term permanent change).[4] Another popular method of assessing effectiveness, *Differential Program Evaluation*,[5] examines a program with respect to its stage of development. All of these evaluative approaches suggest management tasks that differ from those required by the business or manufacturing plant. Because of their "softness," they also are often regarded suspiciously by members of a hostile task environment.

The Prime Beneficiary Issue

Another major difference exists between the business/corporate sector and most human service agencies that goes a long way toward explaining the unique emphasis of the management functions of the social worker. It is so important to our understanding that we will give it special in-depth attention.

In their classic 1962 study, Blau and Scott first introduced the concept of prime beneficiary.[6] They identified four categories of individuals as potential beneficiaries of any organization:

1. the members
2. the owners
3. the clients or customers
4. the public-at-large

While more than one of these groups may benefit from the product of the organization's activities, Blau and Scott suggest that there tends to be one *prime* beneficiary that can usually be identified. An organization is expected to be most accountable for its actions to its prime beneficiary. Any benefits that accrue to other beneficiaries are usually viewed as cost and tend only to reduce the profit or surplus that the organization experiences.

In the ideal world of concepts and constructs, identification of the prime beneficiary is quite simple. In "mutual-benefit associations" such as social clubs, credit unions, or other organizations where members share equally in costs and benefits, the membership is the prime beneficiary. In most businesses that are privately or publicly owned, the prime beneficiary would be the owners or stockholders. Service organizations, including most social agencies, see the client as their prime beneficiary. A police department or public utility would have as its prime beneficiary the public-at-large. The AT&T monopoly that we discussed earlier was a rare example of a situation where there appeared to be more than one "prime" beneficiary. It was allowed to exist as long as it seemed that both the stockholders and general public were benefitting equally from its favored position. When the federal government saw the balance being shifted in the direction of the owners as prime beneficiary, its privileged status was revoked through antitrust action.

The right of the owners to be the prime beneficiary of a business or industry is rarely challenged by the public in our society. A sense of outrage may occur if profit is very high while a corporation rapidly raises prices under the rationalization of rising costs (for example, U.S. oil companies in the early 1980s or wholesale food companies during the drought of 1988). Or the public will become upset if profits appear to be made at the expense of the public-at-large (e.g., environmental pollution, labor exploitation). But the right of a business to make a reasonable profit (unreasonable is viewed as "gouging") is generally defended in our country.

We don't expect a business to operate at a loss, and we expect its managers to make decisions that will contribute to the production of a profit. Managers need not apologize for their actions. Owners demand profits. The prime beneficiary of a business (the owners) has a right to "call the shots." They have invested capital with the hope that it will increase; they also run the risk that it will diminish or be totally lost. Public service was not the objective. If a business engages in public service, it is viewed as an investment in community relationships. It is hoped that the goodwill generated will ultimately result in more profit (extra sales will exceed the cost of service).

The presence of a clear-cut and societally sanctioned prime beneficiary (owners) puts the business sector in a position that is envied by most social agencies. There is only one master to please. As long as sales and profits increase, the prime beneficiary will be pleased with the organization. There is general agreement between the business and its prime beneficiary about what is a desirable goal. Business managers can work to improve efficiency, knowing that if they can, the prime beneficiary will be pleased.

A key difference in the situation of most social agencies is the lack of consensus regarding the identity of the prime beneficiary. The social work manager must spend great amounts of time trying to gain acceptance for the client as being the legitimate occupant of this role. The public-at-large that (sometimes reluctantly) contributes money through the tax structure and/or private contributions to support agency services may think, logically, that they should be the prime beneficiary. The battle over this difference in perception may be ongoing.

Social work managers employed in a state psychiatric hospital regularly have their activities shaped by a lack of consensus regarding the identity of the prime beneficiary. To a social worker, the organization is there to treat and to serve the patients. The patients' best interests should always take precedence over other factors. For example, professional staff members believe that a patient should be released when, in their judgment, discharge is a more therapeutic alternative to continued hospitalization. Occasional errors in judgment, present in all professional decision making, are tolerable and inevitable. From this perspective, a social work manager might work toward changes in facilities to make them more homelike, less threatening or oppressive, and more conducive to treatment.

The public-at-large, viewing *itself* as the prime beneficiary, may take a very different attitude. While giving lip service to treatment goals, it may express opinions that belie its real priorities. It may demand protection and react with outrage when a former patient is released "prematurely" and engages in violent or embarrassing behavior. (One wonders, sometimes, whether premature is not synonymous with "prior to death" as evidenced by the comments of some members of the public-at-large.) It may see no reason to spend public funds to make hospital settings more "friendly." Security is often an obsession. Basically, walls around the institution (in some cases, literally) rather than bridges to the community are seen as desirable.

Social workers employed in correctional settings see even more extreme examples of the same attitude on the part of elements of the public-at-large, who, believing themselves to be the prime beneficiary, insist on punishment for offenses against the public. Staff, who view the prisoner as the prime beneficiary, view rehabilitation as a principal goal. This basic disagreement in perception undoubtedly explains, at least in part, the position taken by both advocates and opponents of capital punishment or chemical castration of rapists.

It is not surprising or even illogical that a similar conflict is played out in many other settings in which social workers are employed. Sometimes the disagreement may not be quite as dichotomous as in mental health or corrections, but the lack of consensus over the identity of the prime beneficiary exists nevertheless. In a private counseling agency that receives most of its funding through United Way, contributors demand a voice. In public child-protection agencies, the public-at-large pays the bills through the tax structure. But its right to "call the shots" takes a slightly different form. As the prime beneficiary, it believes it has a right to shape and control the actions of social workers. It also believes that its definitions of a client, or family, or even a community should be the accepted one. Social workers who view the child as the client and prime beneficiary see their functions as child protection and child advocacy. The public-at-large, while not denying the need for child protection and not beyond rage and charges of incompetence when a child is severely injured or killed, will often fight against "precipitous" removal of the child from the home or investigations that may embarrass the family and/or the community.

Many social workers labor in settings where a lack of consensus regarding the prime beneficiary is inevitable. There is a prevailing and persistent belief in Western nations that "they who pay the fiddler get to call the tune." As long as social agencies receive primary funding from tax revenues, or private contributions, the public-at-large will continue to view itself as the prime beneficiary and will demand a say in how, when, where, and to whom services will be delivered. Social workers in their role of managers cannot simply deny the legitimacy of the public-at-large's claim and go about their business as if client satisfaction is all that really matters. An agency that fails to respond to the public-at-large's demands will soon cease to be an agency.

Human service organizations that are not tax-supported also face similar problems because of disagreements over who their prime beneficiary is. For those organizations that are publicly owned (e.g., nursing homes that are part of a for-profit corporation; prisons that are being operated through contract with the private sector), the issue may be whether the prime beneficiary is the client or the owners and managers. Professional staff, possessing social work values and ethics, may tend to view the client as the prime beneficiary. But the stockholder cannot be ignored. As we noted earlier, empty beds or empty cells do not generate profit. The issue becomes especially problematic in private psychiatric facilities when a patient or client is viewed by professional staff as ready to go home and there is not another patient awaiting admission.

Long-term treatment in private, for-profit outpatient clinics also provides certainty to the organization in the area of cash flow. Short-term crisis intervention may be a treatment of professional choice, but it leaves the organization more vulnerable to client no-shows and vacant treatment time. So what is a manager to do? Frequently, social work managers in this dilemma decide that, for their own professional integrity, they must continue to view the client as the prime beneficiary—the client's needs must come first. But they also acknowledge that the financial needs of staff to earn a decent living cannot consistently be ignored.

In those agencies where employees have organized into unions or other groups designed to advocate for better salaries and benefits, another interesting phenomenon may exist. The prime beneficiary struggle may appear to be between those who say it is the client and those who at least *act* like it is the members. The issue can evolve into such questions as whether staff can be required to work evenings and weekends when clients are most available for services or whether overtime pay or compensatory time should be awarded for work performed after 5 PM. Social work managers frequently find themselves in the middle of conflicts over these matters. If they naively assume that all employees just naturally adhere to the belief that the client is the prime beneficiary and that self-interest should always be of lesser importance, they will continue to be puzzled by many staff activities. To some staff in highly unionized settings, particularly those at lower administrative levels, their own interests may sometimes take precedence over those of the clients. This is a reality that a manager cannot afford to ignore.

Misuse of the Prime Beneficiary Concept. The concept of prime beneficiary is helpful in understanding the feeling of being "caught in the middle" that a social work manager often experiences. While it can help to explain a manager's problems, we do *not* want to propose it as a convenient rationale for poor management. Some managers have attempted to justify inattention to the demands of the public-at-large or of employee unions on the grounds that they have done their job by concerning themselves primarily with their prime beneficiary—the client. They have run a very inefficient, but client-loved organization and react with indignation when accused of mismanagement or undermanagement. Especially in the public sector but in other settings as well, managers need to remind staff and themselves of who the prime beneficiary *should* be, while taking actions and making decisions that will successfully negotiate with those groups who think they *ought to be* the prime beneficiary.

Social work managers may also find the concept of prime beneficiary to be a convenient alibi for a lack of sensitivity to client needs and demands. This misuse is especially common in publicly supported agencies. Some managers have done a good job of playing the game in a way that will make themselves and the agency look good to the public-at-large. This may be accomplished at the expense of needed client services. The "creaming" approach to client selection—choosing only those clients where the potential for demonstrated success is high—is a good example of a way in which managers court the favor of the public. While demonstrating an approach to management that is fiscally sound, they place a low priority on client need. They have, in effect, bought into the commonly held idea that the prime beneficiary is the group that pays the bills. They use the need for good standing with the public to justify management that is insensitive and unresponsive to clients and inconsistent with social work values. If challenged to defend their behavior, they rely on the rationalization that, in their role as manager, they must concern themselves primarily with those groups that are responsible for the organization's long-range survival.

Managers who use the concept of prime beneficiary (whether they call it that or not) to justify a lack of attention to either client needs or the pressures exerted by the agency's outside environment or internal forces do not fully understand the role of the social work manager. The discussion in this chapter and Chapter 1 should have communicated to the reader that good social work management is an ongoing balancing act in which trade-offs are inevitable and satisfaction with management decisions on the part of all parties rarely exists. A good manager can derive satisfaction from maintaining the balance. In some situations where it seems like the best decision will end up pleasing no one, this may be the *only* source of satisfaction for the manager.

Accountability Implications of the Prime Beneficiary Question. Social workers often find themselves walking a narrow path. In their role as managers, they recognize the need to be accountable, but to whom? Should they demonstrate efficiency and effectiveness to clients or to the public-at-large? Efficiency relates to cost of services, usually relative to the costs of other agencies or organizations that offer similar services. Effectiveness relates to an agency's ability to demonstrate that it does what it says it does and the degree to which it accomplishes its goals.

Most social workers recognize that social work services are, by their very nature, not very efficient. Counseling services, for example, are very costly in comparison with the benefits that can often be documented. Effectiveness is not easily measured, as we have suggested earlier. For example, can we really prove that our counseling has resulted in improvement in Ms. Gonzalez' self-concept? How much? Can we say that we are responsible for any improvement that occurred, or were other factors such as the birth of her grandchild the real reasons for change? Can we even say with certainty that her "having to see a social worker" hasn't been a negative contribution to how she feels about herself? There are many difficulties that relate to problems of measurement.

The public-at-large is used to using business yardsticks to assess efficiency and effectiveness. In recent times, social agencies have had business evaluation techniques such as PPBS (Programming, Planning, Budgeting System)[7] applied to social agencies. The public demanded it as proof of accountability in the use of tax money. Social workers have cried foul, and while grudgingly acknowledging the fiscal power that government has over them, they have fought for the use of other evaluation methods that are based on the client as the prime beneficiary. Such methods as Differential Program Evaluation[8] and social tests[9] of efficiency and effectiveness, which compare a social agency with other social agencies rather than with the business sector, have received only limited legitimization by the public and by government-funded organizations.

The accountability emphasis that preoccupied and struck fear in the hearts of social work managers in the 1970s and 1980s stressed responsibility to the general public. Many social workers believed that the focus of the "age of accountability"[10] was not sufficiently concerned with client welfare. They feared, among other things, that concerns over efficiency would dominate agency activities and that professional standards would become less important than the economics of "people processing." An "anti-efficiency" climate developed in some organizations.

Demands for fiscal accountability arose in the early 1970s, in part in response to what was perceived as social workers' failures to reduce welfare caseloads during times of relatively generous funding for counseling during the Johnson administration.[11] Waste and inefficiency in social agencies were exposed with glee by John Ehrlichman and others who announced that social workers and others would "have to make an honest living"[12] in the future.

The presence of inefficiency and even ineffectiveness within social agencies was not totally the imagination of a vindictive group of federal officials. A lack of accountability over the years had resulted in some services and practices for their delivery that were dubious. The emphasis on accountability and, in some cases, the application of business evaluation methods were not without some value. As organizations tightened up, the social worker's prime beneficiary, the client, sometimes benefited. Those agencies that really were delivering effective services in an efficient manner had little problem in demonstrating accountability. Those that were not were forced to improve their management methods or risk loss of funds. While undoubtedly some good agencies were evaluated out of existence and some good but inefficient services had to be discontinued, in retrospect the accountability focus may have been more beneficial than harmful.

Emphasis on accountability has certainly not disappeared. Its legacy continues to contribute to conflicts over the identity of the prime beneficiary within both public and private social agencies. Social workers as managers cannot ignore the prevalent belief that the agency must demonstrate accountability to the public-at-large or at least to that part of it that provides funding. They must make management decisions that will meet the needs and wishes of the client *and* of the public. While it may not be easy, they need constantly to find ways to demonstrate to the public that they are both effective *and* efficient in expenditure of funds. In response to demands for evaluation, it is no longer enough to simply provide professional assessments that clients are being well served. The manager must constantly balance client need with the public's demands for more accountability, especially for greater efficiency. Social workers as managers must avoid soft data and seek out those indicators of success that will have credibility within the business mentality that is prevalent among the public-at-large. In the process of doing this they will also learn how to better serve their clients. Accountability and good client service are not incompatible or mutually exclusive. A good manager will function in a way that a delicate balance is maintained. Methods to demonstrate accountability can become vehicles for better services.

SUMMARY

In this chapter we have examined the external environment of human services in order to better understand the unique role of the social work manager. The presence of a task environment that is not always friendly, and sometimes quite hostile, suggests why the tasks of management in social work take certain directions that would seem illogical to many people in business. Ways to try to make the task environment more friendly were discussed.

We reviewed the ways in which businesses differ from many social agencies and how these differences shape the actions of their respective managers. We singled out an old but still very serviceable concept, namely prime beneficiary, to explain an especially important difference. The lack of consensus regarding the identity of the prime beneficiary presents problems and occupies much of the energies of the social worker as manager, particularly in public and nonprofit private agencies, but in proprietary settings as well. We looked at a related issue, accountability, and at the special problems faced by the manager who must demonstrate effectiveness and efficiency to the public-at-large that regards itself as the organization's prime beneficiary.

REFERENCES

1. William R. Dill, "Environment as an Influence on Managerial Autonomy, *Administrative Science Quarterly*, 2 (1958):409–443.
2. Peter M. Blau and Richard W. Scott, *Formal Organizations* (Scranton, PA: Chandler Publishing Company, 1962), pp. 194–206.
3. James D. Thompson and William J. McEwen, "Organization Goals and Environment: Goal Setting as an Interaction Process," *American Sociological Review*, 23 (1958):23–31.
4. Ruth E. Weber and Norman A. Polansky, eds., *Social Work Research* (Chicago: University of Chicago Press, 1975), pp. 185–187.
5. Tony Tripodi, Phillip Fellin, and Irwin Epstein, *Social Program Evaluation* (Itasca, IL: F. E. Peacock Publishers, 1971), pp. 41–60.
6. Blau and Scott, *op. cit.*, pp. 42–44.
7. Marc L. Miringoff, *Management in Human Service Organizations* (New York: Macmillan, 1980), pp. 119–123.
8. Tripodi, Fellin, and Epstein, *op. cit.*, pp. 41–60.
9. James D. Thompson, *Organizations in Action* (New York: McGraw-Hill, 1967), pp. 85–87.
10. Scott Briar, "The Age of Accountability," *Social Work*, 18 (1973):2, 14.
11. See, for example, Daniel P. Moynihan, *Maximum Feasible Misunderstanding: Community Action in the War on Poverty* (New York: Free Press, 1969), pp. 75–101.
12. See, for example, John Ehrlichman, *Witness to Power: The Nixon Years* (New York: Simon & Schuster, 1982), pp. 207–241.

ADDITIONAL READINGS

Brawley, E. "The Mass Media: A Vital Adjunct to the New Community and Administrative Practice." *Administration in Social Work*, 9 (1985/86):63–73.
Gruber, M. "A Three-Factor Model of Administrative Effectiveness." *Administration in Social Work*, 10 (1986):1–14.
McGowin, M. "The Hustle-Butt Society (Is American Society Too Competitive?)." *Business Social Review*, 61(1987):52–54.
Schneidman, D. "Values-Added Marketing Emerging as Key to Competitiveness." *Marketing News*, 21 (1987):3.
Stoner, M. "Marketing of Social Sciences Gains Prominence in Practice." *Administration in Social Work*, 10 (1986):41–52.
Turem, J. "Social Work Administration and Modern Technology." *Administration in Social Work*, 19 (1986):15–24.

CHAPTER 3

Historical and Theoretical Influences on Social Work Management

Classical management theories are much more than an amusing anachronism; they are the historical antecedents of today's management theories. Current management theory reflects an evolution of thought about the nature of human beings in the workplace and about the role of the manager. While few current social work managers would admit to being a product, say, of the scientific management or administrative management schools, their behavior as managers suggest that earlier theories are alive and well. Earlier conceptualizations of workers and of the role of managers continue to have an unmistakable influence on management within social agencies.

In our examination of historical approaches to understanding management we will attempt to identify both what they have to offer today's social workers as managers and where they fall short of their needs. With relatively few exceptions, management theories developed in the late nineteenth and early twentieth centuries were based upon research conducted within work settings where efficiency was a desirable means to an even more desirable end—profit. As we discussed in Chapter 2, most human service agencies reflect some very basic differences from organizations in the "for-profit" sector. But these differences do not preclude our learning from the work of those who have studied management in the business sector. Past, present, and emerging business management theories have great importance for social work managers charged with demonstrating the efficiency and effectiveness of programs and services.

When family businesses and cottage industries were the norm, there was little interest in the development of a systematic body of knowledge relating to management. The coming of the industrial revolution to North America produced a new phenomenon, namely the large-scale economic enterprise. Individuals found themselves working with hundreds and sometimes thousands of other employees in the production of goods and services. An impersonality, heretofore unknown, characterized many working relationships.

The growth of large and complex businesses and industries prompted the arrival of a new kind of specialist—the manager. The manager's role was neither that of worker nor owner. Managers neither produced the product with their own hands nor stood to gain directly by its sale. They were paid to oversee the work of others and were evaluated on their ability to perform this task. In especially large organizations, some managers had no direct dealings at all with workers; they performed only higher-level management tasks. Those who found themselves in roles as managers stood to benefit from the development of a systematic body of knowledge to help them perform their work.

SCIENTIFIC MANAGEMENT

The earliest identifiable theories of management, collectively labeled *scientific management*, really had their origins in the apprenticeship methods of the nineteenth century. Frederick W. Taylor (1856–1915), an engineer by profession, is the name most generally associated with scientific management, although the label was first applied to his theories in 1910 by Louis Brandeis.

Taylor was heavily influenced by the work ethic that was prevalent in his time. Scientific management was based on a number of assumptions about people and their behavior in the workplace. Taylor assumed that workers are motivated primarily by economic concerns. They act rationally. They prefer simple tasks, and they require and want guidance and supervision to help them with their work. What they are really seeking in their work is financial security and a stable work environment that guarantees good, regular pay.

If one subscribes to this view of human beings, certain management principles and behaviors follow. The work of the manager should involve the design and application of better ways to increase worker productivity. To accomplish this, scientific management relied heavily on methods of reward such as incentive pay, commissions, and piecework (pay based on number of units of work produced). All of these methods provided financial incentives to workers under the belief that, because of the presence of these incentives, they would devote more of their time and effort to production. If someone works primarily to earn money, that person will work harder if more money is offered as a reward. It makes sense, particularly if your perception of human beings is that of Frederick Taylor, that is, "economic man" (sometimes referred to as "machine man").

Because workers, managers, and owners *all* tend to benefit when efficiency and productivity increase, proponents of scientific management argued that conflict within an organization ought to be minimal. If it existed it was only because of a lack of scientific knowledge and management expertise. Again, there was a compelling logic to this line of thought, given Taylor's basic assumptions about people. Why would any rational, economically motivated worker *not* want to be productive, contributing to organizational profit as well as to one's own financial well-being?

Scientific management theory, because it believed that employees wanted work to be simple and financially rewarding, placed great emphasis on the selection and careful training of workers. It emphasized careful division of labor with "hands-on" workers performing simple tasks and managers relieving them of the responsibility to think and make decisions. Each worker does his or her specific task. Because their work is so uncomplicated, employees quickly learn to do it correctly and become increasingly more productive. Managerial and worker roles are clearly differentiated. The assembly line, first widely publicized for its efficient production of Model T and Model A Fords, was one of the applications of scientific management theories. It relied heavily on strict adherence to the principle of division of labor.

A phrase that is commonly remembered as critical to an understanding of scientific management is the "one best way." If one assumes that people are rational and that their motivation is uncomplicated, it is only logical to conclude that cause-effect knowledge can be obtained. This knowledge will suggest to the manager a best way of performing a task. The role of managers was to discover that way through a combination of their own scientific research and the application of the scientific studies of management performed by others. Scientific management assumed that the best way (often the most efficient way) exists; it must be found. Managers aspired to making management a science, based upon an accumulation of knowledge about the best way to perform tasks. A popular application of the scientific method to the business sector was time-and-motion studies that sought to identify and eliminate waste and to increase quantity of worker output.

Limitations of Scientific Management

Scientific management theory did not evolve without a basis in research. Taylor and his followers conducted studies that seemed to lend empirical support to the positions that they advocated. Later theorists sought to discredit their findings based in part on the researchers' methods.[1] It was pointed out that Taylor and his followers generally did not use a control group when "testing" for the effectiveness of the application of scientific management principles. It was also suggested that the findings were influenced by what later became known as the Hawthorne effect,[2] a measurement bias that is introduced by the presence of the researcher. Taylor himself was a convincing salesperson. When he conducted research (some critics argue), his personality and charismatic presence may have had more to do with a rise in worker productivity than did the management methods he employed.

Other criticism of scientific mangement focused on the basic assumptions about people on which it was based. Some critics saw it as condescending and insulting to workers, viewing workers as interchangeable parts. Taylor was accused of a lack of sensitivity to the possible long-term physiological and psychological damage that can occur to an individual who, day after day, must perform repetitive tasks. This accusation may be a little unfair, as at least one author points out.[3] Taylor was not totally insensitive to human needs or to the potentially damaging effects of routinized tasks on the worker. His writings do reflect a beginning understanding of group dynamics and their influence on productivity. His emphasis on individual motivation through economic incentives was probably more designed to overcome group influences rather than an indication of Taylor's naivete about them.

The "one best way" focus of management met opposition from both contemporaries and later critics. Employees and managers were used to making decisions based upon "art" factors such as instinct, experience, and tradition. They therefore resented what they saw as an effort to develop a body of scientific knowledge that might suggest that some current practices were simply wrong. Identifying what Taylor believed to be the "best way" had the potential to limit their available options as managers. Later, criticism was leveled at the idea that there could ever be a "best way" to perform mangement functions that would be universally best in different situations and with people who differ markedly from each other.

Critics also questioned Taylor's contention that conflict was unnecessary within organizations if managers just did their jobs well. Especially as unionization spread, organized resistance to Taylor's methods grew. Workers often argued that they were not sharing equally with owners in the profits of their productivity. They began to resent the constant pressure to produce more and more. Labor union leaders argued that scientific management methods were used to undermine the limited progress that had been made by workers.

In fairness to Taylor, his conception of human beings, particularly his ideas about economic motivation, may not have been as far off-base in his time as they appear to be today. Many of us have grown up with the belief that our work should be interesting, challenging, varied, and should be something we genuinely enjoy, at least some of the time. Many workers in the late nineteenth and early twentieth centuries probably had quite different expectations for their jobs than many of us have today. Many of the workers of Taylor's time were recent immigrants who came to the United States primarily to better their economic lot in life. They were inclined to see their jobs as a means to escape poverty, to get a financial start that would put them on the road to prosperity. They didn't come to work expecting to be challenged, just to get paid. They wanted financial security first (having generally had little) and were less inclined to seek higher-level need gratification. They didn't look for a career; they wanted a job that would pay well. In short, Taylor's perception of "economic man" may have been largely accurate (if a little overgeneralized), given many of the workers that he encountered. It would be a mistake to precipitously judge his assumptions and methods based on our understandings of the dynamics of human behavior as they exist in the 1990s.

Current Application of Scientific Management

Based upon the many problems related to scientific management that we have just mentioned, it would seem that the theories would offer little to social workers in their roles as managers. However, Taylor and his colleagues made major contributions to management that are still valid and useful today. We must remember that scientific management was a major departure from management practices of the pre-Industrial Revolution era. Prior to scientific management, managers operated and made decisions based primarily on rule-of-thumb, their instincts, and experience. They functioned with little regard for principles of management or any other conceptual framework. Profit, and whatever it took to produce it, guided management decision making. As a result, workers were often abused and made to feel powerless. Managers often appeared to be arbitrary and capricious in their handling of individual employees. Scientific management was at least based upon certain assumptions and principles; it was a step in the direction of a more objective approach to management.

The search for the one best way, the belief that people are motivated by money, and other assumptions of Frederick Taylor did not disappear with his death in 1915. Social workers in the role of manager continue to see the presence of scientific management ideas, sometimes in the management of others and occasionally in their own management practices. These are not always inappropriate. For example, there are occasions where there *is* a best way and there are times when financial considerations *are* powerful influences on staff behavior. Scientific management theory contributed many insights into organizational behavior that remain relevant today.

ADMINISTRATIVE MANAGEMENT

Another approach to management also was taking shape during the first half of the twentieth century. The theories collectively referred to as *administrative management* evolved from the writings of Henri Fayol (1841–1925) and others. Fayol was a French industrialist (mining) who believed that there are certain management principles that are universally appropriate for higher administrative levels in different settings. He first published his observations in 1916, but they were not generally known in the United States until the 1940s when they were widely discussed among management theorists.

Fayol has been widely misunderstood. While it was probably not ever his intention that his 14 management principles should be perceived as rules or laws, common misunderstandings of them were that they were meant to be quite rigid. Such supervisory principles as "span of control shall not exceed eight" (no one should supervise more than eight people) or [sic] "one man—one boss" were assumed to be prescriptive. They are what is generally remembered about administrative management while the broader principles of Fayol are less well known.

Fayol believed that good management could be taught. Persons who applied his principles, so he argued, could be successful in performing the tasks of the manager. His list of managerial functions (see Chapter 1) consisted of planning, organizing, commanding, coordinating, and controlling. He observed, as we have noted earlier, that management is not confined to the workplace. We engage in management in all human activities. But, Fayol argued, people can be taught to do a *better* job of management wherever they manage if they adhere to his basic principles. These principles are outlined below:

1. Division of work (specialization belongs to the natural order).
2. Authority and responsibility (responsibility is a corollary with authority).
3. Discipline (discipline is what leaders make it).
4. Unity of command (men cannot bear dual command).
5. Unity of direction (one head and one plan for a group of activities having the same objectives).
6. Subordination of individual interest to the general interest.
7. Remuneration (fair, rewarding of effort, reasonable).
8. Centralization (centralization belongs to the natural order).
9. Scalar chain (line of authority, gangplank principle).
10. Order (a place for everyone and everyone in his place).
11. Equity (results from combination of kindliness and justice).
12. Stability of tenure of personnel (prosperous firms are stable).
13. Initiative (great source of strength for business).
14. Esprit de corps (union is strength).[4]

It might be logical to conclude that Taylor's scientific management and Fayol's administrative management were rival theories that were incompatible. In fact, they were neither. Fayol's principles were designed primarily to assist higher-level administrators in performing their management functions. Taylor's approaches focused on ways for managers to affect positively the productivity of individual workers. Both contributed to management theory, but from a slightly different perspective. Actually, their insights are quite complementary. They shared (along with advocates of the bureaucratic model) very similar beliefs about human beings and how they are motivated.

One of the theorists who took some of Fayol's ideas and developed them a little further was Mary Parker Follett. She relied heavily on the idea of universal management principles, but her writings are based on different experiences and, therefore, have a somewhat different emphasis. Follett knew and understood government and business administration. She also understood the importance of psychological and social factors in the practice of management. While not quite a behavioral scientist per se, her writings reflect more the need for a manager's sensitivity to human individuality than do those of Fayol or most other writers identified with administrative management theories. Not surprisingly, the social work manager is likely to feel more at home with Follett's work than with the others. Her insights are especially remarkable, given her lack of significant formal education in the social sciences.

Limitations of Administrative Management

As suggested above, much of the criticism of Fayol and those who extended his work was based on a misunderstanding of just how rigid his principles were intended to be. If mistakenly viewed as laws, it is not hard to discredit them. It was pointed out, for example, that in real life the principles didn't always work for the manager. The limits of each (the situations in which they fail) were not defined. There was also little effort to identify the consequences of noncompliance.

While the principles are logical, they are not always factual in the real world of work. One writer, Herbert Simon, went to great pains to demonstrate the lack of consistency of some principles with others. He demonstrated that, in some situations, compliance with one principle would require the violation of a second one.[5]

Although critics of administrative management may have been somewhat unfair in their attacks, the contention that not all of management can be accomplished based on 14 or even 400 principles is probably valid. Overemphasis on principles can pay insufficient attention to some very important situational variables, especially the unique human beings affected by management activities and the unique person who *is* the manager. Follett reflected a beginning recognition of the importance of these, but her insights still fell short of those needed by the social work manager of the 1990s.

Current Application of Administrative Management

While the 14 principles of administrative management have their limits, they are still worthy of our study today. We have chosen to include them as worthy of discussion and of frequent application by the social work manager. They are far more valuable than misleading. In fact, adherence to them will result in management decisions that will be sound far more often than not. Many of the ideas implicit in this and other current texts are consistent with them and probably evolved from them, at least indirectly.

The reader will also note that Fayol's five functions of management are reflected in current literature. We might argue, for example, that organizing and coordinating are not discreet functions. The functions as described in detail constitute a rather complete description of management activities in any environment, whether personal or professional.

The idea that management can be taught may be administrative management's most relevant contribution to current management theory, at least for our purposes as current and future social work managers. It is consistent with a social work value that says that people can change, that they can learn to function better if given a chance and some assistance. It would be most unfortunate if we still adhered to earlier beliefs of the nineteenth century that good management practice is a gift, given to some and not to others. Because all social work practitioners are placed in the role of manager, as we contend throughout this book, such a belief would not bode well for many of us. However, believing that we can learn to become better managers not only provides justification for the study of management but it affords optimism that we can become successful in our roles as managers. We can thank administrative management theorists for this assumption.

BUREAUCRATIC MANAGEMENT

It is relatively easy for us to assign many scientific management and administrative management concepts to a place in history. But the third identifiable component of what is collectively referred to as classical management theory, namely *bureaucratic management*, is not so easily dismissed. Bureaucracies are very much in evidence within the human services. It is even a fairly common practice among those who are not social workers to use large social welfare bureaucracies such as public welfare agencies as examples of everything that can go wrong when bureaucratic principles dominate within an organization.

As with the two theories discussed above, one name is most frequently associated with bureaucracies—Max Weber (1864–1920). While Weber's writings begin to appear at the same time that scientific management and administrative management theories were taking shape, translation and serious implementation of his ideas did not occur in the United States until after World War II. The bureaucracy, as conceptualized by Weber, remains the most dominant model seen in American organizations today.

To Weber, the bureaucracy was the ideal organization for twentieth-century needs. Above all, it promised a high degree of efficiency and control. We need to think of a bureaucracy as an organizational design, specifically constructed along certain principles that promise to promote efficiency. The principles are probably not new to anyone who has ever worked in a social agency. They are logical and, at this point, time-honored and time-tested. Bureaucracies are usually characterized by:

1. A vertical organizational hierarchy. The person on the top is the boss; power decreases at each respective lower level of the hierarchy. Everyone's behavior is monitored by somebody else.
2. Well-defined rules that limit functions. There are rules for everything. A bureaucracy will make frequent use of methods such as procedure manuals, job descriptions, and even decision-making rules to govern and control behavior when no other rules exist. The idea is that rules will function within organizations much as habits work for individuals.
3. Promotion and other rewards are based on demonstrated technical competence. Do your job well and you will be rewarded.
4. Communication channels are formal and rigid. There is strict adherence to the chain of command in communication (and in other activities).
5. Job security for full-time employees. Do your job and you can't be fired.
6. Division of labor. People have very specific jobs to do. They know exactly what their job entails and so does everyone else.
7. Emphasis on written documentation. When in doubt, always put it in writing.

A bureaucracy is very logical. Its strict adherence to rather impersonal, unresponsive principles makes it a natural for many human service agencies, especially those large ones that serve great numbers of people. Organization around bureaucratic principles makes it possible to retain control over large numbers of people and their activities. A bureaucracy offers a high level of certainty to employees who might otherwise have difficulty navigating their way within a large organization. Adhere to rules, policies, and procedures (you can look them up if you have to) and you can be pretty certain that you will be rewarded with job security and promotion. Please your immediate supervisor and you will be okay.

As many social welfare programs receive financing from federal sources and the federal government is itself a highly structured bureaucracy, it is not surprising that bureaucracies would also occur at the agency level. Internal rules and other controls can be tailored to meet federal guidelines and requirements. This promotes more certainty—the certainty that funding and reimbursement will be forthcoming.

Bureaucracies are even credited with providing a desirable level of certainty to clients. Client advantages of bureaucracies include uniform treatment (no favorites) and protection of clients from discrimination by those who might try to withhold needed services. The impersonality of a bureaucracy *can* work to assure clients that they will be treated no differently from anyone else and that they will get all that they are entitled to, assuming that they meet all eligibility requirements.

Higher-level administrators, those most responsible for the long-range survival of the organization, find bureaucracies to be an especially useful way of dealing with what is frequently a hostile task environment. If, as in the case of public assistance, the primary enterprise is the distribution of tax dollars to those often stereotyped by the general public as lazy or unworthy, the manager needs all the protection from the task environment that he or she can muster. It is not surprising that bureaucracies have evolved in organizations that live under constant assault from a hostile task environment. A bureaucracy can insulate and buffer out criticism. It does this through the use of organizational principles that promote and communicate to the task environment a sense of control and accountability. Careful and rigid adherence to federal guidelines, documentation, voluminous record keeping, close monitoring of everyone's work, rules that control behavior even when the supervisor is unavailable—these and other bureaucratic methods minimize embarrassing mistakes and keep criticism by the general public down to a tolerable level. An organizational structure that promotes efficiency and the reduction of errors (e.g., in eligibility determination) is far less likely to risk critical attack from a hostile task environment than one based on principles of individualization of clients, flexibility, or professional judgment in decision making. A bureaucracy is ideally suited to silencing those critics who are eager to accuse an organization of overly zealous distribution of public funds and publicly supported services. When challenged, a record of strict adherence to rules can be presented in the form of statistics, records of correspondence, and other data.

Limitations of Bureaucratic Management

Anyone who has ever experienced the frustrations of working in a bureaucracy is well aware of the limitations of bureaucratic principles. While bureaucracies are logical, rational, and would, on the surface, seem to have high potential for promoting efficiency, sometimes just the opposite occurs.

We will mention some of the most commonly acknowledged flaws; the reader can undoubtedly add to the list.

Spheres of Confidence. The principle of specific spheres of confidence in which all jobs are carefully defined is often problematic in the real world of human services and, to a lesser degree, even in business. What if, as so often happens with client services, there is a need for a service that falls within *no one's* job description? Ethically, it is difficult to deny a person in need because the services the person needs are not our responsibility. For example, a social work bureaucracy tightly structured into spheres of confidence might not have been able to address the specific needs of AIDS patients or their families in, say, 1983. The nature of our work as social workers is constantly evolving along with the needs of our current clients and those that we will serve next year. The manager who relies too heavily on strict adherence to bureaucratic principles fails to recognize both the inevitability of some overlap in function and the need for some openness in job descriptions to meet the everchanging demands for services.

Put It in Writing. This principle also seems like a good idea but it sometimes can cause problems. While designed to promote efficiency, it can result in a very inefficient use of time. Effort and resources (secretarial, clerical supplies, data storage capacity) that could be used for client services frequently are expended in the support of unnecessary documentation and record keeping. The "memo barrage" that frequently is seen in bureaucracies presents a clear example of this kind of waste. Employees have been known to exchange dozens of memos in a work week with another employee whose office is 10 feet from their own! They could have gone over, talked directly to the co-worker, and completed the communication in two minutes or less, but bureaucratic principles discourage this type of behavior.

Promotion Based on Proven Competency. This principle also has a compelling logic; but it is also flawed. As we suggested earlier, different knowledge skills, motivation, and abilities are needed for different jobs. There is no guarantee that a good direct-practice worker will be successful as a supervisor or that a good planner will be equally competent as the administrator of a community-based agency. Sometimes the principle results in people being promoted out of jobs where they perform well and into other jobs where they struggle.

Stability. Bereaucracies probably are effective in relatively stable, unchanging environments. This, of course, is not characteristic of most human service enterprises. Bureaucracies have a way of breeding conformity and stifling creativity. The reward system promotes behavior according to the book; this behavior may or may not be consistent with the needs of changing situations.

Frequently, the heavily bureaucratized organization seems to be populated by survivors, namely those willing to learn and comply with the rules and to "make no waves." Those seeking new and better ways of doing things and who agitate for change in order to adapt to new situations inevitably find themselves at odds with the bureaucratic power structure. They remain frustrated or go to work elsewhere where they believe that their flexibility will be more appreciated.

Job Security. Like tenure in an academic setting, job security theoretically should provide workers with the freedom to do their work without danger of losing their job. Sometimes this is the result. There are some very able civil service employees whom, we would all agree, deserve to know that their job is secure. However, there are those who have been awarded permanent employee status based upon evaluation of a brief probationary period and who have become a liability to their organization. Job security can promote good job performance, but it can also result in apathy, complacency, and a feeling of invulnerability for those who lack the necessary dedication and motivation to perform well. Bureaucracies can become overpopulated with the latter, particularly if work conditions and rewards are so limited that the more marketable and more creative employees tend not to stay around long.

Growth. Bureaucracies seem to want to grow and to become increasingly inflexible. A rule when reinforced by tradition over time seems to take on even more controlling force. Even solutions to problems and structures that were intended to be only temporary seem to become institutionalized. For example, committees and task forces are a common solution to problems in bureaucracies. They are especially recommended for those situations where involvement of all persons who have an interest in solving the problem is logistically impractical and would be an inefficient use of staff time. Again, the principle is a good one, but, in bureaucracies, it is far easier to form a committee or a task force than to dissolve one. Both seem to be self-perpetuating, always identifying additional work that needs to be done or issues that need to be discussed. A committee seems able to meet for thirty minutes to produce nothing tangible other than a time and place for the next meeting. Unfortunately, lack of productivity rarely leads to the termination of a committee in a bureaucracy. As members invest more and more time into its functioning, there is a tendency to perpetuate it—dissolving it would be an admission that it was a waste of time.

Of course, committees and task forces are not the only "temporary" structures that outlive their usefulness in bureaucracies. This is why they continue to grow so large. Programs also sometimes exist long after a need for their services has dissipated. Because of vested staff interest and the overall tendency of bureaucracies to grow rather than to diminish, some social programs have remained and continued to drain needed funds long after they could have been phased out. For example, the drastic reduction in influx of Southeast Asian immigrants into the United States in the late 1980s as a result of declining immigration quotas had little effect on the size and scope of many programs in state bureaucracies that had been created to address an earlier critical need. The frequently discussed but rarely required "sunset provisions" provide for programs to be terminated at a given time unless a convincing new demonstration of need could be provided. They are an effort to address the tendency of programs in bureaucracies to exist beyond the point where they are needed.

Goal Displacement. We would be remiss if we did not mention one other problem that seems to pervade most bureaucracies. Just the sheer size of many bureaucracies makes it difficult to retain a focus on an organization's purposes and broader objectives. But bureaucratic emphasis on paperwork, documentation, and objective evaluation of worker performance tends to exacerbate this problem. The vehicles that were originally designed to achieve goals and objectives more efficiently can quickly become goals themselves. This specific type of goal displacement is what is referred to as a *means-end displacement.* (Another type of goal displacement occurs when a goal is perceived as unattainable and a *goal shift* is consciously made.) The means-end displacement is common in bureaucracies. It often occurs subtly and incrementally over time. It is not planned and often goes unnoticed until someone (usually an outsider) calls attention to it. It can be extremely detrimental to the kind of services that social workers hope to promote in their role as managers. Persons immersed in meeting the requirements of their job may be unaware of its presence and may even resist "changing the rules" to regain a focus on what was the original goal or objective.

CASE EXAMPLE: GOAL DISPLACEMENT IN A BUREAUCRACY

When she was promoted to Child Protection Supervisor, Arlene set out to do a good job. While employed as a worker in the same public agency, she frequently had been frustrated when she had to pick up cases from other workers who had been reassigned or who left the agency. She inherited case records from workers who were months behind in their recording. As a result, she did not know what work had been done with her clients and she felt that continuity of service suffered badly. She determined that, as a supervisor, this type of irresponsibility would not be tolerated.

Arlene received excellent support from the district director when, as a new supervisor, she implemented strict new rules about case recording. The director recently had received a call from an angry and prominent citizen who wanted to know why his brother-in-law was being "harassed" by a caseworker about how he punished his child. The director called for the case record and was unable to document and defend the caseworker's actions because there was no record of an investigation. The rules were in the best interest of defending the agency from outside criticism. Besides, how could anyone argue against rules that were a means to better client services?

Arlene clearly communicated the rules to her workers. A minimum of a 100-word summary would be placed in the record for each telephone contact or in-person interview with clients or other persons contributing relevant information about the alleged abuse incident. All recording would be completed within 72 hours of the contact. Adherence to recording rules would be a major focus of semiannual employee evaluations. Arlene was rather proud of her approach to a problem that had been negatively affecting client services.

Within a short time most workers in Arlene's unit were in compliance with the new recording rules. Over a period of three years, a means-end displacement had occurred. New workers quickly learned the importance of timely compliance with the rules. One individual who provided good services was denied a merit raise because her records were not up to date. Others began to believe that complete, up-to-date records were evidence of competence; they were rewarded with good personnel evaluations. Workers spent a considerable amount of time counting words in their records. Certain cliche phrases occurred regularly to pad a note to the 100-word minimum requirement. One very good worker left the agency when she felt that she no longer had time to conduct thorough investigations because of the heavy demand for paperwork. Others who were less conscientious simply made fewer collateral calls to avoid having to write notes in the record. Useful calls that were made were often described by workers as "providing no relevant information" so that there was no requirement that a summary should be made in the record.

The director expressed pleasure with Arlene's rules. She now felt that she was in a much more defensible position when complaints from the community occurred. She rewarded Arlene with public compliments and high evaluations. Other supervisors, perceiving the high value placed on Arlene's methods, implemented even more demanding rules for recording. They rewarded those workers who anonymously reported rules violated by others that they observed. An implicit message was sent out at all levels of the agency—a good worker is one whose records are up to date; an incompetent one doesn't comply with the rules. Employees who could accept this definition stayed on and were rewarded for their attention to rules. Those who couldn't, because they saw other child-protection services as a higher priority than record keeping, soon left. Before long, the professional community learned of the agency's priority on record keeping; some very good potential employees didn't bother to apply.

Finally, the agency administrator retired. The new director was dismayed to observe that the need for record keeping had gotten all out of perspective. It had become synonymous with good child-protection work. What had begun as an appropriate means to an end had become the objective for many workers. Record keeping had taken on a higher priority than services themselves. The director moved quickly to regain an agency focus on professional services. Service priorities were outlined and it was made clear that, while timely and complete recording is desirable, this should never take precedence over service needs of children.

The director's reminder of the appropriate place of recording as a means to an end (services) brought relief to some employees and produced anger and anxiety in others. Some of those who had fared well in the earlier environment were able to adjust their priorities, but they feared that their best qualities would no longer be valued. Some, who had little investment in the retirement plan, simply resigned.

Arlene, who had recently recognized the problem but felt powerless to do anything about it because of lack of higher-level support from her former boss, welcomed the refocusing on objectives. She made a mental note to herself to remember that reminding workers of organization goals and seeing that they don't lose sight of them is an important function of the manager. She also reminded herself just how easily means-end displacements can occur within bureaucracies.

Current Applications of Bureaucratic Management

We must acknowledge that the bureaucracy is not the ideal organization envisioned by Max Weber. It may result in over-conformity, it may promote mediocrity, and it may, in fact, promote inefficiency. Other than that it's not bad!

The continued widespread use of bureaucratic methods in human services cannot be totally in error. Bureaucracies can and do work effectively for the delivery of human services. The fact that certain undesirable phenomena tend to occur naturally within bureaucracies does not negate their value. Their existence, however, underlines the need for alert and skilled management on the part of social workers. The social worker as manager must be adept at deriving the benefits from a bureaucratically oriented agency while using his or her knowledge and skills to prevent the problems that can readily occur.

A bureaucracy can be a very effective vehicle for coordinating activities within organizations that must, of necessity, be large and/or possess a variety of functions. Problems in bureaucracies occur when bureaucratic methods are allowed to feed on themselves and to hamstring the service functions that deserve top priority. A bureaucratic structure imposed on an organization that is small and uncomplicated and that does not need the tight control and accountability benefits that the model offers can similarly result in problems. Bureaucracies work best in those situations where tasks are fairly routine and standardization is generally desirable.

Not surprisingly, few social workers have much good to say about bureaucracies. But bureaucracies are not inherently bad. Most of our negative experiences with bureaucracies have occurred when principles were used inappropriately or overzealously applied—over-bureaucratization for the needs of the situations. Skilled social work managers who understand the merits and the shortcomings of the bureaucratic model can make decisions that will minimize these abuses of a very serviceable body of theoretical knowledge.

COMMON SHORTCOMINGS OF THE CLASSICAL MANAGEMENT CONCEPTS

In addition to the problems noted above, four common problems can be seen in the scientific, administrative, and bureaucratic approaches to management. We will discuss each of the four in greater detail in other contexts within this book and only briefly mention them here. All three classical management theories tend to ignore (1) the power of group norms on individual behavior, (2) the degree of individual differences that exist among people, particularly in regard to their motivation, (3) the irrational side of human beings that results in their doing things that are not always in their best interests, and (4) the existence of an informal but very powerful force, namely the informal organization, that may bear little resemblance to what appears on a tidy organizational chart. Limited attention to these factors resulted in a great amount of false confidence regarding what behaviors will succeed for the manager. If one views people as relatively simple and easily understood, various prescriptive approaches to management will result. Classical theories tend to ignore the complexities of human behavior. Later concepts, based more on those ideas closer to social work's understanding of behavior (multiple causation, systems theory, etc.), are less presumptive. They focus more on description of patterns of behavior and do not presume to be able to demonstrate 100 percent success in influencing it.

RESPONSES TO CLASSICAL MANAGEMENT THEORY

Taylor, Weber, and other classical theorists saw managers as rational people capable of possessing the necessary knowledge to make the right decisions. They identify the various available alternatives and project the consequences of each. Based on previously identified priorities, they then decide and act. The idea is to seek out the perfect solution (referred to in the literature as "optimizing").

Based chiefly on a recognition of the complexity of human behavior, those writers who have been especially critical of the classical theorists have a somewhat different perception of managers. Managers are viewed more as pragmatists, making acceptable decisions based on limited information and with the knowledge that even good decisions cannot guarantee success. As opposed to the optimizing of the classical theorists, Herbert Simon[6] viewed managers as "satisficing," that is, searching until they find an acceptable solution, what is good enough rather than optimal. The term "bounded rationality" is used to describe managers' approach to decision making. Because they can't consider all possible alternatives and can't fully understand all the variables involved, limits (boundaries) are placed around the amount of information that will be processed prior to making a decision.

Bounded rationality is not unlike the kind of decision making that we make every day of our lives. If, for example, we need to buy a used car, we first identify the most important criteria that must be met. It must cost under $4,000, get at least 25 mpg, seat four or more people, be any color but red, etc. Many cars would qualify. Obviously we cannot afford to examine every car in the Western Hemisphere that might meet our criteria in order to be able to identify the best one overall. We never would be able to make a decision because new ones would keep becoming available, some would be sold, etc. A reasonable approach to the decision of which car to buy would be to go to five or ten local dealers regarded as relatively reputable, see what they have, and choose from their best available cars. This is satisficing through the use of bounded rationality. Optimizing would be more than just costly; it would be impossible. Any effort to seek the *best* car would only leave us incapable of making any decision. Other more important decisions in life—for example, selection of a college, a career, or a mate—also must be made through a process of satisficing. Any other approach will result in the decision maker becoming immobilized and unable to decide.

There are several identifiable "schools" of management theory seen to address the perceived shortcomings of classical management theory, and there is considerable overlap and a lack of consensus in the literature as to how they relate to each other, which school is a variation of which other one, etc. We will briefly mention several. They are those most frequently discussed in the management literature. We will identify only the more important concepts usually associated with them and note the major contributions of each to our current study of management functions of the social worker.

The Modern Structuralists

Structuralist writers describe the organization as heavily influenced by its outside environment. This is consistent with much of our discussion in Chapter 2. Managers, particularly those at the higher levels, spend much of their time addressing the demands and pressures of the ever-changing task environment.

Structuralist theorists also assume that there is inevitably a lack of goal congruence among persons who work in an organization. Some employees, but certainly not all, share the goals formally espoused by the organization. Others have their own quite different goals and agenda. This, necessarily, results in conflict. The inevitability of conflict, it is proposed, need not be destructive or unhealthy for the organization. Lewis Coser has suggested that conflict has many positive functions including the identification and solution of problems that exist.[7] An important function of managers at all levels, the structuralists suggest, is the control and management of conflict to keep it at a tolerable and productive level.

Insights into conflict within organizations and the inevitable stress between the organization and its external environment are important contributions to our study of management. They help us to better understand the importance of managers and their role in relation to these phenomena.

Human Relations

Those theorists generally associated with human relations theories of management stress the complexity of human motivation. They especially focus on the ways in which levels of productivity, attitudes toward one's work, and various behaviors on the job are socially determined—that is, influenced by group norms. Social needs, largely ignored by people like Taylor, Fayol, and Weber, are viewed as important influences. They are used to explain, at least in part, why people in organizations behave in ways that appear irrational given the classical theorists' limited perception of what motivates people. The contention that nonmonetary factors influence behavior would explain, for example, why a person might decline a promotion in order to avoid having to supervise those who are best friends. Taylor would have been puzzled by such a decision.

Human relations theorists also depart drastically from classical writers in their attitudes toward specialization. Simple tasks are not regarded as necessarily better. Instead, more complex and integrated (with those of others) work is seen as more consistent with human social needs. The production line is viewed as a demeaning, stultifying way of organizing work that tends to make people hate their jobs and to devalue productivity.

Unlike the structuralist theoreticians, human relations writers do not see conflict as inevitable within organizations. They note that it occurs frequently but that sensitive and responsive management can prevent much of it and resolve the rest, primarily through creating an environment that promotes open communication and trust.

Human relations theorists based their understanding primarily on empirical research that studied the behavior of persons in formal organizations. Their theories formed the basis for the field of industrial psychology and contributed a major component to our understanding of systems. There was a heavy emphasis on problem solving and decision making that are based on a manager's understanding of both the rational and the more irrational (that is, social, affective) determinants of human behavior within organizations.

The contributions of the human relations management theorists are, of course, very consistent with the social work knowledge base and with our professional values. In fact, many schools of social work rely heavily on content taken from human relations research, particularly in discussing the influences of the organization as just one system that impacts on individual behavior.

Contingency Approaches

Another loose grouping of ideas about management became identified as the contingency school of management. It also was largely a response to the classical emphasis on optimizing and, specifically, to the "one best way" approach of scientific management. In contrast, contingency approaches to management argue that there is no one best way or no correct decision that will work for all situations. Different situations require different decisions and managerial behaviors. Managers will, however, make good, acceptable decisions if they have the sensitivity to make a valid assessment of the needs of a situation and have some skill in decision making.

Contingency approaches seem quite relevant to social work management needs. We rarely find ourselves in identical situations—a correct managerial response in one situation is by no means certain to work in another. We make most of our decisions in a "one-time-only" environment. We also make managerial decisions that affect professionals who are definitely not interchangeable parts. Contingency approaches to management emphasize decision making that considers the individual person affected and the likely impact of the decision on that person's behavior. A given decision may be right for one staff member and wrong for another. Contingency approaches would, of course, be less appropriate in those relatively rare situations in human service organizations where we must make the same decision again and again in identical situations. Overall, contingency approaches to thinking about management have much to say to the social work manager. Their basic concepts are woven throughout much of the content of the chapters that follow.

Participative Management

Another identifiable approach to management is based heavily on the application of the democratic process. While there are certain techniques associated with participative management,[8] it is probably better understood as an application of a manager's belief that human beings are more productive, more loyal, and are more trustworthy if they are granted a role in decision making in areas that affect them and their job. Participative management is believed to promote better consensus between individual goals and the goals of the organization.

A prerequisite for participation in decision making is that individuals must have knowledge, experience, and/or expertise that they can contribute to a decision. If not, they should not be involved. Consequently, the involvement of other employees in management decision making will vary, depending on the decision to be made or the problem to be addressed. Even the type of involvement will vary—an employee's role may be chiefly advisory in regard to one decision but may have a vote in another. However, certain areas of decision making are off-limits (for example, expenditure of funds in another organizational unit; evaluation of individual staff competence).

The inclusion of staff members (not normally involved in certain decision making) into the decision-making process can do wonders for morale, it is argued. This approach is based on certain assumptions about human beings—for example, that they are more likely to support a decision when they have been involved in the decision making. It does not work when staff members perceive their involvement as little more than a manipulative attempt to co-opt them by presenting a charade of caring what they think or desiring their input. Theorists insist that it must be a genuine approach to management based upon strongly held beliefs about the higher nature of people.

Most of the criticisms of participative management are based on observation of misuse or overuse of it and the consequences that have ensued. It is argued that, in addition to knowledge and experience, an individual should also express an *interest* in involvement in decision making or a particular problem area. The concept of "zone of indifference"[9] is relevant here. It is based on the assumption that we all have many areas of our life where we really don't have much investment. In situations where a decision affecting them must be made, we would rather that someone just go ahead and make it for us. Most students, for example, may have some preference regarding whether they would rather write a term paper or take an examination in a course, but they are unwilling to organize a protest march over what the professor states as the requirement. That decision (and probably the one about when exactly a break will occur during class time) is within their zone of indifference. They will simply defer to the professor to make the decision. Other students in the same room *may* have a much greater interest in the decision (for example, they lack access to a typewriter or word processor) and very much resent the professor's decision not to consult them before requiring a term paper. For them, the decision is *not* within the zone of indifference.

Critics of participative management note that many managers who employ it underestimate the scope of their employees' zone of indifference. The manager may inappropriately tend to ask for a vote on decisions where interest is low, using up the time of employees to cast a vote on whether No. 2 or No. 3 pencils should be purchased or whether monthly or weekly calendars should be ordered. In some cases, where individual preferences may be strong, it is individual wishes, not the wishes of the majority, that are important. If they can all be accommodated, the participatory decision-making approach is inappropriate anyway. Consensus is neither desirable nor necessary.

Participative management is also misused in situations where other influences of which the manager is aware—for example, some political necessity—limit the decision that can realistically be made. If a certain decision must be made anyway, why involve others in it? You might be fortunate and staff *may* come up with the inevitable decision. But they may also vote for another alternative. They will then become angry, frustrated, and resentful of the time that was wasted when, ultimately, their decision was not implemented. Correctly applied, participative management is used only in those situations where all reasonable decisions can be seriously considered and potentially implemented.

Another criticism often leveled against participative management methods is that they tend to confuse (some would say corrupt) the role of the manager. If used to excess, group decision making can make a manager feel and be perceived like more of a chairperson than a leader. Managers might even be perceived as abdicating their leadership responsibilities. Most importantly, their ability to possess the required respect to make necessary but unpopular decisions may be weakened by too much participative management. The question is, What is too much? There is no easy answer.

Participative mangement can also create an environment of uncertainty that can interfere with morale and productivity. It should be possible to figure out and to predict the behavior of the manager. Decisions tend to follow a pattern based on the manager's priorities, style, etc. There is fairly good certainty for employees who learn regularly to predict the manager's response to a situation. If a decision is delegated to a work group, many different and unpredictable results can occur. Politics, friendships, power groups, and other characteristics and dynamics of groups can take priority over agency needs or client services. Employees are sometimes subject to decisions that may be based more on loyalties to others in the group than on what is rational or sound. This can leave everyone uneasy. The group process may preclude irrational decision making, but sometimes it can also promote it.

Participative management methods can be very appealing to the social worker as manager. Knowledge and experience are widely distributed throughout the administrative hierarchy in most human service agencies. The greatest knowledge in an area (e.g., a particular intervention technique) is as likely or even more likely to be found with a newer, lower-ranking employee than with a higher-level administrator. Some of those people may have gained knowledge during prior employment elsewhere. Participative management is a useful method for bringing the best expertise to bear on a problem.

Professionals tend to feel insulted and constrained when their input is not sought in areas where they have knowledge and expertise. Involvement can help to create a greater climate of mutual respect within human service organizations.

A note of warning is in order. Many social work managers state that their philosophy of management is participatory. (It is difficult in our democratic society to be opposed to it.) But a much smaller percentage actually practice it. Some may try it initially and then retreat from it when they find themselves having to live with decisions that they oppose or when their authority or control is threatened. The author knows of at least one high-level administrator who when hired announced publicly that his style would be one of participatory management. Within one year, all traces of participation had vanished, along with the open-door policy and several other practices that were found to be unworkable given the needs of the situation. A residue of anger remained. There would be far less resentment today if assurances of employee input into decision making had never been made in the first place.

Participative management can work, but only in certain situations involving certain staff and certain managers. There are some managers who never should attempt it (they need to control too much) and others for whom it is just a logical extension of their style and personality. The latter may find it ideally suited for use, at least in some situations.

Variations on Participative Management

Ironically, approaches to management that emphasized wide worker participation in decision making initially were not well accepted in the United States. They were given a second look and more careful consideration in the 1970s and 1980s largely because of their successful application in Japan. The so-called Japanese management, Theory Z, and other related concepts are applications of participative management ideas originally developed in the United States, where they had met with a lukewarm reception by North American industry. But success has a way of getting the attention of the for-profit sector.

The effectiveness of Japanese management techniques was seen most dramatically in the automobile industry. During the past several decades, American car sales were drastically hurt by the import of Japanese automobiles. Import quotas and heavy import taxes were required to limit foreign car sales and to drive foreign car prices up to a point where American cars would be able to compete. Despite easy American explanations about cheap Japanese labor and a temporary obsession with gasoline costs, it soon became apparent that the North American car buyer really preferred Japanese cars largely because they perceived them to be better made. There were fewer flaws and defects. Quality control was better; Japanese workers seemed to care more about the quality of the product they produced. They did not, for example, deliberately drop bolts into inaccessible door panels to annoy prospective car owners as American workers were known to do. Such behavior was unheard of among Japanese workers who viewed their job as a career, had considerable input into decision making that affected production, received rewards and extensive fringe benefits tied to the quality of their work, and generally took pride in their association with their employer. The 1980s were years of experimentation with application of Japanese management techniques within American industry and, to a lesser degree, within human service organizations. At this point, the verdict is not yet in on the effectiveness of these new-old methods.

Probably the best-known of the Japanese management methods is the use of quality circles[10] (known as *quality control circles* when they were first discussed earlier in the United States). As a means of solving problems, these methods have been credited with changing the meaning of "Made in Japan" from a connotation of shoddy product quality in the 1950s to one of high quality in the 1980s. A quality circle is a voluntary group led by a supervisor and consisting of fewer than 15 (seven or eight is ideal) workers. The group might meet one hour per week at a regular time (on paid time) to discuss problems that have been identified. Circle leaders are trained in step-by-step problem-solving methods. The circle members discuss possible solutions to the problem and decide on the best one. If it can be immediately implemented, it will be. If it can't be implemented without higher-level approval, a presentation to sell it to the next level is developed. The emphasis is on developing solutions to problems, not simply complaining about them. In turn, higher-level management assumes a position of receptiveness to ideas and solutions proposed.

Problems for quality-circle work must be production related (work flow, product defects, etc.). Such areas as salary, promotions, grievances, personalities, or anything outside of the group's work responsibilities are not discussed. (Sound familiar?) The group leader (supervisor) must be a good facilitator. This person must be comfortable in stepping out of and back into an authoritarian role. Leaders must be able to create a group climate of trust where even "half-baked" ideas can be proposed by the most timid of members without fear of ridicule or reprisal. Leaders must be able to give recognition to the group for solutions that work while not blaming group members for solutions that do not work. Clearly, quality circles require the type of manager, staff, and work situation conducive to other forms of participative management. At this point we cannot say with certainty when conditions for their use are right and when they are not. Experimentation with quality circles continues into the 1990s. The social worker as manager needs to know more about quality circles and all aspects of participative management and to be sensitive to the presence of situations where they can be appropriately and productively employed.

SUMMARY

This chapter has presented an overview of management theory that has influenced the behaviors of managers during the late nineteenth and early twentieth centuries. By understanding the principles and ideas that have been and continue to be prevalent, we have gained a perspective on how we have arrived at some of the current ideas presented in this and other management textbooks.

Each of the respective theories has left a rich legacy. To some degree, all continue to affect how managers think, how they perceive situations and people, and why they respond to situations in the ways they do. All the theories that we examined had a compelling logic for the times in which they were developed. None are totally obsolete or have nothing to offer us. The classical theories may have been based on a different perception of human beings and their motivation, but they contributed objectivity in management, some workable organizational structures, and other ideas that are still useful. Other theories and approaches offered better insight into social and psychological influences on behavior while stressing the limits of what a manager can know and process in order to make decisions. We have not finished with any of the theories examined in this chapter. Their influence will continue in all the chapters that follow.

REFERENCES

1. David Whitsett and Lyle Yorks, *From Management Theory to Business Sense: The Myths and Realities of People at Work* (New York: American Management Association, 1983), pp. 221–241.
2. Ibid., pp. 221–241.
3. Ibid., p. 223.
4. Daniel Wren, *The Evolution of Management Thought* (New York: Ronald Press, 1972), p. 218; Claude George, *The History of Management Thought* (Englewood Cliffs, NJ: Prentice-Hall, 1972), p. 113.
5. Herbert Simon, *Administrative Behavior* (New York: Macmillan, 1976), pp. 20–44.
6. Ibid.
7. Lewis Coser, *Functions of Social Conflict* (New York: Free Press, 1956), pp. 151–157.
8. Alfred Marrow, *The Failure of Success* (New York: American Management Association, Inc., 1972), pp. 83–102.

9. Chester Barnard, *The Functions of the Executive* (Cambridge, MA: Harvard University Press, 1938), p. 167.

10. Howard Smith and Carl Doeing, "Japanese Management: A Model for Social Work Administration?" *Administration in Social Work*, 9(1), (Spring 1985):4; Sud Ingle, "How to Avoid Quality Circle Failure in Your Company," *Training and Development Journal*, 36(6), (June 1982):54–59.

ADDITIONAL READINGS

Brown, D. "Management: How and Where It Originated. *Bureaucrat*, 16 (1987): 28–30.

Durlabhji, S. "Japanese-style American Management: Primary Relations and Social Organizations. *Human Relations*, 36 (1983):827–840.

Keys, P., and Ginsberg, L. *New Management in Human Services*. Silver Spring, MD: National Association of Social Workers, 1988.

Merrill, H., ed. *Classics in Management*. New York: American Management Association, 1960.

Reisman, B. "Management Theory and Agency Management: A New Compatibility." *Social Casework*, 67 (1986):387–393.

Wren, D. "Management History: Issues and Ideas for Teaching and Research." *Journal of Management*, 13 (1987):339–350.

Wren, D. *The Evolution of Management Thought*, 3rd ed. New York: Wiley, 1987.

PART II

Performing Management Tasks

Chapters 4 through 11 provide an in-depth look at the planning, staffing, organizing, controlling, and leading functions of the social worker in the role of manager. Each of these functions is envisioned as a way of influencing organizational outcome. More than anything else, management *is* influence. *Positive* influence on the work environment is the goal of a social worker's management behaviors.

Four chapters (Chapters 5 through 8) are devoted to issues that relate to the function of staffing. The person-to-person behaviors of the manager are those that seem most closely related to the knowledge and skills possessed by the social work practitioner. Yet the staffing function often presents a wide array of problems for the social worker as manager. This paradox is examined.

The five functions of management clearly overlap to some degree. By the time we discuss influencing through control (Chapter 10) and influencing through leadership (Chapter 11) the topics have already been introduced in other contexts. This should not be surprising. After all, the social worker as manager is a complete person who frequently is called upon to perform two or more functions of management simultaneously. On occasion, such individuals cannot even be certain whether what they are doing is planning, staffing, organizing, controlling, or leading. They would like to know so that they can have a clear picture of what they are trying to accomplish. But this isn't always possible. Usually this causes no problem, especially if the social worker at least possesses a keen awareness that he or she is *managing*.

CHAPTER 4

Influencing Purpose and Direction (Planning)

Planning by managers within organizations is critical to the delivery of client services. It is also important to the creation and maintenance of an organizational climate in which staff will *want* to work and will commit their activities to the goals of the organization. There should be nothing mysterious about planning. It involves the use of some very natural and familiar structures and activities. We use them every day in both our personal and our professional lives.

Planning requires an understanding of past events and the capacity to envision the future. In order to plan successfully, the social worker as manager must be able to learn from past mistakes. Lessons learned are a valuable asset for future planning and for avoiding a repetition of mistakes. The social work practitioner is very conscious of this truth.

Planning also requires a good understanding of people and the origins of their behavior. As is true of all management activities, successful planning also depends heavily on the manager's having a high level of self-awareness. In many ways, good planning is more a "people skill" than a technical skill. It involves a careful matching of plans to the needs of situations, but also to those of the manager and to their subordinates and co-workers.

WHAT IS PLANNING WITHIN AN ORGANIZATION?

When we talk about the planning functions of social work managers, we are talking about those structures and activities that are used to shape future events in an organization. Plans are designed to take us from where we are today to where we hope to be tomorrow. Planning is the opposite of simply allowing events to unfold; it is an active process, not a passive or reactive one. Managers cannot afford to leave too much to chance. They must be involved in setting into motion a variety of activities and in creating structures that increase the likelihood that the organization and its staff will move in an orderly, unified way toward achievement of goals. A social agency manager cannot, for example, assume that a general commitment to quality client services on the part of staff will necessarily result in attainment of this goal. In fact, experience tells us that activities and energies will get sidetracked unless active planning for goal achievement is undertaken. Plans must be created and implemented at many levels to help coordinate activities for goal achievement.

Up to now we have deliberately not used the word *control* in describing planning. Yet planning and control (a function of the manager described in more detail in Chapter 10) are very closely related. In fact, some types of plans that we describe in this chapter (for example, policies and budgets) are also included in most discussions of management as methods of control.

Chronology is important in understanding the difference between planning and controlling as management functions. Control of activities within organizations in order to keep them goal-focused is virtually impossible unless careful planning has preceded it. Plans suggest and shape the kind of controls that should be used. Planning is decidedly future-oriented. It involves "selecting from among alternative future courses of action."[1] It is also described as "a rational approach to preselected objectives."[2] It entails deciding in advance just what needs to be done, what are the best ways and times to do it, and who is the best choice to do it. Planning carefully establishes individual and group efforts in a way that they are supportive of each other and that they contribute significantly to higher-level goal attainment. When this has been accomplished (and only when it has), methods of control can keep activities on the track that has been laid out by the planning functions of the manager.

Planning is a continuous process. While it precedes control, it does not end when controls are set up. It requires constant monitoring and revision to assume that it remains effective and efficient.

Planning, like every other function of the manager, is expensive. It requires both human and material resources to create and to put plans into effect. Ideally, of course, planning should be worth the effort; like other management functions, it *should* generate a surplus. Surplus in planning is the amount that it contributes to goal achievement minus the cost of resources used that might have been used in other ways to contribute to goal achievement.

Planning can be inefficient; it can result in a financial loss if not performed well. It is important to remember here and elsewhere, that not all costs carry an obvious dollar value. For example, planning can and should make a positive contribution to the organizational climate. It can result in such environmental factors as confidence, certainty, trust, or other organizational characteristics that contribute to healthy group morale and that make people more likely to want to work toward goal achievement. But *poor* planning can exact a cost in such areas as morale, motivation, and negative attitudes of staff toward their work. These can certainly interfere with goal achievement. They can also result in financial losses. If staff members become unhappy, they tend to waste more time in nonproductive activities on the job, call in sick more frequently, or even quit their jobs, necessitating costly retraining of new workers. We must remember too that overplanning (and overcontrol) can quickly harm the morale of social work professionals, most of whom value and protect their professional freedom and discretion and wish to work in an environment of reasonable autonomy.

THE PLANNING MENU

There are many different types of plans. While some are more likely to be used for planning at one level of management or another or in one situation or another, all have potential for use by all levels of managers.

Within human service organizations, there exists a considerable amount of misunderstanding about exactly what is meant by the labels applied to different types of plans. We all use them, but we may have something quite different in mind than does a colleague who uses the same term. In the discussion that follows we will use terminology that is applied fairly consistently in business and less consistently within human service organizations.

The reader may notice disparities between the ways that we will use some terms and their usage in some of the social work literature. For example, the use of the terms *goals* and *objectives* interchangeably may be a little disconcerting to the student of macro-social-work practice. For our purposes here (and for the sake of the communication needed to understand planning) we will use the terms as they appear in what is probably the most widely used business management text.[3] The authors describe eight major types of plans: purposes or missions; objectives and goals; strategies; policies; rules; procedures; programs; and budgets. Each takes on a rather distinctive character when applied to human service agencies, especially those in the nonprofit sector.

Purposes or Missions

The purpose or mission of an organization represents the broadest, most general type of plan. Most social work managers are not involved in formulating the purpose or mission of an organization; they inherit them when they take a job within the organization. Managers are, however, constrained by them in their planning and in their other activities as managers. All other planning is shaped by the purpose or mission that a society has legitimized for the organization.

The idea of societal legitimization of a purpose or mission is important to understanding this type of plan as it operates within human service agencies. It suggests a political component to planning. Unless a society sees a purpose or mission as desirable and appropriate for that organization, the organization will fight a never-ending battle with its task environment. That is why mission statements are often stated broadly and in such a way that hardly anyone would challenge their legitimacy. Who can argue with a mission statement like "we help others help themselves" or "ensuring equal opportunity"? Mission statements tend to be general, idealistic, altruistic, and often even "cute." They provide only the broadest of direction for an organization as it moves from the present to the future. Missions and purposes must, of necessity, be vague enough to be palatable to most everyone. Their vagueness, while necessary, is also their biggest limitation. They are of only limited use in providing any specific guidance to influence staff behavior.

Objectives or Goals

A somewhat more specific type of plan is an objective or goal. Organization-wide objectives or goals are the observable and measurable outcome toward which activities of persons in an organization are (or should be) aimed. Objectives and goals can be quite specific (for example, "to increase the number of minority clients by 25 percent within 18 months") or more general ("to reflect greater service to minority populations within the service area"). Either statement represents the end to which other management activities (for example, organizing, staffing, controlling, leading) are supposed to be directed. Theoretically, any management decision should be able to be evaluated by using organization-wide objectives and goals as a yardstick. The manager may ask, "Will the decision produce results that are consistent with the goal or objective?" or "Will it contribute to its attainment more than other decisions might?" While this is an unrealistic approach to all of a manager's decision making, it demonstrates the ways in which the highest-level objectives and goals can shape a variety of management activity.

The higher-level objectives or goals of a human service organization are usually set years before the individual social worker arrives on the scene. Like purposes and missions (the other components of what is sometimes referred to as "strategic planning"), we frequently inherit them. However, goals and objectives are not meant to be written in stone. Social workers employed at all levels can have input into planful (usually incremental) shifts in high-level objectives and goals.

Sometimes there may be a rather dramatic shift in objectives and goals.

This may occur when an organization is especially successful in its goal achievement. This desirable phenomenon, which involves a conscious abandonment of one objective or goal and its replacement with another, is called *goal succession* (as opposed to goal displacement, discussed in Chapter 3, which is an undesirable and inadvertent goal shift). A goal shift that occurs because of successful goal achievement is a rare phenomenon in human service organizations, where we frequently lack the resources and the technology to ever accomplish our goals. But it does occur. In the 1940s and 1950s, the March of Dimes had as its objective or goal the finding of a cure or method of prevention for poliomyelitis ("polio"). The development of an effective vaccine all but eliminted new cases of the disease; the goal of the organization was essentially accomplished. Stripped of a viable goal, the March of Dimes had to choose between going out of existence or finding a new goal. As we know, it chose the latter, and now the organization is devoted to the goal of elimination of birth defects. The new goal is sufficiently like the old one that it seems natural and appropriate for this organization, which has always stressed fund-raising for research, to enhance the health of children. But, given the current state of genetic knowledge, it is not likely to be attained in the foreseeable future. The shift in goals at the March of Dimes meant that an effective, well-managed organization was kept in place and remained viable. Of course, the shift in goals also necessitated major changes in other types of plans and in other managerial functions aimed at attainment of the new goal.

A less favorable organizational goal switch can occur if an organization has to admit defeat, that it has no hope of goal achievement. Usually this will occur because of some outside factor such as the total elimination of funding being used to support the achievement of a goal. Another goal may be substituted if, for example, grant funding becomes available to support attainment of the new goal.

Objectives and goals are types of plans that are used by managers at all levels, not just by those planning for the total organization. They are formulated for employees who work primarily in direct services to clients, for supervisors, and for work groups and units of all sizes and varieties.

A well-known method of integrating the activities of all persons within an organization is known as Management by Objectives (MBO).[4] This relies heavily on planning by goal-setting at all levels and has been employed within social agencies with mixed results. MBO is characterized by written objectives (referred to as targets) for each employee. Targets are supposed to be measurable; they should also be realistic, but challenging. They contain statements of how and when something is to be done. There is ongoing assessment of progress toward goal achievement. Targets are supposed to be negotiated, not assigned, by supervisors.

With MBO, integration of objectives within the organization is accomplished by selecting targets for individual staff that, if accomplished, will provide the means whereby the individual at the next level (the supervisor) will be able to accomplish his or her objectives. Actually, the target-setting begins at the top levels. Each successive supervisor (moving down the hierarchy) works with those below to set targets that will assist in the successful achievement of objectives. In theory, at least, it makes for a tight organization in which goal displacement is not as likely to occur. It is also very useful for building more objectivity into the manager's task of employee evaluation; evaluation is based almost exclusively on an assessment of the attainment of each individual's negotiated objectives.

MBO illustrates just how useful objectives and goals can be in performing the task of planning. They can be a powerful influence in shaping the course of activities in a human service organization as they occur at all levels. A primary task of the social worker as manager is to remind others of objectives and goals in a subtle and sometimes not-so-subtle way. Like all plans, their mere presence alone does not guarantee productive activity. Ideally, objectives and goals of individuals and work groups are consistent with and contribute to achievement of those of the organization. In the real world in which we live, managers need to do what they can to move organizational objectives and goals and individual and group objectives and goals closer to congruence. This is done through a combination of emphasis, restatement, and reminder of just what employees are supposed to be doing. Particularly in the large bureaucracies in which many social workers work, goal displacement will readily occur unless the manager is conscientious in use of objectives and goals.

Strategies

The word *strategies* seems to imply a kind of purely intellectual type of plan. We tend to think of chessboards and complex cognitive exercises. The word also has certain military connotations. We have images of generals surrounding a topographical map, deciding how and when and where to deploy their infantry, armor, artillery, and air power to defeat the enemy. The image is not totally inaccurate in describing strategies as a type of plan employed by the social worker as manager. What are the elements in the military analogy? A general plan of action is evolved. The plan does not specify exactly how tasks are to be performed. It requires a carefully integrated use of resources (always limited), committed in order to overcome an opponent.

Do social agencies really do this? Yes. Our opponent might be public ignorance of sexually transmitted diseases, apathy about child abuse, political intervention in the agency's budget allocations, inefficient use of professional staff, or employee burnout. For large government programs the opponent might be a little more general, like institutional ageism, racism or sexism, inferior housing, overcrowded prisons, or even poverty within a nation of wealth. When we identify an opponent, resources available to do battle with them are always limited. We must hold some back, set priorities, and select and carefully expend those that we believe will do the most damage to the enemy. We develop plans to do this; they are our strategies. We might, for example, develop a strategy to improve our poor public image as an agency with the local press. It might involve a coordinated plan of expenditure of our version of troops, tanks and artillery. There could be staff time devoted to public speaking or part of our printing budget to develop a public relations brochure. We might commit time to review carefully a case record of a relative or friend of the local newspaper publisher's that might help us to better understand why the paper is so hostile toward the agency. Whatever the strategy, it involves the careful exploration of options and costs and the coordinated use of resources that can be committed.

Strategies seem especially appropriate when designed to attain an objective that involves the elimination or reduction of an existing problem (enemy). But they can also be used to plan in situations where there is no identified opponent currently present. A social work supervisor could, for example, develop a strategy aimed at maintaining subordinates' interest in expanding their direct treatment skills. It might involve the use of tangible and intangible rewards for participation in continuing education, granting of release time, use of case staffings in staff meetings, and other resource commitments that would reinforce positive attitudes toward ongoing learning. In this example, the strategy is one of *prevention* of the presence of an enemy that does not yet exist. Not a real opponent, but the specter of a stagnant, apathetic, and ineffective treatment staff is what provokes a coordinated plan of commitment of resources. While social agencies may sometimes lack the obvious opponents of the corporate sector (competitors), real and potential enemies abound everywhere. Identification of them frequently suggests the value of strategies as plans for use by social workers in their role as managers.

Strategies, like the other types of plans that we are discussing, are no stranger to the social worker. In our personal lives, we might develop a strategy to obtain a graduate degree or even to get the attention of another person in whom we are interested. Professionally, we might develop strategies to promote family involvement in treatment of our clients through deployment of resources (transportation, telephone calls, etc.) to assist relatives to be able to participate in treatment sessions. We might develop social-action strategies to reduce exploitive rent rates charged to members of a community. Somewhere, perhaps because of their military associations, strategies have gotten a bad name in social work practice. They can be seen as manipulative or deceptive. They can be both, but they need not be. They should be thought of as one of the useful planning tools of a manager.

Strategies can increase the likelihood of moving an organization's activities in a desirable direction so that clients can be better served.

Policies

Probably the most misunderstood type of plan is *policies*. Most of the confusion centers around how they differ from rules, which will be examined a little later. To define policies we can say that they are "general statements or understandings which guide or channel thinking and action in decision making."[5] To understand policies we will need to look at the full meaning of several words in this definition.

The word "general" suggests that policies are not meant to give specific instruction as to what a staff member is to do or not do. Rather, policies set broad parameters for decision making. Policies are used for situations where the specific unique nature of a situation cannot be anticipated. An organization may, for example, have a policy against promotion from within (hiring a current staff member as a high-level administrator when a vacancy arises). If the choice of a policy (rather than a rule) to address this issue—which is related to some future need for decision making—was a conscious, deliberate one (as it should be), we can infer something about the intentions of the manager who made the policy. The manager wanted others to know about the strong preference that exists in the agency. But being unable to anticipate all future hiring decisions relating to higher-level administrators and the variables involved in each, the manager left open the possibility that there might be some rare instances when hiring from outside might *not* be the best decision. The manager did not want to tie the hands of the personnel director and force that person to make a decision that would not be in the best interest of the organization and the clients it serves. Policies must be general. Otherwise you would need an infinite amount of them to cover each situation that might occur. Also, policies could not possibly be appropriate for use by all those who are expected to abide by them.

The phrase "statements or understandings" in the definition of policies suggests the variety of ways in which policies are communicated. Policies can be written. But the "policy manual" in many organizations frequently contains more of other types of plans than it does policies. Memos are a common written way of communicating a policy. Policies are also found in job descriptions. Here, the word "expected" is usually a tip-off that a policy will follow.

Policies are also communicated verbally in both formal and informal ways. Orientation sessions contain many policies. Other policies are communicated by supervisors or administrators in staff meetings. Others are learned through verbal communication that occurs in the coffee room, over lunch, or in myriad other informal ways. They can come from persons on the same level, from above, or even from below.

Many policies are simply implied by the actions of others, usually superiors. Certain patterns of behavior and decision making are observed consciously or even unconsciously over time and are perceived as policies. The manager's preferences or philosophies are gleaned from that person's behavior and copied by other staff, further solidifying a policy. The dangers of this type of policy communication should be apparent. Managers who do not want their behavior copied need to be abundantly clear that they are not implying a policy. There are situations where the behavior of a manager and the kind of decisions made are right for the manager, but not for other staff. Unless this is communicated, overly zealous staff members may perceive a policy, act on it, and respond with resentment if later criticized for their actions.

The phrase "guide or channel thinking and action in decision making" in the definition tells us more about policies. Policies are an effort to shape the way others think and act. They also attempt to use the valuable experience of the past by communicating to the less experienced employee what has usually been the right decision in the past and, therefore, is likely to be the right one in the future. Even more than that, employees are expected to make a certain decision or think and act in a certain way most of the time. Implicit in this is the idea that a decision that is not consistent with policy may require justification.

Policies are meant to constrain (and they can become frustrating), but they are also meant to help workers, facilitating certain types of decision making and freeing them up to use their energies in other areas. Policies have been equated with social roles and, more specifically, with role expectations. They perform similar functions. Social roles make moving into a new situation easier; so do policies. Both tell us what is generally acceptable practice in a situation and when our behavior could get us into trouble. Similar to role expectations, policies are sometimes not even noticed until they are violated. We may be unaware that a greeting to a fellow student whom we pass on the sidewalk is an expectation of our role of student or friend until that person goes by without speaking. Then we start asking how we might have offended the person or what problems he or she might be having. Similarly, we may be unaware that there is a policy that discourages secretaries from being invited to staff holiday parties until we invite one and observe the discomfort and resentment of the other professional staff. Both role expectations and policies can save us time, effort, mistakes, and embarrassment.

Policies are made by managers at all levels, but they also are made by persons not technically in the role of manager. Particularly in those organizations where participative management principles are evident, policies are made by work groups based on the democratic process and by the principle that "the majority rules." Policies made in this way are likely to be written as approved motions within the minutes from the meeting. Of course, policies are only one type of plan that can be reflected in the minutes of the meeting of a work group.

Policies are designed so that they contain some flexibility. It is assumed that there will be exceptions made to policies in some situations. The author knew one administrator who mistakenly insisted that a policy is no longer a policy once an exception is made. He based this on the realities of our current age of litigation in which, if you do it for one, you'd better be prepared to do it for all. While the manager must be concerned with equal treatment of staff and clients, this in no way means that an exception to a policy causes the policy to cease to exist. On the contrary, many good policies have been refined over the years to the point that not only the general policy but also the likely situations in which exceptions should be made are now communicated to staff. The exceptions have further refined the policy, but they have not erased it.

Is there a point where the number or percentage of exceptions to a policy becomes so great that the policy no longer exists? Probably. Just where that point exists (10 percent? 20 percent? 30 percent?) is a matter of judgment for the manager. It is probably safe to say that when a policy is no longer a helpful shortcut to decision making for employees and when it begins to require too much thought to be able to consider all desirable exceptions before implementing it, its effectiveness as a plan disappears. It is time to consider a new policy or policies or some other methods of planning and/or control.

Policies are especially popular in human service organizations, and for good reason. They are flexible. Because they are designed to allow exceptions, they leave room for the exercise of professional discretion in decision making. Given the knowledge and education level of most human service professionals and the many unique situations in which they find themselves, this can be very useful. There are many gray areas of decision making in social work practice in which there is no obvious right or wrong decision. Policies are helpful, but they often are not sufficient in themselves to give adequate direction for decision making. We must also consider, for example, individual client welfare, professional values, political and morale issues, and common sense. Because of their flexibility, policies allow for this.

Let us look at a few policies often seen in human service agencies. In clinical-type micro-practice agencies, a common policy relates to accepting gifts from clients or patients. It might be fairly precise, such as: "Social workers will not accept from a client a gift that is of any significant monetary value." This policy is stated in such a way that it makes it clear that gifts from clients are generally discouraged (employees are certainly not expected to solicit them), but that (as with all policies) some exceptions are expected. It even communicates the type of exceptions that are clearly tolerable and that are expected to constitute the great majority of exceptions made. But as a policy (not a rule) it implies that rare exceptions may be made, at the discretion of the social worker. The word "significant" in the policy statement is probably deliberately vague. To anyone but a statistician it is open to a limited range of interpretations. To a staff member, it might suggest something in the $2 or $3 range, adjusted for inflation. The term "significant," while usefully vague, manages to convey the intention of the creator of the policy that employees should not subsidize their income through receipt of client gifts.

The use of a policy with its implied potential for exceptions makes it possible for a staff member to exercise professional discretion. For example, what if a patient wants to give an especially nice piece of pottery made in occupational therapy to his or her social worker? It might have a fair market value of $10 or even more. The social worker, if a policy were not designed to be flexible, would have to refuse to accept the pottery. The patient's feelings might be hurt and a good treatment relationship might be endangered. But because a policy (and not a rule) was in effect, the social worker can make an exception, exercising professional judgment as to what is best overall for the client. In another situation, the worker might refuse a gift of very little monetary value from a patient when, in the worker's professional judgement, the giving of the gift is designed to manipulate the social worker or to resist the establishment of an appropriate and productive social worker–patient treatment relationship.

Another policy commonly seen in human services might relate to moonlighting (outside employment). Realistically, it is virtually impossible within most human service organizations to forbid an employee from taking an evening job or from having a business on the side. However, policies sometimes exist to discourage certain types of behavior that would be considered as bad public relations for the organization or inconsistent with professional ethics. A policy might exist, therefore, that would make it clear that bartending within the community served by the alcohol treatment agency is not generally acceptable or desirable behavior. The question of the ownership of rental property within the same community might be the subject of another policy. Professional discretion on the part of the employee (owner) would be needed to determine at what point the role of landlord might have a negative effect on work within the organization, its image, and that of its professional employees. Clearly, the manager cannot simply take the position that what an employee does after hours is nobody's business. But employees may require a policy to provide guidance if their decision is likely to have an effect on organizational goal achievement.

As a plan, a policy is appropriate in many social agency situations. The major problem with policies is that they tend to be confused with rules. We will look more at this phenomenon in the discussion that follows.

Rules

In contrast to a policy, a *rule* is used to *disallow* the exercise of discretion. A rule spells out the required decision or action in a situation that tends to recur in an organization. Rules either require or forbid a particular behavior. Implicit in a rule is the idea that those persons who violate them are subject to some kind of sanction or punishment.

When managers choose to use a rule for performing a planning function, they are making a statement to other staff. They are saying that "only this is acceptable" and/or that "this is not acceptable." Rules are very useful in those situations where it has been determined that the consequences of any action other than the desired ones cannot be tolerated. A rule would be used, for example, when noncompliance might result in legal action against the organization, when severe financial loss might occur, when there might be severe harm to the community image of the organization, and, of course, when there is the possibility of a violation of professional and ethical standards for treatment of clients. Rules are frequently used to forbid a behavior (for example, sexual involvement with clients) that would potentially result in all of these negative consequences and more.

Rules are more commonly used in large public bureaucracies than in smaller private agencies or in private practice, but they are seen in all human service organizations. Generally, the more hostile the task environment, the more likely that rules will be used to avoid giving those critical of the organization and its functions even more reason to find fault.

In large federal bureaucracies, rules may be tailored to enforce compliance with federal requirements. For example, a public assistance organization is likely to have strict rules regarding the frequency of mandatory home visits. A child-protection division will have carefully defined rules for timely investigation of alleged incidences of child abuse. Noncompliance in the first example would risk federal reimbursement for AFDC benefits paid out. In the case of the child-protection division, a lawsuit or even the death of a child creates a specter that just could not be allowed to occur.

A smaller organization may have a special need for rules, too. For example, small agency professional staffs may lead to rules such as "No more than two employees may be on vacation at any one time." The need for adequate professional coverage necessitates the rule. In a larger bureaucracy with many more staff, a less rigid approach (a policy?) might suffice.

The rule that "All lunch breaks must occur between 11 A.M and 1:30 P.M." may be needed and enforceable in a large public agency; it may be neither in the small public agency. If, because of other factors that take priority, a rule is not enforceable, it soon ceases to function as a rule. It is, in effect, a policy. This is probably all right; in such circumstances a rule was probably not appropriate in the first place. Remember that rules are usually designed for situations in which there is only one correct course of action and when no special conditions will change the overall needs of the situation.

Sometimes social workers as managers choose to use a rule when they originally *thought* a policy was best-suited to a situation. But they learned that the exercise of professional discretion led to abuses and/or more problems than would a hard-and-fast rule. Employees may have sought the loopholes provided by a policy rather than constructively using the policy as a guide for action, as intended. In such cases, a rule may be exchanged for a policy, effectively removing a decision or an action from the realm of professional discretion.

Like policies, rules can be laid out in great detail. They can also cover several different situations that might indicate different correct courses of action. Rules, like policies, can be time-savers for employees and for the manager. With a rule in place, very little if any direct supervision may be needed. For the person bound by a rule, no real thought is required. Just comply and you will be correct. Rules have a way of freeing up the time and cognitive processes of employees so that they can better devote them to other decisions where they are needed (for example, in application of policies).

If all staff members fully understood the differences between rules and policies and always read the manager's intentions correctly, there would be far fewer problems in human service organizations. Unfortunately, this is often not the case. The terms *rule* and *policy* often are used as if they were interchangeable, which, of course, they are not. Often managers fail to make themselves clear as to their meaning and/or intentions. Sometimes, even if managers clearly communicate which of the two is in effect, the receiver of the communication may not *choose* to hear correctly or may not receive the message for some other reason. If one or both is confused about the difference in meaning, situations can become chaotic.

There is no shortage of real-life examples of confusion over policies and rules. Here are a few:

1. A rule may be in effect that "employees may not accumulate over 30 days' leave." An employee who has "heard" this as a policy fails to take vacation time because he or she is trying to get caught up on work or to see a client through a crisis. The employee becomes outraged when the employee's pay stub reveals that he or she has lost four days of leave time.
2. A social worker knows about the rule that requires that "complete medical coverage information must be collected and recorded during

the initial patient contact." But the worker perceives it to be a policy. Fearing the reaction of a particularly hostile client, the worker fails to get the details of the client's coverage as required. After five interviews, the client terminates treatment and leaves the state with no forwarding address. The worker resents the reprimand given by the agency director for behavior that the worker perceived as involving the use of professional discretion.

3. A social worker is aware of a policy that limits the size of treatment groups to eight clients, but the worker perceives it as a rule. The worker refuses to admit the son of a prominent local politician into the smoking-cessation group that he or she leads because the group already has eight members. The worker becomes perplexed and angry when the supervisor is highly critical of the worker's behavior.

There are other potential problems with the use of rules by the social worker as manager. Because of their rigidity and the fact that they are designed to disallow the use of discretion, rules are often resented as insulting, condescending, or a form of "one-up" game played by professional staff. Rules can be an unpleasant reminder of rank and power differentials that exist within organizations. While rules are probably universally disliked, they seem particularly repugnant to social workers who value autonomy in their decision making. They are one of the most frequently mentioned sources of frustration among social workers employed in large bureaucracies. Policies are much preferred to rules by both managers and staff.

Some rules are inevitable in any organization. Some tasks must be done the *only* correct way; some decisions cannot be left to individual judgment. The social worker as manager should view rules as useful planning methods of choice for some situations. But, because of their disadvantages, rules should be used sparingly and with special attention to communication of the manager's intent.

Procedures

A type of plan that is designed to influence the sequence or chronoloy of events is called a *procedure*. The use of procedures is most appropriate for situations where the best results are achieved (or results are best achieved) when a step-by-step method is followed. Procedures are rarely used in shaping the sequence of events in individual social work treatment or in macro-level social work practice. For example, we don't usually have the kind of knowledge available to prescribe the best order of methods to use in counseling a client who has just sustained a personal loss or in influencing the power structure to support legislation to provide funding for group homes. Our clients also are not interchangeable parts to be worked on using a "correct" chronology of behaviors in the way that an automobile mechanic might rebuild a fuel pump or an automatic transmission. There will never be a cookbook approach to social work practice that details the chronology in which social work methods should be used. Nevertheless, procedures are a useful planning tool for the social worker as manager. They can serve to standardize activities within human service organizations. This can have real advantages for both staff and clients. For example, we might use a procedure for the intake of new clients that will assure that data on the client are available and have been collected in a logical sequence prior to a staffing conference (social worker performs intake history, then medical work-up, then psychological testing). Or we might employ a procedure for applying for vacation time that will assure that all the right people will be notified that a particular employee will not be at work January 3 through January 7, and that those who need to plan for the employee's absence farthest in advance will be notified first, those who need little warning will learn of it last, etc. A medical social worker may function most effectively and efficiently if procedures for discharge planning tasks are spelled out by the chief social worker.

Unlike policies—where exceptions are implict; and rules, where they are not—procedures seem to run a wide range from very flexible to very rigid. Some procedures are quite loose and are meant to serve as general guidelines for shaping the sequence of events. Others are meant to allow no flexibility. Because of the ambiguity regarding the place of discretion in using procedures to govern the chronology of activities, it is critical that managers make their intentions abundantly clear when procedures are presented and clarified to staff. If it is intended that exceptions will occur, it might be useful to give examples of when they might be appropriate and what criteria might be used in determining when an exception will be acceptable to the manger. If no exceptions will be tolerated, this must also be made very clear.

Like rules, procedures sometimes can be viewed as too restricting by some professional staff. They prescribe the right sequence of events to perform tasks and suggest that other sequences are incorrect. The social worker as manager considering the use of a procedure should ask, "Does it really matter in what order the events occur?" If it doesn't matter, procedures may be viewed as an unnecessary harassment and should not be used. If it does matter, use them. Procedures can be very helpful for shaping organizational behavior in order to increase the likelihood of effective service delivery.

Programs

Most social work practitioners have a thorough understanding of what a program is within a human service organization. But we may not think of a program as a planning tool of the social worker in the role of manager. Programs are a complex system. They may consist of all the other planning tools that we have just discussed. A program as a type of plan is really a package of goals, policies, procedures, and rules. It is put together in a special way to facilitate achievement of an organizational goal or of the goal of a subunit of the organization.

An organization usually has many programs that are *supposed* to interact supportively or at least cooperatively with each other. Sometimes managers find themselves immersed in the difficult and thankless task of trying to coordinate and keep peace among the various programs that exist within an organization. Competition among them can be fierce. For example, higher-level managers may need to find ways to integrate a new program of group counseling for abused wives with other existing programs whose staff are aware that the new program will necessarily divert needed financial and staff resources. Overlap between existing programs (for example, alcohol treatment and family counseling) can also present territorial problems that a manager must try to iron out.

For the social worker as manager, programs are more easily understood and used if there exists an understanding of systems theory and concepts. For example, a manager, tuned in to the systems concept of "interface," can anticipate the effect of a new program on all other components of the supra-system, and can thus head off many potential problems before they occur.

In the business literature, programs are often described as time-limited. This is logical, because they are regarded rather naturally as packages put together to address and eliminate a problem. In social work, we often use programs to confront problems that can be addressed but that will not go away. We are not so presumptive as to believe that any program will meet all the needs of the victims of child abuse or will be 100 percent effective in eliminating the consequences of a lifetime of discrimination or economic or psychological deprivation. Therefore, while some of our programs are time-limited, many are not, and these should continue. Others began as time-limited and perhaps should have been eliminated, but, bureaucracies and people's vested interests being what they are, still continue to exist (Chapter 3).

A program that continues to exist primarily for self-serving reasons rather than for client service contributes little to goal attainment and is an example of a misuse of a plan. A program that is of little use can also be very demoralizing for the staff associated with it. No one can feel very good about work that is of little value. Managers need to be sensitive to the different situations that require time-limited programs and those that do not. Sometimes, in addition to setting up and monitoring programs, managers will need to make unpopular decisions as to when a program should be terminated because of its limited contributions to needed client services. This is a decision that managers find very distasteful because it may involve the loss of jobs for friends and colleagues.

A program can have a wide influence on the future course of events within an organization. Social work practitioners who deliver client services cannot help but have their behavior shaped by programs. In their role as managers, social workers make frequent use of programs in planning.

Budgets

We don't often think of a budget as a planning document. But a budget is really little more than a projection of future activities expressed in dollars and cents. When we make up budgets, whether for the management of our personal finances or for an agency's upcoming expenditures, we are anticipating what financial resources are needed to support the various activities that we hope will achieve our goals and objectives. We then allocate limited resources, which, in turn, constrain the scope of the various activities. The planning function of budgets relates most to the task of constructing the budget; the limitations on activities that result from it relate more to the management function of control that we will discuss further in Chapter 10.

In using budgets to perform the planning function of the manager, it is useful to be aware of the dangers of constructing budgets that are too rigid or too detailed. Especially in our areas of work, we rarely can predict the exact financial support needs of our various enterprises a year or more in advance. Rigid budgets that disallow transfer of funds from one area to another can sometimes run at cross-purposes to goal attainment and client services. They promote a "spend it or lose it" mentality that results in some organizational units wasting money while others lack sufficient support to be as effective as they might. This undesirable phenomenon is even more likely to occur when next year's budget allocation relies heavily on full expenditure of monies earmarked for the previous year. When staff either are not allowed to turn back or are discouraged from turning back unneeded funds that might be needed elsewhere, budgets can detract from delivery of effective services rather than promote them. Flexibility is a desirable quality in budgets used for planning.

SELECTING FROM THE PLANNING MENU

In planning, as in performing other management functions, there is no perfect or universally applicable approach. We have chosen to describe the list of various types of plans as a menu in order to suggest that there are many acceptable choices available to the manager.

A hungry diner, presented with a menu at a restaurant, could select many different foods from it. Most would alleviate hunger, at least in the short run. Some foods would do the job longer. Some choices are more palatable to the diner than others. Some would be viewed as more appropriate or acceptable to fellow diners or significant others. Many considerations might enter into the final selection.

The choice of a menu of plans for use by the social worker as manager involves consideration of many of the same variables that the diner considers in contemplating the menu in a restaurant. (This is a slightly different use of the term "menu" as we see it in computer jargon.) Some types of plans, as we have discussed, are best suited to some situations, whereas others are better for others. Some are good for long-range planning; others have a shorter focus. The manager, as a person with a style and a personality of his or her own, is an important consideration. For example, some social workers functioning as managers find rules quite palatable as plans. Others are more comfortable with policies. Some staff members will find some types of plans offensive. They will more readily accept and tolerate one type of plan over others. All these variables are important in the selection of a single type of plan from the menu and in assembling what should be an ever-changing package of plans used by the social worker as manager.

It is probably easier to identify problems in selection of a planning package than it is to know when the package is a good one. Managers who rely almost exclusively on one or two types of plans are immediately suspect. If, for example, they seem to use rules and procedures but rarely employ policies in management involving professionals, we immediately wonder whether their intrapersonal needs for control may have gained predominance over the needs of staff or the situation. Usually, a mixture of plans suggests a healthy balance. We are less likely to suspect that the manager has lost sight of the purposes of planning (ends) and has become enamored of the means.

The Planning Menu

1. Purposes or missions = very broad statements of why the organization or its subunit exists. They should be legitimized.
2. Objectives or goals = descriptions of the end to which other management activities are supposed to be directed.
3. Strategies = specific plans of action designed to achieve goals or objectives. They involve deployment of resources.
4. Policies = general statements or understandings that are designed to guide or channel thinking, decision-making and behavior. Policies may be written, but often they are not.
5. Rules = specific requirements that are designed to standardize behavior and decision-making and to eliminate the use of judgment and discretion.

6. Procedures = structure provided to influence the nature and (especially) the chronology of events.
7. Programs = packages of goals, policies, rules, procedures, and (sometimes) strategies assembled in a unique manner to facilitate the achievement of a goal or objective.
8. Budgets = projections of future activities expressed in dollars and cents.

THE BENEFITS OF PLANNING

Planning contributes to the effectiveness and efficiency of an organization in several ways. In the previous discussion we suggested that attention to planning can help staff to maintain a focus on what should be our objective, namely delivery of effective client services. Specifically, it can help to avoid a means-end displacement.

Before using any type of plan, managers should ask what its contribution to overall organizational objectives is likely to be. They should be prepared to explain to themselves or to others why a plan is necessary and how it will contribute to attainment of objectives. If, for example, an organization's long-range goal is to move toward widespread use of crisis-intervention services, plans should be designed to contribute to achievement of this objective. Plans should help staff members seeing clients for extended treatment to sense that they are out-of-step.

Plans are useful in promoting a more efficient operation. They promote anticipation of resource needs so that it is possible to make decisions today that will help quickly and economically to accommodate changes that are needed tomorrow. In the example of an agency moving toward a case-management focus, planning will help a manager to avoid hiring too many MSW's for tasks that might be easily addressed by persons with a bachelor's degree. A cost saving can occur. If changes can be anticipated, it is less likely that personnel and other resources will be misused or wasted.

Planning makes control easier. While it really is primarily a means of controlling the future, planning also provides a yardstick for a retrospective evaluation of what has occurred. It provides criteria for determining whether the work that individuals and groups have done is commensurate with what was envisioned for the future. If there is a discrepancy between plans and past performance, the fault may be in the work of subordinates. But we should also remember that the problem may lie in the poor planning of the social worker as manager that resulted in unrealistic expectations. This is especially useful to keep in mind in those organizations that make heavy use of planning systems such as Management by Objectives (MBO) for evaluation of employee performance.

Probably the most important benefit of planning for social workers in their roles as managers is planning's capacity to help us to deal with uncertainty and change. As we have suggested earlier, many of those employed in human services work in an environment that can be quite uncertain, at least in part because of a lack of consistent support within the task environment. Many social agencies, for example, are vulnerable to fluctuations in funding received from federal, state, and private sources. Even the needs of our clients can change rapidly as either other sources of help become available or as new problems emerge that require our assistance. Social work professionals are also highly mobile as a group; we can't even depend on staff stability to assist in responding to changes within our organizations and within their task environment.

The uncertainty of our work environment makes it especially important that managers use planning to minimize the chaos that change can trigger. Even some of the most frightening change scenarios become less formidable if we have thought through (in an earlier, less emotional moment) what would be the best courses of action should they occur. This is what is generally referred to as *contingency planning*. It involves asking ourselves how we will respond or what we will do if "it" occurs. What if, for example, we must take a 10 percent budget cut, or what if we do not get a grant renewed for next year? What if we no longer receive referrals from a primary referral source or what if we no longer qualify for third-party payments? What if a senior staff person takes another job or what if a client decides to sue? Contingency planning is a kind of insurance. We carry malpractice insurance to protect us from the $5 million lawsuit. But we also seek insurance in the form of contingency planning so that we will not be caught off guard, unprepared to act, and likely to make bad decisions in a moment of pressure and emotionality. We need the help of contingency planning to ensure that, if some event occurs, we will not make too many impetuous decisions or become so immobilized that we cannot decide at all.

How much contingency planning can and should a manager attempt? Everyone would agree that there is some need to plan for contingencies. But we could spend our entire day, evenings, and sleepless nights planning for contingencies and still not cover all events that might occur. There would be no time left for carrying out our other functions as managers (and as people). Overplanning for contingencies is as dangerous as underplanning because contingency planning is costly. Some happy medium must be struck.

Because we must plan and because we cannot and should not plan for all contingencies, it is logical to focus most of our planning energies on those possible future events that appear to have a reasonable likelihood of occurring. It might, for example, make sense to consider the probable needs of a situation should we have to sustain a 5 or 10 percent cutback in funding or, if there are reliable rumors on the horizon, even a 20 or 30 percent cut.

The likelihood of a 75 percent cut is so unlikely and would be so disruptive to even the existence of the organization that contingency planning around it is not a productive use of our time. Certain "doomsday" scenarios may occasionally need to be considered. But most human service organizations have enough realistic threats to occupy most of the time that a manager can devote to contingency planning.

In the role of manager, a social worker will sometimes have access to information that suggests the need for contingency planning. However, this information may have the potential to be very destructive to morale or otherwise cause the preoccupation of other staff members if shared with them. The decision as to whether to share negative (and sometimes even positive) information about what may occur is a difficult one. On the one hand, foreknowledge of a potential problem can sometimes help staff to prepare and to adjust gradually to needed changes. However, there is another compelling argument against sharing information about impending problems: If it is shared, staff members can become upset and overly concerned about something that may never materialize.

As a general policy, it is probably best to do most contingency planning without sharing concerns until the likelihood of occurrence of a situation requiring change is quite great. The decision of just how likely the occurrence of the event must be to suggest sharing knowledge about it is strictly a judgment call. It would depend on a manager's assessment of the likely impact on productivity and goal achievement of the knowledge, the time required to prepare for it, and many other factors. No formula can be applied. But we should remember that open contingency planning can have its costs. Sometimes staff and the organization (including clients) are better off not knowing what might occur, especially if it is too early for them to need to begin doing much about it anyway. It may be better in many situations to plan for contingencies by ourselves, or, if we need help in thinking through a plan, by not involving subordinates and/or those likely to be directly affected by a possible future event. Persons at the same level, particularly those not directly involved, are a safer source of assistance in developing and evaluating our plans.

> ### CASE EXAMPLE: CONSEQUENCES OF
> ### OPEN CONTINGENCY PLANNING
>
> Sheryl was the Director of Casework Services for a large state agency. She was very competent in her role as manager and recognized the importance of contingency planning. She also occasionally acted impulsively.
>
> One of her case supervisors, Jo, informed Sheryl that she was pregnant, would be quitting work in three months, and would not be returning after her baby was born. Sheryl began to plan for Jo's resignation. Shortly after her meeting with Jo, Jim, a competent caseworker with 10 years' experience working under Jo, asked

for a conference with Sheryl. He explained that he wanted to know if he could have Jo's job as supervisor when she left. Sheryl told him that she had already considered her options and decided that he was the best choice for the job. Jim was obviously very pleased at hearing this news. He revealed that he had recently received another job offer and was considering leaving, but that he would now stay. He no longer felt that he was "career blocked." Learning this, Sheryl felt even more convinced that her plan was a good one. She felt good about herself and enjoyed the obvious happiness that she brought to Jim. She was even more gratified to learn that he intended to take a short course at his own expense to prepare for the job of supervisor. The conference was extremely enjoyable for both parties.

As the euphoria of the conference began to fade, Sheryl began to have some second thoughts about the fact that she had shared her plan with Jim. She recalled a favorite warning of a previous administrator who had been fond of telling his staff to "never respond to a question about a hypothetical situation." As she thought even more about the possible consequences of her openness, Sheryl felt even more unsure about how wise she had been. True, if everything went as planned, no harm might be done by her candor and Jim would be better prepared for the job. However, many other possible events could occur, and virtually all of them would cause her to regret having promised him the job. Sheryl began to speculate:

If Jo left as planned, several negative events could occur. Jim, a good caseworker, might give indications that he did not have the qualifications necessary for the job of supervisor. Even if Sheryl's perception of Jim remained unchanged, a new and experienced caseworker might be hired in the subsequent three months who would be a better choice for the job. Or, other valued workers whom Jim told of his selection might rebel and threaten to leave if he got the job, either because they aspired to it or because they did not want to work for him.

Any change in the situation that would result in her no longer seeing Jim as the best choice would leave Sheryl in an untenable situation. If she kept her word and gave him the job, she would not have the best person in the position and would not be operating in the best interests of the organization. She would antagonize and possibly lose some good staff.

If Sheryl were to select someone other than Jim, he would be humiliated, furious, and would feel double-crossed. He might promote the idea that Sheryl was untrustworthy. He might resign or file a grievance with the agency. (He might even win a grievance suit.) At best, Sheryl would be seen as indecisive, even by those who would agree with her decision to select another supervisor.

Jo also might not leave. She might change her mind and decide to take a brief maternity leave and then return to work. Many negative consequences of Sheryl's conference with Jim could then occur. Jim would be disappointed and might resent Jo when she returned to work. Those caseworkers who had looked forward to Jim getting the job would also be disappointed at Jo's return, although they may have been satisfied with her supervision in the past. Jo would eventually learn of Sheryl's plan to replace her with Jim, and she would wonder if Sheryl didn't actually prefer Jim in the job. All of these phenomena could harm Jo's effectiveness as a supervisor, especially in her relationship with Jim.

If Jim didn't leave when Jo returned, he might have morale problems. He would certainly expect to get the next available supervisory job, a choice to which Sheryl might not prefer to feel obligated. Other good workers who might aspire to supervisory jobs might now assume that they were no better than second in line and might decide to take a job in another agency where chances for promotion would be better.

After thinking of the possible results of her having shared her plan with Jim, Sheryl felt a little like the football coach who had just called for a forward pass. There might be a good result, but the likelihood of one or more negative consequences was much greater. She vowed that, in the future, she would not respond to questions about hypothetical situations and that she would keep the results of her contingency planning to herself.

Three variables are especially important for social workers in deciding whether they should devote their limited managerial time to planning for a possible event: The likelihood of the event, the cost versus the benefits of planning, and the severity of the consequences of *not* having planned for the event should all be considered. As with all managerial activities that we have discussed and will discuss in this book, the personality of the manager and of other personnel should also play a part in deciding whether contingency planning should take place in regard to a possible future event. Some managers and some other personnel can function well in an environment of considerable uncertainty. They can react calmly and quickly when a need for change occurs and prefer not to know about or plan too much for events that may never materialize. Others are quite the opposite. They have little tolerance for uncertainty and need to spend more time in anticipation of and preparation for possible future events. Most people fall somewhere between these two extremes. Judgment of the appropriate extent of and need for contingency planning depends heavily on managers' knowledge of themselves and their co-workers. There is no sure prescription for success in contingency planning, but there is one for failure. Social workers as managers are certain to fail if they try to plan for all contingencies or for none.

SUMMARY

In this chapter we looked at why planning is often misunderstood, and we tried to view it as a natural and familiar management function of the social worker. A variety of types of plans were discussed. In giving in-depth attention to the differences between rules and policies, we tried to help the present and future manager avoid some of the many pitfalls that can result from misuse and misunderstanding of these types of plans.

All plans have a common purpose—they are ways to shape the future in a way that will increase the likelihood of our achieving what we hope to achieve. Planning is a rational approach to our work that recognizes the danger of leaving the future to chance. We have examined the benefits of planning and placed special emphasis on how contingency planning can help to reduce some of the uncertainty that inevitably seems to exist in great amounts within human service agencies. In Chapter 5 we will see how selection and use of staff by a social worker as manager will help to shape further the future and also to help reduce uncertainty within an organization.

REFERENCES

1. Harold Koontz, Cyril O'Donnell, and Heinz Weihrich, *Essentials of Management* (New York: McGraw-Hill, 1986), p. 73.
2. Ibid., p. 73.
3. Ibid., pp. 76–84.
4. See, for example, Rex A. Skidmore, *Social Work Administration* (Englewood Cliffs, NJ: Prentice-Hill, 1983), pp. 22–23, or Koontz, O'Donnell, and Weihrich, *op. cit.*, pp. 102–113.
5. Koontz, O'Donnell, and Weihrich, *op. cit.*, p. 79.

ADDITIONAL READINGS

Friedmann, J. *Planning in the Public Domain*. Princeton, NJ: Princeton University Press, 1987.

Hax, A., ed. *Planning Strategies That Work*. New York: Oxford University Press, 1987.

Newman, H. *Self-evaluation and Planning for Human Service Organizations*. New York: AMACOM, 1987.

Seville, M. "Accounting and Auditing of Human Service Organizations." *CPA*, 57 (1987), p. 34.

Turner, A. "The Planning Process: Human Problems and Solutions." *Optimum*, 16 (1985):7–23.

Vogel, L., and Patterson, I. "Strategy and Structure: A Case Study of the Implications of Strategic Planning for Organizational Structure and Management Practice." *Administration in Social Work*, 10 (1986):53–66.

CHAPTER 5

Influencing Through Knowledge of and Use of Staff

In the ideal world, social workers in their role as managers would be able to select those persons with whom they will work. They would identify the jobs to be done and would seek and hire persons with the necessary attributes for doing those jobs. In reality, most social workers assume managerial roles with relatively little choice as to which staff will be available to them. Unless the agency or organization is newly created, they find themselves with a staff made up of individuals with widely varying backgrounds, abilities, and motivational levels. These individuals may have been hired in a rational manner, but they are more likely to have joined the organization based upon a hurried perception of a current need and an apparent match with the applicant's attributes. The specific need for which they were hired may no longer exist. (They also may have been someone's unemployed brother-in-law.)

The management function term *staffing*, for most social workers in their role as managers, is really a misnomer. It is far more likely to involve, among other functions, the assessment and deployment of existing staff (some of whom may possess more job security than we have) than the assembling of a team of new employees. It is the former activities that will be the focus of much of our discussion in this chapter. Other staffing functions will be discussed in Chapters 6 through 8.

ISSUES THAT AFFECT HIRING DECISIONS

When, on occasion, the social worker as manager is fortunate enough to be involved in hiring a new employee, a number of issues must be considered. The selection of a new staff member is not and should not be a unilateral decision by any one individual. Input can be gleaned from a number of sources (there is no shortage of advice available for personnel decisions), but difficult decisions must be made regarding the appropriateness of available help and advice.

One issue relates to the question of whose input should be sought and/or used. Politically, it is impossible to ignore the wishes of a high-level administrator who wishes to be involved. Frequently, this person's wishes in regard to a staff vacancy will be consistent with the social worker as manager's perception of what is needed. But they may not be, and for good reason. It should be remembered that, whoever makes the final choice from among applicants (it may be a personnel specialist rather than a social worker in some organizations), a high-level administrator has a valuable perspective to add to the decision. An executive director, for example, must be especially concerned with the long-range survival of and planning for an organization. Such individuals are also likely to have strongly held beliefs about the kind of image they wish to project in the community and may, therefore, have specific ideas about the qualifications and style of employees that would be most consistent with that image. Both the power and the perspective of high-level administrators suggest the need for some vehicle for their input into hiring decisions.

When new employees are hired, they will assume a place somewhere in the organizational hierarchy. The person who will be their direct supervisor will undoubtedly have preferences and needs that cannot be ignored. (Of course, the social worker as manager may *be* the supervisor.) Frequently a supervisor will wish to meet and interview applicants, even if someone else is actually doing the hiring. Applicants may also insist on knowing under whom they will work. Even if a face-to-face meeting is not used, the style and preferences of the potential supervisor provide valuable input for a hiring decision. A question for which there is no easy answer is, Should a supervisor have to approve the hiring of a new employee? Generally, a rule that requires approval of the supervisor can cause problems. A particularly competent and hardworking applicant can threaten a supervisor who might wish to veto that person being hired despite the fact that the person would be a valuable asset to the organization. A veto or implied veto is always dangerous in hiring situations. A *policy* regarding guaranteed input may be preferable, in that it does not imply the power of rejection by a supervisor. This should be clarified in advance to avoid resentment when an employee is hired who, for one reason or another, was not liked by a supervisor or when one who was well liked was not hired. Once again, we see the danger of confusion as it relates to rules and policies.

The input of potential co-workers may be important but should usually be limited. Few organizations could tolerate an approach that allows future peers to vote on the hiring of an applicant. There are many subjective and self-serving reasons why future co-workers might dislike a competent applicant or might favor one of dubious knowledge and skills. For example, the work group could benefit from a new employee who is more hardworking and dedicated than a majority of current staff, but future co-workers might not enjoy the prospect of hiring that person, who might tend to "show up" the more senior staff members.

Future worker compatibility is an important consideration in selection of a job applicant. Particularly if the new employee would be joining a productive group of competent staff, a style that would easily mesh with that of the group would be an advantage. The new hire would adjust quickly and with little disruption to the group.

The need perceptions and preferences of other people in the organization are only part of what serves to influence hiring decisions made by the social worker as manager. A number of other concerns and constraints help to narrow the number of acceptable choices to fill a staff vacancy. An obvious one is the salary that can be offered. The needs of the job and the preferences of other staff may suggest the need for a graduate-school educated, experienced professional. But the amount allocated for salary in the budget may indicate that it may be more realistic to think of hiring someone with lesser academic credentials or whose experience can justify only an entry-level position. While persons employed in human services tend to exhibit an above-average level of dedication, they will not generally work for less than the salary range dictated by the market, unless they have another major source of support. However, it is not unheard of for those in human services to take a particularly challenging or professionally gratifying position when they could have made much more money elsewhere. If there is time, it may be worth seeking the optimal employee, knowing that a lowering of sights may be necessary if none can be found who will work for the remuneration offered. A permanent position that offers job security versus one that is "soft" (funded by grant or contract money that may disappear) sometimes also can make a lower-paying job more attractive.

Professional standards may leave the manager with little choice regarding the qualifications of the person hired. In recent years, an increase in certification and licensure requirements for practice have removed some of the judgment from personnel hiring decisions. Accreditation guidelines of, for example, the American Hospital Association (AHA) or the personnel standards of professional organizations like the National Association of Social Workers (NASW) have different degrees of enforceability. But the desire for good-standing dictates the need for conforming to the wishes of these groups whether they actually can threaten the existence of the organization or can do little but impose a more symbolic "slap on the wrist." No organization that depends on its professional reputation to hire new personnel or to receive client referrals can afford to regularly ignore the personnel standards set by outside organizations and, in some cases, even the legislative and judicial arms of government. In those regions where labor unions are established and powerful, additional standards may further limit the hiring choices of the social worker as manager.

Federal restrictions play an important role in hiring decisions. Over the past three decades we have seen an evolution of constraints that have been designed to counteract forces of discrimination in hiring and other personnel practices. In the United States, the Equal Pay Act of 1963 was designed to prevent discrimination based on gender. Title VII of the Civil Rights Act of 1964 was another step in the direction of nondiscrimination; it required that organizations with 15 or more employees must specify and justify hiring criteria. In 1968, Executive Order 11246 (revised later as Executive Order 11375) was a major milestone in the increasing role of government in personnel matters. It became generally known as "affirmative action."

The influence of the presence of affirmative action legislation on hiring practices has tended to ebb and flow with the attitudes and priorities of subsequent presidential administrations. During the Carter administration enforcement in the courts became quite vigorous. Several landmark decisions provided support; some challenges to it were also successful. During the Reagan administration, affirmative action underwent a period in which enforcement in the courts was frequently not in evidence. As we enter the 1990s, it remains in effect, but a number of successful challenges and opposition by various interest groups (including conservatives and labor unions) seem to have weakened its influence. Nevertheless, social workers as managers need to understand the basic thrust of affirmative action and what it means to their staffing function. Both as a social worker concerned with the problems of discrimination and social justice and as a manager seeking to comply with federal guidelines in order not to put an organization in jeopardy, such individuals must be prepared to address affirmative action concerns.

Affirmative action takes the concept of nondiscrimination a step further. It requires that organizations that have federal sources of funding (as is true of most human service organizations) must initiate steps to correct employment inequities that exist. Specifically it requires the development and implementation of a plan to grant preferential treatment in hiring and other personnel actions to women and minorities in order to increase their representation in an organization. It may sometimes involve the use of quotas, a method that opponents find particularly offensive. Other criticisms leveled center around the potential within affirmative action plans to create a situation of reverse discrimination. In fact, in one sense, that is exactly what happens. There is a certain underlying philosophy to affirmative action that the end justifies the means—short-range discrimination against white males may be necessary to correct the underrepresentation of women and minorities in many areas of the workplace that currently exists.

Not surprisingly, affirmative action often has met with considerable resistance. Those charged with enforcing it sometimes have seemed to look the other way or have accepted compromises that allowed for statements of intent and good intentions rather than actual implementation of plans. Various other means of getting around affirmative action also have been tested. A popular one has used a "clear the decks" approach whereby reasons to judge all women and minorities who apply for a job as not qualified are sought so that white males then can be freely hired.

Central to an understanding of affirmative action legislation is the difference between the concepts of *fully qualified* and *best qualified*. The former means that persons are judged to meet the requirements of a job or not; the latter involves an additional rank-ordering of all those who are fully qualified. Under an attitude of best qualified, hiring the person judged to be the top applicant for a job traditionally has been an unchallenged practice. But under affirmative action guidelines, the principle of hiring the best-qualified applicant has only limited applicability. Qualifications for a job must be carefully studied to be certain that they are really needed and not sex-linked, culturally linked, or unnecessarily discriminatory toward a minority group. If they pass this test, all fully qualified applicants are reviewed, but preferential hiring is given to women and minorities over white males. The fact that a white male might appear to have additional, desirable, but not required qualifications (for example, an additional graduate degree) cannot enter into consideration. (A woman or minority with the "bonus" could be chosen over other women or minorities without it.) The shift in emphasis from best qualified to fully qualified is a departure from what, to many people, has been a very logical and time-honored approach to employment decision making. To many, it represents a government's infringement on a manager's assessment of what is in the best interests of an organization. Advocates of affirmative action would reply that a more heterogeneous work force *is* in the best interest of the organization, as well as of the society as a whole. Some social workers who favor professionalization with its emphasis on advanced credentialing find themselves in conflict. They also favor affirmative action, which sometimes will not allow "credit" for the advanced credentials that, historically, have been more frequently held by white males.

Affirmative action and other legal protections against discrimination in hiring can also constrain social work managers in their staffing function by requiring that certain hiring procedures must be followed. Standards may require, for example, that all candidates must be interviewed or that a job opening must be advertised for a certain length of time and/or an announcement must appear in widely circulated state or national publications. Jobs that are learned about by word-of-mouth can be dangerous for an organization. Because such practices can easily lead to charges of discrimination through networking, it is usually necessary to require that job announcements are widely disseminated and that all evidence of a fair and open search is available for review. Charges of jobs being "wired" to hire a white male acquaintance can be particularly damaging to an organization that is committed to the values and ethics of social work.

We have only scratched the surface of the list of the many constraints that operate and must be considered when staff members are hired. Social work managers will need to learn what they can and cannot do (both legally and ethically) or at least they will need to find out what they need to know if they are in the position to hire staff. Even if the actual interviewing and hiring are performed by personnel specialists or managers at another level, every social worker needs to become sensitized to the fact that hiring decisions involve much more than simply choosing the job applicant that is best liked or appears to be the best qualified. Both social work values related to fairness and nondiscrimination and good, sound management practice require it.

TYPES OF STAFF WITHIN ORGANIZATIONS

One point that we make repeatedly throughout this book is that social work managers should not engage in stereotyping in working with their staff. Managers and employees are unique individuals; thus, an approach designed for the "typical" employee is almost certain to fail. We will discuss the various types of staff within organizations with this in mind. When we review various employee categories, we will limit ourselves to some very broad generalizations that usually (but not always) characterize members of that group. The categories give us an initial insight into what we can generally expect in the way of knowledge and other attributes of an employee and help to suggest how those with various backgrounds might be appropriately deployed. They will in no way substitute for the kind of firsthand knowledge of any one employee that will make possible an individualized approach to management.

Professionals

In social work practice, we are most likely to think of professionals when we think of agency staff. In beginning social work practice books, there is usually a discussion of social work as a profession. Two of the most widely used quotations in our literature[1] are used to present the issue of whether social work meets the criteria in order to be considered a profession. We will not take time away from our study of management to get involved in this never-ending debate. For our discussion, we will assume that social workers, along with physicians, psychologists, nurses, dentists, and many other groups, qualify for the label *professional*, based on the fact that we generally act more like professionals than we do nonprofessionals.

While the lists of qualifications for the label "professional" tend to vary, they usually include:

1. Decisions based on client best interest, not self-interest or personal preference.
2. Professional organizations for maintaining ethical and quality standards.
3. Specific expertise in some area of specialized learning.
4. A body of knowledge for use in practice.
5. A condemning of personal involvement with clients.
6. A single standard of conduct for working with clients.
7. Extensive formal preparation in a program of advanced study required to achieve full professional status.

What do these criteria tell the social worker as manager about what to expect from a professional? What do they say about how managers can best use the attributes of professionals to contribute to organizational objectives? The manager *should* be able to expect a high level of commitment to clients and their welfare. Professionals already have been socialized to certain values and ethical behavior that are probably consistent with those fostered by the organization. They should be able to perform their jobs with less close supervision than other staff. Professionals are likely to want to use the knowledge and skills that they have acquired in situations that require professional judgment. They may resent requirements for mindless obedience to rules and procedures. They may seek opportunities for further professional development and for receiving the kind of intellectual stimulation that can be obtained from regular contact with other like-minded professionals. They can also be expected to be critical of certain ways in which things are done in the organization, particularly if these practices are perceived to be in violation of professional ethics and standards. It is probably a cliché, but educated professionals really are the "backbone" of an organization. As long as they view the organization positively, they are a valuable asset. But they can also quickly represent a threat to an organization and its stability if their professional ire is aroused. Managers will fail in their jobs without the support, trust, and respect of their fellow professionals.

Because professionals usually function with a relatively high degree of autonomy and tend to be involved in nonstandardized activities, they often lack very specific job descriptions. Their roles may be vague and ambiguous and there may be considerable disagreement among staff at all levels as to what behaviors are expected from them. This can result in a type of role strain that sometimes leads to high absenteeism, dissatisfaction, "burnout," and high turnover among professional staff.

Other factors seem to point to the inevitability of some type of role strain for professionals within organizations. While all types of staff members that we shall discuss have the potential for role problems, professionals seem to be vulnerable to it from many directions. One source of role strain is the discrepancy between client role expectations and professionals' perception of their roles. Especially with social work professionals, there is frequently a misunderstanding on the part of clients about what a social worker does or should do. A common misconception is that professional social workers provide tangible assistance in the form of cash or commodities or that at least they are supposed to provide specific and effective solutions to problems. To many clients, "How do you feel about it?" or some other professionally acceptable response designed to help clients find answers for themselves can be viewed as inappropriate for one who claims to be so knowledgeable. An "if you know, why don't you tell?" reaction can reflect client frustration and rage that can be very stressful for professionals. Credentials can be challenged, and professionals can be made to feel as though they are on the defensive.

Professionals can also experience role strain when having to work alongside others who do not value or accept their professional credentials. Social workers employed in medical or psychiatric settings often feel that their work is not valued and that they are not viewed as "real" professionals by physicians and staff trained within other disciplines. Role strain may also be felt by professionals in their relationships with other social work staff who lack their professional education. There may be overlap in roles with nonprofessionals who may be perceived as seeking to take over ever more and more of the seemingly "glamorous" tasks that professionals wish to keep for themselves. Professionals tend to believe in the value of professional education. They generally have invested a considerable amount of time and money in acquiring it, and they may be resentful of those who seem to be performing many of the same tasks without benefit of advanced study.

Particularly for those professionals working in highly bureaucratized settings, there is likely to be conflict between organizational requirements and professional values and priorities. Paperwork, rules, procedures, and attention to lines of communication and authority can be especially maddening to professionals who see these as interfering with rather than facilitating delivery of services to clients. There may be the feeling that their professional autonomy is being restricted and that use of professional judgment is not valued, or is even discouraged. There may be annoyance that persons who, in their opinion, lack their professional knowledge and skills can nevertheless exert great influence over what they can and cannot do, simply because they occupy a high position in the organizational hierarchy.

Still another source of role strain for professionals lies in the existence of different role perceptions held by themselves and their supervisors. A supervisor can easily see a client situation and the appropriate response to it one way; a professional working directly with the client or client group may see it another. Client demands made on professionals may influence their perception of what their role should be. There may even be legitimate disagreement between the professional and his or her supervisor on the appropriate application of professional values and ethics. This can easily occur because values and ethics tend to be stated in a general way and, therefore, are open to interpretation.

Even the very nature of the role of the supervisor can cause role strain in relationships with professional supervisees. Unlike the role of supervisors in business or industry, supervisors of professionals have a heavy responsibility for the educational development of those they supervise. They spend a considerable amount of time in the role of educator. This can inevitably (and inappropriately) come very close to and sometimes can overlap into the role of counselor or therapist, creating additional role strain for the professional who may not want to be "treated." But how do you tell the person who writes your evaluation to "back off"? This problem is especially likely to occur if the supervisor has begun to miss the experience of direct client contact and wants to get involved in a more treatment-oriented relationship with the supervisee. Even if the assistance is welcomed or even sought, the respective roles can become blurred, making it difficult for both parties to have a clear understanding of their role and interfering with their ability to meet more appropriate role expectations. If the supervisor happens to be from another discipline where the expectations of the supervisory role are different, even more severe role strain can develop.

Social workers as managers need to understand the unique knowledge, skills, values, and perspectives that professionals bring to organizations. In deciding whether to hire a professional or in considering how best to use one to contribute to achievement of objectives, they also must understand the role strains that frequently exist and impact on the performance of the professional. The manager's insights should also include a knowledge of the differences in preparations and values held by different professional disciplines that may coexist within many human service organizations.

CASE EXAMPLE: PROFESSIONAL ROLE PROBLEMS IN AN INTERDISCIPLINARY AGENCY

When Mark resigned his job as chief social worker in a community mental health center after only six months, Marcia wasn't too surprised. After all, Mark took a job that paid more in a neighboring state. As the Director of Social Services for the entire state mental health system, Marcia understood that some good employees simply could make more money elsewhere. But when three highly recruited and well-recommended social work managers—Joel, Chris, and Andrew—each took the chief social worker job and resigned shortly thereafter, Marcia concluded that something must be amiss. She made an appointment to interview all three of the former employees to determine why they found their work intolerable. She hoped to be able to correct whatever problems existed before seeking to hire another replacement.

What Marcia learned from her interviews quickly confirmed her suspicions. All three presented a similar picture. They believed that the job placed them in a position of considerable role strain, both in their relationship to those employees that they supervised and in their relationship with their own supervisor. They had found that the attitudes of co-workers made them hate their jobs.

The position, which entailed the administrative supervision of the other eight MSW and BSW social workers, was supposed to be 95 percent management. The chief social worker saw patients only on rare occasions in order to handle complaints or problems about staff or to back up the other social workers who might have been unavailable. The position carried no caseload. Primary responsibilities included the hiring, evaluation, firing (if necessary), and continuing education of social work staff. The chief also served as social work liaison to the state office. This entailed regular weekly meetings with counterparts in another city, attendance at national symposia, and active participation in client advocacy and other social action activities deemed appropriate for a mid-level management social work professional working in mental health. At least, that was the way that Marcia and the series of chief social workers perceived the job; the perception was also reflected in the job description that was on file.

Unfortunately, the other social workers and the center's director had different perceptions that had put the chief social worker under a great amount of role strain. Other social work staff members deeply resented the fact that the chief did not see patients; they blamed their heavy caseload on this fact. The staff became very annoyed when they looked for the chief and were told that the person was not in the office. They constantly sought clinical case supervision despite the fact that this function was supposed to be handled by the senior worker. They kept records of days that the chief was out of town at meetings, conferences, and other activities and sarcastically referred to them as "vacation time." No matter how frequently efforts were made to explain and clarify the respective roles of the chief social worker and the other professional staff, the resentment continued. It even seemed to get worse, Marcia surmised, after each successive occupant of the position attempted to address the problem. Workers even began to leave anonymous notes for the director to be certain that she knew each time that the chief of social services was out of the office.

While the director of the center, Sally, a psychiatrist, could have helped to alleviate the role strain between the chief social workers and their staff, she did not. In fact, she tended to agree with many of the misconceptions held by the other social workers and even had a few of her own. She regularly tried to impose limitations on the actions of her chief social worker in order to make that person's role more consistent with what *she* believed it should be. She held a belief common among physicians that, as a social worker, the chief should really be spending time seeing patients, or preferably, families of patients. She was annoyed when the chiefs were not in their offices and shared the feeling of the other social workers that time spent out of the office was time off from work. She perceived their activities on behalf of client rights as disloyal to her and to the organization.

She made them take personal leave time in order to present papers at national social work conferences, yet did not do the same for her presentations at medical and psychiatric conferences. She frequently invoked a policy that allowed her to deny them permission to attend weekly social work meetings in the state office if, in her judgment, their presence was needed in the center. All three chief social workers had been told that their work was unsatisfactory and that, in the future, Sally would be doing what she could to see that they stayed in the center to begin seeing patients and their families.

After learning of the role strain experienced by Joel, Chris, and Andrew, Marcia concluded that *no* chief social worker (at least not one that had the professional characteristics that she valued) could remain in the job for long. She immediately set out to alleviate the problem in a series of meetings with the State Director of Mental Health, with Sally, and with the social work staff at the center. She told the social work staff what the chief social worker's role was to be and what it was not. She clearly laid out her expectations for them in their interaction with the next chief. While she did not hesitate to explain the rationale for their respective roles, she made it clear that, generally, what she was telling them was not negotiable. However, she did agree to consider whether case supervision might not be a more appropriate role for the next chief social worker than for the senior worker (who really didn't want the responsibility and preferred to see more of her own cases). She later presented this to the next chief, who was happy to take over this responsibility.

Marcia met with the State Director of Mental Health and with Sally individually and then together. She believed that, primarily because of the director's support of her position, Sally ultimately reflected a noticeable shift in her beliefs and attitudes about the role of the chief of social services. When the new person, Paula, was hired, she found both Sally and her staff to be much more cooperative, and she experienced much less role strain than had her predecessors.

Nonprofessionals

The term *nonprofessional* is used in our discussion to differentiate certain staff members from professionals. It is not used in a derogatory way or to imply that the staff members that we are describing are somehow less important, that their contributions are necessarily less valuable, or that they are likely to behave in inappropriate ways. We are also not suggesting that the term nonprofessional should be used by the manager in dealing with the staff. In fact, in some organizations, the terms *professional* and *nonprofessional* are avoided altogether in order not to suggest a kind of caste system—all staff are just referred to as either paid or unpaid. This is probably not a bad idea as it does not lend additional support to the elitism that sometimes exists among professionals.

One subgroup of persons who are not professionals are sometimes referred to as *preprofessionals*. They are individuals who share an identification and commitment to the same goals, values, and ethics with professionals, but they fall short on one or more professional criteria. Usually they have not yet completed the professional degree or have not received some other credential that the profession requires for full status. Preprofessionals may be students (for example, they may be completing an internship or field placement), they may have had their formal education interrupted and have not yet gone back to complete requirements, or they may simply have not yet passed an examination or board. They have been brought into the organization because they possess certain knowledge and skills that contribute to achievement of objectives. In most cases they will become professionals someday, probably quite soon.

Preprofessionals generally require more supervision and monitoring than do professionals. Because of credentialing regulations, they also may be more limited in the work that they are allowed to perform than are professionals. Paid preprofessionals may be very productive. Students may be somewhat less productive in terms of actual units of work produced. Their primary role as learners will also put an additional drain on the time of professional staff. Both groups, but particularly students, are likely to ask many questions, some of which professional staff may struggle to answer. Preprofessionals enhance accountability and, by questioning all aspects of the way work is done, often promote needed changes. They can breathe fresh ideas into an organization; this is especially useful in relatively stable settings where staff turnover is low and behaviors have become routinized and unlikely to go challenged. Of course, preprofessionals also can easily threaten the manager and other staff who have slipped into certain behavior patterns that lack a logical rationale.

A second type of nonprofessional, first widely used in the 1960s and 1970s, is the *indigenous* nonprofessional. A frequent criticism of social agencies during that time was that they were staffed by persons (usually white, upper middle class) who were out of touch with and unable to relate well to clients. The consumer movement was demanding more client participation in organizational decision making. Indigenous nonprofessionals were hired, not because of their formal training or professional skills (though some did have these too), but because of certain demographic characteristics that had the potential to contribute to the effectiveness of the organization while defusing community resentment.

Indigenous nonprofessionals may bring to an organization a cultural affiliation with client groups and/or problem experiences that are shared with clients. If they share a culture, they are likely to possess the same values, customs, beliefs, general life experiences, and insights as clients. They will be better able to communicate with them and will be more readily accepted and trusted. They will understand and be able to have access to the informal power structure that exists within a community. If they have had similar problems, they can understand the difficult process of overcoming them. They can't be accused of not knowing how it really is. If they have overcome a problem (for example, alcoholism or drug addiction) they can serve as a role model while giving valuable help to those still struggling with the problem. Their credibility is much better than those who have never "been there." When they challenge or confront a client or client group, they are usually less likely to be resented for their behavior.

There are obvious political reasons why managers hire and use indigenous nonprofessionals. They have been used to gain acceptance and credibility within a community and to attempt to improve an agency's image. While there is nothing inherently wrong with using them for these purposes, their most valuable contribution is as instruments for change. If indigenous nonprofessionals are given little real input into decisions and if their activities are tightly controlled, they can quickly become hostile and resentful. They may actually harm the image of an organization within the community, especially if they are perceived as little more than "tokens" or "window dressing." But if used appropriately, they help an organization to stay "in touch," serving as a communication channel between an organization and its clients. If given reasonable autonomy, they can be instrumental in promoting timely changes that will ensure that services offered are those that are needed and are well received.

The manager who has a strong need to control and who does not take criticism well may experience difficulties in the use of indigenous nonprofessionals. The very characteristics that make these people valuable to an organization can easily put a manager on the defensive. Candid and direct criticism of a manager from indigenous nonprofessionals, criticism not clothed in the tactful verbiage of the professional, can appear abrasive. Even though the criticism may hurt, it should be remembered that those who provide a critique of how well a social worker functions as a manager usually offer more valuable input than those who submit praise. Indigenous nonprofessionals who are doing their job will definitely keep managers on their toes.

Support Staff

A social worker usually does not need to be convinced of the importance of good support personnel. Secretarial and other clerical staff can keep work flowing smoothly or they can seriously impair the functioning of others. They can present an image of competence or dedication or one of disorganization and preoccupation. The work of custodial and maintenance staff can likewise reflect either pride in an organization or apathy that is easily conveyed to clients and the public at large.

In their role as managers, social workers know the importance of hiring and keeping good support staff, but they frequently are frustrated in their efforts. Human service agencies often are notorious for their low pay for all staff, but particularly those who have little recognized claim to professional status. Organizations can become training grounds for entry-level workers who, if they are competent, frequently move on to private, for-profit settings that can offer far better pay and fringe benefits. Yet some very good support staff members remain despite better offers. The task for the manager often is to identify the intangible benefits that are helping to keep the long-term good worker and to try to offer more of these benefits to others whom they wish to keep.

A human service organization may be able to offer job security to a member of the support staff that is not available in the profit-oriented private sector. In the latter, if business deteriorates, support staff are often the first to go. Human service organizations also sometimes tend to be a little more egalitarian than are businesses. Support staff may be treated with a little more sensitivity and respect. They may even occupy positions of considerable power that are not reflected in their official slot on the organizational hierarchy. For example, a competent senior member of the secretarial staff is often a most important part of the staff. This person represents continuity and the source of knowledge and experience that others turn to as professional staff come and go. Such individuals are often privy to a considerable amount of information and insight into political issues that keeps their job interesting and makes them a valuable resource. These phenomena are less likely to occur in a for-profit corporation where higher-level staff may pay more attention to the fact that such people are "just secretaries" and may be more condescending in their treatment of them.

Much of the work performed by support staff is unstimulating and repetitive. If a manager can find ways to introduce variety into their day, staff members will find their work more pleasant. The time spent in socializing and other technically nonproductive activities may also perform a function of relieving boredom, thereby keeping a good worker around. The social worker as manager will want to carefully assess the cost-benefit ratio of establishing rigid controls to reduce this behavior. It may not be a good idea, unless the behavior represents a serious loss to efficiency for the organization. Elsewhere in this book we will discuss the dangers of the use of rigid controls and other issues affecting the use of support staff. For now, it will suffice to say that support staff are an important and sometimes very difficult group for social work managers to work with in their staffing functions as managers.

Volunteers

Some organizations depend heavily on the use of volunteers and have used them for many years. For example, adult Red Cross volunteers, candy stripers, and other volunteers have long been an integral part of patient services within hospitals. Other organizations only recently have begun to use volunteers, a decision influenced in part by a renewed emphasis on volunteerism during the 1980s. Despite a recent increase in the number of women involved in paid employment, the number of individuals active in voluntary activities continues to grow. Both young adults and elders in particular were reflecting a greater involvement in volunteerism as we entered the 1990s.

There are obvious benefits to the social work manager in the use of volunteers. The most obvious of these is that volunteers can perform many jobs at minimal costs. While they are not "free" in the sense that they require supervisory time and are usually reimbursed for some of their expenses (travel, meals, etc.), volunteers offer many services, thereby freeing up paid staff to do other work.

Some benefits of using volunteers are more subtle. In a way similar to indigenous nonprofessionals, volunteer staff can provide greater credibility for the organization within the community. They can provide a valuable communication linkage with the consumer. They can help to avoid some of the barriers that an overly professionalized organization sometimes seems to construct. Somehow, a client entering an agency and seeing a volunteer who is also a part of the community can provide a kind of legitimization for the organization. Volunteers also can do something that paid staff often cannot. They can offer "unhurried attention, one-to-one caring and community input in planning."[2] Finally, some contracts and grants from federal, state, and even private sources may require citizen involvement if certain programs are to be funded. Volunteers can help to meet these requirements.

The social worker as manager should recognize that there are also many potential dangers and costs in the use of volunteers. Generally, volunteers are more difficult to control than are paid staff members. They don't have an economic *need* to work in a given organization; others would probably welcome their services if they were to become unhappy and leave. Volunteers are usually not professionals and may not share the same values and ethics as professional and even nonprofessional staff. For example, confidentiality and punctuality may be a problem. A healthy curiosity about what goes on in an agency can become problematic if interest in clients and internal organizational problems exceeds the need to know and is shared with others outside the organization. What seemed like such a clever political coup in bringing the spouse of a prominent politician on the staff as a volunteer can quickly turn to regret and problems when the volunteer talks too much about potentially sensitive material at home.

People volunteer for many different reasons. A manager needs to understand the complex motivation that prompts individuals to volunteer their time without compensation. Their reasons for volunteering often reflect a mixture of personal need and altruism. Sometimes it is hard to identify the primary motivator. Some volunteers may enjoy the education and intellectual stimulation that a professional work environment provides. They also may gain considerable gratification from working with others toward a common goal. The social interaction also frequently is mentioned as important to those volunteers who have a need to be with others.

More altruistic reasons for volunteering may be found in a strong feeling about a need to help others and a wish to contribute something. Volunteers also may hold a conviction that a change is needed and that they should do their part in working toward it.

Some people volunteer because they seek responsibility, want to contribute to the happiness of others, or are simply happier when they are productive. Others may wish to share what they've learned over the years. Sometimes they wish to do for someone what they were never really comfortable in doing for those close to them. Even alleviating personal guilt in this way is not necessarily bad for an organization. But the manager needs to be able to assess just what it is that the volunteer is seeking.

The complexity of the motivation of volunteers (about the only thing that we can be sure of is that they are not doing it for the money) can set limits on their deployment by the social work manager. Generally, volunteers want to do what *they* want to do (jobs consistent with their motivation) and will strongly resist or simply refuse to do anything else. Unlike a paid employee, they don't *have* to do the less pleasant job that has to be done. If pushed hard enough, they will simply leave. (For the volunteer who hasn't worked out well, a manager sometimes may deliberately provoke such a response.)

Some tasks are, by their very nature, appealing to volunteers. Others aren't much fun and have fewer takers. For example, in a hospital setting, there is usually no shortage of volunteers to read to patients or to assume a "friendly visitor" role. More strenuous or less rewarding jobs such as assisting in rehabilitative therapy are less vigorously sought. Fortunately, the complex needs that drive people to volunteer result in widely varying volunteer preferences. Some jobs, where the needs of patients and clients are very great, are not outwardly attractive for the volunteer, but there may be significant intrinsic benefits. Volunteers, once they become aware of these benefits, may find the job most rewarding. For example, hospice volunteers who offer a variety of assistance to terminally ill cancer patients report a great feeling of satisfaction derived from their work. This kind of experience and others similar to it are not for every volunteer or even for the majority. The manager who fails to recognize this and assigns volunteers to needed work as if they were paid staff may soon find that they have an abbreviated list of volunteers.

The roles of volunteers in human service organizations vary widely. They might offer direct individual or group services to clients, participate in citizen action groups, serve on advisory boards of public or private agencies, take part in self-help or mutual aid groups, or do any number of clerical and semiskilled or even unskilled jobs that need to be done. The nature of the task or tasks will determine the amount of training, education, and supervision that will be required. Larger volunteer programs suggest the need for a staff member assigned full-time to oversee the program. Even volunteer programs with only one or two members will need a person clearly designated to supervise them. There is also a need for a sincere commitment to preparing and assisting volunteers in their work on the part of other staff. Happy and productive volunteers are those who know what they are doing as a result of appropriate training and a clear job description. They also receive regular help and feedback by a designated person, a fairly common role for a social work manager.

In deciding whether to use volunteers or how to use them, the manager must be able to see beyond their obvious financial advantages. Volunteers can be a real asset or a liability to an organization. They can either do wonders for public relations or they can be a major source of embarrassment. Before choosing to use volunteers, several questions should be addressed. These include:

1. Are there tasks that lend themselves to the needs and interests of available volunteers and are these tasks easily defined?
2. Can volunteers be recruited who will appropriately meet the needs of the organization?
3. Will other staff accept and work comfortably with volunteers or will they be resented or be allowed only token participation?
4. Will volunteers' contributions be recognized by staff as valuable or will there be a tendency to put down their work as of lesser value than that of paid staff?
5. Is there sufficient available staff time for training, staff development, education, and supervision of volunteers?
6. Can the organization tolerate the uncertainty and unevenness of service that volunteers sometimes bring, and would high volunteer turnover be a problem?
7. Will staff reflect tolerance of a wide range of volunteer demographic characteristics and motivation or do they have narrow attitudes about just how a volunteer should look and act?
8. Will staff accept volunteers in many different levels of input, and how will they receive volunteer efforts to change the way things are done?

The presence of conditions that would argue against the use of volunteers should not necessarily preclude their use. For example, paid staff can be helped by the manager to change some of the beliefs and attitudes that would currently sabotage their productive use. Sometimes only the presence of volunteers will convince some of those who are most resistive and initially resentful of them. While the manager cannot afford to cause too much disruption in the work environment, a little incremental change can often be desirable. The experimental use of one or two carefully chosen volunteers (two is better for mutual support) placed where their potential for success is high sometimes can be a good first step in the development of a viable volunteer program.

There is every reason to believe that volunteers will become an even more integral part of the staff of human service organizations in future decades. Because of volunteers' potential to enhance efficiency, social work managers need to be sensitive to areas where volunteers can contribute to achievement of organizational objectives. Managers also need to be aware that, as a group and as individuals, volunteers have unique assets and liabilities. The manager needs to be able to assess these objectively in considering their use and in providing the necessary support for their activities.

TOWARD THE OPTIMAL STAFF MIX

We have briefly discussed some of the categories of staff that exist within human service organizations and their similarities and differences. There is no formula or recipe for providing the exact proportion of each staff category that is best for all organizations or even for any given organization. Even if we could obtain that kind of knowledge, just about the time we were successful in achieving the optimal mix, the needs of the organization would change and we would have to make staffing changes anyway. Nevertheless, managers will make better staffing decisions if they recognize and understand some of the issues that influence what is a good balance of different staff types in an organization.

The Professionalization Issue

For social workers, professionalization generally has been seen as a desirable goal. However, the issues of just how many professionals are best and how much professionalization is desirable and when professionalization can become nonproductive or cause more problems than it prevents are important to consider. Before a manager rushes to upgrade the credential level of staff and engages in other activities designed to professionalize, the manager needs to recognize both the pros and the cons of such an effort.

An important question to ask is: In this work environment, *for whom* is professionalization desirable? The question is best answered with reference to a concept that we mentioned earlier, namely prime beneficiary. Undoubtedly there are benefits to staff in professionalization. It can lead to higher status and rewards and to a greater pride in one's work. However, professionalization can also represent a threat to staff. Just as physicians have found in recent years, claims to professional status have convinced the general public that treatment is a science based on cause-effect knowledge. As a result, mistakes tend not to be tolerated; they can land a professional in court facing a malpractice suit. Those with less claim to professional status are usually less vulnerable. It appears that there has been a direct association between social work's success at gaining recognition as a profession and the presence and threat of malpractice suits. The point is, even from the perspective of staff, professionalization is probably at best a mixed blessing that should not be regarded as universally desirable.[3]

Of course, based on social work values and ethics, the client or client groups served should be regarded as the prime beneficiary. Again, on the surface, professionalization of staff and of service delivery would seem to be nothing but desirable. What could be bad about the delivery of services by highly educated professionals using a single standard of quality regulated by a professional organization? It would seem difficult to argue that professionalization is anything but good. If a manager is fortunate enough to work in an organization that can pay the cost of highly professionalized service delivery, why not? The problem sometimes can lie in too much of a good thing. An overly professionalized organization actually can create barriers to client service while it should facilitate them. Frequently, professionalization carries with it some undesirable baggage. Professionals and other staff who are encouraged to look and to act like professionals *may* provide assurance of competence and objectivity to clients, but their behavior also can tend to accentuate differences between clients and staff and to weaken staff credibility. Particularly when cultural and social class differences already exist, a highly professionalized organization can seem to create even more distance between the organization and those whom the organization would serve. Some of the symbols of professionalization (for example, attractive offices, efficient receptionists, white coats) can serve to underscore differences between how clients live and how staff function.

The decision as to how much professionalization is desirable both in assembling a staff and in influencing their behavior and work environment is a difficult one for social workers as managers. No generalizations are possible. Managers must decide what is best for their work situation. Specifically, they must ask, What level of professionalization will best facilitate the efficient and effective delivery of services? Their answer will give clues as to the directions that they should take. In some organizations, a highly professionalized work environment is desirable. In others, more casual, laid-back approaches that emphasize similarities between client and staff and that emphasize a dedicated but fallible approach to offering help may be desirable. Whether in selecting staff or in shaping an organizational climate, the manager must remember and must help others to remember that client interests must be the first priority.

Organizational Staff Types

Sometimes it is helpful for the manager in making staffing decisions to look beyond the descriptive criteria that allow us to place staff into one of the categories that we have discussed. Staff may seem to be influenced in their work by factors that seem to transcend their educational achievements or job category. Bearing in mind that any categorizing and stereotyping of human beings always is a dangerous and misleading activity, there is still some value in looking at another way of categorizing staff that has been discussed in the business literature for many years. It offers some insights that still have utility for the social work manager.

In 1957, Alvin Gouldner's research suggested that paid staff tend to fall into one of two categories. He called one group "locals" and the other "cosmopolitans." He proposed three criteria for determining whether a staff member is a local or a cosmopolitan. They are (1) the object of the individual's loyalty, (2) their primary reference group, and (3) their degree of commitment to skills.[4]

A local owes primary loyalty to the organization. The local's primary reference group is those persons who appear as immediate supervisors on the organizational chart, whether or not the supervisor was educated in the same discipline. Locals have a relatively low commitment to the skills of their discipline. If, for example, a promotion were offered that would change their job to require primarily supervision of other staff rather than use of their professional skills, locals would eagerly accept it in order to move up within the organization.

Cosmopolitans reflect the opposite characteristics. Their primary loyalty is to their profession and to its values. For example, if a conflict were to arise between the demands of the organization and their professional values or ethics, they would take a position consistent with the latter. Their primary reference group is their fellow professionals, not necessarily the person who occupies the position on the organizational chart immediately above their own. A colleague's opinion of their work is more important to them than that of a supervisor whose identification is with another discipline. Cosmopolitans are highly committed to professional skills and demonstrate a desire to use them. For example, they would not be interested in a promotion to an administrative position where they could no longer practice the skills that they learned as part of their professional education.

While professionally educated persons are more likely to be cosmopolitans than locals, there are numerous exceptions. If we apply the Gouldner typology to a common social work practice situation, we can illustrate this point. Two social workers who are graduates of the same MSW program and who both majored in micro-practice methods may be employed as medical social workers within a hospital setting. They are assigned to work on different medical services, one in pediatrics and the other in obstetrics. The first social worker is a professional and a cosmopolitan. She has a reputation for fighting the discharge of patients when, in her professional opinion, family members have been inadequately prepared for their roles in home care. While she values the opinion of the physician who oversees most of her work, she places a higher premium on the opinion of her work that is held by the Chief of Social Services, with whom she regularly staffs all of her problem cases. She likes and values her direct service to clients and has little interest in moving into supervision, unless she can be assured that she will be allowed to carry a partial caseload.

The second social worker is a local. He is highly loyal to the hospital and supportive of its policies. He is very proud of his association with it. He accepts the fiscal necessity of DRG's (diagnostic categories that determine third-party reimbursement and that often result in limits on length of hospitalization for patients with certain diagnoses) and has never opposed a physician's recommendation for discharge of a patient. He identifies himself as an "obstetrical social worker" to friends and neighbors and values the opinion of his work held by the Chief of Obstetrics much more highly than that of the Chief of Social Services. He would like very much to move up in the organizational hierarchy in social work or some other administrative area and would not be concerned if the promotion meant that he could no longer use his direct practice skills.

The local/cosmopolitan typology is, of course, an oversimplification of the real world. Critics of it have pointed out that the two types are not inclusive of all staff that exist within organizations. Some people seem to have some characteristics of both locals and cosmopolitans. Some seem to meet the criteria for both. Others (the ones whom the manager hopes are few) seem to be largely self-serving, lacking in loyalty to anything but themselves, not valuing the opinions of others, and having little commitment to either professional skills or to moving up within the organizational hierarchy. However, even those persons who suggest the shortcomings of the Gouldner typology acknowledge that it is helpful and has at least limited utility in understanding and deploying staff.

It should be noted by the social worker as manager that persons who tend to have the characteristics of cosmopolitans are not necessarily more desirable employees than locals or vice versa. Both have a contribution to make, as suggested by our example of the two medical social workers. Both also represent risks and potential problems for the manager. Locals are likely to do what they are told without much questioning; they will want to please their immediate superiors. They are not likely to debate the professional ethics of what needs to be done to meet the requirements of the organization. They usually will not object if asked to perform a task that is outside their job description or what they claim as their professional area of expertise. Locals tend to make a career within a single organization; they are not likely to leave as long as promotions and other rewards occur on a fairly regular basis. They can be depended on to speak well of the organization within the community and to try to cover for its embarrassing mistakes. They tend to respect such bureaucratic features as the chain of command, and they pay close attention to rules and procedures that, they believe, are in everyone's best interests overall.

On the negative side, locals can tend to be too agreeable and compliant. They don't speak up or offer valuable critique when it is needed. Their deference to those in authority can make life easy for the manager in some ways, but it also cheats the manager of the negative feedback that is sometimes needed. Managers who are especially insecure or in need of validation for their decisions have a tendency to surround themselves with locals who are almost always complimentary of what they do. A mutual admiration society can develop. Managers get a distorted idea of their skills and abilities and, making matters worse, start to discount the opinions and advice of those who are even mildly critical. Before long they listen to nobody *but* locals, who may lack a kind of professional conscience. Because of a lack of commitment to professional skills, locals may not have much interest in continued professional growth and are less likely to remain current on emerging knowledge in their field than are cosmopolitans (but they know the current policy manual!).

Cosmopolitans provide a needed critical perspective on the activities of persons and activities within an organization. They insist on adherence to professional standards. In human service organizations, they often provide needed advocacy for clients and the protection of their rights. They offer fresh new ideas that emanate both from their contacts with professionals outside the organization and from their efforts to continue to practice and upgrade their skills. They are not preoccupied with moving up in the organizational hierarchy and never lose sight of the primacy of client needs. They are less likely to get involved in means-end displacements than are locals, as long as they agree with the objectives of the organization.

As with locals, the negative contributions of cosmopolitans to organizations are really just the other side to their positive contributions. Cosmopolitans tend to challenge and question a little too much, sometimes failing to accept the realities of politics, fiscal limitations, and a need for efficiency as valid reasons to offer services that are less than perfect. They may share their criticisms of the organization with community members. They may have little respect for authority and tend to ignore the administrative hierarchy and the chain of command. In service to clients, they may frequently take an "end justifies the means" attitude that tends to ignore rules and procedures and makes overly liberal use of exceptions to policy. They may advocate for change based on new ideas and approaches to practice, sometimes even if there is nothing essentially wrong with the way work is currently being performed. There may be a tendency on their part to think that conditions are better elsewhere. Because they are not committed to a career within the organization, cosmopolitans tend to be highly mobile. If they become too unhappy, their colleagues within the professional community will help them to find work elsewhere. They may give adequate notice about leaving or they may not, especially if they are very unhappy with the organization. They may exert considerable influence over other cosmopolitans, agitating them to the point of leaving with them or at least making them more dissatisfied with their work than they had previously been.

No social work manager would ever wish for a staff consisting of all locals or all cosmopolitans. The two types tend to complement each other—both offer needed attributes and perspectives. Clearly, some mix of the two (and of less pure types) is most desirable.

What factors influence the mix that would be optimal for a given organization? Generally, those organizations that are dependent on adherence to rules and procedures for funding and reimbursement function best with a majority of staff who are locals. A public-assistance agency, for example, could not tolerate too many cosmopolitans (and would not attract them). Neither would a state correctional facility. In contrast, a private adoption agency or private psychiatric clinic might require (and attract) a majority of cosmopolitans. A certain amount of natural selection takes place: People tend to want to work in settings that value their attributes. If they don't perceive that they are appreciated, they leave to find another place to work where what they have to offer is more consistent with the needs of the organization. Social workers as managers should not be alarmed to observe that they have a preponderance of locals or cosmopolitans on their staff. It is likely to be a result of the natural selection process. Of course, if they clearly have the *wrong* majority, they may have a problem.

As a conceptual model that is not always consistent with the world as it actually exists, the local/cosmopolitan typology is of some use. It does a better job of labeling and of identifying potential problem areas for the social worker as manager than it does of suggesting ways to address them.

SUMMARY

In this chapter we looked at some of the factors that affect a manager's understanding of the hiring and use of staff. We have examined the various types of staff frequently seen in human service organizations and have presented their general characteristics.

Problems of professionals within organizations were examined as well as broader issues related to the desirability of professionalization. A categorization of staff (local/cosmopolitan) that has been around for a long time was "resurrected" to illustrate one of the many personnel typologies available to the manager for assistance in gaining insight into the mix of people who function within a given work situation. We will examine the issue of staff motivation in greater depth in Chapter 8.

This chapter has examined only part of what is generally regarded as the management function of staffing. In the next three chapters we will focus on other staffing activities.

REFERENCES

1. Ernest Greenwood, "Attributes of a Profession," *Social Work*, 2(3), (July 1957):55; Abraham Flexner, "Is Social Work a Profession?" *Proceedings of the National Conference of Charities and Correction* (Chicago: The Hildman Printing Company, 1915), pp. 576–590.
2. Robert Clifton and Alan Dahms, *Grassroots Administration* (Monterey, CA: Brooks/Cole, 1980), p. 113.
3. Robert Weinbach, "Accountability Crises: Consequences of Professionalization," *Journal of Sociology and Social Welfare*, IV(7), (September 1977):1011–1024.
4. Alvin Gouldner, "Cosmopolitans and Locals," *Administrative Science Quarterly*, 2 (1957–58):281–306 and 444–480.

ADDITIONAL READINGS

Bowes, L. *No One Need Apply*. Cambridge, MA: Harvard Business School Press, 1987.

Moffat, T. *Selection Interviewing for Managers*. Madison, WI: Science Technology, 1987.

Netting, F. "Ethical Issues in Volunteer Management and Accountability." *Social Work*, 32 (1978):250–251.

Pierce, J., and Dunham, R. "Organizational Commitment: Pre-employment Propensity and Initial Work Experience." *Journal of Management*, 13 (1987): 163–178.

Smart, B. "Progressive Approaches for Hiring the Best People." *Training & Development Journal*, 41 (1987):46–53.

Sutton, R., and Lewis, M. "How Selecting and Socializing Newcomers Influences Insiders." *Human Resource Management*, 26 (1987):347–361.

CHAPTER 6

Influencing Employee Growth

No matter what credentials and experience employees bring to the organization, they will start to change beginning with their first day on the job. As social workers, we are well aware of the influence that the organization, work groups, and other systems have on the knowledge, attitudes, and behaviors of workers. As managers, we must assume an active role in shaping the changes that inevitably take place so that they are in a direction that is consistent with the organization's goal achievement. While many factors promote desirable professional growth among employees, we will focus upon the two most powerful influences available to the manager—supervision and continuing education.

Both supervision and continuing education form a source of support and of learning for employees in human service organizations. By providing them, managers are telling employees that they value and are willing to commit necessary time and other resources to promote more effective work performance. They are communicating a message that emphasizes the importance of learning to do more, to do it better, and to do it more autonomously. In earlier chapters and those that follow, we have referred to how the social worker as manager can contribute to the creation of a desirable climate for work. Supervision and continuing education can provide the knowledge necessary for employees to do their job within a climate of reasonable certainty. It is impossible for anyone to know everything that is needed to know in order to approach every task and decision confidently. But supervision and continuing education help to reduce to a tolerable minimum the number of decisions where employees feel lost and unprepared. They rarely will find themselves totally without the knowledge necessary to make an intelligent decision or to perform a task. Even when it appears that employees have had little preparation for a specific decision, the presence of good supervision and the resources identified through continuing education will provide sources of help.

GROWTH THROUGH SUPERVISION

There are many good recent texts that prepare the reader for the job of social work supervisor.[1] This is not our purpose here. As we have noted before, social workers as managers may actually hold the job of supervisor, but they may also hold any other position within the organization. A manager at any level in the organization needs to understand what supervision is and to be aware of some of the options available for its provision.

One problem that is frequently encountered in understanding supervision is the different functions that are encompassed under the term. The social worker who is a direct service practitioner is most likely to envision supervision as a process designed to provide workers with insights and assistance in working with individual cases. This is commonly referred to as *case supervision* and, sometimes, as *case consultation*. While this is a legitimate area of supervision and a necessary one, we really cannot understand supervision as managers unless we broaden our understandings to include many other interactions between supervisors and workers that have only an indirect relationship to treatment offered to specific clients. There exists another whole group of supervisory activities that more closely resembles our focus of study—management. It includes the use of management functions as applied to subordinates to shape, support, and enhance their job performance.

Traditional Supervisory Roles

Confusion over case supervision and administrative supervision permeates our literature. One author[2] helped to differentiate supervisory roles by dividing the functions of the supervisor into three slightly overlapping activities: administrative supervision; supportive supervision; and educational supervision. This author, Alfred Kadushin, addressed a related area, consultation, in another text.[3] The three roles (along with consultation) provide a workable overview of supervision for social workers as managers who recognize the need to assure that good supervision is provided, whether by themselves or by others whom they designate.

Kadushin's description of administrative supervision comes closest to what we are referring to as management. It involves such important functions as work assignment and review, overseeing, communicating, serving as a buffer between higher-level administrators and workers, and matching of workers to tasks.

The second role, supportive supervision, spotlights a major difference in emphasis between the role of the social work supervisor and supervisors in many businesses and industries. The type of job stresses and tensions inherent in many human service organizations (for example, in child protection, investigation of charges of family violence, or hospice work) often dictate that much of the supervisor's time is spent in providing psychological support to a supervisee. With this support, workers can continue to function on the job without being overwhelmed by the types of stresses that exist within their work.

The third major role described by Kadushin, namely educational supervision, also represents somewhat of a departure from how business or industry defines supervision. The role of teacher or mentor usually is not emphasized in a manufacturing plant. If anything, such a role may be perceived as inappropriate in that it might compromise the objectivity required to perform the major supervisory function, which is administrative supervision. But in human service organizations, the supervisor is expected to take on the role of educator, partly by facilitating continuing education for a supervisee, but also by providing direct instruction. It is the supervisor who is supposed to pass on the combination of "humanitarian impulse, occupational folklore and common sense" that have frequently been relied upon by practitioners in their work when empirical knowledge is not available.[4]

As a case consultant, the supervisor recognizes the need for professional autonomy of subordinates. But supervisors also acknowledge that some particularly difficult cases may require the assistance of a senior professional with more experience and/or a different perspective. In this role, the supervisor may be an employee of the organization or may be brought in from the outside on a regular basis as a kind of troubleshooter. The role of case consultant would not be totally inconsistent with the role of consultant as used within some large corporations. However, it would be unlikely that a business in a highly competitive task environment would ever seek consultation from those employed by a competitor to gain assistance in addressing problems of a technical nature. Human service agencies do this.

Supervisory Options

The word "supervision" usually tends to connote a one-to-one type of relationship, as illustrated in our past discussion. The manager should know that, in making provisions for the supervision necessary for employee growth, there are several viable options to the traditional social work supervisor–supervisee model. Each option should be seriously considered; each may offer time and cost saving advantages as well as a format that may be preferred by some professionals. We will examine two of them.

Interdisciplinary Supervision. Although ideally it might be best for an employee to be supervised by a person who is from the same discipline and who has engaged in or is currently engaged in performing the same tasks, this is not always possible. As managers, social workers sometimes recognize that opportunities for growth of an employee can be limited by the employee receiving professional supervision from any one supervisor. The supervisor may lack the knowledge and experience to supervise the employee in activities that are important to that individual's professional development. For example, a relatively new employee in an inpatient mental health setting may be interested in learning more about a certain type of group treatment being offered in the hospital. The group leader may be a psychologist, and the employee's social work supervisor (a senior-level social worker) admits to little knowledge of or interest in this type of treatment. In order not to preclude the employee from having this experience and growth opportunity, a manager may assign a portion of the supervision to the psychologist. However, supervision of all other professional activities and all administrative and supportive supervision will remain with the social work supervisor. Only a small portion of the task of educational supervision has been "farmed out."

Depending upon the number of desirable interdisciplinary learning opportunities available and the supervisory capacities of staff, the scope of interdisciplinary supervision may be far more extensive than that described in our example. Because of either choice or necessity, most, and sometimes nearly all, professional supervision is provided by someone from another discipline or by an interdisciplinary team consisting of persons from various disciplines. When this situation exists, it is imperative that the social worker as manager recognizes both the inherent dangers and educational advantages that can exist. There is the potential for professional identity to become confused. The employee may even contribute willingly to this phenomenon, especially if the other discipline is a more attractive one or one possessing higher status. Social workers as managers will need to stress the importance of each staff member maintaining a professional identity consistent with an employee's formal educational preparation. They will need to make every effort to assure that some supervision is provided by persons within the staff member's discipline (perhaps through outside consultation). They should also assure that the employee is evaluated by a person who understands both the functions and the values and ethics that are appropriate for the staff member's profession.

The social worker assigned to work on a medical specialty floor in a large hospital illustrates both the advantages and dangers of interdisciplinary supervision. The Director of Social Services must be extremely skillful in handling the supervision of the social worker who is assigned to, for example, pediatrics, neonatal intensive care, or eating-disorder units. These assignments offer the kind of growth within a specialized area that is not available within a more generic assignment. Clearly, the physician who is in charge of the unit is more knowledgeable than is the Director of Social Services in his or her area of specialization and is a logical choice to assume a major portion of the supervisory role. But how much and at what cost? How does the Director of Social Services avoid a situation where the social worker assumes the identity of "pediatric social worker" or some other attractive role that suggests a primary loyalty to the discipline of the physician in charge? How can one assure that when value conflicts occur between medical and social work values (for example, regarding discharge plans), the social worker will seek professional consultation and support from the Director of Social Services rather than simply deferring to the physician? Can the Director, as manager, avoid having a work environment populated by social-work locals without the desirable balance of cosmopolitans?

Interdisciplinary supervision is a logical and a desirable alternative to traditional supervisory structures, especially in some work settings, but it also has the potential to weaken or sabotage desirable authority relationships. Annual evaluations and recommendations for promotions or merit raises, for example, are best left to those from the same discipline who understand, appreciate, and share the values, knowledge, and skills of an employee. The subordinate can lose respect for the supervisor who maintains administrative supervisory authority but has assigned most of the functions of supervision to someone of another discipline. Especially when evaluations are unfavorable, a tendency exists to respond with a kind of "what do they know?" resentment that does not promote improvement in job performance.

Social workers as managers must weigh the advantages of interdisciplinary supervision with the potential costs. They must remain sensitive to problems in its overuse that can either threaten to undermine supervisor authority or reduce the potential for employee growth.

Group Supervision. A supervisory structure that retains the responsibility for supervision within the discipline of the employee is the use of group supervision.[5] A supervisor may choose to carry out supervisory activities in a group setting with all or some of the supervisees present. Group supervision is an appealing alternative to the manager for a number of reasons. Many of the learning needs of supervisees are held in common. By addressing them in a group, a supervisor can save the time and effort necessary to conduct the same instruction individually for each employee. The more standardized the need for instruction and the more standardized the communication that is indicated, the more appropriate the group supervisory approach seems to be.

Group supervision also can provide the opportunity for employees to learn from each other and from the supervisor in a relatively nonthreatening environment. They can share relevant learning experiences, pooling knowledge in a way that provides more access to knowledge than the supervisor alone could provide.

On the negative side, certain supervisory requirements may not be appropriately addressed using group supervision. While the approach can be comfortable for some employees, it can be uncomfortable for those who are less experienced, more vulnerable to group sanction, or who do not wish to share their failures and problems with peers. For example, a worker encountering the stresses of the job can find support through group supervision *if* others admit to having similar problems. But if others deny having the same difficulties, the worker can be made to feel even more overwhelmed and embarassed. Individual criticisms also can be more painful if given in front of others than if communicated in one-to-one supervision.

Another major problem of group supervision from the perspective of the social worker as manager relates to its potential for loss of control by the supervisor. A too-egalitarian approach to supervision can be popular with supervisees, but it can quickly cause problems. The supervisor's advice, admonition, or even directive can begin to be perceived as having no more force than the opinion of other persons in the group and, sometimes, even less than that of an outspoken co-worker. It can become difficult for group members to discern when the supervisor speaks from a position of expertise or of power (which supervisors continue to possess) and when the supervisor is just offering an observation.

A competition for power and influence also may develop among supervisees as individuals seek to assume the position of most knowledgeable or most competent (even to the point of not reporting situations accurately if they might reflect negatively on themselves). This can threaten supervisors and their role, making it more difficult for them to function, particularly in their role of administrative supervision. For instance, how do supervisors tactfully provide a critical evaluation of supervisees' work when a peer of theirs who has claimed the role of expert has complimented their performance? Or how can the supervisor criticize a worker's performance that is not satisfactory when the worker's deficiencies were first pointed out by a peer? Will it look like the peer influenced the supervisor's judgment? These and other issues reflect the danger of a kind of role-blurring that can occur if group supervision is not used with extreme caution. Many managers who recognize its advantages also realize its potential for creating problems. They advocate a combination of group, individual, and other supervisory approaches to capitalize on the advantages inherent in each and to minimize the likelihood of difficulties that can occur when too heavy a reliance on one approach exists.

Attributes of Good Supervision

Whatever supervisory structure or structures a social work manager chooses, it is necessary that managers keep in mind the importance of promoting employee professional growth. If growth is to occur, the supervision package chosen should reflect certain essential characteristics.

Administrative supervision components should be fair and objective and should be consistent with appropriate personnel standards and practices. If an employee is a social worker, for example, supervisory procedures should be consistent with the current NASW Standards for Social Work Personnel Practices and/or other local, state, or federal standards that apply. Not only is this in the best interests of the employee but it also leaves the organization and its staff in a defensible position if employee grievance procedures are later initiated.

Good supervision constantly stresses the need for high-quality and ethical client services. To this end, employees are encouraged to acquire the knowledge and skills to become ever-more competent in their work. Subsequently, they are assigned tasks that require the use of newly acquired professional knowledge and skills. Whenever possible, they are encouraged to exercise professional judgment in decision making and are supported in their decisions. They should be recognized and accepted as competent professionals who may, in fact, know more about some areas of practice than does the supervisor. Yet good supervision does not absolve the supervisor from continuing objectively to assist their professional growth and from contributing to the learning of the supervisee whenever possible.

Good supervision provides both a reference point and a role model for the employee. It also provides a perspective not available to the supervisee who is frequently immersed in the everyday requirements of his or her job. It can remind employees of their responsibility to perform in a way consistent with organizational goals and objectives. Good supervision may also serve as a reminder to employees that they have a responsibility, not only for their own growth, but for the development of knowledge for others who work in the field. It can stress the need for employees to base their work on available knowledge and to evaluate their work regularly in order to move toward the ideal of empirically based practice.

If supervision is to be effective in promoting employee growth, it should create a climate for problem-solving in which errors can be freely discussed in a candid manner. Both the supervisee and the person or persons doing the supervising should feel comfortable in giving and taking suggestions. However, it should be clear that some decisions cannot be delegated to the supervisee or the supervisory group and that the administrative hierarchy will not be undermined by whatever supervisory models the manager employs.

GROWTH THROUGH CONTINUING EDUCATION

The background of formal education and experience that an employee brings to a human service organization will quickly become obsolete and inadequate for his or her job responsibilities unless some form of formalized ongoing learning opportunities are provided. Social workers as managers frequently find themselves in the position to be able to choose or at least to influence the choice of present and future learning experiences of staff members.

In fact, ongoing learning within organizations is inevitable. Employees *will* learn every day. They learn from co-workers, supervisors, subordinates, clients, clerical staff, and anyone else with whom they have contact. The issue for the manager is, *What* do they learn, and is what they learn desirable for promoting effective and efficient client services? Sometimes it is, and sometimes it most definitely is not. Informal learning from a co-worker may, for example, suggest a shortcut to record keeping that will result in more time for client service. The saving may have no negative costs *or* it may result in a disastrous loss of federal reimbursement, if detected. Other well-meaning informal orientation of a new employee by a senior worker may result in quickly undermining respect for an administrator who might otherwise have been respected without the biasing input by the "old hand." If a manager fails to provide for formal learning, other learning will take place to fill the void. But it could just be learning that should never be allowed to occur.

Just simply providing learning will not guarantee that it will "take," at least not in the way intended. For example, a training orientation designed to assure that employees follow appropriate procedures whenever they must be out of the office can inadvertently suggest ways to cover for oneself to conduct personal business on agency time. Just *what* is communicated in programs of formalized learning must be verified by the manager, or the continuing education expenditure can quickly become counterproductive.

Differential Continuing Education Needs

Staff members have a wide variety of learning needs. They range from technical skills to theoretical knowledge to instruction in appropriate values. Certain continuing education methods are appropriate for some learning needs, but inappropriate for others. Three terms—training, education, and staff development—are often used rather freely and even interchangeably to describe the varieties of continuing education methods that exist. Understanding how they differ in purpose, content, and process is very helpful to the manager in identifying what response might be needed by staff for continued growth. We will use a chart to summarize the distinctive characteristics of each of the three types of continuing education and then discuss each individually.

Training. Unlike the other two types of continuing education, training is designed to provoke a standardized and correct response from staff. Like a rule (as discussed in Chapter 4) it is designed to prohibit the exercise of professional discretion. You can train people to respond in a prescribed way to a predictable and recurring situation. It is possible and desirable to train in

TABLE 6.1. CHARACTERISTICS OF THREE TYPES OF CONTINUING EDUCATION

Distinguishing Characteristics	Type of Activity		
	Training	Staff Development	Education
Purpose	Socialization (orientation to the organization), standardization of activities to meet a standard	Acquiring and applying new knowledge (to increase professional competence in service delivery)	Career advancement through advanced study (within context of the profession)
Content	Specific "how-to" knowledge (application of policy to procedures)	Emerging knowledge and insights	Theoretical knowledge
Process	Instruction in and exposure to needed knowledge	Application of new knowledge to a problem situation	Providing knowledge that is generalizable

Adapted from Robert W. Weinbach and Karen M. Kuehner, "Trainer or Academician—Who Shall Provide?" Journal of Continuing Social Work Education, I, 3, (Summer 1981): 5.

those situations where we know in advance that an event will occur, that there is one acceptable way to handle it, and that we can be reasonably certain that the way will be effective. Training is appropriate when we know what must be done and wish to make sure that there is no deviation in the way it is done. Training usually involves hands-on experience in performing a task in the approved way. We can and should, for example, train staff to answer the phone in a professional manner, to fill out a form correctly, or to comply with the new federal requirements for client eligibility determination. As socialization, training helps employees achieve a basic identification with an organization and how its tasks are performed. It helps them to achieve a basic role competency and to represent the agency to the public in a standardized manner. It imparts knowledge and provides experience in use of skills that are of immediate value on the job. It helps employees meet role expectations.

Training can be a very cost-efficient and valuable form of continuing education for the social worker as manager.[6] With training, workers come on-line quickly and make fewer mistakes. This, in turn, produces less embarrassment for the agency and its staff and makes staff feel better about their work performance. They are then less likely to engage in absenteeism, complain less, and are less likely to resign from their jobs, which results in costly retraining of new employees. Well-trained workers need less on-site supervision. Once correct methods of responding to situations that can be specified in advance have been learned, staff members can function with more autonomy and feel certain that their handling of a situation is correct. The supervisor, in turn, may be able to supervise a larger number of workers.

If employees are well-trained, they will provide better services. As behaviors for which they have been trained become "second nature," the behaviors function like habits. This allows employees to devote more time and energy to addressing those situations and decisions where training could not prepare them because of the uniqueness of the situation and/or its unpredictability.

Employees may complain about going to training or they may welcome it as time off from work. But if performed effectively, employees almost always appreciate it when learning is later put into practice. They also tend to appreciate the message that the manager conveys through the provision of training—namely that management values competent staff performance and is willing to commit resources to support it.

Unfortunately, in a time of fiscal cutbacks, training sometimes may be viewed as a luxury. It is often one of the first activities to be reduced or cut out. This is a gross error on the part of managers. At a time when there are funding reductions often accompanied by nonreplacement or "rifting" of staff, it is more imperative than ever that remaining staff are well trained in order to assure the highest possible quality and quantity of production.

Education. In many ways, education is designed for learning needs that are almost directly opposite those addressed through training. Education is learning of generalized empirical and theoretical knowledge. It is designed to equip the learner to be able to act competently in some future situation, the specifics of which cannot be clearly envisioned. Only the broadest of knowledge and skill requirements can be anticipated. The idea is to provide the general knowledge necessary to make a decision and/or to act appropriately in unique situations. The requirements of a given situation and the persons involved will require a one-time-only response. Education hopes to prepare the employee with the knowledge resources necessary to act competently, despite the specific and unique requirements of the situation. It is the only preparation possible; if we knew what the situation would require or could have learned from its regular occurence, we could do more than educate—we could train for it.

There is widespread confusion regarding the respective purpose and meaning of the terms *training* and *education*. It exists both among the general public and among professionals in our field. This confusion has led to some angry disagreements that would have been avoidable, at least in part, if the differences had been understood. For example, the awareness of the AIDS crisis in the 1980s resulted in a renewed conflict and polarization of public opinion over sex education in public schools. As in the past, much of the opposition seemed to originate in misconceptions about sex education; opponents described scenarios that clearly indicated that they expected training in sexuality to occur if sex education became more widespread. While the need for the practice of safe sex did suggest the need for learning that was more specific than ever before, advocates of sex education were, in almost all instances, proposing the introduction of generalized knowledge—that is, education. This knowledge would assist young people in making intelligent decisions about their sexuality in some unpredictable situation sometime in the future. Advocates of sex education were not supporting the use of classroom instruction in sexuality—that would be training, not education.

Social work students and educators are also familiar with the confusion generated over the meaning of training and education and the problems that arise. Faculty perceive themselves as educators, preparing their students by providing them with generalized knowledge designed to assist them in functioning in some future, unspecified practice situation. While social work education may have some training components (most commonly within field agencies and, sometimes, in practice courses where skill-building takes place), the preponderance of curricula are designed to educate, not to train. There is a compelling logic to this emphasis. We cannot anticipate the precise needs of a client or client group in some future situation or the correct decision or response of a social worker. Furthermore, no two practice situations and no two social work practitioners are identical. The social worker needs to be able to assess the situation, draw on experience and generalized knowledge acquired through education, and to apply professional discretion in a unique, one-time-only manner. If social workers were trained and not educated, no social worker who attended college before 1980 would have received the formalized learning necessary for working with AIDS patients or their families or for providing services for new categories of the homeless. However, much of the dissatisfaction of social work students seems to arise from concern that they are not getting enough "how-to-do-it" (that is, training) to prepare them for practice. They may enter a program of professional education expecting training which, most faculty would argue, cannot be offered. Just how much training is appropriate within social work curricula remains open to debate, even among educators.

Generally speaking, managers tend to be supportive of education for their employees, but they may not choose to or be able to provide it. Staff usually receive this form of continuing education by enrolling in short courses, individual formal courses, or in advanced degree programs. If resources are available, released time and even tuition expenses are much appreciated by staff. In this way, a manager can communicate a belief in the value of continued employee growth. Some caution is in order for the manager, however.

As staff members acquire more education and particularly if they are awarded advanced degrees, they are likely to expect increased work responsibilities and continued career advancement. For an employee, nothing demoralizes quite as quickly as investing the time, effort, and expense to go back to school only to return to one's old job, sometimes even with a loss of seniority for time spent in getting a degree. The manager will need to plan to reward the better-educated returning employee with more or different responsibilities and perhaps even promotion. If these cannot be offered, at the very least it should be communicated why the manager is unable to do so *before* any such expectations are allowed to develop.

Regardless of the rewards offered, the social worker as manager should recognize that one likely result of additional education may be that staff members might leave the organization to attempt to better themselves by taking a job elsewhere. This is an unavoidable phenomenon as employees make themselves more marketable through advanced credentialing. The manager should recognize this and bear no resentment toward the staff member should it occur. After all, some other manager has probably supported the advanced education of the new employee who will be replacing the one leaving.

Staff Development.   The third form of continuing education, *staff development*, can be especially useful to the manager in addressing problem situations or in providing staff with the new or updated learning required to function in their changing work environment. Staff development contains some elements of both training and education.

What distinguishes staff development is its problem focus. Changing knowledge, changing service needs, and changing standards for their delivery are likely to create practice knowledge gaps and stress among staff. In past years, certain problems have demonstrated timely and appropriate topics for staff development. In the 1970s a staff development focus frequently was the use of case management or implementation of affirmative action guidelines. In the early 1980s, it was often burnout or detection of child abuse. In later years, it has been the use of nonsexist language or various topics related to AIDS. Generally, staff development tends to address the needs of practitioners for current knowledge relating to a recently identified (or at least recently spotlighted) problem in the field. It usually employs a short-term intensive format with a fairly narrow focus. State-of-the-art knowledge is presented and discussed along with practical suggestions for addressing the problem. Sometimes, experiential learning is a part of staff development. Overall, it provides the manager with a useful and well-received vehicle for influencing employee growth. Staff members tend to like spending time acquiring new and emerging knowledge and in addressing topics that are widely discussed in both professional and lay circles.

Who Can Provide Continuing Education?

Many different sources can provide continuing education. The task for the social work manager is to weigh the pros and cons of the various options and to find the best match between continuing education needs and provider. Generally, education is the domain of college or university educators. Training is more likely to be conducted by staff within the organization, at least in the larger bureaucracies. Staff development is a highly contested area that is claimed by those possessing various professional affiliations.[7] In recent years, however, these boundaries have become blurred, if not alto-

TABLE 6.2. CONTINUING EDUCATION PROVIDERS: ADVANTAGES AND DISADVANTAGES

Provider	Advantages	Disadvantages
Agency Employees	Agency loyalty Knowledge of agency Accountability for performance Simplicity of agreements Control over content Low cost	Lack of full-time availability Inbreeding of ideas Questions of credibility Professional training
Established Social Work Continuing Education Organizations or Private Contractors	Monetary incentive Experience Full-time involvement Control over content through purchase Credibility of "outside experts" Identification with practice values, methods	Cost to agency Coordination/distance factors Unreceptivity to smaller contracts/agreements
Newer Continuing Education Programs in Social Work Schools	Monetary incentive Receptivity to smaller contracts/agreements Local availability Identification with practice values, methods	Orientation costs Inexperience leading to misunderstanding Product flaws Inappropriateness for changing roles
Other College/University Units	Specialized knowledge Monetary incentive Aura of the "other discipline"	Lack of knowledge of social agencies Lack of identification with practice values, methods Orientation costs
Professional Organizations	Identification with practice values Knowledge of issues and development in the field Credibility of "outside experts"	Limited resources (time, topics, personnel) Cost to agency

Adapted from Robert W. Weinbach and Karen M. Kuehner, "Selecting the Provider of Continuing Education for Child Welfare Agencies," Child Welfare, 64(5), (September/October 1985): 478. (Discussion that follows relies heavily on text from this article.)

gether obliterated. Fiscal necessity and opportunity increasingly have moved academicians into the training arena within organizations. Professional organizations and private, for-profit contractors have seized upon opportunities to contract for training and staff development. The current environment can be a confusing one for social work managers who are unclear as to just what they want in the way of staff development and what they are able to pay in the way of monetary and nonmonetary costs. We will explore the costs and benefits of available options.[8]

Agency staff. Certain obvious advantages exist for the social worker as manager who selects in-house providers of continuing education. Agency employees are less costly to use, although subtle costs exist in the form of time taken from other activities. Persons already on the payroll are generally committed to the organization; a certain level of loyalty can usually be assumed. They should know the agency and its unique needs, political constraints, and clientele better than an outsider.

Managers who opt for in-house continuing education usually have good control over content. If agency-training staff members are used, accountability pressures are present. Trainers' job performance is judged by the success of their efforts. They cannot walk away without knowing the results of their work or without being held accountable for its quality.

Accountability is less in evidence when supervisors and senior-level line staff members are used, but they are still agency employees subject to in-house evaluation. A major advantage is their specific job knowledge. No one, including agency trainers, can know the needs of first-line employees as well as they do. The likelihood of truly relevant content is increased if line staff members are granted some control over selection of curricula and methods.

Using in-house staff requires only simple arrangements and agreements, and a minimum of paperwork and red tape. Contracts involving complicated budgeting and time-consuming approvals at several levels are largely unnecessary. This may be the greatest plus of all for the social worker as manager who chooses to use his or her own employees.

The extensive use of agency employees and the short-circuiting of multi-level review and approval procedures can be costly, however. It can weaken the continuity of curriculum development, the broad-based reinforcement of agency goals, and the monitoring and evaluation capabilities inherent in the contracting process. The extensive use of in-house training programs may result in fragmented and shortsighted approaches to addressing continuing education needs.

Too heavy a reliance on one's own employees can also result in inbreeding problems characterized by a shortage of new ideas or creative approaches to situations. The agency employee may lack familiarity with the theoretical knowledge in a given subject area that is readily available to the academician. Supervisors and lower-lever employees are especially likely to lack the time for preparation that otherwise might compensate for this deficiency. They may also lack experience and skill in the use of teaching methods.

Full-time in-house training personnel may not be close enough to a specific job to understand its requirements fully. They may, for example, never have worked in direct client service. Trainers, however, are likely to be experienced in training techniques, use of audiovisuals, and other necessary skills. This is a big plus. They are seasoned "performers" who probably took the job because they liked leading groups in various methods of learning.

Ironically, the greatest strength of agency employees as providers of continuing education also is their greatest liability. They are clearly identified as agency persons with all the advantages that this entails. But this identification also threatens their credibility and, therefore, the effectiveness of their teaching. Will employees accept their expertise as they would that of an outside "expert" who may hold high academic credentials? Will their employee status make them suspect as continuing education participants? Will trainees seek hidden meaning in what they say or do because they are viewed as agents of the organization? They may bear the dual liability of being perceived as both "prophet without honor" and "spy." Even the most accepted fellow employee may not experience a productive candor from participants. The usefulness of employees as providers of continuing education (especially of supervisors and other nontrainers) may be limited to activities where suspicion and doubts about competence and loyalties are least likely to exist.

Generally, when we think of agency staff as potential providers of continuing education, we tend to think of persons employed as trainers or of senior-level supervisors or line staff. But social work managers (particularly those at lower levels of the administrative hierarchy) have another valuable resource at their disposal. As providers of certain types of continuing education—for example, orientation training—an employee's peers may be the option of choice. Peer trainers may be relatively "junior" and even quite new to the organization themselves. Peer training is defined as "the use of a more experienced fellow employee to teach specific knowledge and skills to a new employee of the same level and job description."[9] Peers are assigned on a time-limited basis under the direction of a permanent agency training staff member. There is an effort to match trainers and trainees as to work style, personal characteristics, and individual perferences. Because the arrangement is temporary, the permanent authority structure is unaffected. Several advantages accrue to the use of peer trainers. These include:

1. *Accessibility to staff.* Local peer trainers based in the county or regional office are more accessible to assist the newly hired worker

than are permanent continuing education prsonnel who, for example, may be located in a state office many miles away, and who must contend with the complexities of providing training with limited on-site interaction. They may be more available than the local supervisor, whose time is consumed by program management and the many needs of other employees.

2. *Individualized attention.* Peer trainers who may have recently experienced the same anxieties and learning needs as the new employee may be able to identify with and clarify potential problem areas. They may be able to listen to and relate better to learning difficulties as they occur than could the full-time continuing education staff. They have probably not forgotten and will not easily dismiss the bewilderment of the employee who must master a vast amount of knowledge and many new tasks in a short period of time.

3. *Greater choice.* With several workers in the same office identified as peer trainers, new employees can be encouraged to engage in a certain amount of approved natural selection. From among a variety of persons, the trainee and supervisor can select the individual who is the best helper or the best resource for clarifying complex policy questions. Trainee input can be used to arrive at the best match of personality and teaching/learning styles.

4. *Trust.* New employees may find it easier to trust and to be candid with a peer. They will be less inhibited about asking what they fear may be "dumb" questions of a peer trainer than they might be in questioning the supervisor or a professional trainer in a classroom setting. The similarity of their status will foster needed candor.[10]

Selection, preparation, management, and evaluation of peer trainers are critical tasks that occupy a good amount of the social work manager's time. But the advantages may justify the effort. Disadvantages of using peer trainers lie primarily in the way in which they can threaten the role and authority of supervision. They should only be employed in a way that it is clear to all concerned that ultimate responsibility for the socialization, job preparation, and peformance evaulation of a staff member remains with the supervisor.

Private Contractors and Larger Continuing Education Programs. Some large organizations (whether private or associated with universities) make continuing education their business. The manager who seeks continuing education from private contractors or the larger continuing education programs is buying economic motivation and experience. The organizations want and need the work; their livelihoods are at stake. They generally have many years of experience in offering continuing education and have learned what sells and what works. They have developed attractive, generally copyrighted packages that do not require time for development or major modifications. These packages include such learning supports as workbooks, transparencies, videotapes, and other aids that are both well liked by participants and have a record of effectiveness.

Larger programs and private contractors can promise something that few of the other alternatives can, namely 12-month, fully staffed operations. They do not operate with reduced staff during summer months and holiday seasons. Contracts always receive high priority. A record of successful continuing education administrative and service contracts is a must for these organizations. It increases the likelihood of future agreements.

The need of the provider for continued work also offers other areas of leverage for the social worker as manager. These programs have less vested interest in the selection of content and curricula than, for example, the academician, who may have a strong personal and professional commitment to a school of thought or method. Established continuing education programs generally will allow the consumer to specify what is needed, but will take the responsibility for the more specific development and packaging phases. To them, continuing education is a business and subject to the rules of the marketplace. They must deliver on time and satisfactorily. Dependence on future contracts—and the threat of possible legal action—guarantees it.

The attractive aspects of agreements with larger social work continuing education programs and private contractors may come with a high price tag. Reimbursement of travel expenses for continuing education staff represents a substantial cost to the purchaser. The use of temporary "outstation offices" (an on-site coordinator assigned to work in the place of delivery) can reduce costs somewhat. The programs must set priorities. They are most interested in those agreements involving the greatest compensation. They most actively seek large, long-term contracts that offer large amounts of money and greater job security for their staffs. Managers looking for a single half-day workshop or other low-cost continuing education item might better seek local providers or be prepared to wait until the large continuing education organization can find time without jeopardizing other commitments. Managers may even be told that the large organization is simply not interested in the job.

Other Social Work Academic Programs. Less established local continuing education programs in social work academic programs may offer continuing education at relatively low cost, particularly in the case of short-term requirements. Public universities often operate under political expectations that their faculty members will provide community services. Social work educators also may need to maintain contact with the practice environment. The need to seek major grants or contracts may result in inexpensive or even gratis agreements for small continuing education requirements, as deans hope to get a "foot in the door."

Because continuing education is only a part-time, occasional function of most educators, programs such as one-day workshops or brief training sessions are especially welcomed. The large number of BSW and MSW programs virtually guarantees that there is one in close proximity to any human service organization. Travel and per diem expenses are a relatively small cost.

Continuing education agreements with social work education programs have a benefit in the form of the aura of the educator. The person delivering the continuing education may have "instant credibility." Academicians are presumed to have knowledge and expertise in their field. Of course, this is not always true. An educator's credibility can be rapidly destroyed by a few comments that indicate that he or she is out of touch with the real world of professional practice.

Many of the disadvantages of agreements with social work education programs stem from inexperience. Confusion about rights and responsibilities involved may result in dangerous misunderstandings. Newer continuing education programs require more agency staff time and involvement in planning and monitoring. Both the manager and the provider should anticipate the need for increased time spent in front-end discussion. The provider must be clear from the outset about expectations for content and format.

Unless similar continuing education already has been offered elsewhere, continuing education packages must be developed. The provider may lack technical support systems such as work processing formats, audiovisual production capabilities, and staff knowledgeable in the nuances of state and federal contracting procedures and regulations. Certain errors will be made that the larger, experienced program would not make. There is less probability of a smooth, well-implemented product.

There also may be a tendency to attempt shortcuts to the development of continuing education curricula by trying to adapt units and materials from existing educational courses. This can result in overly theoretical, esoteric materials that may have little pertinence to the needs of employees. Educators also are accustomed to guarding principles of academic freedom vigorously. They may resent and resist agency efforts to influence the content and/or format of delivery. The social worker as manager may have little control over what is actually presented when contracting with academicians who are accustomed to exercising a good ideal of autonomy in curriculum development.

Although the motivation of individual providers is an important variable among all provider groups, it is a special concern in continuing education agreements with academicians. College and university reward systems of tenure, promotion, and merit increases are structured so that some faculty members have less to gain from continuing education activities than others.

Identifying those who have the most to gain from providing the best learning experiences is an important task. Whenever possible, the manager should request that continuing education is delivered by these individuals. Those who perceive little personal reward for themselves other than a salary supplement are best avoided.

The recent thrust toward reprivatization in public agencies has called into question the entire assumption that schools of social work can offer continuing education appropriate to the changing jobs of agency staff in these settings. As social workers do less "people serving" and more "people processing" as a result of increased purchase of services, much of the counseling focus that a school of social work offers may no longer be needed by or appropriate for a large percentage of workers. The applicability of continuing education delivered by university social work educators should be carefully scrutinized by the social worker as manager before those individuals are selected to be the providers of continuing education.

CASE EXAMPLE: WHEN ACADEMICIANS TRAIN

During a recent funding cutback, the continuing education staff of a large public agency was reduced from 16 to 6. Because seniority considerations were used, those remaining were persons who had not performed training in several years. They were senior people who had been active in development of materials, contracting, scheduling, and in the overseeing of the training activities of junior staff who were dismissed as a result of the current fiscal crisis. As partial remedy for their acute personnel shortage, the remaining staff members were granted a moderate increase in their budget for contracting with outside sources to deliver training.

One of the six members, Del, was assigned by the Director of Continuing Education to begin negotiating with outside providers. He was to develop a contract for basic skills training for new adoption workers and those transferred into adoptions from other areas as a result of reorganization caused by the funding cutback. After a number of preliminary discussions, he concluded that only one local organization, the Hamilton School of Social Work, had the expertise and support systems necessary to do the job. After checking with his agency's legal counsel, he concluded that a "sole source" contract could be justified and that it would not be necessary to issue a request for proposals to other possible providers.

Del's negotiations with the dean of the school went quite smoothly. The dean had actively sought grants and contracts ever since taking her job, and the possibility of bringing in additional funding for her program was appealing. She suggested that, having taught in the child-welfare area for many years, Dr. James, a senior faculty member, would be a logical choice to design and implement the training.

The proposal was promptly developed and submitted by the school. It was well written and costs were generally appropriate for the services offered. After some minor changes were negotiated, the contract was awarded to the Hamilton School.

Del knew of Dr. James by reputation and through personal experience; he had attended one of his staff development workshops on burnout. As he knew Dr. James to be a bright, entertaining, and very competent educator, Del had no misgivings about his being selected to design and implement the training.

The curriculum design component of the contract seemed to support Del's belief that Dr. James was an excellent choice. In meetings with him, Del found that Dr. James was very knowledgeable in the subject area but yet readily admitted his lack of insight into agency functioning. He invited and responded well to suggestions from continuing education staff.

Del and the Director of Continuing Education were very pleased with the curriculum model that was developed. It seemed to contain a good blend of current knowledge and opportunity to gain controlled experience in its application. The current issues section that Dr. James included seemed certain to be professionally stimulating for trainees, even if it was not training *per se*. Del had every reason to believe that the entire package would accomplish his and the agency's objectives.

The training turned out to be a disaster that was costly to the agency for years to come. Dr. James was a seasoned educator who genuinely enjoyed the stimulation of the classroom. He stuck carefully to the curriculum during the first (of two) day's training. The trainees asked few questions, took copious notes, and were polite but distant. By the end of the day, Dr. James felt himself struggling to get any discussion started. He used every educational device at his disposal, but nothing seemed to work. Even his good-natured but sarcastic humor didn't get much reaction, at least not the kind of appreciation that he usually experienced.

In a moment of desperation, Dr. James told a marginally related anecdote about gross mismanagement of an adoption program that had occurred in a public agency in another state. Several trainees pointed out parallels with their agency. Seizing on the first glimmer of excitement that he had seen, Dr. James countered with a joke about an incompetent agency director; the group laughed uproariously. It soon become apparent from trainees' comments that the group had been preoccupied. They were seething over the recent reorganization that had required several of them to be demoted from supervisory jobs in other areas into direct service positions in adoptions.

The second day, Dr. James had little problem in holding the group's attention or in promoting lively discussion. While he thoroughly covered the required content and successfully taught the necessary skills, his delivery of training came with a heavy cost to the agency. His sarcastic humor was eagerly appreciated whenever it was targeted at the insensitivities of bureaucracies and those who rise to the top within them. The group came to view him as extremely knowledgeable and supportive of their complaints. One trainee even stated that he would be welcome as an administrator any time that he decided to leave education. While Dr. James humbly denied a knowledge of management skills, he obviously enjoyed the flattery and did little to discourage disparaging remarks about agency management that were made. While he carefully avoided any criticism of administrators because "I really don't know the facts," his negative generalizations about bureaucrats were consistently perceived as "on target" by the trainees for their work situation. While delivering the needed learning, his sensitivity to feelings of staff, humor, articulateness, and down-to-earth manner seemed to stand in stark contrast to the style of the agency director and other high-level administrators. His invitation to "please call me Ralph!" went unheeded but was, nevertheless, appreciated as another indication of his egalitarian style.

When he entered the adoption issues section at the end of the second day, Dr. James was really "on a roll." He was clearly within his element as he discussed his ideas about adoption placement policies, adoption studies, single-parent adoptions, and special needs adoptions. The trainees' obvious respect and liking for him resulted in almost unanimous agreement with his positions, many of which were in opposition to agency policy. At the end of training, many of the trainees remained to thank him personally for all that they had learned.

When Del computed the trainees' evaluation of the training, he at first felt that the contract had been a resounding success. The scores on the knowledge posttest given to trainees even seemed to confirm this feeling. However, some of the open-ended comments of trainees caused him to begin to question the soundness of using Dr. James. The praise heaped upon the academician was almost too much to be believed. What's more, the compliments frequently were accompanied by negative comparisons with staff trainers and agency administrative personnel.

Over the next year, Del's worst suspicions about Dr. James' training session were confirmed. Staff morale seemed to decline to a new low among those who attended the session. Supervisors complained that the trainees regularly cited Dr. James as they resisted compliance with agency rules and procedures. Words like *antiquated* and *anachronistic* were frequently used to describe policies. Petitions demanding changes were widely circulated. An attitude of "we" (the direct service staff) and "they" (the administrative staff) that had not been seen previously was now in existence. When Dr. James was replaced by an agency continuing education staff member for a subsequent training session, the trainer met with open hostility and resistance. Trainees saw the decision not to use Dr. James again as evidence that Del had "sold out" to the administration.

It took nearly two years after Dr. James' training before staff morale approached its previous level. Del concluded that, in the future, he would be far more cautious in using university faculty for training. He would interview potential trainers to explore carefully their personality, teaching style, and needs. If using them for any form of continuing education, he would personally meet with them to stress his concerns about their potential disruptive influence on morale and staff compliance with policies, rules, and procedures. In general, he would look more to in-house trainers to deliver training and would contract with educators for staff development or education. Under no condition would he use educators to train when trainees were experiencing a high level of dissatisfaction because of recent events within the organization.

Other College/University Units. If administrators of human service agencies seek continuing education services from college or university units other than programs in social work, they have a wide range of choices. Some of the specialized knowledge and expertise needed within social agencies is only minimally taught in social work programs. Study of such knowledge areas as adult learning (a specialty of education) or organizational behavior (a focus in business schools) may be viewed as desirable for the continued growth of staff members. The social worker as manager may decide to seek continuing education that is delivered by people who are acknowledged to be "experts" in these areas.

Staff may find it refreshing to be taught by those from another discipline. They previously may have experienced frustration with in-house staff and with social work academicians. The aura of the other discipline can, of course, work against providers if they are perceived as unaware of the unique characteristics of human service delivery systems. For example, most human service agencies are not run as businesses. The manager who uses a business school academician to deliver continuing education should be certain that providers recognize the many important differences that exist and that they are capable of adjusting content to the world of social workers. If they cannot understand the special situations encountered by most human service organizations (Chapter 2), their contributions to continuing education learning may be very limited.

A lack of identification with social work values and methods also can be a major problem when using providers from other academic disciplines. Before choosing them, the manager should ascertain whether individuals who will deliver continuing education are likely to perceive clients and services in a way consistent with social work values. The best continuing education methods can be of little value when delivered by a provider who, for example, clearly views single-parent adoptions as unacceptable, or corporal punishment as the right of parents and has little patience with those who believe differently. Although it is possible for the social worker as manager to teach continuing education providers what employees do and what they value, this is a time-consuming and costly endeavor. The briefing time required may make the cost of any but long-term agreements prohibitive.

Being an academician—that is, somewhat removed from practice, and a non-social worker besides—can be "refreshing." It can also be a dual liability for continuing education designed to assist employees in the everyday delivery of human services. As a general rule, these specialized academic units may be more appropriately used as continuing education providers for staff other than those involved in direct client contact.

Professional Organizations. If social work managers select a professional organization (for example, the National Association of Social Workers) to provide continuing education, there is no question about identification with social work values and practice. Professional organization staff are also likely to be attuned to practice issues and political and legislative developments that affect service delivery.

Providers from professional organizations can form a linkage between the practice community and the knowledge base of the profession. Many of them are employed as practitioners. They can be assumed to be knowledgeable about new developments and practice methods. They can also serve as good role models for employees.

The biggest disadvantage in the use of professional organizations for continuing education is their limited capacity to deliver continuing education. They can offer continuing education services in only limited topic areas and can provide limited support materials (usually in the form of publications). Where staff from national offices are involved in delivering continuing education, distance and travel costs can be prohibitive. Local staff serve largely on a voluntary basis and may be unavailable to provide continuing education.[11]

When we discussed the different types of continuing education available to the social worker as manager (training, education, and staff development), we suggested that they really represent a group of options, each of which is more or less desirable for a given learning need of staff. Similarly, the various provider options represent a kind of menu for managers from which they can choose based upon a variety of factors relating to preferences and situational needs. It should be clear that, as a manager, much more than simply what staff need to know should enter into the decision process. Such factors as morale, loyalty, credibility, and other potential concerns are important to consider. A pattern of regularly turning to one provider may suggest that the manager is not adequately considering the advantages that other providers can offer. Usually some package involving a combination of continuing education methods and different provider categories will prove best for supporting employee growth.

Arranging for Continuing Education

Three basic types of agreement are used for the delivery of continuing education services that are provided by persons outside the organization. Confusion regarding their meaning results in problems and a great deal of resentment on the part of those involved. The three types of agreement are: consultation agreements, grants, and contracts. Whether in negotiating with providers of continuing education or in monitoring agreements made, a manager should be careful to avoid using the three terms as if they are somehow interchangeable—they are not.

Consultation Agreements. A consultation agreement is designed to bring a person or persons into the organization for a limited purpose. These people are hired because of some specific expertise that is needed. Consultants also are hired because they are believed to possess objectivity. This is particularly important when they are hired to arbitrate in situations of internal conflict. They should have no allegiance to any staff (at any level) and no preconceived biases as to the rightness or wrongness of anyone's position.

In human service organizations, it is sometimes stated that we hire "consultants" to provide regular ongoing services (for example, certain types of supervision) if no one on staff possesses the necessary credentials or expertise. But this is really a misuse of the term. These persons are really more like part-time employees. True consultants are more likely to be involved with an organization on a very time-limited, problem-focused basis. They might, for example, be brought in to help to revamp an agency's personnel practices, to computerize a record system, to design a needs assessment survey, or to help develop a new program for battered wives. Consultants should have knowledge and experience in performing the tasks for which they are hired, attributes not available within the organization.

Actual written agreements for consultation can be quite formal (for example, the Veteran's Administration requires extensive paperwork and clearances), but they frequently involve little more than a letter of agreement outlining the purpose, duties, and compensation involved. Because the consultant is assumed to be the expert, the specific nature of consulting services may not be detailed; these are left to the judgment of the consultant, who should be in the best position to know how to do the job. It is in the best interest of the consultant to keep the agreement as vague as possible. However, the social worker as manager who hires a consultant may wish to make the agreement as specific as the consultant will allow in order to be certain that the agency gets "its money's worth" of needed services.

Grants. Grants are really most accurately understood as a reward or a subsidy given to an individual or organization. Grants are awarded because the applicant is believed to possess the necessary credibility, skills, and identification with a given subject area to be able successfully to undertake research or continuing education in the area. Frequently, grants are awarded to researchers and academicians to enable them to continue their work or to allow them to pursue some area of inquiry on a large scale. A common source of grants is federal agencies (for example, National Institute of Mental Health, Department of Education, Bureau of Maternal and Child Health).

Grants are characterized by a relative amount of autonomy for the recipient, but grants for continuing education generally allow the recipient less freedom than do research grants. University faculty like and actively seek grants because they can provide a significant salary supplement in the form of summer pay as well as other attractive benefits such as budgets for professional travel or purchase of computer hardware and software. As long as faculty demonstrate a reasonable degree of accountability in expenditure of funds, the grantor will allow them to use discretion in specifically how, for example, they will design and implement a new curriculum or will analyze their research data. Some confusion occurs because federal agencies use the term "training grant" to describe awards of money to develop and deliver programs of continuing education that include what we have described as training as well as education and staff development. No matter what type of continuing education is purchased through a grant, a fair degree of trust in the provider to develop and deliver a quality product is implied. Social workers who, in their role as manager, are instrumental in offering a grant award for continuing education services should be aware that they may have relatively little input or control over the selection of specific content and teaching methods that will be used. A grant, like consultation, assumes that the expertise lies with the recipient and that such decisions are most appropriately left to that person. Unlike consultation, grants are likely to be awarded on a competitive basis. Despite the fact that grants frequently involve long written agreements and notarized signatures, they are deliberately vague in some areas where the purchaser defers to the superior knowledge and experience of the grantee.

Contracts. Because of the freedom implicit in the use of consultation agreements and grants, persons in organizations who are seeking continuing education services usually prefer to use contracts. Contracts simply are more enforceable. They hold the provider of continuing education directly responsible for delivering what has been promised in a manner acceptable to the organization. Contracts are legally binding; if continuing education is not delivered as specified in the contract, the recipient may not be paid. In contrast, dissatisfaction with services based on a consultation agreement or grant only will result in the provider not receiving future agreements. Sometimes, third parties (outside evaluators) are used to guarantee full compliance with the conditions of a contract.

A contract is awarded on a competitive basis—that is, several organizations or individuals usually "bid" for it by submitting a proposal in response to the organization's Request for Proposals (RFP). A "sole source" (no competitive bidding) situation occurs only if it can be demonstrated that only one organization or individual is qualified to deliver the desired service.

A contract for continuing education services is best understood as being virtually comparable to, for example, a contract a homeowner might sign to have new carpeting installed in the home. Material quality, time of delivery, and quality of work must be that which was agreed upon and must be approved by the homeowner or the homeowner is legally not bound to pay; full or partial payment may be withheld. The contract is designed to protect both parties should events unfold in a way that one or the other did not envision or if it is later learned that their perceptions of what the job entailed were not in agreement.

If a social worker as manager chooses to contract for continuing education, he or she has many protections. The primary protection for providers is that they will be paid promptly if their work is completed and perceived as satisfactory. Contracts tend to be negotiated and written out in legal jargon and in great detail. Authorized signatures are required. Unlike grants, little is left to the discretion of the provider or the purchaser; at least it shouldn't be.

For obvious reasons, managers prefer contracts to grants or consultation and tend to use them if they can get the provider to agree to their use. Unfortunately, even the use of contracts sometimes does not preclude problems if the provider of continuing education does not understand the difference between a contract and a grant or consultation agreement. Educators are particularly notorious for confusing the three types of agreements. The large, established facilities and private, for-profit organizations are well aware of the differences. A contract with an educator or educational institution relatively new to agreements for continuing education may lead to many difficulties. The mind-set of many educators is toward grants or consultation agreements. They may mistakenly believe that any agreement for continuing education services provides for similar autonomy and exercise of professional discretion. When they learn that they are wrong, a strained relationship between personnel at the two organizations can occur.

Another frequent source of trouble is the belated realization on the part of educators that a contract usually grants ownership of materials and teaching aids developed under the contract to the purchaser (organization). Professors using treasured course notes developed over the years may be shocked to learn that they no longer own their "material" after being paid for their part in delivery of continuing education. In fact, under agreements contained in most contracts, the educator need not be invited to return to deliver the continuing education a second time. An agency staff member can take notes while sitting in on the professor's instruction and use them to teach subsequent educational units.

While contracts with universities for continuing education are generally an organization-to-organization agreement, it would be naive not to understand contracts also as an arrangement made at the human level. Such agreements are more or less desirable for individuals who must provide the actual learning experience. Their attitude toward doing the work is likely to be affected by ego needs, financial considerations, career status, and other factors that can either enhance the quality of learning offered or detract from it. For this reason, the manager should, whenever possible, influence the choice of the provider as well as the choice of the organization awarded the contract.[12] (Del learned this important lesson in our case example.)

The social worker as manager may, on occasion, have the opportunity to choose from among consultation agreements, grants, and contracts to provide outside instruction for employee professional growth. Because of their limited applicability and their inherent potential for dissatisfaction, consultation and grants are used less often than contracts. Overall, contracts provide the best assurance that the organization will receive the kind of quality instruction that is needed. However, until there is greater understanding of the differences among the three types of continuing education, some problems and resentment probably are inevitable when contracts are used. Because of this, managers have a heavy communication responsibility on the front end of any contractual agreement. If agreements for continuing education services are allowed to produce bitterness on the part of providers, it is the potential beneficiaries (staff) who will suffer a loss. They will not receive the quality learning required to enhance their professional growth.

SUMMARY

In this chapter we looked at a second important responsibility of the social worker as manager that is part of the staffing function—continued professional growth of staff. We concentrated our analysis on two major vehicles for promoting staff growth, supervision and continuing education.

It is useful to understand the traditional one-to-one supervisory tasks as that of administrative supervision, educational supervision, supportive supervision, and case consultation. While we did not explore these in detail, we used them to help us as managers conceptualize the various ways in which supervision can promote employee growth. Interdisciplinary and group supervision models also were described and discussed as options available to the manager in enhancing growth through supervision.

In the examination of continuing education, several important distinctions were made. First, we emphasized the important differences in purpose, content, and process that are present in training, education, and staff development. The task of selecting a provider for delivery of continuing education was given thorough consideration. Options proposed for the manager's consideration included agency staff at all levels (including peers), both private and large public-supported continuing education organizations, newer continuing education efforts in social work BSW and MSW programs, non-social work academic programs, and professional organizations. The advantages and disadvantages of each were discussed.

Finally, the various agreement options for acquiring continuing education were examined. Consultation agreements, grants, and contracts were examined both individually and in comparison with each other. Common sources of misunderstandings and problems encountered by the manager in their use were noted.

In Chapter 7 we will continue our discussion of the staffing function of the social worker as manager. We will focus on how social workers as managers evaluate staff and take personnel actions that have potential to affect the quality of services to clients and the overall health of the organization.

REFERENCES

1. Eileen Gambrill and Theodore Stein, *Supervision: A Decision-Making Approach* (Beverly Hills, CA: Sage, 1983); Ruth Middleman and Gary Rhodes, *Competent Supervision* (Englewood Cliffs, NJ: Prentice-Hall, 1985); Carlton Munson, *An Introduction to Clinical Social Work Supervision* (New York: The Haworth Press, 1983); Carlton Munson, ed., *Social Work Supervision* (New York: Free Press, 1979); Lawrence Shulman, *Skills of Supervision and Staff Management* (Itasca, IL: F. E Peacock Publishers, 1982).
2. Alfred Kadushin, *Supervision in Social Work* (New York: Columbia University Press, 1976).
3. Alfred Kadushin, *Consultation in Social Work* (New York: Columbia University Press, 1977).
4. Richard Simpson, "Understanding the Utilization of Research in Social Work and Other Applied Professions," in *Sourcebook on Research Utilization* (New York: Council in Social Work Education, 1979), p. 24.
5. Kadushin, *Supervision in Social Work*, op. cit., pp. 320–357.
6. Joseph Olmstead, *Working Papers Number Two: Organizational Structure and Climate: Implications for Agencies* (Washington, DC: U.S. Department of Health, Education and Welfare, 1973), p. 158.
7. Robert Weinbach and Karen Kuehner, "Trainer or Academician—Who Shall Provide?" *Journal of Continuing Social Work Education*, 1(3), (Summer 1981): 4–5.
8. Robert Weinbach and Karen Kuehner, "Selecting the Provider of Continuing Education for Child Welfare Agencies," *Child Welfare*, 64(5), (September/October 1985):477–488.
9. Robert Weinbach and Karen Kuehner, "Improving the Use of Agency Resources through Peer Training," *Social Work*, 32(3), (May/June 1987):222.
10. Ibid., pp. 222–223.
11. The discussion of private contractors and larger continuing-education programs, other social work academic programs, other college/university units, and professional organizations is taken chiefly from Weinbach and Kuehner, "Selecting the Provider of Continuing Education for Child Welfare Agencies," *op. cit.*
12. Robert Weinbach and Karen Kuehner, "The Agency-Academic Program Training Contract: A Critical Examination," *Journal of Continuing Social Work Education*, 2(4), (1984):17–22.

ADDITIONAL READINGS

Brinkerhoff, R. *Achieving Results From Training*. San Francisco: Jossey-Bass, 1987.

Cumstock, T. *Modern Supervision*. Albany, NY: Delmar Publishers, 1987.

Doucek, H., and Austin, M. "Improving Agency Functioning Through Staff Development." *Administration in Social Work*, 10 (1986):27–37.

Handy, C. Management Training: Perk or Prerequisite? *Personnel Management*, 19 (1987):28–31.

Schnake, M. *Principles of Supervision*. Dubuque, IA: Brown, 1987.

Silverman, W. "Agency-Based Staff Development." *Administration in Social Work*, 12 (1985):284–292.

CHAPTER 7

Influencing Through Staff Evaluations and Personnel Actions

The social worker as manager influences the selection of the type of staff assigned to do a job (Chapter 5) and helps to create opportunities for their professional growth and development (Chapter 6). Both of these management activities assume that there are many potentially competent individuals available to perform needed tasks and that they will respond well to support that is provided to help them to develop their competence. Frequently, these assumptions are both correct. However, even if they are, some staff members will reflect more rapid growth than others. Some will aspire to greater responsibilities and higher-level positions within the organization. Of these, some will be capable of advancing; others will not. Still other individuals, despite all efforts to support their competent performance in their present roles, will be found to be unwilling and/or unable to meet expected performance standards. In the best interests of the organization, its staff, and the clients served, they may require reassignment or termination of employment.

Evaluation of employee performance is a critical task that is performed by the social worker. It also is one that frequently has been dreaded by persons who hold professional values that emphasize that they should be nonjudgmental and should seek to build upon strengths while not focusing on the weaknesses of others. But evaluation is a necessary and valuable prerequisite to management decisions regarding promotion, merit raises, reprimands, and other corrective action and staff termination. The social worker as manager needs to understand the issues that relate to staff evaluations and the personnel actions that can follow them. These issues will be the focus of this chapter.

152

STAFF EVALUATIONS

Formal, periodic evaluations of employees tend to be disliked by both those being evaluated and by those doing the evaluating. For the mature, adult professional, the idea of being evaluated often is viewed as insulting. It may reawaken all kinds of humiliating feelings associated with the powerlessness of childhood and of student roles. We tend to think that people should arrive at a point in life where their competence is assumed by all. They should no longer need to be evaluated or to prove their capacities and achievements to others. However, if we think about it, *everyone* continues to be evaluated by someone, no matter at what level the person is employed. Evaluations provide needed feedback. Consumers of services provide an evaluation of our staff when they return or don't return for additional assistance or when they discuss our services in the community. Why, then, should staff be resentful of having to be evaluated by a professional peer who is most likely to be an experienced professional who occupies a higher level in the administrative hierarchy? In part, it may be because of the attitudes that frequently are conveyed by the evaluator and the way that evaluations often tend to be handled.

Much of the mutual dislike of employee evaluations may result from the attitudes of those doing the evaluations, namely social workers in the role of manager. We evaluate clients and their situations in our role as practitioner. We evaluate political climates or community strengths and resources. But when it comes to evaluating the work of a colleague with whom we must work, we tend to react with great distaste. It is as if there were something unseemly or inappropriate about such a practice.

The dislike of performing and sharing of staff evaluations that frequently occurs among social workers as managers necessarily gets communicated to those being evaluated. How? If we don't like evaluating and find the entire task distasteful, there is a normal tendency to present the evaluation process as a necessary evil imposed upon us in our role as manager. We even might convey our belief that evaluations are really of little value and that they are best performed to meet a requirement of the organization and then quickly filed away. Such an attitude confirms the fears and resentment of evaluations held by those being evaluated. It creates a mind-set on the part of both parties that any staff evaluation will be an unpleasant necessity that is of little value. What ultimately results is likely to be a self-fulfilling prophecy. The evaluation probably *will* be of little value. The negative experience will then create a negative mind-set for the next evaluation. The vicious circle will continue on indefinitely if not stopped.

What we have described is a scenario that is fairly common within human service organizations. It may be that being a social worker represents an obstacle to performing staff evaluations and eliminating incompetent personnel. Social work values stress tolerance and a nonjudgmental attitude toward the behavior of others. But for a social worker, evaluation should *not* be simply a necessary evil. It is consistent with social work knowledge, skills, and values. Performed correctly by persons who recognize its value to all concerned, it can and should be viewed as a valuable opportunity and an essential contribution to both employee growth and organizational goal achievement.

Value to the Employee

The employee who is being evaluated has much to gain from an evaluation performed by the social worker as manager. Employees will have the opportunity to learn about others' perceptions of their areas of strength and weakness. The latter will suggest places where continuing education needs are greatest. For future reference, they also will know where they stand with those doing the evaluating. Is the evaluator fair and objective? Do evaluators appear to value role performance in some areas more than in others? Do they use evaluations to punish? Do they allow personality factors to enter into their assessments? To what degree? In this respect, even an unfair evaluation should be a valuable learning experience for the staff member being evaluated. Staff are likely to learn more about the evaluator in one annual evaluation session than in hours of staff meetings, casual conversation, or sharing of tasks. Evaluations have a way of exposing the evaluator's values, identifications, priorities, and sources of motivation. These are important for employees to understand. Even if they choose not to change their behavior to accommodate a supervisor's wishes, employees will be able to operate with more certainty, knowing what future reactions and evaluations they can expect.

Some social workers as managers tend to handle their discomfort with their role as evaluators by being unrealistically favorable in their evaluations of staff. They find it much more enjoyable to give good evaluations than to confront a colleague on his or her shortcomings. While we are *not* advocating this practice and will discuss its liabilities elsewhere in this chapter, an inflated evaluation or even one that is realistically positive becomes a valuable commodity for the employee who has been evaluated. It presents a legal and ethical safeguard against later precipitous or capricious negative personnel actions. Persons receiving "excellent" evaluations one month are protected from being fired the next. They also find themselves in a position to receive greater margin for error when they make mistakes or greater tolerance for behavior that is in conflict with policies, procedures, or other types of plans adopted by the organization. "Excellent" personnel evaluations are a buffer that can protect staff members. They allow them to act in ways that they choose without fear of dismissal or other punitive action.

We deliberately used the term "excellent" to describe the kind of evaluation that can provide a buffer of certainty to an employee ("outstanding" is another favorite). Merely "good" evaluations, because of evaluation inflation (the tendency of human service evaluators to be overly flattering in evaluating staff), are now of little "insurance" value. In fact, "good" can be a bad mark against an employee, for it may communicate a warning about a lack of job security. "Excellent" or "outstanding" evaluations are about the only ones that offer much security.

Value to the Manager

Formal evaluations of subordinates can perform several valuable functions for the social worker as manager. They provide a periodic vehicle to call staff attention to individual and organizational goals and objectives. As we observed earlier, large human service bureaucracies have a tendency to foster the phenomenon of means-end displacements. Staff can become immersed in keeping paperwork up to date or in compliance with the many rules and procedures that exist. A formal evaluation provides both the manager and the employee with the opportunity to stop, step back, and assess just how well the individual's daily activities contribute to the organization's client service goals and objectives. If a means-end displacement seems to be developing, it can be identified early and steps to eliminate it can be initiated.

Of course, if the manager doing the evaluating has "lost sight of the forest for the trees" and has become preoccupied with a supervisee's performance of tasks that were intended to be means to an end, an evaluation conference will benefit neither staff, manager, nor the organization. Evaluation in this type of unfortunate situation only may tend to reinforce a means-end displacement. The social worker as manager bears a heavy responsibility not to lose sight of goals and objectives, even if other staff may have lost sight of them. Evaluation conferences can help to refocus activities and priorities of both the evaluator and of the individual being evaluated.

The person doing the evaluating (manager) is required to apply objective criteria to judge the work of staff members. In doing this, he or she sometimes can obtain some new and valuable perspectives. In the casual interaction that occurs among employees of an organization, personality traits sometimes can distort the manager's impressions of the abilities and achievements of staff. For example, a personable, confident, outgoing, and articulate employee tends to leave a general impression of being knowledgeable and competent. The quiet, withdrawn loner is more likely to elicit doubts about that person's competence. In fact, the contributions of the loner to organizational goal achievement may be comparable to or even greater than those of the more socially adept individual. But this may not be revealed until a formal evaluation forces the manager to apply an objective yardstick that neither adds nor subtracts points for personality factors that may not be relevant to one's performance on the job. Gregarious individuals may, in fact, be using their attractive style as a smoke screen for the fact that they really do very little of a constructive nature. The evaluation can serve to point this out, along with the true value of the more socially withdrawn individual. This payoff from the evaluation process will only occur, however, if irrelevant personality factors are not allowed to intrude into the evaluation process where they can distort it.

Evaluation time should be one event in the activities of staff when superfluous factors (no matter how pleasant) are not allowed a place in interaction between manager and staff. If a staff member's personality is a verifiable asset or liability to the delivery of services or to promoting a productive work climate, it has relevance. Otherwise it does not, and it has no place in the evaluation process.

The careful selection or development of a written evaluation instrument will go far toward eliminating the potential for personality bias to occur. Both the business and the social work professional literature contain examples of evaluation forms that can be used as is or adapted for use by the social worker as manager.[1] Specific recommendations for productive use of evaluation conferences are also available.[2] However, in some organizations the manager has little choice and must use certain required instruments and procedures. This can seriously detract from the value of an evaluation because standardized forms and methods of this type are usually not completely appropriate for any one employee or his or her job.

In large organizations where work roles tend not to overlap—for example, where supervisors do nothing but supervise, only workers see clients, etc.—the evaluation affords the manager (the supervisor) the opportunity to get to know staff better and to better understand their jobs. Evaluation time may be the only time that a staff member receives the undivided attention of a supervisor to focus on that person's performance, career goals, and attitudes toward work, unlike ongoing supervision that generally touches on these only in the context of difficulties that the worker may be having in dealing with specific clients or client groups. While this is beneficial to the person being evaluated, it is especially valuable to the person doing the evaluating. It provides the chance to assess the motivation of an employee, to evaluate the employee's potential for promotion, and to compare the employee's career goals with opportunities within the organization. An evaluation also helps the social worker as manager to predict the likelihood of subordinates fitting into long-range organizational plans or of their seeking employment elsewhere. It offers many other related insights that facilitate the future decision making of the manager.

For those staff performing well and making valuable contributions to the organization and to its goals and objectives, evaluations provide the manager with a way to reinforce desirable behavior. While an employee may sense or even know that he or she is doing a job well, there is something about written and verbal kudos within the context of a periodic evaluation that is especially gratifying for the recipient. This is particularly important in smaller, closer organizations (for example, private practice, satellite clinics) where role differentiation is likely to become somewhat blurred by the necessity for all staff to work closely together, frequently performing the same or comparable tasks. In their role as evaluators, social work managers assume (or should assume) greater credibility than in the informal communication that occurs in the day-to-day work interaction. A very positive formal evaluation using objective criteria provides a more powerful reinforcement for good work performance than does any general sense of approval that a manager can convey on a daily basis. It also allows the manager to propose areas where even a good employee can improve performance.

On the less pleasant side, evaluations when performed properly lay the legal and ethical groundwork for reassignment, denial of merit pay increases, demotion, or even termination of employees who are not performing up to standards or who represent a liability to the organization, its clients, and/or its image within the community. Optimistically, we hope that an evaluation of an employee who is not performing well will provide an impetus for change and improvement. Initially, the manager must proceed on the assumption that employees are capable of improvement, must suggest specific areas where improvement will be required, and must provide support for improvement in the form of supervision and/or continuing education. But there may come a time when it is clear that an employee lacks either the ability or the motivation to improve to the degree necessary and must be dismissed. At that point, written evaluations must be available to provide documentation of an employee's inadequate job performance, that the employee has received the required warnings and all due process. Evaluations can be used to provide evidence that the decision to fire an employee is neither arbitrary, capricious, unfair, impulsive, nor in any way unanticipated by all parties involved.

As we have suggested earlier, evaluations should be firmly based on objective criteria. While tact and sensitivity have their place in the evaluation process, that place relates primarily to *how* the manager's assessments of an employee are communicated to an employee, and, perhaps, to the nature of corrective action chosen, *not* to the substance of the evaluation itself. Managers, for example, might use their social worker's insights into human behavior to select their words carefully in conveying their critical assessment of the work of an employee who has recently sustained the loss of a partner or close relative. As much as possible, managers would avoid contributing to existing feelings of depression, rejection, debilitating anger, or helplessness. But accurate communication of the assessment of a worker's performance must occur. To provide an unrealistic, glossed-over assessment, even at a time of worker "vulnerability," would be a disservice to the employee (it doesn't suggest areas that need work). It also could prove to be a real problem for the manager if the employee later demonstrates that, even without unusual stress, the employee is incapable of meeting job requirements. To a social worker who is also a manager, the life situation of the employee would suggest a realistic but tactful assessment with assurances of support for help in overcoming performance deficiencies. Some special consideration may even be appropriate, but it should be clear that any "period of grace" will be time-limited. The needs of the organization and its clients must remain the top priority, and the manager must communicate this to all employees through whatever evaluation methods are used.

CASE EXAMPLE: THE COST OF KINDNESS

Scott was a case supervisor in a large, well-established family agency offering a variety of counseling services to client families. He came to the Jefferson Family Service Center from a mental health clinic where he had been employed as a psychiatric social worker for six years. He came highly recommended as a replacement for the previous case supervisor who had retired.

When he took the job at Jefferson, Scott looked forward to the additional responsibilities that go with the job of supervisor. He thought that he would enjoy splitting his time between direct services (he would continue to see some clients) and supervisory management responsibilities.

Overall, the social workers that Scott supervised were a dedicated and competent group. He found that they responded well to advice and suggestions and could usually be counted on to function with little day-to-day case supervision. There was, however, one notable exception. Mildred was 57 years old when Scott came to Jefferson. In her first supervisory conference with Scott, Mildred pointedly but pleasantly reminded him that (1) she had grown children older than he and (2) that she planned to work eight more years, doing essentially what she had been doing, and then retire. He learned that she had, in fact, been doing very little. She had been hired 27 years earlier along with Scott's predecessor—her former supervisor—and continued to have regular contact with her. They remained the best of friends.

As he learned more about Mildred and got to know her better, Scott's anger at her approach to their first conference subsided. He found himself genuinely liking her. While he had intended to insist that she be more productive, he quickly concluded that she was probably incapable of doing more anyway. When he had assigned several new cases to her, she missed appointments and seemed to become overwhelmed. The other staff became resentful and suggested, without actually stating it, that he just leave her alone until retirement. Her duties consisted of seeing a few clients whom she had carried for many years, doing occasional intake histories, watering the plants in all offices, and keeping the waiting room tidy and uncluttered. On those occasions when Scott needed to use her for work more appropriate to her job level, she generally proved herself to be totally incompetent.

According to policy, Scott conducted regular six-month evaluations with all of his supervisees. The first time that one was scheduled, he seriously considered rating Mildred as unsatisfactory and confronting her with her shortcomings in the evaluation conference. He revised and tore up the written evaluation that he had prepared. He finally decided that Mildred would be devastated if he rated her objectively, especially since she had always been rated "excellent" by her friend and previous supervisor. She also had become very complimentary of his supervisory skills. He envisioned a hurt, tearful evaluation conference, painful to both parties, and resentment from the rest of the staff for how insensitively Mildred had been treated. He couldn't imagine how she could possibly use a critical evaluation for improvement anyway, given her sensitive nature and her pattern of performance developed over many years. He chose the road of least resistance with a slight effort at compromise—he rated her "excellent" in eight performance categories and "needs improvement" in two. In their conference he quickly explained to her that everyone (even himself) "needs improvement" in the two areas, punctuality and attention to detail. They laughed together about this and, overall, the conference was a pleasant interchange.

Scott was relieved. He had dreaded the conference with Mildred and expected that even the two slightly critical ratings would hurt her feelings. Her reaction was far better than anticipated; it made him even more fond of her and seemed to confirm that he had chosen the right course of action. He decided not to assign her to any new duties. This would make her happy and would allow him to continue to give her high evaluations on what she did, without grossly distorting reality. She *did* do an excellent job of plant care, didn't she?

For the next two years, Mildred continued to do very little. Her co-workers continued to cover for her and Scott continued to give her very favorable evaluations. Then a new Executive Director was hired. Private funding had declined drastically, and the board of directors had given him the specific charge to reorganize the administrative structure of the agency in an effort to do more with less funding. Among other obstacles that he would face, the board denied funding to replace social work staff members who had recently left the agency.

The Director wasted little time. He called his three supervisors together and explained the situation. He instructed each to develop a plan that would represent no reduction in client services while making full use of remaining staff. The other supervisors had a difficult but inevitable solution available to them. They reassigned cases previously handled by the workers who had left to newer workers carrying smaller caseloads and they began to see more clients themselves. Scott considered all possible alternatives. None were ideal and all involved some change that Mildred would see as punitive and that would force her to have more client contact. He finally concluded that the best solution was to assign her full-time to do intake histories, freeing up the other remaining social workers and himself to do more treatment. Predictably, Mildred reacted with incredulity, hurt, and even a little anger. She suggested that she might retire early, a thought that gave Scott no small amount of false hope. But before she could follow through on her threat (which most people doubted would occur anyway), another situation arose.

The Jefferson reorganization resulted in reassignment and/or a heavier workload for eight other employees in addition to Mildred. Six of them were those most recently hired who were given a full caseload immediately. This was a departure from the usual agency practice of giving new social workers a 3/4 load for their first six months on the job. All six were women. One of the six convinced the others and, eventually, even Mildred, to lend their names to a sex-discrimination suit against the agency.

The addition of Mildred's name to the legal action gave the suit more credibility. Mildred's reassignment involved a very senior employee. The fact that the Executive Director, Scott, and the one other supervisor were male lent even more credence to the complaint.

When he learned just how incompetent Mildred had been for years, the Director grew optimistic. Scott told him that neither he nor his predecessor felt that they could trust her to handle higher-level professional duties and had used her for only routine tasks. The Director asked for documentation of Mildred's limitations. Scott had to respond that he had none. The Director asked to see her six-month employee evaluations; they were, of course, very favorable. The Director was furious, refusing to accept the only explanations that Scott could offer.

The board, not wanting to risk the public reaction to a lawsuit charging sexism in a social agency, agreed to a substantial financial settlement for participants in the lawsuit. Jefferson's financial problems were compounded. The subsequent resignation of Mildred and all but one of the staff involved in the suit left several new vacanies, most of which could not be filled because of new budget deficits. Another painful reorganization had to be implemented.

Scott's next six-month evaluation of his own performance was no surprise to him. The Director rated him as "unsatisfactory" in performance of managerial roles, the first bad mark on his personnel record. He left the agency shortly afterward to take another supervisory position in a public agency. He vowed that, in the future, he would be sensitive and tactful in conducting evaluations. But he also would do whatever was necessary to document the actual performance level of his staff, no matter how unpleasant the task might be at the time.

Fairness as a Goal of Evaluation

An evaluation, whether it is regular, periodic, and formalized or whether it consists of a mixture of formal methods and informal, regular communication of a manager's assessment of an employee's work, has the potential to seriously affect group morale. All evaluations must be perceived as fair and objective. This perception should be shared by the individual being evaluated as well as by other staff. While evaluators must maintain the strict confidentiality of an evaluation, in most organizations individuals being evaluated often discuss all or part of their evaluation with peers. They are especially likely to share those negative communications that they did not like because they thought that they were unjustified. This type of behavior can be reduced by the social worker as manager through careful attention to the fairness issue. The way that evaluations are conducted can enhance the manager's reputation for fairness. Or they can do it irreparable harm. While a few co-workers may rejoice in a manager's evaluation that is perceived as unfairly critical of a peer (if they don't like or respect the employee themselves), a more likely reaction is to conclude that "if the manager was unfair to them, the manager may be the same way with me." If this occurs, group morale will suffer.

Even evaluations that are not fair in that they reflect a tendency to be unrealistically complimentary of all staff can result in morale problems. A student who works hard for an *A* tends to resent anther student who gets an *A* but who did *C* work; that same student also resents the professor who awarded the undeserved *A*. Employees react similarly when they learn through the grapevine that their "excellent" evaluations by a supervisor reflect very little if any difference from those received by a peer judged by all to be only marginally competent. Their own excellent rating communicated very little. It also underwent depreciation in their eyes and those of others if virtually everyone was rated about the same. Staff members know that there are differences in the motivation, knowledge, skills, and professional values of their peers. They have a right to expect that a manager's staff evaluations will reflect these differences. If they do not (and staff almost always find out), they will resent the lack of differentiation and morale can be seriously damaged.

When is an evaluation fair? It is fair to evaluate an employee based upon objective standards that are predetermined by the manager, usually with input from the individual being evaluated. It is unfair to change the rules between evaluations. If, for example, an employee demonstrates the capacity to do more than was anticipated and required or is able to complete a task more quickly than previously anticipated, performance on additional work assignments should not be considered for subsequent evaluation purposes. That would be unfair. It is quickly perceived as unfair by staff if the reward for good work is more work or if new standards for evaluation are added that might result in an unfavorable evaluation for individuals who did what was expected of them and did it well.

While some comparison of staff by a manager is inevitable and even desirable in performing some functions (for example, selecting an employee for promotion), other types of comparison have no place in an evaluation of an individual. It is fair to evaluate individuals using objectives and standards previously set for them. It is unfair to evaluate them using another employee as a reference point. This erroneous practice is just another variation on the previous discussion of the inappropriateness of changing standards after objectives are set. A statistician will confirm that the use of a normal curve to assign grades to students is, in most all cases, unfair. It leaves the individual student less likely to be evaluated based upon his or her learning or demonstrated knowledge than upon the chance that placed the student in a particular class section. (The student in a "curved" course of 15 students who attends the first session and hears 10 classmates explain to the professor after class that they are taking only one course and would like additional reading assignments had better drop the course fast—they are working their way down from a *C*!) The supervisor or other social worker as manager who evaluates using comparisons with other staff creates both a statistical and a managerial error. No group of employees is large enough to produce the normal distribution that might assure a fair evaluation using comparisons. If evaluations are "curved," all employees and their evaluations are vulnerable to the strength or weakness of the group in which they find themselves.

Comparative staff evaluations also create excessive competitiveness among staff. This may produce results in the short run, but it is unhealthy over time. Staff will usually see such a practice as manipulative on the part of the manager. It can also be insulting. Adult professionals should not be placed in a position of "sibling rivalry." What matters is how well *they* do *their* job and contribute to achievement of organizational goals and client services. Any evaluation based on anything else is inappropriate and potentially destructive of an environment of trust.

Still another good reason why a manager should avoid comparative evaluation relates to issues of confidentiality. It is impossible for a manager to convince employees that they are being fairly compared with others without revealing parts of the other staff members' evaluations. This practice is unethical. It can also discourage the productive and candid discussion of a worker's performance that should be a part of any good evaluation. A staff member may fear that what he or she reveals and discusses will be shared with others. Evaluations depend on honest communication, and their value is diminished when discussion becomes guarded.

The selection of objective criteria and instruments for evaluation, the adherence to prenegotiated standards, and the avoidance of comparison with other employees do not in themselves guarantee fairness. The nature of employee tasks also must be considered. The goal of an evaluation that is neither too severe nor too lenient (that is, one that is fair) can only be accomplished if managers introduce other considerations into the evaluation process.

Evaluation must include an assessment of what is a realistic expectation for each employee. Such factors as employee's stage of career development, professional background, stated career objectives, and previous work experience are logical variables that should be considered. No one can fairly expect the same level of performance (in terms of quality or quantity) from, for example, a new graduate as that expected from a senior, experienced counselor. A certain kind and number of mistakes are expected from the new graduate; the same mistakes might be indicative of apathy or motivational problems for the seasoned professional. Evaluation should reflect consideration of these factors if fairness is to be perceived.

Another factor to consider is the nature of the job itself. The amount of cause-effect knowledge available to help in performing tasks may be considered in evaluating performance. Was the job one for which our professional knowledge base virtually guarantees success if a method is employed correctly (a rarity in our field)? Or is the level of knowledge so tentative (for example, in treatment of families of AIDS patients) that a high tolerance for a lack of demonstrated success is indicated?

Having assessed what performance standards are reasonable—given knowledge available for use—still another variable must be considered. A fair evaluation should reflect whether or not there is consensus on what is the desirable outcome of an employee's work activities and whether this has been clearly stated. For example, how should an evaluator construe the fact that few of a social worker's clients return for a second treatment interview? Is it indicative of an inability to form treatment relationships or of the successful application of crisis intervention methods? Or is the dissolution of the marriages of three of a social worker's cases an indication that the worker's role as marriage counselor was performed successfully or not? What is a desirable outcome? In evaluating the work of human service professionals we frequently encounter situations where there is a lack of consensus as to what is successful goal achievement.

The social worker as manager must be prepared to use practice knowledge, values, and skills to provide an employee performance evaluation that is perceived as fair. There is really no reason to proceed on the mistaken assumption that the injection of the "soft" knowledge of the professional social worker as manager will compromise the objectivity of an evaluation. Objectivity is not synonymous with rigidity; it implies fairness and lack of bias, both of which can coexist in an evaluation process that takes into consideration both personal and situational factors that impact on the performance of an employee. It represents a conscious effort on the part of the manager to eliminate certain biases from evaluations. Managers cognizant of mitigating circumstances will be less likely to, for example, rely on themselves and their own knowledge and skills as a reference point to evaluate others. They also will be less likely to make a general assessment of an employee first and then proceed to rate all aspects of the employee's performance in a way that is consistent with that assessment.[3] Employee evaluations, like virtually all management tasks, can be made easier by the knowledge and skills possessed by the social worker.

MANAGEMENT ISSUES RELATING TO PROMOTION

In their role as manager, social workers frequently have the opportunity and the responsibility to make promotion decisions or to influence the promotion decisions of others. As we have observed in our discussion of the general topic of employee evaluation, staff perception of a manager's fairness in making decisions related to promotion can greatly affect group morale, the organizational climate, and the manager's future capacity to manage. Will the decision or recommendation reflect objectivity and what is believed to be best overall for the organization? If so, trust in the manager is likely to be enhanced. Or will the decision or recommendation appear to be tainted by self-serving motivation or personal allegiances of the manager? If this occurs, trust and respect for the manager can be seriously damaged.

Outside or Within?

A decision that must precede the final selection of the best individual for a promotion but that is heavily influenced by individual staff characteristics involves whether to fill a position at a mid- or upper-organizational level with a current employee of the organization or a person not currently associated with it. Sometimes policies and, occasionally, even rules make this decision an easy one for the social worker as manager. But if a policy invites consideration of both alternatives or if no organizational guidance is available, assessment of the costs and benefits of either choice is indicated.

We will use a common situation to illustrate the mixed blessings of the two alternatives. Consider the selection of a replacement for a case supervisor who has resigned. On first blush, a promotion from within current staff appears to be the logical option to choose. A pattern of continued looking beyond current staff when opportunities for advancement arise can have a demoralizing effect on staff attitudes. If, however, the usual practice is to promote from within, employees not only feel that they have a chance to get ahead but they also feel that their employee status gives them a better opportunity for advancement. What's more, managers considering their own employees for promotion are much more likely to make a knowledgeable decision (they are more likely to know candidates' strengths and weaknesses) than if they were to consider persons outside the organization about whom little is known. Why not tap the management potential of one's own employees? Why should an employee with management potential have to leave the organization in order to be promoted?

While a practice of promotion from within has a compelling logic to it and several distinct advantages, a number of cautions regarding its use are in order. In human service organizations, perhaps even more so than in business enterprises, a large number of employees (cosmopolitans?—see Chapter 5) wish to exercise the professional skills (often treatment) that they possess and do not aspire to promotion. To assume that everyone seeks this kind of advancement may be an error; to assume that anyone seeks it even may be a false assumption.

Generally, staff tend to agree with the principle of promotion from within and its implicit potential for upward mobility. But among those who seek promotion, it is not unusual for them to object to and resent a promotion recommendation that rewards a co-worker or acquaintance other than themselves. Jealousies and rivalries can develop within organizations that have a policy of promotion from within. Competition for a promotion that may become available sometime in the future can be a stimulus for productivity. But it can also promote an attitude that discourages sharing of essential information with colleagues (potential rivals for a job) and offers of needed assistance. Staff may tend to engage in largely self-serving behaviors.

It should also be remembered that a promotion of a competent and proven staff member from within may weaken the ranks from which that person was drawn. Can an adequate replacement be found within the organization (a double disruption) or hired from outside? Sometimes not.

Arguments for filling higher-level vacancies from outside the organization relate primarily to how this practice can avoid the problems related to promoting from within, which we have described. Outside promotions do not directly deplete existing staff, but staff may feel career-blocked and leave anyway. Jealousies and rivalries may be less likely to occur when a policy that favors outside promotion is announced. In such situations, it may be less personally embarrassing for employees to have someone outside selected over themselves than it is to have a co-worker given the promotion that they had sought. While staff may disagree with the principle of filling higher-level vacancies from among those outside the organization, the selection of a nonemployee is less likely to humiliate rejected applicants. They can easily rationalize to themselves and others that "they obviously wanted to hire from outside."

A compromise policy that often works well is one of open competition. Advantages to this kind of policy include the opportunity to hire the best possible applicant from among all possible candidates and it also "motivates the complacent heir apparent"[4] who might believe that he or she has a lock on the promotion if promotion from within were to be the policy. It also avoids the morale problems associated with the belief related to promotion from outside—that no one currently employed need bother to apply. Open competition, however, puts a heavy burden on social workers as managers to demonstrate that the competition is indeed open if they are to maintain a reputation for fairness. Despite the existence of such a policy, employees tend to want to believe that one of the other two policies is *really* in effect or that a job was "wired" from the start.

Selecting the Individual

Organizations that fill higher-level vacancies with nonemployees tend to place decision making more in the hands of personnel specialists and less in the hands of social workers in their roles as managers. If promotion from within or open competition is the policy, the manager is more likely to have valuable input to offer. What should managers consider in making or influencing the decision of whom to choose?

From one perspective, a promotion of an employee can be viewed as a reward. But it should also be considered as a show of confidence in an individual based upon projections about that person's future performance in a new role. The past is a good indicator of the future, but it is far from perfect. We don't know how an employee will perform if promoted, but past and present behavior and attitudes give us some good hints.

The concept of a reward suggests that someone selected as the best candidate for promotion (in the manager's perception) ought to have been doing a good job in his or her present position. While it is conceivable that an employee functioning marginally in a current assignment would rise to new heights if promoted, it is highly unlikely. The idea of "promotion to motivate" rarely works. In addition to the fact that it is unlikely to be successful, it sends an unfortunate message to other staff, namely do a good job and we will overlook you; don't do a good job, and we may promote you. This same message is conveyed when a highly competent employee is passed over in favor of one less competent because the competent one is viewed as too valuable in his or her present position to be moved. Some managers have received a less than grateful response when they have paid an employee this kind of "compliment" after denying the person a promotion.

Projections about an individual's ability to function in a higher-level position usually tend to be based upon the person's demonstrated or assumed personal attributes. Certain characteristics such as initiative, intelligence, conceptual abilities, problem-solving skills, interpersonal skills, integrity, communication skills, and commitment to organizational goals tend to be frequently mentioned as indications that an individual is capable of "moving up." These are all important characteristics to possess, but the problem with all of them and most of the others suggested in the literature is that they are desirable attributes for employees at all levels.—Besides, how *much* intelligence, for example, is necessary? We know that it is helpful to be a little brighter than those you supervise, but is *very much brighter* an asset or a liability? We also can identify persons who, for example, are good supervisors but who seem to lack one or more of the characteristics often suggested as prerequisites for successfully assuming higher-level positions.

Use of checklists of desirable attributes are of only limited value for the manager in considering candidates for a promotion. One attribute sometimes mentioned is an especially useful assessment tool for the manager, however. It is absolutely essential for individuals seeking promotion. It is the desire to perform the functions of manager. Any promotion will almost certainly result in more time spent in management activities and the likelihood of involvement in a wider variety of management functions. The question for the social worker as manager charged with choosing or recommending someone for a promotion must be, "Does this person really want to manage?"

Many people want to assume management positions, but they lack the desire to manage. The two are not synonymous. Higher-level positions carry with them a greater amount of status, autonomy, power, and (usually) pay more. They generally also involve fewer routine, repetitive, lower-level tasks. Individuals promoted to supervisory positions in social work counseling agencies, for example, can expect a number of immediate attractive changes in their workday. They may no longer have to perform social histories or do intake interviews. They are likely to assume either a greatly reduced caseload or none at all. If they see clients, they may be able to choose the cases that they wish to follow. They will be far less accountable for their time and activities, but they will be able to hold others accountable for how they spend their day. They will be the object of subtle and less-than-subtle deference from those whom they supervise, will be treated as peers by other supervisors, and will be given more respect by higher-level administrators. As supervisors, they may be entitled to a larger, better-furnished office, more vacation time, better secretarial support, reserved parking space, their own computer equipment, private phone, and/or other indicators of their place in the organization. The title of "supervisor" will now appear on the signature block of their correspondence. Who wouldn't aspire to having these "perks"?

When we think of promotion we usually think of more money and all the outer signs of success that accompany it. If we are an academician, we tend to think of the benefits of becoming a dean, not of the activity of "deaning." If we are a caseworker, we think of becoming a supervisor, not of the tasks of supervising. We may fantasize telling our relatives or friends about our promotion and of how they will be impressed with our obvious success. We may even think of how we will "rub it in" to someone who predicted that we would never succeed or who once seemed to relish exercising power over us.

In our upwardly mobile society, there is also a tendency to feel obligated to seek a promotion if we think we can acquire it. After all, others want it, we can get it, so why not take it to show that we are better than they are? It would be embarrassing to let them have it and to wonder if we could have really had it. Worse still, others might actually think someone else was chosen over us. This kind of thinking has led some people to seek promotions to positions that they really did not want. What they really wanted was the outer signs of success that go with a movement up within the administrative hierarchy.

There is one major problem for the individual who makes a career move based primarily on the promise of tangible rewards and the outer shows of success that accompany it. The benefits soon lose their impact. Relatives and friends are most impressed when they learn about a promotion; after that, it is no longer news. Parking one's car in the reserved parking place becomes habit after about two weeks; it soon provides little satisfaction. The large office soon fills up with dust catchers, which have miraculously expended to fill the greater available area. One soon forgets about the tasks one used to hate and focuses on those one currently hates. People may even learn that they miss some old tasks—for example, client contact. When 95 percent of the "goodies" that go with the promotion have lost their glow—after about six weeks—they are left with *the job* of supervisor or whatever higher-level position was assumed. They may wake up one Monday morning to realize that most of the fun is now over (the paycheck is larger, but somehow there's still nothing left) and what really matters is the function and performance expectations that the organization now has for them.

Social workers as managers should carefully help candidates for promotion explore their motivation. One of the best services that they can provide is to remind candidates of the other, longer-lasting effects of a promotion, of how their workday will be different. By using skills familiar to the social work practitioner, the social worker as manager can help to relieve employees of some of the pressure felt in our society to take any promotion that is accessible to them. Many academicians capable of becoming a dean *choose* not to become one; many caseworkers who could become a supervisor *choose* not to accept a promotion. There is no shame inherent in such a decision. On the contrary, it may reflect a depth of insight into one's own needs and preferences that may be lacking in those who do take a higher-level job chiefly because it exists and is available to them or because of the tangible rewards it may offer.

What kind of people turn down the opportunity for a promotion with all of its tangible and intangible benefits? Who *should* turn one down? How can a social worker as manager sort out the motivation of different promotional candidates to determine who wants the promotion for the right reasons (including a desire to manage) and who is simply seeking the ephemeral benefits? We find ourselves right back at our understandings of management as discussed in Chapter 1 of this text.

In assessing the motivation of candidates for promotion, the manager must ask whether the candidates seem to have the attributes of a manager and whether they would like to do what a manager does. Would they enjoy a job that requires that more of their day be spent in tasks of planning, staffing, organizing, controlling, and leading? Would they, for example, be able to handle making unpleasant personnel decisions or providing critical evaluations of others' work performance? Would they be comfortable with developing and implementing rules, policies, procedures, strategies, and programs? Would they find these tasks stimulating or deadly boring? If we understand our roles as managers, we are in a perfect position to help others to explore whether they want to assume the increased management responsibilities and tasks that inevitably go with a promotion. If we know what management requires, we are well qualified to determine whether others have what it takes.

Choosing or recommending a staff member for promotion is an important task of the social worker as manager. On the surface, it would seem like a most pleasant activity. Performed correctly, it is hard, time-consuming work. It can also result in unpleasant feelings and confrontations. Fortunately, the job is made much easier for us because, as social workers, we have insight into both human behavior and the motivation of others. We also have interviewing skills. As managers ourselves, we can understand better than anyone else how a promotion can change the workday of an employee who must assume added managerial functions.

The Fairness Issue Again

The selection or recommendation of a staff member for promotion requires that the manager look beyond the motivation of individual candidates. As managers, we have a perspective that should always give highest priority to the good of the organization and of the clients that it serves. In respecting these priorities, the person ultimately chosen or recommended sometimes may not be simply the individual who seems to have the greatest amount of desirable personal attributes and motivation. Other factors must be considered.

The formal job description of a position may give only a limited hint as to the best person to assume it. If, for example, it is a case-supervision job that involves overseeing a productive, cooperative, self-motivated group of professionals, one type of supervisor may be appropriate. Another opening, though identical on paper, may require a supervisor who can exert the control and "hard hand" necessary to bring to productivity an apathetic or passive-aggressive group who apear to have retired on the job. Especially in the task of selecting a supervisor, the matching of potential supervisory style and attributes with subordinate needs becomes extremely important. Among the myriad other situational factors that may influence the decision of who should be promoted are such diverse considerations as whether the organization is in a period of relative stability or change, the political visibility of the specific position, the characteristics and success of the previous occupant, the type of informal support network available to assist the newly promoted employee, and the likely reaction of the candidate's present co-workers who will be left behind and who may have sought the promotion themselves.

Other realities that exist also may affect the selection or recommendation of a candidate for promotion. For example, in unionized organizations, managers may not have free rein simply to pick the person they deem to be best for the job. In order to maintain good labor relations, managers may need to adhere to union guidelines. Affirmative action restrictions and other legislative and judicial rules and policies may also influence who may be chosen. It is not unusual for social workers as managers to find themselves caught between labor unions with seniority-based requirements on one hand

and federal nondiscrimination requirements on the other. Women and particularly minorities of color may possess the least seniority, having been recently hired within many organizations. By union standards, they are not likely to be in line for promotion. Yet efforts to eliminate discrimination (as well as our professional values as social workers) would suggest that, in the interest of achieving equality, we should promote them. This dilemma once again illustrates why Taylor's "one best way" is not well suited for today's manager. These *is* no perfect candidate for a promotion or a perfect solution to the opposing forces that sometimes influence the choice of a candidate for promotion. The social worker as manager must seek a satisfactory solution, not a perfect one, relying at least in part on the knowledge, values, and skills of his or her profession.

HANDLING INADEQUATE STAFF PERFORMANCE

Despite the hard work involved and the potential to create resentment and a loss of trust for the manager, the selection of an employee for promotion is, overall, a relatively pleasant management task. It is, after all, a confirmation that at least one staff member is believed to be capable of even greater growth and of more responsibility. Unfortunately, both formal and casual evaluations of staff also reveal that some other individuals are falling short of meeting the expectations of even their present positions. The social worker as manager must consider a number of available options to address this problem.

Transfers

For the employee judged to be not functioning at an acceptable level, transfer should be considered. If used inappropriately, it creates its own problems in that it may seem to reward those who are not performing satisfactorily by reassigning them to another job that other staff members may perceive as more desirable. Used appropriately, however, a transfer may represent a good problem solution for the manager. A failure to function in one job (particularly if there are unique situational factors such as personality conflicts that negatively affect performance) may not preclude success in another job.

Transfers may not always be an option in very small organizations or in situations where the employee clearly lacks the credentials for any job other than his or her current one. Where possible, transfers should be used cautiously by the manager. The potential impact on morale of other employees in both the old and new work groups should be carefully evaluated. If the decision is made to transfer, it should be made abundantly clear to the employee that being transferred should be viewed as a second chance and not an indication that he or she has been absolved of responsibility for a previous level of functioning. Careful setting of acceptable standards and the use of regular, comprehensive employee evaluations in the employee's new job will also be required.

Use of Reprimands

If, for whatever reason, it is not possible or desirable to transfer to another position within the organization an employee who is not performing satisfactorily, the social worker as manager will need to do whatever possible to communicate to the employee his or her deficiencies, provide support for change, and prepare the employee for the possibility of termination. If periodic employee evaluations have been performed conscientiously and honestly, they will go a long way toward assisting in all of these activities. But evaluations may lack the specific criticism and direction that staff members require to tell them exactly what they need to do to improve or they may not offer the manager the needed documentation to prove that due process has existed. Reprimands may be required. Negative evaluations can be somewhat general, especially if the manager is limited by the use of highly structured forms and criteria. The employee who so chooses can ignore them or not hear the messages that they convey. Reprimands are not so easily ignored, if communicated properly.

A reprimand, to be effective, must be a direct, one-to-one, private, and confidential communication of an employee shortcoming. It flows from one at a higher administrative level directly to the deficient subordinate. It is generally written and includes a warning of the consequences if the deficiency is not corrected, usually within a certain time period. Copies of the written reprimand are kept, usually in the employee's personnel file. If a verbal reprimand is used, a written record of the conversation is retained. A reprimand is very specific. It spells out in detail what was done wrong or inadequately, and it states what the expected acceptable level of performance is. It leaves no room for misunderstandings or claims that the recipient was not adequately warned of the perceived shortcomings or the consequences of their continuation.

Social workers as managers have often tended to avoid the use of reprimands, for they represent the unpleasant critical confrontation that seems almost antithetical to good social work practice. There is nothing nonjudgmental about a reprimand; it is based upon a judgment that has found another human being to be deficient in some respect. It communicates an expectation of change. Because of their distaste for one-to-one reprimands, social work managers sometimes have relied on a substitute that is both inadequate and creates new problems of its own—the group reprimand.

The group reprimand is essentially a contradiction in terms. Unlike an individual reprimand, it is public, not private and confidential. It has the potential to embarrass rather than to protect the offending individual from the gossip and ridicule of one's peers. It may be easier on the manager than an individual reprimand, but harder on the rest of the work group.

Group reprimands rarely work. For example, a supervisor may be having a persistent problem with a subordinate who spends several hours a day on the phone with family and friends. The supervisor might choose to address the problem by means of a group reprimand delivered during a staff meeting. The supervisor stands to gain little and lose much. A typical group reprimand in this hypothetical situation might consist of a stern voice, a scowl, and a statement such as, "Some of you are spending too much time on the telephone handling personal business. This is against agency policy and must stop immediately! You know who you are." The supervisor might feel relieved to have avoided an unpleasant direct confrontation and would feel that a particular concern had been effectively communicated.

What is the likely result of the use of a group reprimand in this situation? Those staff members who rarely or never use the phone for personal business will speculate on just who the culprit is, if they don't already know. They also will likely be angry that they had to listen to the supervisor's insulting display of parenting when they were not the guilty party. They will resent the time wasted by this action and will lose some respect for the supervisor who seemed to lack the courage to confront directly their peer who was misusing the phone.

Some other productive and competent staff members who occasionally use their work phone for necessary personal calls may believe that the supervisor was referring to them. They will feel chastised, a little surprised and hurt at the severity of the supervisor's reaction. A distance may develop between them and the supervisor. They will probably not make any personal calls from work, taking time off the job to use the pay phone in the lobby if a call is absolutely necessary.

Meanwhile, the real object of the reprimand may simply assume that the supervisor wasn't talking about him (or her) anyway. Even if the culprit recognizes that he (or she) was the target of the reprimand, the person will be somewhat reassured to think that he (or she) is not the only one using the phone for personal business, and will be unlikely to stop the behavior. There will be no written record of the group reprimand, either to serve as an ongoing impetus for change for the employee or to provide the manager with proof of due process, should the employee ultimately have to be fired.

Overall, group reprimands are less than worthless; they can be destructive of morale and the kind of productive organizational climate that the manager is expected to create. They are not a discharging of managerial responsibility; they are a shirking of it. Appropriately used, direct, one-to-one reprimands are an unpleasant but absolutely essential part of a social worker's job as manager. They should not be perceived as unfair or insensitive. They represent what is needed by the employee who receives them; that is, specific, honest communication about where and how they need to improve in order to avoid future unpleasant consequences or even to retain their job. If improvement is insufficient and the employee must be terminated, reprimands help to expedite the smooth performance of this task. If ultimately necessary, they make it easier to remove a deficient employee fairly from the job and to replace the offender with one who has greater potential to deliver the kind of client services that we as social workers value and which clients have a right to expect.

Exit Interviews

Even the decision to dismiss an employee following unsuccessful efforts to bring the employee's performance up to a satisfactory level does not conclude a social work manager's responsibilities to the employee. Despite due process, the departing staff members are likely to bear hostility toward the manager who judged them to be a liability or at least not an asset to the organization. An offer of an exist interview is usually appropriate. If employees choose to avail themselves of an exit interview (and it is difficult to force them to do anything at this point) it can be beneficial for all concerned. Managers may tend to dread exit interviews but they should not. If all legal and ethical obligations have been met and the dismissal is an appropriate action the manager is on firm ground. As social workers, we should recognize the possible value of employees having the opportunity to vent their feelings, no matter how negative and hostile. An exit interview also gives the manager the opportunity to stress the fact that the discharged employee has not been rejected as a person, but as an individual who did not happen to meet the requirements of a particular work role.

As managers, the exit interview can be very valuable. We may have the opportunity to defuse some of the anger toward the organization that the staff member is likely to have. This makes the dismissed employee less likely to present the organization in a bad light in the community or to distort the reasons for his or her dismissal. In addition, even bitter, angry, about-to-be former employees may provide us with some valuable insights and knowledge. Perhaps some of the stress that they were asked to work under was at least partially avoidable. Probably not all of their shortcomings were totally their fault. We may be able to learn much from the exit interview that will allow us to increase the chances for successful job performance of the next person who will occupy the position. Of course, not only dismissed employees but also those who leave voluntarily with good feelings can provide us with useful ideas for improvement when an exit interview is used.

The social worker as manager who approaches the task of confronting inadequate employee performance as a vehicle to improve client service is less likely to dread it. If approached in a fair and objective manner, the exit interview, along with performance evaluations, can be a constructive activity for both the manager and for the staff member who is leaving. It is important to remember that while social work values may initially make the job uncomfortable and not sought, the knowledge and skills of the social worker are of great assistance in performing these tasks, and they increase the likelihood of their success. If pursued with sensitivity and a high level of professionalism, even the termination of an employee can contribute much to a productive work climate and to high group morale among those staff members who remain.

SUMMARY

In this chapter we discussed the third element of what we have loosely labeled the staffing function of the social worker as manager. The formal periodic evaluation of employees is not a task that the social worker usually enjoys. Various perspectives on the value of evaluations were presented. They were described as extremely useful to all concerned when conducted objectively and as an essential prerequisite to either promotion or dismissal of staff. They also have the potential either to enhance the manager's reputation for fairness or to damage it. The fairness issue was explored in some detail.

The topic of promotion of staff was examined in relation to three options —promotion from within, promotion from outside, or open competition. The importance of matching individual characteristics to the needs of an available position was emphasized. It was stressed that the social worker as manager needs to determine how much a candidate for promotion really wants a job that is likely to entail increased management responsibilities. Sometimes employees merely wish to have the benefits that go with the position, most of which are transitory.

The employee who is not meeting performance expectations requires special action from the manager. The value and the appropriate use of transfers and reprimands were discussed, along with a strong warning against the use of group reprimands, Finally, the termination of the services of an employee was presented as a necessary management function that can result in gain for the organization in several ways. Exit interviews were advocated as valuable for all parties involved.

In the last three chapters we have focused on the manager's involvement in the selection of staff, their professional growth, and in personnel actions that affect staff members' movements within the organization. In the course of these discussions we have frequently touched upon the topic of employee motivation and how it relates to decisions made in performing these functions. In Chapter 8 we shall look at motivation in greater detail, thus enabling social workers as managers to acquire a better understanding of it and thereby facilitating their ability to promote a desirable and healthy organizational climate.

REFERENCES

1. Walter Christian and Gerald Hannah, *Effective Management in the Human Services* (Englewood Cliffs, NJ: Prentice-Hall, 1983), pp. 213–241; Eileen Gambrill and Theodore Stein, *Supervision: A Decision-Making Approach* (Beverly Hills, CA, Sage, 1983), pp. 39–106.
2. Alfred Kadushin, *Supervision in Social Work* (New York: Columbia University Press, 1976), pp. 286–313.
3. Ibid., p. 287.
4. Harold Koontz, Cyril O'Donnell, and Heinz Weihrich, *Essentials of Management* (New York: McGraw-Hill, 1986), p. 287.

ADDITIONAL READINGS

Eldridge, W. "Coping with Accountability and Evaluation: Some Guidelines for Supervisors of Direct Service Staff." *Administration in Mental Health*, 11 (1984): 195–204.

Heller, L. "Corporate Compassion (Survey: Managers' Reactions to Staffers' Personal Problems)." *Executive Women*, 10 (1987):26–31.

Kelley, N. *Personnel Management in Action*. St. Paul, MN: West, 1987.

Merwin, S. *Effective Evaluation (Employee) Strategies and Techniques*. San Diego: University Association, 1986.

Reece, B. *Effective Human Relations in Organizations*. Boston: Houghton Mifflin, 1987.

Sandefur, G. *Workbook for Evaluation*, 3rd ed. Beverly Hills, CA: Sage, 1986.

CHAPTER 8

Influencing Work Performance

Social workers as managers are responsible for positively influencing the productivity of those around them, but they should not and cannot do others' work for them. Managers also cannot create a desire for productive activity where none exists. They *can*, however, identify what motivates a given employee and appeal to the employee's sources of motivation.

We have all probably heard a manager remark in disgust that, "That person has no motivation." The manager may have been a teacher, a parent, an agency administrator, or a therapist describing a client. The remark provides a bit of therapeutic ventilation for the speaker, but it is not an accurate description of the truth. It might have been more accurate for the manager to have said, "I can't seem to identify what motivates that person" or "I haven't yet been able to use my knowledge of people's motivation to increase their productive activity." The point is, people with no motivation at all would not survive for long. They would not get out of bed, would stop eating, and would soon die. So, everyone has his or her source of motivation. We frequently become frustrated as managers because others do not seem to share the same motivators that we possess or because of our inability to understand and work with motivators that are different from our own.

Throughout this book we have emphasized that the knowledge and skills required to perform the management functions of the social worker often are more similar to those needed for performance of other roles of the social worker. Effective use of knowledge of motivation is a "people skill" that is certainly an asset to the counselor or therapist or to the macro-level practitioner as well as to the manager. As we examine the topic of motivation from the perspective of the social worker as manager in this chapter, the reader will probably experience a slight feeling of *déjà vu*. It will be evident that social workers already know a great deal about motivation that is applicable to successful performance within their role as managers.

SOME CLASSICAL THEORIES OF MOTIVATION

There is no shortage of studies of human motivation in the literature. It didn't take long for managers and students of management to notice that workers do not all seem to be driven by the same needs and forces. This realization came in part as a response to the Scientific Management theories of Frederick Taylor and others (see Chapter 3). Taylor's theories, the reader will recall, were dependent on a belief in the existence of "economic man," that is, the belief that money is the primary motivator of workers. The eventual recognition of the limits of Taylor's theories led other scholars to the conclusion that this concept of motivation was at best an overgeneralization and at worst a gross misunderstanding of workers. Subsequent beliefs about motivation tended to emphasize the diversity of needs and forces that influence an individual's behavior. We will look at a few of the better-known conceptualizations of motivation to see what each has to say to the social worker as manager.

The Hierarchy of Needs

One of the more familiar theories of motivation is attributed to Abraham Maslow.[1] It is a theory that has great utility for the social work practitioner; but it is also frequently misunderstood. Maslow's *needs hierarchy* is generally illustrated by a pyramid containing five categories or levels of needs. They are, in ascending order, physiological, security, social, ego, and self-actualization (see Figure 8.1). The choice of a pyramid to illustrate the various need levels is a reflection of Maslow's belief that many persons find themselves stalled at the first (physiological) level, fewer are functioning at the second (security) level, fewer yet at the third level, and so on. In fairness to Maslow, his hierarchy was developed at a time (around 1945) when this may have been a more accurate description of the distribution of workers and their motivation than is probably true today. We now believe that many more than just a few persons are motivated by a need for self-actualization.

The five levels reflect what Maslow believed were the primary motivators seen among individuals. Persons who have not satisfactorily acquired the basic necessities of life (food, clothing, shelter) are motivated by offers that promise to help meet their physiological needs.

Having met these most basic of needs, people might "graduate" to the

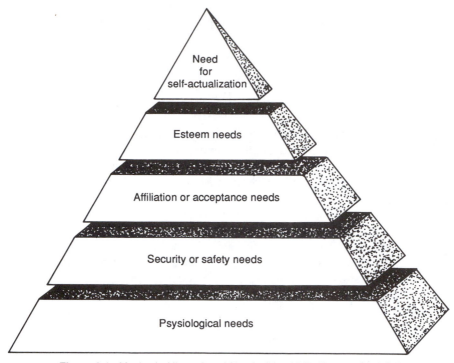

Figure 8.1. Maslow's Hierarchy of Needs (Harold D. Kootnz, Cyril O'Donnell and Heinz Weirch, *Essentials of Management*, 1986, McGraw-Hill Publishing Company. Figure 18.3, p. 377. Reprinted with permission of publisher.)

security-need level. Here, motivators take the form of protection from threat or danger or loss of what has been acquired.

For individuals who reach the third (social) level, needs reflect a pre-occupation with the question "What do others think of me?" Affiliation and acceptance are perceived as primary motivators at this level. Belonging is of utmost importance, and the promise of being able to fit in is a powerful influence on behavior.

At the fourth (ego) level, the important question is more likely to be, "What do *I* think of myself?" An individual at this level is expected to be driven by a need for self-esteem. Recognition, status, and prestige are important, but only because of their potential for enhancing what is most sought, namely self-confidence and a good feeling about oneself.

The fifth level (self-actualization) is the highest and last need level. It involves the use of one's talents, creativity, and the opportunity for working to full potential. A person operating at this need level would have satisfactorily met lower-level needs; appeals to lower level needs would not successfully influence behavior.

That people are motivated by different needs, or that the needs are hierarchical in nature, was really not the theoretical contribution of Maslow. His major contribution was the conclusion that human beings are only motivated by unmet needs, specifically by the need *above* the highest one in the hierarchy that has already been adequately met. Implicit in the idea of adequate need fulfillment is the recognition that what is "enough" for one person may not be "enough" for another. People tend to have different thresholds for their need gratification. Some require relatively little in order to move on to the next level. Others appear to be fixated at one level and never seem to be able to meet that need. For example, some of our parents or grandparents who lived through the Great Depression seem to exemplify persons for whom security needs will always be the major motivator. They find it virtually impossible to understand why people would choose a low-paying profession for their life's work or why they would give up job security in order to take a new position that is more challenging or less structured. Sometimes a crisis or setback also can cause a person to slip back into to a need level that was previously adequately gratified.

Social workers have usually encountered Maslow's needs hierarchy somewhere in their education, staff development, or training. It is a useful way of explaining client behavior. For example, it would provide understanding of why a welfare client who lacks the basic necessities of life (operating at the physiological need level) might derive limited benefits from insight therapy or counseling efforts aimed at promoting personality change. How could appeals to higher-level needs be expected to motivate a person who has not yet progressed beyond the first need level? Conversely, the Maslow conceptualization would also explain why an affluent client in a private residential care setting might be more enticed by the affiliation with others afforded by a Friday night bingo game (an appeal to the third need level) than by the possibility of winning the $10 grand prize. After all, a satisfied need (according to Maslow) is no longer a motivator.

Application of the needs hierarchy concept to the social worker's management activities is readily apparent. One worker might be operating at one need level; another may be at another level. It is not inconceivable that all five levels might be represented in a single work unit. It is incumbent on managers to know their employees well enough to assess accurately for each employee which needs have been met and which (the next higher level) have not and, therefore, are a potential source of motivation. For example, a manager should be reasonably certain that a staff employee is operating at the highest (self-actualization) level before expecting the employee to respond positively to an offer of new work responsibilities that will allow for creativity and innovation. If managers misjudge workers and are unaware that they are motivated primarily by social needs, they may be surprised by a reaction of resentment and "no thanks" to the offer of a job that will require that they demonstrate their creativity in an isolated work environment.

Maslow's theory, not unlike others that attempt to conceptualize human motivation, is, of course, a bit of an oversimplification. Who of us doesn't feel that, upon different occasions, any one of the five levels represents our need of the moment? Social needs may seem to predominate today but self-actualization may be more important next week. Some critics of Maslow—for example, Lawler and Suttle[2]—concluded that there was little to document even the existence of a needs hierarchy. They saw only two distinct types of needs, biological and nonbiological, with nonbiological needs emerging only after biological needs were met. Other researchers[3] noted that, as people move on through the life cycle, higher-level needs predominate. This may occur as a result of career progression, however, rather than as a result of gratification of lower-level needs. Certainly, situational changes can create needs or at least can change the focus of how we meet our needs and, therefore, the point of leverage for appeals to motivate us. But even if we as managers believe that Maslow's theory is flawed or lacking in total documentation in the real world, it still offers us some basic insights worthy of repetition. Specifically, if we accept the idea that a satisfied need is not a motivator and that unmet needs are potential sources of motivation, we will be more likely to avoid costly mistakes that can damage individual and group morale. We will be less likely to fumble in our offer of rewards to staff as an effort to appeal to their sources of motivation in order to improve or increase their contributions to organizational effectiveness and to client services. We will more consistently offer those rewards that appeal to workers' potential sources of motivation when we don't try to offer gratification for needs that are already met or are not yet felt by them.

McClelland's Needs Theory

David McClelland viewed individual motivation a little differently from Maslow. His early research suggested that there are basically three different organizational "types"[4] whose behavior suggests the type of need that is predominant for each. McClelland's conceptualization is an appealing one for social workers who have likely seen clients, co-workers, professors, and relatives or friends who seem to be very good examples of the three types.

According to McClelland, people tend to be motivated by a need for power, for affiliation, or for achievement. Power-needing individuals are likely to move toward positions and situations that promise control and influence over others. They enjoy exercising power and never seem to get enough of it. As personality types, they are outspoken, forceful, and demanding;

these characteristics frequently are revealed in their interactions with others. Friendships are pursued as devices to be used to acquire more power rather than as a source of pleasure or gratification in their own right.

The second type of individual has an approach to human relationships that is almost 180° different from that of the power-motivated individual. Because they have a predominant need for affiliation, activities of these individuals seem to be aimed at being loved and at avoiding rejection. They enjoy all kinds of *friendly* interaction and are extremely uncomfortable when interpersonal conflict occurs. They do not seek to have power over or to control others, because to do so might damage a friendship or get in the way of forming yet another one. Persons with a need for affiliation are inclined to be nonjudgmental and giving, but, of course, they give primarily in order to receive. Their need is readily apparent in the extremes to which they will go in order to be liked and to avoid offending another.

Individuals driven by a strong need for achievement are, like the first two types, never satiated. They crave success, but never really believe that they have achieved it. They fear failure more than most anything, and it is this specter that drives them on when, by most outside assessments, they have "made it." They often have some unattainable ideal for a definition of "real success" that guarantees that they inevitably fall short, but they keep trying.

As we observed in our discussion of Maslow's theory, examples abound of persons who seem to reflect indications of the presence of two or more of these needs simultaneously. But that does not negate the value of McClelland's conceptualization for our examination of motivation and its messages to the social worker as manager. If we assume that, at least for a sizable number of staff members, one of the three needs predominates, certain implications emerge. First, it should be noted that all three types have the potential to make large contributions to organizational goal achievement and to client services. As we suggested in our discussion of the merits of locals and cosmopolitans in Chapter 5, it is indeed the unfortunate manager who finds himself or herself with all of one type or of another. But a reasonable mixture has the potential to constitute a very effective work group. Thus, it is critical that managers recognize the existence of each of these types and that they tailor their motivation-enhancing strategies for them accordingly.

Staff members with a strong need for power can be expected to work hard in a position that grants them limited control over the activities of others. However, it should be understood that, if their motivation is particularly transparent, others over whom they have authority may quickly grow to resent them for their personality traits and the ways in which they seem to enjoy their exercise of power. If the manager chooses to "play to" their needs by giving them authority, they had better be prepared to monitor their activities closely to be certain that they are not unnecessarily heavy-handed or abrasive in their interaction with peers and subordinates. The high morale of a work unit is, after all, preferable to the high level of motivation of one power-hungry individual.

Individuals high in need for affiliation generally have acquired social skills that can be advantageous to the organization, both internally and dealing with others within the organization's task environment. Their diplomacy can be a real asset. They will work extra hard and display a high level of motivation in activities that promise the reward of close friendships and pleasant social interaction. But they also may be virtually unable to function if the environment is *too* hostile or if conflict is frequent and/or severe.

Individuals with a high need for affiliation will often make sacrifices and give much of themselves in order to please superiors and to help out when needed. In client treatment, for example, they might welcome telephone calls at home or not resent unexpected five o'clock walk-ins from those who seem to need their help. The negative side of this behavior is that excessive dependency (actually it is more like interdependency) can easily occur with clients and other staff because of the strong affiliation need. This individual might have difficulty in saying no when "no" is the correct response given organizational or client needs. Their need to give and to receive can occupy great amounts of time and effort that can interfere with efficiency. They also can be resented by co-workers who eventually recognize their particular need and begin to tire of their continuous courting of acceptance.

Social workers as managers can prevent many of these negative phenomena by recognizing a worker's need for affiliation and by providing situations for its gratification that do not jeopardize collegial relationships or client services. The potential to engage in nonproductive social interaction can be addressed by the use of additional structure if absolutely necessary, but it should be recognized that fostering motivation, not frustrating it, is a goal of the manager. Any unnecessary structure that prohibits the development of friendships is likely to be deeply resented by this individual. The secret (as with the other two types as well) is to channel the need-meeting into activities where motivation will naturally flourish and where the organization and its clients will benefit from it.

Staff members who possess strong needs for achievement are, like the other two types, a mixed blessing for the manager. These individuals are likely to work hard at tasks that promise recognition or some tangible indicator of their success. But the manager may experience frustration at their incessantly critical approaches to their own and others' achievements. They are likely to accomplish much in their efforts at need-meeting, but they may also demand an unreasonable amount of achievement from subordinates and co-workers. This can be useful as a source of relief for the manager in that it allows someone else to play the "heavy" for a while. But it also can cause real morale problems. Co-workers quickly resent it. While it is tempting for managers to relinquish their role as taskmaster and to look relatively considerate in contrast, allowing an achievement-oriented staff member to play boss is dangerous. It can quickly communicate weakness on the part of the manager to staff and can undermine the manager's authority and ability to manage.

McClelland continued to do research and to refine his theories of motivation during the many years since he first published his conceptualization of the three primary motivators. In a recent book[5] he suggested that there may be another group of motivators—avoidance motives—that also may provide the primary impetus for a person's behavior on the job. He noted that, for example, an obsession with fear of failure, fear of rejection, fear of success, and fear of power seem to be accompanied by behavior not generally seen in individuals who do not possess them. McClelland concludes, however, that evidence that avoidance motives are distinctly different from "the big three" is not yet present.

McClelland's theories are useful to the manager in assessing individual staff motivation and in promoting appropriate and productive behavior. They also have at least one other practical use—as a mirror. The social worker as manager is little different from the therapist or the community worker in his or her need for insight. Thus, it is useful for managers occasionally to ask whether their own behaviors and decision making are based on organizational needs, management principles, and other appropriate influences or whether they might be emanating from a more inappropriate and less desirable source, namely their own predominant need. Managers at all levels are vulnerable to strong needs that can get in the way of good management. It is probably worthwhile for social workers as managers to occasionally review the typologies of McClelland, Maslow, and others to assess just how much their own predominant needs may be interfering with sound management decision making.

CASE EXAMPLE: MOTIVATION MISREAD

John was a bright, energetic, and upwardly mobile man. At 28, he was the director of a large employee assistance organization that had contracts with three major manufacturing organizations and appeared to be on the way to negotiating lucrative contracts with two others. Based upon the excellent reputation of his organization and on the high income that he received, John would have to be regarded as a success, a high achiever. He took pride in his achievements, but also in his organization's strict adherence to social work values and practice standards.

John's Employee Assistance Program (EAP) organization had begun only four years earlier when the first contract was negotiated. At the time, three social workers were hired to provide services. All were personal friends whom John knew well and respected. As the demand for services increased and as new contracts came along, John continued to take an active part in all personnel matters and in any major decisions relative to assignment of staff. While he could no longer know his staff as well as he once had, John believed that he was a good judge of people and relied on his own judgment to reward staff through promotion and pay increases.

It didn't take John long to notice Bruce, a counselor who was a recent graduate of an MSW program. Several of the more senior staff had nothing but praise for his attitude and his performance. Not only was Bruce exceptionally well-liked but he was also highly productive. He volunteered to take on new cases for other staff who were claiming to be overworked. He came to work early to chat informally with other staff members about their jobs. He never seemed too busy to offer help to others or to just allow co-workers to vent their frustrations. John found himself wishing he could hire 10 other social workers just like Bruce, people who possessed Bruce's high motivation, cooperativeness, and dedication. John was not surprised when Bruce's employee evaluations (completed by his supervisor) were the best that he had seen.

As a manager, John knew the importance of rewarding his staff for good work. He perceived Bruce as very marketable elsewhere, and he did not wish to lose him to another organization. He also perceived that Bruce had a great need for achievement, and he decided to do what he could to provide gratification for this need without Bruce having to go elsewhere.

John called Bruce in for a conference to discuss his future with the organization. He began by mentioning Bruce's high evaluations and the other favorable comments that had been made by co-workers, clients, and corporation personnel officers. He told Bruce that he really appreciated his work and his positive attitude toward it, and he assured Bruce that it would not go unrewarded. Bruce clearly savored the praise heaped upon him. John went on to describe the other two contracts that he hoped to acquire. He volunteered that, while he could make no promises, Bruce was the current front-runner to be the coordinator of the next contract received, a promotion that would entail considerably more money, status, and the supervision of four or more other staff members. Bruce's response to this information—"I'm not sure that I'm ready for that!"—puzzled John at first. But as he thought about it shortly afterward, he interpreted it as humility, or, perhaps, just a way of fishing for another compliment in the form of a statement of confidence (which John quickly provided). At any rate, John had little doubt that a person as highly motivated as Bruce would jump at the chance for a promotion if it were ultimately offered.

One new contract was successfully negotiated in August for full implementation on April 1. The staff were informed about it in early September. Three of them immediately applied for the coordinator job, but Bruce did not apply until after John asked for his letter of application. During September, October, and November, plans proceeded for the new EAP. During that time, John began to receive complaints about the quality of Bruce's work. Bruce seemed far less enthusiastic; he took several sick days with no evidence of suffering from any medical problems. What had once been the organization's most highly motivated employee now looked no better or worse than any other staff member. When the time came to make a decision on the choice of the new coordinator, John could not in good conscience support the selection of Bruce. He chose someone else.

Not one to avoid the unpleasant tasks of management, John called each of the applicants that were not selected (including Bruce) into his office to announce and explain his decision before it became public knowledge. While he didn't relish this task with any of the three, he especially dreaded it with Bruce because of their earlier conference. His concerns proved unfounded. Bruce seemed genuinely to appreciate this gesture of consideration. If anything, he seemed relieved that another had been chosen, and he used the occasion to confide to John that he had not looked forward to functioning in the role of supervisor and very much liked just what he was doing.

Shortly after their second conference, John again began to receive rave notices about the quality of Bruce's work. After he got to know and to understand Bruce later and after a conversation with a senior co-worker who was one of Bruce's best friends, John began to make some sense of Bruce's behavior. He realized that what seemed to really motivate Bruce was a very strong need to be liked. His high level of work performance was designed to please others; it was not a means to move up. While Bruce's motivation, like that of all of us, was a complex blend of needs, for him the need for affiliation was clearly stronger than the need for achievement.

John had misjudged Bruce's motivation. By mistakenly assuming that Bruce was very similar to himself, John attempted to appeal to what he believed was Bruce's motivation by offering him an incentive. It would have further motivated John but that was not at all what Bruce sought. On the contrary, the thought of assuming a supervisory role terrified Bruce, not so much because he thought that he could not do the job, but because of the likelihood that the new position would offer him little hope of social-need gratification. He perceived that as a supervisor, he would have to distance himself from those over whom he had authority. Current friendships might suffer from his having to assume a different place on the organizational hierarchy. He would have less contact with clients, cutting himself off from the gratification that he received from being in a helping relationship. He had speculated that potential supervisees, because they were aware of his own high standards of productivity, would not look forward to working under him. He feared that he would have difficulty in being tough or in negatively assessing the work of others when it was necessary.

Because of his great need to please others (including John) and to be liked, Bruce felt that he dared not show his true feelings about the promotion when it was first brought up or when John later pressured him to apply. His subsequent decline in work performance probably resulted from the increased anxiety that he felt as the possibility of the new job began to loom closer. It also may have been a partially unconscious way of sabotaging the promotion or of communicating to John what he could not say verbally for fear of offending. Freed from the threat of moving into a job where affiliation needs have less opportunity for gratification, Bruce once again was free to meet his needs in a way that contributed positively to organizational goal attainment.

Herzberg's Job Enrichment Theories

As suggested earlier, some of the later critics of Maslow did not accept the triangle conceptualization of relatively few persons progressing to the level where self-actualization is a potential motivator. Frederick Herzberg is one well-known theoretician who argued that persons who are motivated by a need for self-actualization are hardly rare. In fact, his approaches to job enrichment[6] are a response to the belief that workers generally tend to be better motivated when efforts to build in ways to increase the self-actualization potential of their jobs are implemented.

Central to an understanding of job enrichment approaches to motivation is Herzberg's conceptualization of two different factors that can exist for employees within organizations. He notes that there are certain *contextual factors*, also called *hygiene factors*, and another group of factors known as either *content factors* or *motivation factors*. Hygiene factors include, for example, high salary, job security, status, good working conditions or fringe benefits. They are, of course, very nice to have. If not present, they can make an individual feel poorly about his or her job. But, and this is the important point, their presence is no guarantee that an employee will be highly motivated. They are not motivators; they are only potential dissatisfiers (if not present).

The second group, namely content or motivation factors, according to Herzberg have the potential to motivate employees because they appeal to employees' need for self-actualization. These motivators include, for example, challenge, interesting work, freedom, responsibility, and potential for growth. They are factors that are intrinsic to the nature of the work.

Herzberg developed *job enrichment* workshops that sought to provide assistance to employers who sought to build more motivation factors into their employees' jobs. The intent was to promote motivation, sometimes even at the expense of hygiene factors. Not surprisingly, labor unions have not always eagerly embraced job enrichment. Job enrichment also is not always applicable to highly mechanized organizations, where tasks are necessarily dull and repetitive.

Herzberg never really suggested that job enrichment is for everyone or all work settings. He acknowledged that some jobs, by their very nature, require routine task performance. We might think, for example, of the work of the file clerk. For this type of job, Herzberg proposed a less desirable alternative to job enrichment: *job enlargement*. It involves building as much variation as possible into a job in order to relieve boredom. Although it was probably not labeled as such, the author of this text was the beneficiary of job enlargement principles many years ago during his part-time employment in a brewery. About every 30 minutes, employees were required to switch from one deadly dull task (such as watching beer bottles pass before a light and removing and discarding any that had an especially disgusting item floating in them) to some other equally non-self-actualizing task (like removing bottles that had jammed in a conveyor). Of course, Frederick Taylor would have viewed such a management practice as job enlargement as unnecessary, as long as the pay was good.

Social workers are likely to have encountered people and situations that seem to support Herzberg's ideas about what motivates people. We may have seen co-workers who seemed to lack motivation despite the presence of a variety of hygiene factors. Job security, relatively high pay, and the best fringe benefits in the world might not be enough to help a social worker "catch fire" in a job that is dull and repetitive and that seems to offer no challenges or no outlet for creativity. The promise of an even larger, more plush office or even one's own personal computer would not help.

We also have seen dedicated, highly motivated professionals who work for low salaries, sharing a work cubicle with another professional, and with virtually no hygiene factors present. They love their work and speak highly of it. Unless they are simply masochistic, we might speculate that their job is probably rich in challenge, freedom, opportunity for professional growth, and/or other motivation factors as described by Herzberg.

What is Herzberg's message to the social work manager? Many of the professionals and preprofessionals with whom we work might be expected to be seeking gratification for their self-actualization needs. After all, few people who are pursuing financial wealth and security choose to enter social work or many other of the helping professions. Social workers as managers may be in a position to engage in a little job enrichment, even if they cannot do much about including more of the hygiene factors that we all would like. This will require both time and thought and the support of superiors. However, it may be easier to let a good employee simply do his or her job in the same predictable way. For those more tedious jobs where only job enlargement is a possibility, it should be considered as a way to make the job at least less boring.

Job enrichment may well promote motivation among many professionals, but the manager cannot assume that even all professionals necessarily seek responsibility, challenge, autonomy, etc. Some don't. For these individuals, opportunities for self-actualization may be more resented than welcomed, especially if it appears to be offered *instead* of such benefits as raises or other hygiene factors.

Some people who feel a strong need for self-actualization also may not be seeking to gratify their needs at work. They may paint, cook, or refinish furniture as an outlet for their creativity. If so, they may seek nothing more than good pay from their job to support the costs of their creative outlet. They would not likely be spurred to new heights of productivity by efforts to enrich their job. The only enrichment they may want is through their paycheck! Unless they are careful, managers can easily err in interpreting and applying a staff member's needs and motivation. They may accurately assess an employee's motivation, but naively assume that the workplace is the place where workers choose to meet their needs, at whatever level they may exist. Not all employees perceive their job as central to their identity or to their gratification. This is all right. Many staff members who think of their work as "just a job" nevertheless make valuable contributions to organizational goal achievement and client service. They ought to be rewarded and supported along with the self-actualizing professionals whom we are naturally more inclined to value and to support through methods of job enrichment.

MOTIVATIONAL PROBLEMS OF EARLY CEILING PROFESSIONALS

In many professions, an employee can look forward to an even better future of increased earnings, responsibility, status, and other benefits in the form of both the content and contextual varieties that Herzberg describes. An attorney, for example, might start out as a law clerk after graduation or as a very junior member of a law firm. But over the next 30, 40, or even 50 years, the attorney's job is likely to get better and better. As senior law partners, such individuals may reach their peak in earnings and status when they are in their sixties and seventies and may have the luxury of setting their own hours and selecting the most interesting cases. Physicians have a similar experience in their career. These two professions are referred to as "late ceiling" occupations.[7] They possess a kind of built-in source of motivation that keeps the professional working with the belief that even "better times are coming."

Not surprisingly, there are also "early ceiling" occupations. One of the best examples is the professional athlete. Relevant to our discussion of motivation, social work and some of the other helping professions also qualify as "early ceiling." People in early ceiling occupations tend to get to the top early in their career. In the case of professional athletes, they may then experience a rapid decline in the status and benefits available to them. Social workers and other professionals usually do not experience a decline after an early peak, but they may experience only minimal improvement in their situation or even a holding action after a point that occurs somewhat early in their career.

It is not unusual for social workers to reach a relatively high level (supervisor, mid-level manager) fairly soon after they complete their professional education. Especially in small organizations, they may perceive that they have little upward mobility left unless they leave the organization, a solution that the organization and its managers would rather avoid if the staff member is a good one. In some settings, it is difficult for the manager to appeal to the motivation of a relatively young employee who believes that he or she has already "peaked out."

Faced with the motivation problems of a good employee in an early ceiling occupation, there are some ways to make a job more rewarding and interesting for the employee. A manager might consider efforts to "raise the ceiling," a type of job redesigning. For example, the employment of pre-professionals or nonprofessionals to relieve some of the more routine, repetitive aspects of the job might help. Perhaps a senior caseworker can be relieved of intake responsibilities or can be granted extra secretarial support for meeting recording responsibilities. And redefinement of one's job that will free the worker from tedious tasks and allow the worker to devote more time to the esoteric or the one-time-only, higher-level tasks would have the potential to appeal to the worker's sources of motivation, especially if the worker appears to have high self-actualization needs.

A second partial solution may exist in what has been called a "dual career ladder."[8] This approach requires the development of support at all levels of an organization because it has high potential for resentment by some employees and because it runs counter to traditional personnel practices. It involves the setting aside of usual salary scales and offers unusually high monetary rewards for persons who lack an opening for promotion or who may even prefer not to move up within the organizational hierarchy. We can best illustrate how a dual career ladder works through comparison with a salary scale that is more typical in many social agencies. Figure 8.2 reflects a traditional single career ladder.

Note that the opportunity to earn more money is available only to those who are able and willing to move to the next higher level in the organizational hierarchy—for example, from Caseworker I to Caseworker II or from Caseworker II to Supervisor I. Employees facing a situation with no opening above them have "topped out" in terms of salary and can only hope for a cost-of-living increase or that an opening above them will occur. Thus, they may engage in frequent inquiries into the health of their superiors.

The skilled Caseworker II who really is not interested in supervision even if an opening occurs remains in the job at a price. Such individuals will sacrifice the opportunity to make considerably more money. They will also probably have to deal with innuendos and beliefs of other employees who may start to question their competence because they are "still a caseworker." These costs may help to motivate them eventually to take the promotion, depriving the caseworker ranks of an exceptional worker and putting them in a job where their lack of interest and desire to manage may doom them to failure. As we have noted earlier, success at one level is no guarantee of success at the next.

The dual career ladder, if the manager can successfully implement it, has

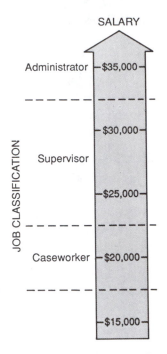

Figure 8.2. The Single Career Ladder

the potential to raise the ceiling for an employee in an early ceiling occupation and, possibly, to provide support for motivation without taking individuals out of a job that they do well. Figure 8.3 illustrates how this alternative might work in the same hypothetical situation.

Note that the dual career ladder rewards employees who are exceptionally good at their job and who either wish to stay there or have nowhere else to go. It suggests, in a way consistent with current thought, that a supervisor is not necessarily worth more or even as much to an organization than a "foot soldier" who is very competent. The caseworker and the supervisor perform different tasks, but their jobs are not inherently hierarchical in nature. Why force the caseworker to "move up?"

An obvious and frequent objection to the dual career ladder is fostered by the traditional belief that an employee can only supervise another if the supervisor is clearly superior in all respects. Specifically, it seems "unnatural" and dangerous for a supervisee to make more money than one's "superior." These beliefs and attitudes quickly can condemn a dual career ladder to failure. This is why it is critical to successful implementation that employees at all levels are sold on it as a concept.

If successfully implemented (and it is gaining popularity within human

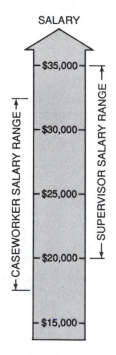

Figure 8.3. The Dual Career Ladder

service organizations), a dual career ladder can provide at least tangible rewards in the form of money and more status for the early ceiling employee. If we accept Herzberg's understanding of motivation, it will not motivate an employee to be more productive or to do better work. It may, however, result in more job satisfaction for the employee and may be enough to keep an employee from quitting in order to seek a job with a higher ceiling in some other organization.

OTHER VARIABLES THAT AFFECT MOTIVATION

Thus far we have viewed motivation from the perspective of most of the theorists who have studied it. Specifically, we have assumed that motivation derives primarily from the needs of the individual. As social workers, we cannot underestimate the importance of human needs and the drives for their gratification. But we also should be aware that the relationship between needs and behaviors is rarely, if ever, a simple case of cause-effect. Human behavior is complex and often unpredictable. However, we know that certain variables in addition to individual needs are very likely to affect motivation of professionals and other staff members within organizations.

Professional Values

One of the objectives of professional education is the socialization of students. It is expected that those who complete professional programs will have absorbed the values of that profession.[9] It is these values that then help to guide both the decision making and the behavior of the practitioner.

The motivation of staff members to perform or not to perform a requested task or to devote more or less energy to its completion can be affected by whether or not they perceive the task's completion as consistent with their professional values. Staff members are likely to be highly motivated if a manager's requests and their own professional values are complementary and mutually reinforcing. A policy that appears to be consistent with the rights of clients is also likely to meet with enthusiastic compliance. However, high motivation can dissipate quickly if, for example, a request is made to a social worker to comply with a policy that appears to impinge on clients' rights to self-determination.

Consistency with professional values must be understood by staff in order to support staff motivation. The message to the social worker as manager is that promoting recognition of the agreement between organizational demands and professional values is highly desirable. Recognition of this agreement may be enough to move staff members to do something they would not ordinarily do or to move them to do a task better than they might have based purely on expectations for their own need gratification.

In those rare situations in which a manager must request a behavior from a staff member that appears to be in conflict with professional values, explanation by the manager is in order. For example, an applicant for counseling must be denied services because the applicant lives outside a catchment area (residence requirement) or because the applicant's primary problem is one that the board has decided not to address through its services. A staff member is likely to view this as a failure to respond to the needs of a person who requires help and probably will not be highly motivated to comply with the supervisor's request not to open a new case. The worker's professional values can become an obstacle to a desirable (from the organizational perspective) behavior. However, if the supervisor in the role of manager makes the extra effort to explain the origin of the agency policy and how it can actually lead to the provision of services to a greater number of clients (an outcome consistent with professional values), motivation for compliance is less likely to be jeopardized and may even gain support.

Professional values may also be supportive of motivation in another way. We know that, at least in part, what people do is a function of the requirements of their situation. Staff who are aware of funding cutbacks, time constraints, or other stresses that jeopardize client service delivery may be highly motivated to do a job, at least in the short run. As professionals, they are committed to the value that services must take priority over self-interest. The client as prime beneficiary of the organization must not pay a price for conditions beyond the client's control. This value may provide extra impetus to do wh t is required in order to avoid shortchanging client services. It may even cause staff members, at least temporarily, to set aside their personal needs in order to place greater priority on the organizational needs to provide services. An appeal to professional values by the manager may result in a "burst" of motivation in the short run. However, no staff person is likely to respond to this type of appeal if it is made too often or if it begins to be perceived as a device to increase efficiency at staff expense. The manager needs to develop and maintain a reputation for advocating for the best interests of staff, not for exploiting staff members through too frequent appeals to professional values.

Influences of the Work Group

Individual workers possess various needs. They also have or acquire professional values. Another strong influence on motivation, namely membership in a work group, is a third powerful influence on motivation. The social worker as manager needs to understand how group pressures can influence work performance and to be able to create a climate where group norms will foster rather than undercut individual motivation.

Individual behavior within an organization is shaped by one's group membership. As a member of a group, a person is expected to adopt certain behaviors and attitudes that are consistent with those of other members. Group norms apply not only to an employee's approach to his or her work but also to the employee's interaction with other work groups and individuals who are defined as outside his or her immediate work group. Relationships with other groups can run the full range from cooperation to a counterproductive, overt antagonism.

Competition and Conflict

No matter how well a manager organizes the activities of a work unit and no matter how much the manager attempts to foster a spirit of cooperation among a staff of dedicated professionals, some competition among groups is inevitable. It also is not always dysfunctional. Some competition promotes a sense of identity and promotes group loyalty in individuals. But, as we have probably all witnessed, excessive competitiveness also can result in antagonism, wasted energy, and the absence of a needed spirit of cooperation.

Social workers usually are not unfamiliar with both the benefits and the costs of competition. The classic studies of conflict performed by Sherif in a children's summer camp[10] are often cited. On the positive side, Sherif concluded that the presence of competition between groups (as long as it remains close) promotes task-oriented behavior, greater structure, and demands for conformity and loyalty. These can be very helpful to the manager. The costs of this kind of competition also were identified. Hostility increases between groups along with decreased communication and stereotyping of members of the other group. These are not helpful to the manager who attempts to foster the optimal cooperative work environment.

Competition among staff members, while inevitable, can and should be kept at a tolerable level where it has the potential to support rather than to sabotage work productivity. Competition is most likely to degenerate into nonproductive conflict if individuals and groups perceive a situation in which the gain of one is necessarily accompanied by the loss of the other individual or group. This situation has been described as a "zero-sum game."[11] A zero-sum game means, literally, that a situation exists in which the net gain for individuals involved in competition must equal zero—one side can gain exactly as much as another must lose. Zero-sum games do exist. Budgeting situations in homes or in organizations are good examples of zero-sum games. If there is only so much money to spend, spending an amount for one activity means that there is that much less available for another activity.

The existence of some zero-sum game situations does not mean that *all* situations in which there is competition are zero-sum games. In fact, much of the antagonism that exists between groups within organizations may occur because persons perceive the existence of a zero-sum game when one doesn't exist. The role of the social worker as manager is frequently to acknowledge the existence of a zero-sum game when it is there and to attempt to reduce competition by helping staff to recognize when it is not. For example, professional staff may be in competition for the assigned services of secretarial staff. Clearly, a secretary assigned to type for one group is not going to be able to type for another simultaneously. This is a zero-sum game situation, and any manager who suggests otherwise is likely to insult the intelligence of staff and to risk his or her own credibility. A fairly high degree of competition is to be expected and may actually result in desirable efforts to be more productive than the rival in order to demonstrate a greater need for secretarial support.

In another intergroup competition, a zero-sum game may be assumed when it is not really present. For example, it is not unusual for professionals in two different service units of a public social agency to act as though there is a limited amount of praise and recognition available to be dispensed by the administrator. Proceeding on this assumption, workers may spend a considerable amount of time trying to discredit the work of those in the other unit.

In such situations, managers need to stress the lack of the existence of the zero-sum game in order to derive the benefits of a controlled, productive environment of cooperative competition. They should help staff see that a good job done by one reflects positively on, and therefore benefits, all members of the organization as well as those clients that they serve.

There is a thin line between motivation-supporting competition and destructive conflict. Some authors have stressed the positive functions of conflict.[12] For example, it can make staff more involved in activities and less apathetic on the job and can spotlight issues and areas of legitimate professional disagreement. It can also reveal professionals at their worst, more concerned with winning an internal struggle than in objectively doing what is in the best interest of clients or of the organization. Even if we are firm believers in the benefits of conflict, we must concede that *too* much conflict or conflict over the wrong issues can be debilitating within human service organizations.

The social worker as manager will, at some time or other, conclude that conflict among staff is preoccupying employees and diverting the valuable energies of those who should be applying them toward organizational goal attainment. When internal squabbles interfere with good decision making and when personal loyalties take priority over the best interests of both the organization and clients, the manager must intervene to reduce conflict. One possible method for intervention involves the identification of a common goal that transcends individual or group interests and the repeated reminder of the existence of that goal. For example, the manager who proposes a move to better facilities has been known to reduce conflict, in part by forcing persons in conflict to work together to do the planning necessary to achieve the goal. If the manager can find a goal that everyone wants (not always an easy task if conflict is intense), the unhealthy and destructive forms of conflict can be set aside.

A second tactic for conflict reduction involves the identification of a common enemy. This approach is not new to students of political science or of world history. It was used by Adolf Hitler to help unify German factions after World War I. Frequently, in human service organizations, it is not necessary to fabricate a common enemy or to vilify some outside group that represents a threat. Budget cuts and other tactics of the hostile task environment can quickly make internal conflict appear trivial if the manager can make staff aware of the threat. A common theme of managers on such occasions is, "This is no time for internal bickering," as it clearly is not. (When *is* a good time?) If no such acute threat or common enemy exists, a skillful manager may still be able to help staff recognize that most social work practice occurs within a chronically hostile task environment whose members like nothing more than to point out the inefficiency of the helping professions. As we stressed in Chapter 2, the task environment is rarely supportive of our efforts. This is a reality that can sometimes be turned to the manager's benefit to help reduce internal conflict and to free up staff energies to be directed toward goal achievement. It can serve as an impetus to force interaction and to begin negotiation between warring factions or at least to help conflicting parties see that "the enemy" stands to gain the most from continued conflict.

Cohesiveness and Motivation. The concept of group cohesiveness is critical to an understanding of how membership in work groups impacts on the motivation of individual staff.[13] Work groups can range from very loosely structured ones with ambiguous boundaries to clearly identified, self-contained units characterized by tight loyalties, clear boundaries, and fierce intragroup loyalties. While a high level of cohesiveness may be present in the former, it is more likely to be present in the latter extreme.

Cohesiveness, as we use the term here, relates to a number of identifiable factors that may be present within work groups to a greater or lesser degree. It refers to the sense of group solidarity that is present. It also suggests the amount of pride in membership in the group that is felt by its members and the desirability of belonging to the group. As we suggested, some groups tend to promote cohesiveness in the way that they are organized. For example, small groups are more likely to be cohesive than large ones, and groups that have existed for long periods of time are generally more cohesive than ones that have been more recently constituted. Employees tend to be more satisfied with their work when they are part of a cohesive work group. They also are more likely to reflect a high commitment to achievement of group goals.

It would seem, on the surface at least, that work group cohesiveness is universally desirable and should be promoted by the social work as manager as a way of advancing productivity. Generally, this may be true. However, it should be noted that cohesiveness accompanied by a commitment to the group's goals may not always guarantee the high-quality work productivity that the manager seeks and that the organization and its clients require. *If* group norms, values, and goals are consistent with organizational goals and objectives, cohesiveness can be very desirable for the manager. Unfortunately, this is not always the case. There exist some work groups that are highly cohesive, yet part of their cohesiveness is based on shared values that promote minimal standards of work performance, antagonism toward other groups, and a hostile, passive-aggressive approach toward the manager. A high level of group cohesiveness can often be found, for example, when needed changes are being resisted or when there are efforts to overthrow an administrator or sabotage a necessary program. In short, cohesiveness is a desirable attribute of work groups, but only if group norms suggest that effective and efficient work performance are valued among group members.

Let us assume that the manager has determined that there is general agreement between group norms and organizational goals and that increased cohesiveness is desirable. What can the manager then do to promote greater group cohesiveness and, indirectly, to promote desired behavior on the part of group members? For a start, it might help to enhance members' awareness of the compatibility between at least some of their group norms and organizational goals. This can be done by enthusiastic support, reward, and commendation for group efforts and by reminding staff members of just how their activities are contributing to the organization's goal attainment. Managers can also communicate clearly that they value and will reward cooperation and that they take a dim view of interpersonal conflict that jeopardizes individual and group productivity. They can emphasize that they expect staff to evaluate ideas and group members' positions on issues from an objective position based on professional values, and not based upon their attitudes toward the individual who presents them or their previous interaction with that individual.

Social workers as managers also can influence activities within work groups in several other ways that will have the potential to promote cohesiveness. They can assign work and structure tasks in such a way that their completion will necessitate cooperation; members will *have* to work together cooperatively to get the job done. For example, the task might depend on expertise that is not available within any one member but that can only be tapped if two or more members are involved. This managerial approach will reduce the likelihood of staff becoming isolated from other group members. Greater cohesiveness may result.

Working together and common experiences can help workers to get to know and appreciate each other's contributions, abilities, and knowledge. They can provide experiences to share and memories about which to reminisce. Of course, cohesiveness will be enhanced only if the collaboration is viewed in retrospect as positive and productive. If the experience of working together leaves one or more group members with the impression that other members are incompetent, don't carry their fair share of the work, or cannot be depended upon, confidence in co-workers can be eroded and the attractiveness of belonging to the work group actually may be diminished. The message to the manager is clear—work to set up tasks that require cooperation and collaboration and that are likely to leave a positive taste for the participants, that is, tasks that will be successful.

As a manager, the social worker at any level of practice is likely to have input into decisions or even total authority regarding how work groups will be structured and how they may be periodically reorganized. Cohesiveness is most likely to thrive when groups remain reasonably stable. Time is required for confidence in co-workers and even for desirable social bonds to develop. A "revolving door" work group with unnecessary transfers of staff in and out of the group can harm cohesiveness.

If the manager is involved in the formation of new work groups, it also might be wise to remember that, all other factors being equal, cohesiveness seems to exist more in groups where members perceive themselves to be similar to other members than where differences in experience, values, and other characteristics are readily apparent. A fairly homogeneous group (or at least one that is *perceived* that way by its members) is desirable for promoting cohesiveness. It might be wise for a manager to make efforts to remind group members of their similarities to each other and to promote the perception of homogeneity.

The cohesive work group that is also effective by the organization's standards possesses a certain internal work climate. It is characterized by pleasant, cooperative relationships where members eagerly assist each other when needed. They volunteer to help because there is a belief that what benefits one benefits the group and, ultimately, benefits all of its members. A member does not want to let the group down or to withhold information that might assist attainment of group goals. Loyalty exists both to peers and to group leaders. There is a respect for the knowledge and competence of others in the group. Interest in and enjoyment of most (but certainly not all) of the work is readily apparent to the outsider. A relaxed, informal atmosphere prevails in which people speak up and feel comfortable to disagree. But members listen to others' points of view and give them consideration. They disagree over positions on issues, not over personalities. Hidden agenda and memories of past personal grievances do not surface when disagreements occur. In short, a climate conducive to gaining the maximum benefits from individual motivation is likely to exist when strong cohesiveness is present in a group whose norms are consistent with organizational goals.

The Informal Power Structure

Life would be much simpler for social workers in the role of manager if factors that affect motivation and productivity of staff all could be easily identified and targeted for influence. The parameters of work groups usually can be drawn, and professional values and standards are available in written form. Yet there is another important influence on employee behavior that is very elusive. It is not easily diagrammed and is constantly in a state of flux. We are referring to what might be called the informal power structure.

Orientation to the formal power structure of an organization usually comes in the form of a handout for new employees accompanied by some verbal explanation. A chart or diagram such as Figure 8.4 portrays the relationship of staff to other staff as they are intended to be. Boxes are used to represent persons or groups of persons who occupy certain positions. Lines often are drawn to denote various types of authority relationships. Organizational charts clearly tell who is accountable to whom. They show lines of supervision and, in theory, are designed to suggest the locus of power, that is,

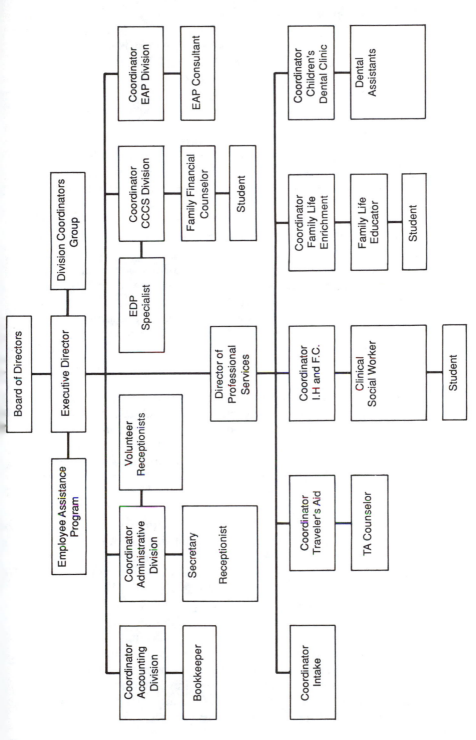

Figure 8.4. A Formal Organizational Chart: Family Service Agency

to show who is able to influence the activities of whom based on official sanction. This type of chart can be very helpful to employees for helping them to understand their work environment. It can also be very misleading if it is assumed that the organizational chart is always synonymous with the way things really get done or with the way power is distributed and exercised in the day-to-day flow to work.

Understanding of the informal power structure may begin at orientation. It rarely occurs in a methodical or planned way. A perceptive new employee may pick up on the subtle communications of "older hands" who seem to imply that the organizational chart should not always be taken too seriously. Learning about the informal power structure continues as time goes on and never really ends. A co-worker's suggestion that "if you really want to get it done, see————" or the revelation that no one really takes a high-ranking administrator's request very seriously begins to complete the picture of how the informal power structure might look. The informal power structure is indicative of how events *really* occur, as learned from experience. It suggests the real locus of power as determined by such factors as seniority, political connections, competence, knowledge, or interpersonal relationships that give some people advantages and that constitute liabilities for others.

In many social agencies, the very senior secretary may be quite powerful because of knowledge, experience, and the confidence of other powerful persons, despite the fact that this individual might occupy a relatively low level position on the formal organization chart. But try ignoring that person or crossing him or her on some issue and uninitiated staff members will quickly find themselves frustrated but respectful of that person's power. As another example, military personnel quickly learn that it is the company first sergeant, not the junior officer or company commander, who is the real power that must be reckoned with and accommodated. This is generally true despite the officer's higher rank and superior place on the organizational chart.

As noted in Chapter 3, classical management theories sometimes made the mistake of ignoring influences that they thought should not be allowed to exist. They often assumed that there was no such entity as the informal power structure because the formal organization was synonymous with the locus of power. If they acknowledged its existence, it was viewed as something that represented a threat to legitimate power and possibly as an indicator that greater control was needed on the part of management.

Current theory suggests that the presence of an informal power structure is inevitable. Efforts to eradicate it or to bring organizational functioning into total compliance with the formal organization chart would be futile. Besides being a wasteful expenditure of time and energy, most theorists now question whether it is even advisable to try to eliminate the informal power structure. After all, it can be a valuable vehicle of support for such tasks as communication of needed information or providing support for goal-directed activities. The message to the manager should probably be to acknowledge its existence, understand it as much as is possible, and use it when appropriate.

The wishes and preferences of persons who possess great amounts of power within the informal power structure cannot be ignored by staff. Employees are likely to seek their approval, perhaps even more than that of the person who may officially be their boss. Sensitive managers who identify the real locus of power in an organization can use these key persons as allies to reinforce their own focus on the attainment of organizational goals. Their potential to influence the motivational level of other employees cuts both ways, of course. If the manager is unsuccessful at achieving their cooperation and support, key persons in the informal power structure can sabotage both individual motivation and organizational goal achievement. Even employees who are strongly motivated to do good work may not feel that they are able to risk the ire of a powerful individual in the informal organization who does not value effective performance and is communicating the suggestion that they had better not become a "curve breaker" by doing more or doing it better than other staff.

SUMMARY

Chapter 8 examined the broad topic of employee motivation. Several of the better-known conceptualizations of individual motivation were presented and discussed. Throughout this chapter, the position was taken that, although individual motivation cannot be created by the manager, it can be sustained or suppressed by a number of factors present in the work situation and how well the manager understands them and responds to them.

Individual motivation was described as emanating primarily from individual needs and pressures for their gratification but also as heavily influenced by the power of other individuals and groups within the organization. Special motivational problems of persons within early ceiling occupations were identified, and two partial solutions to the problem were proposed. Professional values and their potential to influence worker performance were also examined. Competition was presented as potentially supportive of motivation but also as a phenomenon that can be destructive of it when it becomes a preoccupation of staff or when it deteriorates into excessive conflict.

Group influences on motivation cannot be understood without recognizing the effects of group cohesiveness. Cohesiveness can support organizational goal achievement if group norms are consistent with organizational goals; it can also present an organized form of resistance to goal achievement if they are not. Ways exist in which the social worker as manager can promote positive group cohesiveness; these were presented and explored. Finally, the existence of the informal organization was acknowledged and suggested as a possible source of support for the manager in enhancing the motivation of individual staff members.

REFERENCES

1. Abraham H. Maslow, *Motivation and Personality*, 3rd ed. (New York: Harper & Row, 1987); Abraham H. Maslow, "A Theory of Human Motivation," *Psychological Review*, 50(4), (July 1943):370–396.
2. Edward E. Lawler III and J. Lloyd Suttle, "A Casual Correlation Test of the Need Hierarchy Concept," *Organizational Behavior and Human Performance*, 7 (1972):265–587.
3. Douglass T. Hall and Khalil E. Nougaim, "An Examination of Maslow's Need Hierarchy in an Organizational Setting, *Organizational Behavior and Human Performance*, 3 (1968):12–35.
4. David C. McClelland, *Studies in Motivation* (New York: Appleton-Century-Crofts, 1955).
5. David C. McClelland, *Human Motivation* (Glenview, IL: Scott, Foresman, 1985), pp. 221–412.
6. See Frederick Herzberg, Bernard Mausner, and Barbara Block Snyderman, *The Motivation to Work* (New York: Wiley, 1959), pp. 3–12 and 126–128; Frederick Herzberg, "One More Time: How Do You Motivate Employees?" *Harvard Business Review*, 46 (January/February):53–62.
7. James D. Thompson, *Organizations in Action* (New York: McGraw Hill, 1967), pp. 109–116. Also see John W. Slocum, Jr., William L. Crow, and Linda C. Young, "Whose Career Is Likely to Plateau?" *Business Horizons*, 30 (1987): 31–38.
8. See Joseph A. Raeline, "Two-Track Plans for One-Track Careers," *Personnel Journal*, 66(1), (January 1987):96–101.
9. Robert B. Hill, "Integrating Relations," in *Encyclopedia of Social Work*, Vol. 1, (New York: National Association of Social Workers), pp. 951–956.
10. See Musafer Sherif, "Intergroup Relations and Leadership: Introductory Statement," in *Intergroup Relations and Leadership: Approaches and Research in Industrial, Ethnic, Cultural, and Political Areas*, M. Sherif, ed. (New York: Wiley), pp. 3–21.
11. Richard M. Emerson, "Power-Dependence Relationships," *American Sociological Review*, 27 (1962):31–41.
12. Lewis A. Coser, *The Functions of Social Conflict* (New York: Free Press, 1954): 15–31 and 151–157.
13. See Joseph A. Olmstead, *Working Papers No. 2. Organizational Structure and Climate: Implications for Agencies* (Washington, DC: Department of Health, Education and Welfare. Social and Rehabilitative Service, 1973), pp. 95–98.

ADDITIONAL READINGS

Davidson, J. "A Great Place to Work: Seven Strategies for Keeping Employees Committed to Your Company." *Management World*, 16 (1987):24–25.

Hackman, R., and Oldham, G. *Work Redesign*. Reading, MA: Addison-Wesley, 1980.

Herzberg, F. "One More Time: How Do You Motivate Employees?" *Harvard Business Review*, 65 (1987):109–120.

Kovatch, K. "What Motivates Employees? Workers and Supervisors Give Different Answers." *Business Horizon*, 30 (1987):58–65.

Merry, U. *The Neurotic Behavior of Organizations*. New York: Garner Press, 1987.

Mook, D. *Motivation*. New York: Norton, 1987.

Steers, R., and Porter, L. *Motivation and Work Behavior*, 4th ed. New York: McGraw-Hill, 1987.

Townsend, Robert. *Further Up the Organization*. New York: Knopf, 1970.

CHAPTER 9

Influencing Work Flow

We have repeatedly emphasized that management, just like other forms of social work practice, involves the use of knowledge of human behavior and human interaction skills. Competent, well-trained, and highly motivated staff, led by a skilled manager who understands them and responds to them as unique individuals, represent major assets to attainment of organizational goals. Clearly, it is not enough for a social worker as manager simply to take the position that "I hire good people and stay out of their way." Such an attitude suggests that the manager is not doing his or her job. Management involves a complex and sometimes overlapping cluster of activities designed to affect positively the delivery of effective client services. In this chapter we shall focus on another of these functions—organizing (we have discussed planning and staffing)—and how it contributes to better service delivery.

Organizing and another management function that we will discuss in the next chapter (controlling) would be less necessary if social workers as managers could merely be available at all times and in all places. If they could only monitor all activities and be available to handle all decision making, it would not be necessary to set up vehicles to structure and shape activities, decisions, and the interaction of staff when they cannot be present. But no method to clone managers has been perfected. Even if one could be invented, too much centralization of thinking and decision making would be involved. No one individual has all the necessary knowledge to be able to make decisions for a work group or groups. Professionals need to learn to evaluate situations and to make decisions for themselves. It is not healthy for an organization to engage in too much centralized decision making.

Given the fact that it is neither possible nor desirable for all decision making to fall to the manager, what alternatives exist? Staff cannot be turned completely loose to select how they define their jobs or how their activities will mesh with those of others. As any student of basic systems theory will recall, organization is an inherent characteristic of any system. It falls to the manager to select from among available ways to structure and to group the activities of staff. The manager must ensure coordination of the efforts of individuals and of work groups. Organizing entails the definition of roles as well as the maintenance of an overall plan where individual and group roles mesh to facilitate attainment of objectives.

BASIC WAYS OF ORGANIZING
HUMAN SERVICE ORGANIZATIONS

Human service organizations tend to reflect one of three general organizing patterns. The pattern is selected by the individuals in high-level administrative positions who are frequently responding to the wishes of the board of directors and to the limits that the task environment has placed on the organization and the activities that it is allowed to perform. The basic way in which the organization is structured tends to shape the organizing function of all social workers as managers, no matter where they are located in the organization's hierarchy.

The Production Line Organization

One way that organizations can be organized is along the model of the production line. This organizing pattern, promoted by early management theorists, involves a system of many individuals performing their own rather specialized tasks in a prescribed sequence. It also has been referred to as "long-linked" or "sequential processing."[1] On first blush, this method of setting up the activities of an organization would seem to be suited for only manufacturing facilities such as automobile plants. It is easy to picture an assembly line where workers perform repetitive tasks, each making their contribution to the construction of the vehicle that emerges at the end of the line. Creative task completion or the use of professional judgment would definitely not be valued and would disrupt the flow of activities. Recent advances in robotics have underlined the fact that the standardization of activities, not innovativeness, is valued in organizations that rely on the assembly line as their primary pattern of organization.

While there are professional values and ethical constraints that would seem to preclude the widespread use of the assembly line approach to setting up an organization for delivery of human services, it is not as foreign to social work practice as we might initially believe. For example, eligibility for economic services has often been characterized by strict adherence to a kind of sequential processing of clients. Similarly, a common method of organizing within some mental health facilities has involved a rather rigidly adhered to sequence of demographic information collection by a receptionist, social history taking by a social worker, psychological testing by the psychologist, medical examination (if medication may be indicated) by a psychiatrist, and staffing and development of a treatment plan by the treatment team. It is important to note that the variation on the assembly line occurs prior to assignment to one professional who then undertakes a course of individualized therapy.

An organization that is set up entirely like a production line may not be suitable to human service delivery. We cannot standardize the treatment of people—individuals, families, groups, or communities. Neither can we hope to nor would we wish to totally standardize the activities of staff who try to help people with their problems. In all likelihood we could not find consensus about how the desirable output of our production line would look. Our clients, staff, and the task environment could probably not agree on, for example, the best product of marital counseling. Even if they could, social work technology is far from an exact science. We lack the cause-effect knowledge required to guarantee that a treatment goal will be achieved if certain activities occur. Production lines would be ideal for only those rare work settings that contain much more rationality and certainty than most human service organizations generally possess.

The Linkage Organization

Other organizations appear to be organized in such a way that their primary function is as a mediator or broker. The activities of persons within the organization and individual's roles make it clear that a goal is to provide a service of bringing people and services together. In the business world, a savings and loan association or credit union mediates between those who wish to invest their savings and those who need to borrow money. A stock brokerage firm functions similarly by making it possible for a woman in Spokane to sell 100 shares of General Motors to a man in Tampa whom she has never met and would likely never meet. The activities of both types of companies center around the linking of people who have something to offer that others need or want.

Do human service agencies ever organize their activities around the goal of linking client to service? Certainly. Adoption agencies offer a service of bringing together those who want a child with a child who needs a home.

Traveler's Aid divisions of Family Service Association of America (FSAA) offer some crisis intervention services but function primarily as mediators between clients and other human service organizations. Any social agency that serves as a mediator or has referral as its principal function may appear to be organized in a way similar to that of a credit union or stock brokerage firm. While social work values require individualized, personalized, and sensitive service to clients, timely and appropriate referrals are important to client well-being. Consequently, activities of staff may center around collection of current data about community resources, networking with intake personnel in other agencies, and even development of contractual arrangements to assure that individuals and services are brought together.

The Custom Service Organization

Most human service organizations are designed to provide services, not to simply broker them for clients. The services cannot be standardized; they must be individualized to the uniqueness of the client or the client group and to their problem situation. Neither input (clients) nor output (ideally, a better-functioning client or other social system) is ever uniform. Neither are the other actors in the system (staff), who work toward problem resolution. The necessity to develop individualized approaches to practice is what makes social work services so expensive. It is also why the delivery of custom services is usually the most logical approach to setting up an organization. Frequently, we lack the cause-effect knowledge required to standardize services, yet we also do not wish to refer people elsewhere for help.

The predominance of custom service orientations within human service organizations suggests the primary focus of the social worker as manager—promoting efficiency and coordination in those areas of activity where it is possible. This frequently is accomplished by the use of clearly defined staff role expectations that spell out what each individual is to do (but usually not specifically how to do it). Role expectations also suggest how individuals are supposed to relate to each other in the course of their job performance.

Despite the fact that services generally require individualization, managers, through skillful use of organizing methods, can work to avoid an organizational climate of chaos and disorganization. Organizing structures can provide purpose to staff activities and can help to create the climate of reasonable certainty that we all require in order to function. The presence of an organization that appears to be generally organized around the use of custom technology provides services that are expensive on a unit cost basis. But while client services are individualized, other staff activities need not be. Social workers as managers are responsible for the identification of those activities where standardization is desirable (to promote efficiency). They are also responsible for the selection of specific organizing structures that will result in the desirable standardization.

ALTERNATIVE STRUCTURES FOR ORGANIZING

The selection of the basic way in which a human service organization is organized often is made when it first comes into existence. Only the highest levels of management may be directly involved in the decision. Furthermore, the choice from among a production line, linkage, or custom service organization model may be a *fait accompli*, given the nature of clients to be served, their problems, and the types of services that are appropriate for meeting client needs. As we have indicated, the basic organizational model for most organizations that employ social workers is far more likely to be that of custom service than either of the other two. Even when, for example, needs for efficiency and the potential to standardize services to some degree result in an organization that starts to resemble a production line (as in some elements of the public sector), it is still likely to be *claimed* that custom services tailored to individual client needs are offered. Public relations require this. Besides, social work values relative to the uniqueness of clients, their problems, and their needs require that every effort to individualize services should be made. This tends to hold true even if one of the other two models seems to dominate the basic organization of an agency.

The inevitability of custom services (to a greater or lesser degree) in human service organizations provides only the most general framework for organizing. Within all human service organizations, but especially in larger ones, the social worker as manager must somehow subdivide the many activities of staff in a logical way. It would be impossible to be aware of, much less influence, the activities of staff unless some way is found to reduce organizational activities into subunits that are sufficiently small to be managed by individuals. This is the organizational activity generally referred to as *departmentation*. It refers to the grouping of people and their activities along some basic pattern or model in order that their activities can be adequately supervised and managed.

Koontz, O'Donnell, and Weihrich,[2] in their text on business management, suggest a menu of different ways that a manager can choose to handle the task of departmentation. On first blush, their methods of departmentation would seem to be so profit- and product-oriented (rather than service-oriented) that they might be of little relevance within human service organizations. But with considerable "translation," most have the potential to suggest a viable approach to organizing, particularly at the level of program design. We will look at seven of them, translate rather liberally, and see what they offer to social workers as managers in their organizing function.

Simple Numbers

One method of departmentation involves simply grouping those who perform the same duties under a single manager (a supervisor in most human service organizations). If there are too many of these individuals for one supervisor to manage effectively, two or more parallel subunits can be created.

The biggest drawback to the simple-numbers method of departmentation may be its lack of recognition of the individual capacities of staff. People are not interchangeable parts with the same knowledge and skills. To treat them as such is to not take full advantage of a staff member's special talents and competencies. Within social agencies, for example, a professional staff member may have a unique aptitude for working with adolescents; another may not relate well to young people, but may quickly develop a productive rapport with the elderly. A counseling agency that features departmentation by simple numbers might not allow sufficient opportunity for specialization or for the use of special competencies. But combined with another method of departmentation that we will discuss a little later (service), it has been used successfully in human service organizations; for example, public child welfare and mental health facilities.

As the *only* method of organizing, the simple-numbers model may have been more functional in Frederick Taylor's day or in an earlier agrarian society when the number of persons required to pick a crop was more important for organizing than the individual attributes of the individuals doing the work. But its utility for today's social agencies is somewhat limited. Perhaps some typing or word-processing pools may still be suited to this single method of departmentation, although full use of individual abilities may even argue against its use for clerical staff. Departmentation by simple numbers is mentioned in this text primarily because it is seen in combination with other departmentation methods within some social agencies. Social workers as managers must be able to recognize and understand it, even if they choose to reject it as inappropriate and to replace it with a more suitable method of departmentation.

Time

For those organizations that must or should operate during evening and/or weekend hours, departmentation by time may be used. While shift work is more commonly seen in manufacturing plants as a means to more efficient use of machinery and to increase productivity, it is not unknown in social agencies. Medical and psychiatric facilities cannot limit patient care to the 9-to-5, Monday-through-Friday model. While social workers are more likely to be part of an on-call roster than part of a night or weekend shift, other professionals such as nurses and aides have come to expect shift work. Some prefer it for a variety of reasons, including higher pay, compatibility with a partner's work schedule, or because the demands of student or parent roles can be more easily met when days are free.

Although social work managers in the health/mental health fields of practice may not use time departmentation for organization of social work staff, they may find themselves with authority over other support staff who may be grouped according to their work hours. Shift work among social work staff is relatively rare, but not unheard of. Many private counseling organizations tend to have clearly identified day staffs and evening staffs. Clients of a Traveler's Aid type of agency are very likely to require professional services during evenings and weekends; it may be logical to schedule professional staff in such a way that two or more distinct work groups (shifts) are employed.

Time departmentation has the obvious advantage of increased availability of client services. It also has several potential disadvantages for the social worker as manager. Hiring and keeping of competent staff on the "night shift" may be difficult. Despite the fact that the important business of client service occurs any time that staff and clients interact, there persists the idea that the "real" business of the organization gets transacted during the day when higher-level administrators and support staff are more likely to be present. Night-shift work can be viewed as less important and, therefore, less attractive to professionals.

Probably the greatest disadvantage of time departmentation for the manager relates to its potential to fragment agency functioning and to interfere with integration of the organization (as a system). Valuable communication between shifts can be difficult, especially if work hours are not structured so that there is some overlap. Generally, anything that the manager can do to promote staff interaction between staff who work different shifts helps to minimize this problem. Staff who know, respect, and like those who work the other shift are likely to facilitate their work by telling them what they need to know about what occurs while they are off-duty. A "that's their problem" attitude or other passive-aggressive behaviors are less likely to exist if the manager has regularly communicated a message that emphasizes the existence of one team. One way of doing this is through the encouragement of social events where staff get to know each other. Occasions during which the valuable contributions of both shifts are recognized also help to minimize the likelihood of nonproductive fragmentation of the organization.

Enterprise Function

Departmentation within for-profit corporations may group employees according to their major activity—for example, production, sales, and finance. To group people by enterprise function is to recognize (especially in larger organizations) that there is room for and value in specialization. It can focus people's activities in that area where they perform best, ideally the same area where they have both preparation and interest. Employees need not be good at everything that falls under the description of their profession or trade, but they are expected to be competent in their area of specialization.

As demands for financial accountability have increased, the differences between for-profit businesses and nonprofit organizations nave tended to blur. Human service organizations have had to pay more attention to efficiency issues, and businesses have become more aware of the relationship between human factors and profit. Some observers have suggested that nonprofit organizations are really businesses in which profits are simply put back into the organization in the form of salaries. The increase in proprietary human service organizations (for example, many nursing homes) and the growth in the private practice of social work also suggest that some variation of departmentation of the usual business enterprises may be appropriate for organizing within human service agencies as well.

What are the human service organization counterparts of production, sales, and finance? Production would logically translate into service delivery or direct practice with clients at whatever systems level (individuals, families, groups, communities, etc.). Sales might equate with the public relations enterprise that is so essential to organizational success within a task environment that is naturally inclined to be unfriendly. It might also involve outreach to potential clients and the building of linkages and networks to other organizations and individuals outside the organization who represent potential sources of referral. Financing requires no translation in today's service environment. Every organization can use people who are specialists in fundraising and financial resource allocation. Grant and contract proposal writing is a valuable skill, as is the development and implementation of budgets.

Departmentation by enterprise function may be a useful way of performing the organizing function of the social worker as manager, particularly at the program-design level. It may have utility for the higher-level manager as an overall method of reducing organizational activities into units that are sufficiently small to be properly managed. It may also be useful for mid-level managers such as supervisors in situations where the activities of staff tend to be specialized and fall into a small number of distinguishable "enterprises" (for example, treatment, public relations, or referral).

A major advantage to enterprise function departmentation lies in its potential to create esprit de corps among staff within each enterprise. People with similar interests and backgrounds—"kindred spirits"—work together toward achievement of similar and/or shared goals. A feeling of camaraderie is likely to result, although the manager should also be alert to the possibility of nonproductive conflict when specialists who sometimes tend to be prima donnas must interact on a daily basis.

Another possible difficulty with enterprise departmentation can occur if interenterprise rivalry is allowed to get out of hand. Human service programs inevitably require the cooperation and mutual support of the various enterprises in order to succeed. If people become too territorial or too obsessed with their own unit's success, organizational goal attainment can be jeopardized. For example, finance persons within human service organizations may be aware that their performance is evaluated by the amount of grant or contract money that they bring in. Unless they remain sensitive to the wishes and needs of staff and clients, they can end up pursuing dollars to offer programs that are outside of staff interests and areas of competence or, even more importantly, do not result in services that clients need or want. The pursuit of grant or contract money can become a near obsession for the specialist. A dollar is a dollar in its effect on a funding specialist's semi-annual evaluation. A grant or contract received for any purpose also has the potential to make the chief executive officer look good and, of course, to pay the bills. So, they are unlikely to object too vigorously if the funding specialist's focus becomes a little misdirected. But the subtle and long-range costs of overzealous grant activity can be great, particularly if staff morale is jeopardized because agency direction appears to be missing. The tail should never be allowed to wag the dog; that is, services require dollars but dollars should not be the primary issue in selection of services. Unfortunately, in recent hard times for human service agencies, the quest for needed funding has led some organizations to venture into areas of service that are inappropriate for their mission.

The manager who selects enterprise function as a method of departmentation will need to remain alert to dangers that include means-end displacements and the development of excessively narrow orientations of the part of staff. The sensitive manager will be able to strike a balance in which staff are conscious of both their specialized function and their place in the overall functioning of the organization. Occasional reminders about staff interdependence and about the superordinate goals of the organization (that all must address) may be useful for the manager who organizes using enterprise functions.

Territory

Departmentation by territory sometimes is employed in human service organizations where similar activities take place over a wide geographical area. Territory departmentation is a way of deciding whom each staff member will serve and whom they will not serve. Particularly in large organizations it may be logical to subdivide the organization by territory in order to reduce it into manageable subunits and to reduce the likelihood of staff heading off both literally and figuratively in all directions. For example, a large public assistance caseload might be divided up based on the place of residence of clients served. Caseworker X would serve all clients in one 10-square block area, but Caseworker Y would serve clients who live in another geographical area. Adjustments might be made so that the number of clients likely to be served would be comparable—the territory with the greater client population density might be smaller than another territory where relatively few residents receive public assistance.

In a similar way, the satellite clinics of a community mental health center might divide up client service by the place of residence of potential clients. If they live one place, they are served by one clinic; if they live one block over, they may have to be seen at another clinic. (The respective territories are sometimes referred to as "catchment areas" in the mental health field.)

Definite advantages accrue to the manager who chooses to use territory departmentation. Questions relative to the issue of "whose job is it?" are less likely to occur than if other methods of organizing are used. Identity and clear-cut responsibilities can be promoted quite easily.

When professionals focus their activities on services to people residing in a relatively small geographical area, they are also likely to become very familiar with that area. For social workers serving a territory, there is increased potential to understand a community and its problems and to get to know, understand, and build relationships with its leadership and other key people. The problems of the individual client also are put into better perspective when they are viewed in the context of problems of other persons, families, and groups that live within an area.

A primary advantage of territory departmentation for the manager may be efficiency. If territories can be kept small, less time and money are spent in travel and less effort is devoted to making contacts, becoming acquainted with community resources, or learning the politics that impact on client social functioning. Overall, concentrated attention and familiarity with an area offer many advantages to the manager and to staff who are likely to benefit from feeling that they are able to really know all that they require to do their job.

Dividing activities by territory also has some major disadvantages. No matter how much planning goes into departmentation, workload is rarely ever in balance for a long period of time. Inevitably, some territories will provide an overload while, simultaneously, staff serving other territories will seem to not have enough to do.

Some territories, based on the nature of the community, its location, its clientele, or other factors, will inevitably be labeled less desirable than others. Someone must be assigned to work there, however. This can lead to morale problems and to charges of favoritism on the part of the manager who makes the work assignments. Skillful managers will find ways to help staff to understand that all territories have their benefits and their liabilities. They may also try to compensate those staff who receive the unpopular assignments. However, the compensation itself may cause resentment by other staff members who feel that they work in unpleasant conditions too and also should be compensated. While services offered may, in fact, be comparable, the conditions under which they must be offered rarely, if ever, are. Managers can quickly find themselves feeling as if they can't win no matter how they try to adjust for these differences.

Another problem of territory departmentation relates to the enforcement of geographical boundaries. In the purest of applications, no exceptions are made. This can lead to situations that, at best, appear absurd. They can also appear to be downright contrary to the best interests of clients and their service. Charges of rigidity will inevitably be made. For example, if Ms. Smith lives in the 800 block of a street and her sister, Ms. Jones, lives across the street in the next block, they may be served by two different social workers. The workers may both make separate home visits to the two clients, perhaps even on the same day. If either client decides to move a relatively short distance, she may have to be reassigned to another (third) social worker.

A social worker as manager will need to respond to the appeals of clients and staff to make exceptions for territory departmentation. In effect, territory lines should be applied as policies rather than rules. Territorial boundaries can be stretched to reduce the number of absurdities, hardship, and inefficiencies that they impose. But where does the manager ultimately draw the line and say no? Eventually, someone will have to conclude bitterly that "they" could have been a little more flexible.

The placement of boundaries can be problematic in itself. The social worker as manager knows that communities don't always conform to streets, subdivisions, or other boundaries that appear on maps. Their parameters are in a constant state of flux. If one of the advantages of territory departmentation, namely knowledge of the community, is to be enjoyed, territories should be formed in such a way that communities are not split up. This may not be possible. Even if a community can be fairly easily defined, it may not be practical to form a territory that has similar boundaries because the community may be too large or too small to be used as a territory for departmentation purposes.

If managers select departmentation by territory as a primary way of performing their task of organizing, they should know that the benefit of clarity of work responsibilities will have a cost. Specifically, they can expect to be the target of staff dissatisfaction over perceived inequities. Unless they are willing to risk the virtual dissolution of territory boundaries, they will almost inevitably be perceived as rigid, both by staff and by clients. A manager is required who can live with more than the usual amount of criticism and challenges to his or her decisions.

Territory departmentation also leaves little room for workers who deliver services to move in the direction of specialization. One's territory *is* that person's speciality. Workers will need to be prepared to offer a wide range of services to a widely divergent group of clients with varying problems. The need to be all things to all people can be a definite disadvantage of this type of departmentation. Few if any of us can do everything well.

Service

Departmentation by service (in the profit sector referred to as "product") should be familiar to the social worker as manager. Service is the antithesis of departmentation by territory in that it is based on a belief in the benefits of specialization. Because of the wide diversity of help offered to clients by social workers, we have usually tended to use subcategories to describe the major types of activities performed. Early in the history of our profession we observed that social workers tended to specialize as to the type of services they offered. Social work education tended to mirror this natural tendency by providing the opportunity to "major" and for students to concentrate their studies in order to prepare for specialized practice. A popular way of doing this in the 1960s and early 1970s was to require students to select among three primary services: casework, group work, and community organization. While it has always been acknowledged that social work practice requires knowledge and skills in all three areas of activity, a service specialization always has been granted legitimacy in social work.

As with other types of departmentation that we have discussed and that we will discuss, the advantages and disadvantages of service departmentation are really two sides of the same coin. If, for example, a manager in a family agency chooses to divide services into referral, individual treatment, group services, and family counseling, the manager will have the reasonable expectation that staff will become very knowledgeable about and skilled in what they do. Who would know the helping resources in the community better than those who do nothing but make referrals? They would very likely have formed valuable networks with their counterparts in other social agencies. It seems logical to conclude that having responsibility for a narrow sphere of activity (services) will result in greater mastery of the knowledge and skills needed to perform that activity.

The narrowness of an employee's tasks, of course, is also the greatest disadvantage of service departmentation. When there is virtually no overlap between one person's job and that of another, there is also likely to be a reduced knowledge of and interest in the activities of others. Desirable sharing of information and a team spirit that includes people in different areas of specialization can be inhibited.

Services to clients may suffer too. Social workers often attempt to help those with multiple problems requiring many different types of assistance. It has been found, for example, that clients in the public sector may need *both* economic assistance and less tangible forms of help such as family or employment counseling. Departmentation that does not recognize this may not provide the coordinated service package that the client requires.

The manager who is considering organizing using only—or primarily—service departmentation should first determine that a high degree of specialization is both possible and *desirable*. For example, while it might be possible for a social worker in a counseling agency to do nothing but group treatment while a colleague offers only one-to-one counseling, this might not be best for either staff, client, or the organization. For staff members, a lack of diversity in their workday could become tedious. They may also lose touch with the knowledge and skills of other specialities. This could become an obstacle to current job functioning while also limiting job mobility.

Clients would have the benefits of having the services of a "specialist," but they would have the usual drawbacks as well. If they require more than one type of service, they would need to see more than one treatment specialist, requiring them to form more than one therapeutic relationship. The issue of primary responsibility for their treatment also could be problematic.

The specialization might also result in an inefficient use of staff within the organization. For example, there might be a waiting list of clients requiring the specialized services of the group treatment worker while the individual treatment specialist might not have enough to do or vice versa.

Clients Served

An alternative to organizing that is based upon services performed would seem to be more consistent with what we as social workers know about the nature of human problems. This would involve departmentation based on a typology of clients and their problems. It is a type of specialization different from service departmentation. It seems to recognize that a problem may require one or many different related services that might most efficiently be provided by the same helping professional.

How might clients be classified in order to use this organizing approach? A hospital provides a good example. Medical social workers are likely to use the various medical service areas in a hospital to identify and classify patients served. A patient is defined as surgery, cardiology, pediatric, etc., and staff may be assigned to work with the patient based on the staff member's "specialty."

While each patient has unique needs, departmentation by clients served carries certain assumptions. It is assumed that, overall, people in the same category will share many of the same service needs. They also are more likely to have certain needs than those in other categories. There is assumed to be some problem overlap (for example, patients in any category may suffer from depression related to their problem) but it is believed that, whatever problems manifest themselves, they are best handled by a single staff member. Occasionally, another social work professional may be consulted or even asked to see the patient based on the professional's special expertise. But this would happen only rarely, because the "specialist" would generally be the individual most familiar with the range of problems likely to be encountered. This person would also be the one possessing the important treatment relationship with the patient.

An outpatient private psychiatric facility or nonprofit counseling facility might also categorize clients based upon their primary problem. Categories might be child-parent conflict, family violence, marital difficulties, employment problems, health-related problems, substance abuse, etc. Whatever the type of services needed, a staff member identified as a specialist in working with the primary problem would be assigned to offer treatment. This individual would work primarily if not exclusively with clients operationally defined as having that problem.

The advantages to departmentation by clients served *can* be great. It can be a clean way to divide up work and to keep it manageable. It can provide the benefits of specialization to clients while allowing them to avoid the necessity of having to relate to two or more helping professionals. Of course, the appropriate conditions do not always exist. We know, for example, that the problem of family violence often is accompanied by substance abuse, parent-child problems, marital difficulties, and many other problems that could just as well serve as the basis for categorizing a client using this method of organizing. Because of the complexity of human behavior, we cannot always say which problem is primary or that one is the cause while another is only a symptom. Problems may interact in such a way that they are mutually supportive of each other. Many human social problems are not easily classified using a primary diagnosis.

In the real world, client departmentation often does not work. This method of organizing may simply not be possible within many human service organizations. Professionals who offer services may find that the ideal of a narrow range of services for each of a limited number of problems cannot be achieved. If they are to serve the diverse needs of clients to whom they are assigned, professionals must be knowledgeable and skilled in many areas, becoming far more "generic" in their practice than they might have anticipated. The manager who chooses client departmentation to better organize activities must be certain that there exist reasonably discrete client groups within the organization who require a limited number of predictable services. If not, this method of organizing is doomed to failure.

Marketing Channels

It is sometimes difficult to think of "marketing" human services. However, a service, not unlike a product, frequently needs to be publicized and needs to be "sold" to potential consumers. There may be several different "markets" in which this can be accomplished.

Some potential clients gain access to a service in one way, others use other methods and channels. What is an acceptable way to receive needed help for one client may not be acceptable (for any number of reasons) for others. For example, we might consider the various channels used to "market" AIDS education, a major concern of the 1990s. As social workers concerned with saving the lives of potential AIDS patients, we are not terribly concerned with how people acquire the knowledge necessary to practice medically safe, responsible sex, just so they acquire it. A variety of market channels might be used. A social work manager might decide to organize staff activities around these channels. Staff might be assigned to work primarily in only one of them.

What different marketing channels might be used? The school system, the media, and presentations to high-risk social groups and clinic populations could all be different channels used to accomplish the same objective. However, the methods used would vary greatly based upon political factors, characteristics of the potential clients who are the target of the population, and other factors. The channel used would suggest the advantage of a degree of specialization. Thus, the social worker as manager may wish to subdivide and organize activities around that market specialization.

In those organizations where services logically can be offered in several different arenas, marketing-channel departmentation can work well. Where education is the service itself, it may be an especially appropriate way to organize. It offers the advantage of creating staff whose specialized knowledge and skills may increase the likelihood that the desired result (knowledge dissemination) will occur.

The major disadvantage of marketing departmentation for organizing is its limited applicability to human services organizations. In manufacturing, it is easy to visualize marketing a product with acceptable success using many different market channels. A wrench, for example, is sold in hardware stores, department stores, appliance stores, and in flea markets as well as in many other outlets. But for many human services, there may be a very limited number of outlets deemed to be acceptable. Although we have broadened our thinking a little in recent years (for example, psychiatric services are now offered in the community, on the job, and in other settings besides hospitals, which were the primary outlets before the Community Mental Health Act of 1963,[3] many services offered by social workers and other health professionals would not seem appropriate for multiple outlets. For reasons of efficiency, professional ethics, and (all too often) inflexibility, we are still reluctant to offer many services anywhere but within the physical confines of an office, usually grouped with similar enterprises. It is unlikely, for example, that in the foreseeable future, public assistance or public adoption services will be regularly offered in shopping malls, through the churches, or in any one of several other innovative ways that have been tried successfully on an experimental basis. These market channels just seem "unprofessional" or inappropriate to many members of the general public and to some of us. Turf issues and the influence of a hostile task environment are likely to continue to constrain the marketing channels available for many of our services. Consequently, only some managers in some settings will find marketing-channel departmentation to be a viable alternative for organizing, at least in the near future.

DELEGATION AS A WAY OF ORGANIZING

No manager can do it all. Even in small human service organizations, managers cannot perform or even directly oversee all activities, collect all necessary data for decision making, or make all management decisions. Organizing entails helping staff members make the best possible use of their time. It also involves the use of activities to ensure that the manager's own time is used efficiently. The manager needs to make those decisions and to perform those tasks that the manager alone can and should perform. Other work can and should be delegated.

One goal of delegation is to maximize the manager's influence while enhancing the quality of the activities within an organization. Delegation empowers staff to make valuable contributions to organizational goal attainment. While everyone would agree that it is a necessary and desirable part of the manager's organizing function, there is far less consensus as to what can be delegated and how much delegation is desirable.

There are a few general principles of management that can be used to sort out some of the confusion that surrounds the topic of delegation. An understanding of certain key terminology is critical to our understanding. When we delegate as managers, we are giving to a subordinate something that would otherwise be associated with the expectations held for our position. If others don't take it on, it falls to us. Simply put, you cannot delegate what you don't have. This may seem patently obvious but, surprisingly, it is a principle sometimes forgotten.

What is it that managers delegate? They can delegate *a task*. The task can be one time only, such as calling managers of other agencies to arrange an emergency meeting, or ongoing, such as recording and transcribing the minutes of a staff meeting or providing supervision to a group of volunteers.

Of course, subordinates cannot perform either task unless they are given the necessary legitimization from the manager to serve as their representatives.

Much of the confusion surrounding delegation centers around the issue of whether or not managers can delegate *responsibility*. When managers assign all or part of a task to other staff members that they would otherwise perform themselves, and *if* the satisfactory performance of that task is a reasonable expectation for staff members given their job description, managers should be able to hold staff responsible for the performance of the tasks. If the task is reasonable (given the job description of the staff member), not too large (given the staff member's other responsibilities), and if the staff member is given the necessary authority to carry it out, the manager is justified in expecting satisfactory performance of the task. If these criteria are not met or some other aspect of poor delegation on the part of the manager exists, fairness suggests that the expectation of a manager that the task is satisfactorily performed is unreasonable. We could argue that the manager cannot legitimately hold the staff member responsible for its completion. Appropriate delegation of a task results in a legitimate expectation on the part of the manager that the staff member will meet a standard; inappropriate delegation would seem to relieve the staff member (at least partially) of responsibility for satisfactory task completion.

Under conditions of appropriate delegation of a task managers can legitimately hold subordinates responsible *to them* for its completion, but the question of ultimate responsibility for a delegated task is another matter. If the task is not completed or is completed poorly, the manager may still be held responsible for the problems created. Why? First, the task was one that was originally within the manager's job description—delegation does not rid the manager of responsibility for its completion as far as the manager's superior is concerned. Second, a manager can be held responsible for all management judgments and decisions. If the decision to delegate or the choice of a person to whom the task was delegated turned out to be bad and the task was not satisfactorily completed, the manager can be faulted. In the broadest sense, a manager can delegate a task, but not the ultimate responsibility for its completion. In some ways delegation brings more responsibility to the manager, not less. Managers are held responsible for the task completion *and* for the decision to delegate.

We have suggested that a delegated task requires the possession of authority necessary to complete it. Thus managers can also delegate *authority*. Before we continue our discussion of delegation, it will be necessary to digress somewhat. We will need to be clear on exactly what is meant by authority and how it differs from the general concept of power.

Power can be thought of as the capacity that people, groups, communities, and other social systems have to influence the beliefs, attitudes, and behaviors of others.[4] Power results in people thinking, believing, and acting in ways that they would not think, believe, or act on their own. Sometimes they don't even want to think, believe, or act in a certain way, but power (closely related to influencing) changes the normal course of these activities for them. The ultimate indication of power at work is when someone does something that he or she clearly would never choose to do.

People acquire power in many ways.[5] The base of power can be knowledge and expertise, or it can be characteristics acquired through education and experience. Society can also confer power; for example, the power of a police officer to direct traffic or to commandeer a private automobile in an emergency situation. Some people have power because of the strength or other characteristics of their personality. Personal charisma has led other people throughout history into behaviors that were uncharacteristic and, in some cases, downright self-destructive.

Social norms can also result in the allocation of power. In a family, the power of parents over young children frequently has been regarded as a given in our society. Unfortunately, as we as social workers know all too well, the power of parents in Western cultures frequently has been so great that it represents a physical and emotional threat to the child.

Parents traditionally have had the power to influence the attitudes, beliefs, and behaviors of their children. But do they always have the authority? Authority is *legitimate* power. Social workers and others now challenge the legitimacy of some of the power that parents possess. Parents of teenagers are well aware that if the validity of parental power is challenged and not granted legitimacy by a son or daughter, they lack the ability to influence their child's behavior to any great degree.

The social worker as manager is concerned primarily with authority as it relates to human service organizations, and there are three different types of authority that exist within organizations. We shall discuss the major advantages and disadvantages of each and how they can assist the manager in accomplishing the managerial function of organizing.

Line Authority

Line authority involves no delegation; it exists without any relinquishment of authority by the manager or any tampering with what is already in place. It is the authority to make certain decisions and to engage in certain activities that exist because of one's job position and its relation to other job positions. Literally, line authority exists because of the line (or box) occupied by one's job title on an organizational chart. It goes with the job.

Line authority provides supervisors with all the legitimacy they need to influence some aspects of the work of supervisees. Line authority is what dictates the respective roles of every employee in relation to every other employee. The formal organizational chart (see Figure 8.4) depicts the relative positions of persons who work within an organization. It implies who has the authority to make decisions affecting others.

Social workers as managers who rely solely on line authority as a primary method of organizing activities are on safe ground in some respects. They will be allowing the exercise of authority that was granted by "the organization." Thus, it is difficult to criticize the manager who relies heavily on line authority and shuns the use of other types of authority. But line authority may not always be best. Total reliance on line authority deprives managers of the needed benefits of delegation. Managers who can't delegate usually end up doing too much themselves and spreading themselves too thin. They also deprive subordinates of the opportunity to grow and to prepare for assumption of more responsibility and use of autonomy.

Differences among staff and situations may also argue against too heavy a reliance on line authority. One disadvantage of line authority is its inability to individualize among those who occupy positions. Any given individual, based on his or her position on the organizational chart, *may* be the best one to make a decision or he or she may *not*. As we have repeatedly emphasized, all individuals have strengths and weaknesses. In fact, the person who might bring the best expertise to bear on a decision actually may be an employee who lacks the line authority to make a decision. Unless other authority options are exercised, managers can find themselves constrained by using only that authority that exists within the organizational chart. They will not be able to use the best person for a job if they adhere too tightly to line authority. Of course, as we shall discuss, too frequent use of alternatives to line authority can create a different set of problems.

Staff Authority

One of the two alternatives to the use of line authority is *staff authority*. Along with functional authority (to be discussed next), it requires delegation and the creation of a particular kind of relationship between manager and staff and among staff that is different from what line authority would suggest as appropriate. The granting of staff authority creates a relationship between a staff member and a manager that can best be described as *advisory*.[6] People assigned staff authority for a task find themselves engaged in activities that will result in their giving advice to the manager. A social work manager might, for example, delegate staff authority to a subordinate to explore options for the location of a new satellite clinic. The manager might ask the staff member to recommend its placement or to advise the manager as to what the staff member thinks the contents of a new "cafeteria" approach to employee fringe benefits should be. In these examples the advice is to be the end product of the work of the person to whom staff authority is granted.

With staff authority it is assumed that the staff member will engage in tasks of research and investigation prior to giving advice to the manager. It is both appropriate and expected that the person granted staff authority will form opinions and will try to sell (without being too insistent) his or her own opinions on the best course of action to the manager. Staff authority does *not* guarantee that the manager will take the advice, or, if the manager does, that the person granted staff authority will receive credit for the advice or be involved in implementing it.

Staff authority is most frequently seen in large organizations, particularly in bureaucracies. It is used frequently in the military and in government circles. Leaders may surround themselves with individuals granted staff authority who do much of the groundwork that makes their decision making possible. Such individuals are even called staff; for example, a general's "staff officer." Staff member are expected never to usurp the decision-making authority of their supervisors.

The advantages of the use of staff authority are obvious. A person assigned to research a topic and give advice can greatly facilitate the decision making of the social worker as manager. The disadvantages of using staff authority relate to what *can* happen if it is not used sparingly and intelligently. If used too frequently with the same subordinates, line authority can be weakened. By definition, staff authority is a relaxing of the usual lines of authority. If it becomes a regular occurrence, lines of supervision can become undermined.

Staff authority can also create accountability problems in other ways. If staff are granted staff authority on a regular basis, they can begin to perceive themselves as primarily thinkers, a breed distinct from the doers. They can start to lose touch with those who must perform the primary work of the organization (that is, those who deliver services to clients). Before long, their advice can become impractical or unrealistic.

Staff authority can also have a deleterious effect on the morale of those granted staff authority. It can be frustrating to be asked repeatedly to research a topic and to make recommendations only to have the recommendations not followed by the manager. Even if advice is regularly taken, frustration can still occur. It is not fulfilling (especially for those with a high need for self-actualization) to have one's authority end with giving advice. Many of us need to "see through" a task and to be involved in implementing a decision that we recommended. Also, there is the problem of who gets credit for a good decision when the research was done by a staff member. Persons assigned staff authority may find it demoralizing to see the manager praised for following their advice. Of course, if the advice is bad, it may be some consolation for the person granted staff authority to know that, as we suggested earlier, the manager cannot be relieved of responsibility for the bad decision.

Functional Authority

The third delegation alternative, *functional authority*, involves a greater range of delegation than does staff authority. Staff members who receive functional authority are given a much larger piece of authority, on a time-limited basis, than that which they would otherwise possess. Authority is granted to research and to plan and, most importantly, to implement as well.

The term functional authority as we will use it is drawn from the literature of the business sector. There it is defined as "the right which is delegated to an individual or a department to control specified processes, practices, policies or other matters relating to activities undertaken by personnel in other departments."[7] Obviously, translation of the concept into a useful delegation alternative for the social worker as manager is needed.

In using functional authority, higher-level social work managers might deprive lower-level managers (for example, a supervisor) of some of their legitimate line authority for a time. They would do this primarily in order to bring the best possible expertise to bear on a limited situation or task. Those with functional authority would be able to make decisions that would affect other employees who are not normally under their influence; that is, they occupy a position that is not under their direct supervision.

For example, let us suppose that a new social worker has been hired as a child-protection worker in a public agency. The manager, the head of child-protection services for the agency, logically would assign the task of orientation of the new worker to the person who is the new employee's supervisor; this would be totally consistent with line authority. But the manager recognizes that the supervisor, recently hired from outside the state, is probably not the best person to handle one aspect of the orientation, namely an introduction to state laws that impact on job expectations. The manager *might* ask the supervisor to work with the unit's legal consultant (a lawyer) using the consultant to advise the supervisor in the development of a package of learning materials and experiences designed to help the new worker acquire the necessary knowledge of relevant state laws. But this strikes the manager as a cumbersome and inefficient way to get the job done. The manager decides instead to grant functional authority to the legal consultant to assume responsibility for developing and implementing a one-day module of the new worker's orientation that focuses on legal aspects of the job. Or, the manager may use another supervisor who is more knowledgeable of and experienced in application of state laws. The manager informs the new worker's supervisor of his (or her) decision and even invites the supervisor to observe the training in order to become familiarized with state laws. The person given functional authority (legal consultant or other supervisor) takes total responsibility for the worker's activities during the legal orientation. This person assigns the worker specific learning exercises, decides when the worker will take a break, and otherwise controls the worker's activities. At the end of the day, the responsibility for orientation shifts back to the supervisor.

Our example of the use of functional authority illustrates both the advantages and the potential disadvantages of the use of functional authority by managers. It might have been illogical for the legal consultant to have taken time to work with the supervisor to help the supervisor develop and implement the legal orientation. Why not simply let the lawyer or another knowledgeable supervisor both develop *and* deliver it? These people have the expertise and, if present, would make it possible for the new worker to ask and receive reliable and correct answers to questions. As long as supervisors are reasonably secure in their role, the temporary suspension of their line authority should not be a problem. The person granted functional authority might even like the opportunity to actually implement the orientation, to be able to identify its strengths and weaknesses, and to learn how future orientations might be made better.

Disadvantages of functional authority relate primarily to dangers associated with its overuse. If used too frequently, it can weaken the capacity of the line supervisor to manage. If, for example, all or most modules of the new worker's orientation were to be delegated out to "experts," the supervisor might lose credibility with the new worker, who might begin to wonder just what the supervisor *does* have to offer.

In many social agencies, functional authority is unavoidable. It is both logical and well-liked by professionals. It is logical because people in the helping professions tend to have special areas of interest and expertise. Why not take advantage of them by letting the "experts" have time-limited line authority over those who may lack their interest and knowledge, even if they are not technically their supervisor? As we suggested in our discussion of problems associated with overuse of line authority, strict adherence to the organizational chart can get in the way of tapping available staff resources.

Professional staff like functional authority for several reasons. It allows a worker to see a task through from start to finish (unlike staff authority) and to get credit for the completed task. It also tends to put less emphasis on the formal organizational hierarchy that many subordinates find demeaning. Some supervisors also find too heavy a reliance on the formal hierarchy uncomfortable because it seems to stand in the way of the formation of collegial relationships. Unlike adherence to formal lines of authority, functional authority says, in effect, "We can *all* learn from each other now and then," an attitude that is very consistent with social work values. To many social workers as managers, functional authority combines the accountability features of line authority with the emphasis on use of individual knowledge and skills present in staff authority.

Desirable Characteristics for Delegation

Delegation of authority is essential both to good social work management and to employee growth. Professionals as well as other staff need experience in exercising discretion. Social work practice in any setting is more than just a technical skill. It requires thought, judgment, and the application of knowledge to situations that are likely to be unique. A practitioner can only acquire competence in exercising judgment if managers are comfortable with delegation and are willing to trust persons other than themselves to evaluate situations and to take necessary action.

One principle of management that exists within manufacturing organizations is that, for purposes of cost-efficiency, tasks should be performed by those at the lowest level capable of performing them. This idea causes problems for many social workers as managers. As professionals, social workers as managers often like to remain close to practice, even to the point of continuing to see clients. They know that they *should* delegate more, but they really don't want to do it.

Delegation of either staff or functional authority requires certain characteristics on the part of social workers as managers. They have to be able to trust subordinates to do a job satisfactorily and to be open to others' ideas and methods that may be different from their own. This involves letting go of tight control and being content with broadly overseeing activities. In the case of functional authority, delegation may also involve allowing others to make mistakes that the manager would probably not make. Managers (and parents!) find it very difficult to see when things are going wrong or to recognize that they will go wrong without jumping in to "rescue" a subordinate. But managers who use functional authority must be able to restrain themselves, recognizing that most errors are not irreversible. Overriding functional authority to avoid a mistake may avoid trouble in the short run. It can, however, be very costly in terms of erosion of staff confidence and morale. It also will jeopardize the potential for its future use. Besides, such a practice leaves little room for staff members to benefit from a learning experience that they might otherwise have had.

Managers who delegate authority must also be skillful communicators. Careful delineation of the type of authority being delegated and its limits must be communicated to both the subordinate and to all others involved. Confusion regarding whether a staff member has been granted staff or functional authority can create havoc in an organization. Workers who thought their role was purely advisory (staff) may feel put upon when asked to make and implement a decision. They thought their work was over when they made recommendations. Conversely, workers who perceived that they had functional authority may become angry and feel insulted when told that their role was to be only advisory. They looked forward to deciding on and implementing a course of action or to assuming responsibilities that they normally do not have. The time for a manager to explain clearly the type of authority delegated and its limits is *before* the task begins. Special skill and tact are also necessary to avoid offending others in the administrative hierarchy who might be inclined to feel that their authority is somehow being usurped or that the person to whom authority is delegated is regarded as "special" by the manager.

CASE EXAMPLE: A PROBLEM IN USE OF STAFF AUTHORITY

Katherine was the Chief of Social Services in an outpatient psychiatric clinic. She learned that, because of another manager's budget oversight, there were excess staff development funds available as the end of the fiscal year approached. She shared this information with the social work staff and encouraged them to inquire into workshops that might be coming up in order that funds could be used prior to being lost. The available funds allowed several supervisors and caseworkers to enroll for short courses.

Katherine was pleased that one of her supervisors, Gilbert, requested funding to enroll in a workshop on a new and controversial approach to working with hostile clients. She approved his request and called him in to discuss his plan for staff development. She mentioned that she regretted not being able to attend the workshop herself because she had heard so much about the new treatment. She communicated to Gilbert her wish that he attend and that afterward he fully investigate the effectiveness of the treatment as reported in the professional literature. He also was asked to present to her a written summary of his findings and to recommend a plan for possible use of the new treatment within the clinic. Gilbert was flattered by the request. He began researching the literature on the new treatment even before he attended the workshop.

In her first meeting with Gilbert, Katherine was careful to use the words *advise, investigate*, and *research*. In her mind, she felt that she had made it very clear that she was delegating staff authority to him. Unfortunately, because of his enthusiasm about attending the workshop and the fact that Katherine had assigned this task to him, Gilbert did not really listen very carefully to Katherine's instructions and explanation of what she was asking him to do. Katherine erred in not reinforcing her message in subsequent meetings with Gilbert. She assumed that he had heard and that it was unnecessary for her to define his authority again.

Two weeks after attending the workshop, Gilbert requested a meeting with Katherine to "let you know how we will be using the new treatment." Katherine rearranged her schedule to see Gilbert as soon as possible, fearful that a miscommunication had occurred. Her fears were confirmed.

Gilbert came to the meeting with his written report in hand. It was immediately apparent that he assumed that the implementation of his recommendations for use of the new treatment was a *fait accompli*. Even worse, he expected to be given functional authority to supervise the implementation of his recommendations throughout all units. Katherine quickly commented that a misunderstanding had obviously taken place. She explained that she had intended that his special assignment would be ending today with the submission of his report and recommendations. But she retained the authority to determine if any or all of the recommendations would be implemented and, if so, by whom. Gilbert's reaction was somewhere between crushed and furious. Katherine admitted to some responsibility for the misunderstanding by not reminding him of the fact that he had been given only staff authority. It did little good. Gilbert threw the report on her desk and left. It was a long time before Katherine felt that she was able to regain his respect. It was also apparent from the attitude of other staff who were his close friends that he had shared with them his perception of how he had been "deceived and misused." When she received additional information about the new treatment indicating that it is probably not effective with the type of clients most served by the clinic, Katherine decided not to implement the recommendations in Gilbert's report. While her decision was a necessary and correct one, it gave Gilbert additional cause for resentment and confirmed his impression that she had just been "playing a power game" with him.

Based upon her experience with Gilbert, Katherine made a mental note to:

1. Use staff authority sparingly with professional staff.
2. Carefully explain what staff authority means while delegating it.
3. Confirm and reinforce the staff member's understanding of staff authority at regular intervals.

THE OPTIMAL AMOUNT OF STRUCTURE

Social workers as managers must remember that organizing is an important part of managing and a managerial function that must be performed. However, it should also be remembered that organizing is designed to help in the achievement of goals and objectives; it should not become an obstacle to their achievement. An "overorganized" organization is just as dysfunctional as a chaotic one that lacks organization. The ideal organization is as well organized as it needs to be, and no more. As is true of all the managerial functions that we discuss in this book, more is *not* synonymous with better.

The decision regarding how tightly organized an organization should be is a difficult one. We must rely heavily on a few general principles, and on common sense and our knowledge of human behavior. In general, large, multipurpose bureaucracies reflect a need for more organizing on the part of the manager. Smaller organizations usually can tolerate some blurring of roles, functions, and lines of authority. They may require less active organizing activities on the part of the manager.

The capacity of staff to tolerate and to accept the need for structure also influences the degree of organization that is optimal. Generally, paraprofessionals, preprofessionals, and clerical staff expect and appreciate the degree of certainty in their jobs that goes with a tightly organized work environment. Professional staff are more likely to value professional autonomy and may be more resistive to many of the organizing efforts of the manager. As we have indicated, however, such organizing activities as the delegation of functional authority provide an acceptable mix of autonomy and structure for professionals.

The personality of managers themselves also can help to determine the amount of structure that is optimal for a work setting. The style of a manager and the manager's approaches to the various tasks of management should be a logical extension of the manager's personality. Easygoing managers will be uncomfortable and will lack staff credibility if they attempt to create a tightly organized work environment. Conversely, managers with a need to organize will not function well if they attempt a more "hands off" approach to organizing. While managers, like all human beings, are capable of growth and change, a total turnaround in style is probably not possible or would at least be very difficult for most of us. This is something to consider before taking a job where much of an individual's time is spend in management. Problems can easily occur in those settings where the organizing needs of the organization are not consistent with the "organizing personality" of a potential manager.

SUMMARY

This chapter examined some of the concepts and issues that relate to the management function of organizing. There are basic ways that higher-level administrators in organizations select to help them organize the delivery of services. There are also many other organizing structures that can be used for program design and for other organizing functions. Available options drawn from the business literature and research within the profit sector were found to be generally applicable to the task of organizing within human service organizations. It was suggested that organizing staff and activities by simple numbers, time, enterprise function, territory, service, clients served, or market channels all have been tried in human service organizations with varying degress of success.

The concepts of power and authority were discussed as a preface to our analysis of delegation as a way of organizing. It was noted that, within an organization, line authority exists with staff based upon the position in the organizational hierarchy occupied by that individual. As a manager, a social worker can also choose to delegate tasks and the authority to accomplish them. But managers cannot delegate the ultimate responsibility for their successful completion. Staff authority and functional authority were presented as two delegation options that have both advantages and disadvantages. Both were proposed as potentially useful. Also discussed were those managerial characteristics that facilitate delegation for the manager. Variables were identified that help to determine what is the desirable degree of organization for a given organization. Chapter 10 will return to some of these variables as we look next at how they can influence the performance of another managerial function, control.

REFERENCES

1. James D. Thompson, *Organizations in Action* (New York: McGraw-Hill, 1967), p. 40.
2. Harold Koontz, Cyril O'Donnell, and Heinz Weihrich, *Essentials of Management*, 4th ed. (New York: McGraw-Hill, 1986), pp. 180–201.
3. Bruce S. Jannson, "Federal Social Legislation Since 1961," in *Encyclopedia of Social Work*, Vol. 1 (18th ed., 1987), p. 594.
4. Koontz, O'Donnell, and Weihrich, *Essentials of Management, op. cit.*, p. 206.
5. Ibid., pp. 206, 383, 409. Also see Joseph Olmstead, *Working Papers Number Two: Organizational Structure and Climate: Implications for Agencies* (Washington, DC: United States Department of Health, Education and Welfare, 1973), pp. 27, 29–30.
6. Koontz, O'Donnell, and Weihrich, *Essentials of Management, op. cit.*, pp. 226–233.
7. Ibid., pp. 209–215.

ADDITIONAL READINGS

Babbitt, B. "To Delegate or Not to Delegate." *Across the Board*, 24 (1987): 56–57.
Baum, L. "Delegating Your Way to Job Survival." *Business Week*, (November 2, 1987):206.
Draft, R. *Organizational Theory*. St. Paul MN: West, 1987.
Imershein, A., Chackerian, R., and Martin, P. "Measuring Organizational Change in Human Services." *New England Journal of Human Services*, 3, (1983):21–28.
Kast, F., and Rosenzweig, J. "General Systems Theory: Applications for Organization and Management." *Academy of Management Journal* (December 1972): 447–465.
Martin, E. "A Flowchart for Evaluation in Service Organizations." *Australian Social Work*, 35 (1982):23–31.
Mintzberg, H. *Power In and Around Organizations*. Englewood Cliffs, NJ: Prentice-Hall, 1983.

CHAPTER 10

Influencing Through Control

It may seem a little redundant to devote one of the latter chapters of this book to the management function of control. After all, haven't all of the management functions that we have discussed to this point contained elements of control? They have. Such activities as planning, staffing, and organizing are designed to help the social worker as manager to shape, constrain, and direct the activities of staff in such a way that they will contribute to the attainment of group and organizational objectives.

Indeed, there is some blurring of boundaries between the management function of control and other management functions. While this may present the student of management with occasional conceptual problems, it really is reflective of life as it exists for social workers as managers, who often are performing two or more management functions simultaneously with little time to worry about what their activities should be labeled or where the boundaries of each should be drawn. In fact, the same activity sometimes can be construed as performing more than one important management function. For example, the activity of employee evaluation (as we shall see) is controlling, but it is also a part of staffing as we noted in Chapter 7. Similarly, the use of a policy or rule performs both a planning and a control function.

THE ELEMENTS OF CONTROL

When we use the word *control*, we tend to think of limits. This is not a bad place to start in order to understand what we mean by the management function of control. The activities of children, adolescents, and even adult professionals occasionally require limits and constraints to assure that their activities are safe, appropriate, and productive. The social worker as manager, whether in the job of first-line supervisor or of agency chief executive officer, has a broader perspective than do subordinates. Managers are in a better position than those who work under their supervision to know when staff activities are contributing to the attainment of objectives and when they are not. Consequently, it falls to the manager to exercise control over the activities of others to assure that their activities are desirable for the organization and for the clients served. Bernard Neugeboren described control as evolving from "the need to integrate individual and organizational goals. Various specific mechanisms may be used to obtain staff compliance."[1] His description of the mechanisms of control available to the human service manager differs little from the control menus described in the business literature. In fact, it is also a comprehensive list of control methods available to managers within most any other social system (for example, families or communities).

Controlling involves both the assessment of staff performance and the setting up of vehicles to amend behavior that is not contributing to attainment of objectives. It involves a three-step process: (1) establishing standards, (2) measuring performance against these standards, and (3) correcting variations from standards and plans.[2] Control is greatly facilitated if good planning precedes it. Planning sets standards that make it possible to evaluate and to make necessary corrections.

Not surprisingly, controlling is another one of those management tasks that many social workers often do not relish, for it requires the assumption of a kind of "parent" role in relation to one's professional colleagues. This does not always set comfortably with social workers or with any other adult workers. Admittedly, controlling tasks sometimes can be unpleasant. Inevitably, they will lead to occasional resentment on the part of staff. But controlling is an absolutely essential part of the job of the social worker as manager, and it is critical for the effective and efficient service to our prime beneficiary, the client.

Many of the words associated with the function of controlling can contribute to the resentment that employees often feel toward it and toward managers who are just doing their job. The vocabulary of controlling includes words and phrases like *curbing*, *restraining*, *indoctrinating*, *exerting authority over*, *regulating*, *checking up on*, *holding to a standard*, or *verifying*. All of these activities *are* a part of controlling. They also are almost universally resented, especially by mature professionals who jealously guard their autonomy and their right to exercise professional discretion. They can easily perceive control as infringing on their autonomy.

One of the most difficult tasks faced by the social worker as manager is finding ways to perform the controlling function in a positive way that neither humiliates staff nor builds unhealthy and counterproductive resentment toward the manager. Fortunately, as in the case of a closely related function, namely planning (discussed in Chapter 4), the manager has a menu of controlling aids available for use. They are often interchangeable, meaning more than one would do the job. They may have quite different effects on the morale of individual staff and of work groups. Sensitive managers who know their staff will be able to develop a positive, dynamic package of controls that can accomplish the task of controlling while not seriously jeopardizing morale and manager-staff relationships.

In some organizations, control is viewed as little more than a necessary evil. It is almost universally resented by staff. When these conditions exist, we must question the effectiveness of the manager in the use of control. Controls that are chosen and implemented with tact and sensitivity need not be resented and are often appreciated by staff. They can *enhance* staff morale and staff-manager relationships. This is most likely to occur when controls are perceived as no more limiting of autonomy than necessary. It should be obvious that they are present because of organizational and client interests (and not because of the psychological needs of the manager for exerting his or her power). Controls can offer a sense of certainty and security that allows employees to know that they are "in the right," thereby freeing them up to concentrate on offering client services. Managers who can successfully create an organizational climate where controls are perceived as a necessary and helpful element will find that these contribute to positive manager-staff relationships. Obviously, some controls are more likely to contribute to this desirable state than others. Some, by their very nature, have a greater potential for resentment. As we look at the control menu available to managers, we will also look at its strengths and weaknesses, with special references to its potential to positively or negatively affect the work climate within a human service organization.

THE CONTROL MENU

The control menu consists of a very diverse collection of influences that a manager can bring to bear to control employee behavior. Some—for example, performance review or punishment—are manager-directed and manger-implemented activities. Others, such as idealism or professional values, are equally powerful influences but seem to "exist" in some degree or other at least in part because of the long-term attitudes and behaviors of the manager. They can be called upon to assist in performing the function of control (but not created) as a need arises. We will view the "mixed bag" of control vehicles available to the manager as a group of alternatives that should be considered for use in situations where control is indicated.

Plans

A plan, by its very nature, is designed to constrain and to control. The reader will recall from Chapter 4 that one of the objectives of planning is to *not* allow events and behaviors to simply happen naturally or at the whim of the actors involved. Plans make it possible to shape behavior in some predetermined direction. They also set standards for staff. They reflect a hoped-for outcome and, as such, they serve as a yardstick by which the manager can evaluate performance of staff and to intervene if necessary to change their behavior. Plans, therefore, are a prerequisite to other kinds of control. You cannot evaluate unless you have a reference point by which to evaluate. Plans provide that reference point. When managers plan, they are attempting to control. They are also laying groundwork for all other controlling activities.

Plans are very powerful control vehicles. For example, "the budget of an organization can be regarded as primarily a planning and control system."[3] One of its two main functions has been described as "to provide a monitor for the financial activities throughout the year."[4] It has the potential to support or to disallow the various activities of staff. If an activity is regarded as desirable and appropriate, that activity is granted legitimacy by provisions made for it within the budget. The budget also can provide the rationale for managers to disallow activities. They can merely point out that the activity has not been granted legitimacy as evidenced by the fact that there is no support for it in the budget.

Formal Guides for Action

Another type of control that we have talked about before is what we will refer to collectively as *formal guides for action*. These include a variety of constraining vehicles that define what is acceptable and what is not acceptable behavior among staff. Examples are rules, policies, strategies, and procedures. The reader will recall that we discussed these in Chapter 4 as types of plans. Here we are concerned primarily with their potential to control the activities of staff. Formal guides are a useful reference for employees. They take some of the guesswork and the risk out of decision making. They are impersonal and designed for use by any individual who occupies a given position within the organization. Consequently, they are less likely to be resented than are controls, which are perceived as aimed specifically at a given individual.

Formal guides are always available to staff. The manager who develops them can be on vacation, on sick leave, or even no longer with the organization. It doesn't matter; their influence and preferences continue to control staff behavior as long as the guide remains in effect. This is a mixed blessing. Staff cannot ignore formal guides by pretending that they didn't know what behavior was acceptable. They can't blame the manager for not telling them what to do. That guarantees that controlling will occur. On the other hand, a formal guide, once in place, will control activities even in exceptional circumstances when the manager never intended for them to apply. Unless the manager is present to override a guide, an employee who complies with it will remain essentially beyond reproach, even if compliance does not result in the correct behavior. Of course, as we indicated in Chapter 4, some guides are inherently more flexible than others. For example, because policies imply more use of discretion than do rules, managers who are concerned with the danger of overly rigid compliance with formal guides in their absence may wish to rely more on policies to control and less on rules.

As with other types of controls, formal guides used in a work environment characterized by trust and mutual respect between manager and staff can greatly facilitate the work of all involved. They can increase certainty for the manager by expanding the manager's potential to control, even when the manager is not physically present. Staff, in turn, can operate with the reasonable assurance that, if they are in compliance with formal guides, they will be "OK" and their decisions and activities probably will be appropriate to goal achievement of the organization. Formal guides also protect subordinates from the use of arbitrary or capricious criteria for evaluation of their performance by the manager.

The very same formal guides used in a climate of distrust and a lack of mutual respect can become weapons to wage war between managers and staff. Managers can use them as a reminder of their superior authority or to stifle the initiative and creativity of a staff member whom they do not trust. In turn, staff members can blindly and rigidly comply with formal guides in situations where they know that they were not meant to apply in order to highlight a manager's "rigidity" or otherwise embarrass the manager in some other passive-aggressive manner.

Formal guides can either promote goal attainment and a healthy work environment or they can sabotage it. The key to their successful or unsuccessful application, as in so much of management, lies in the nature of the relationship that exists between the social worker as manager and the subordinates. Once again we see that management and other areas of social work practice are far more similar than dissimilar. A positive working relationship is critical both to successful social work practice and to effective management.

Training

We last discussed training in Chapter 6 as one way to support employee growth. But training is also a very effective control vehicle available to the manager. While in some situations it is desirable for the manager to promote initiative and creative solutions on the part of staff, other situations suggest the need for standardization through training. For example, there are certain right and wrong ways (legally and professionally) for a child-protection worker to handle a report of suspected child abuse or to respond to the sexual overtures of a client. Creativity and initiative are *not* desirable. On the contrary, managers need to assure that workers are sufficiently socialized so that there is little room for discretion in those situations where discretion simply cannot be tolerated. They want to convert and standardize staff to think and to act in a way that is regarded as *correct*. "Indoctrination" is required. Staff are expected to possess the same values, to operate on the same premises and priorities, and to absorb these to the point where they are, for all intents and purposes, their own.

Training makes people look and act more alike. In some work situations this is desirable if not absolutely necessary. Particularly when direct supervision is not always possible, training is useful. It allows a manager's controls to be exercised even when the manager cannot be physically present. If an employee has internalized the correct sequence for doing a job, for example, there is every reason to assume that the job will be done correctly. What's more, the employee who is well trained will probably not even be consciously aware of the manager's control and will, therefore, not resent it. Because the behavior is so well internalized, it will just seem natural, correct, and an extension of one's own work habits and style. For example, it is training that makes it possible for social workers to obey protocol while making home visits even though they don't take their supervisors along with them. Workers are made to feel more free and able to function autonomously when they are well trained. A manager uses training to standardize employees so that they can be turned loose with less supervision. Training actually can allow staff to feel *less* controlled. It provides "alternatives to the exercise of authority or advice as a means of control over the subordinate's decision."[5]

Training is an expensive (in terms of dollars and time) method of control, but it is one that is usually appreciated by employees. Confident, well-trained employees have a tendency to feel better about their job and are more likely to be positively predisposed toward the manager who provides the training. What's more, as we suggested in Chapter 6, the cost of *not* training is often much greater for both the employee and the organization (in errors and embarrassment) than is the cost of training.

Performance Review

Performance reviews or performance evaluations (as distinguished from program evaluations)[6] can exert a considerable amount of control over the behavior of employees. As we suggested in Chapter 7, review of employees' work tells the manager how they compare with expectations that have been established for them. If certain types of very precise plans are in use within an organization (for example, management by objectives), performance review provides the manager with a clear reading of when work has been satisfactory and when it has not. Review of work suggests where changes in employees' work performance are indicated and where additional control over their performance needs to be added. For example, it may suggest what type of training an employee requires or which activities need to be more carefully supervised. The performance review may suggest that inadequate performance was not the fault of the individual evaluated. For example, the identification of poor decisions may suggest that inadequate information was available or that the employee was inadequately prepared for decision-making responsibilities.

Performance reviews suggest better ways to control future employee behavior. But the promise of future performance reviews also exerts a considerable amount of control over employee behaviors. Staff members, knowing that there will be a regular, periodic day of accounting, are less likely to engage in behaviors that they will not be able to justify or that will leave them vulnerable to poor evaluations. All of us (including those of us who are classroom teachers) tend to a greater or lesser degree to carry our evaluation forms in the back of our minds. Their presence and the inevitability of their application are likely to curb those behaviors that we know are likely to result in critical reviews.

While the threat of performance reviews can be a useful and constructive control on employee behavior, an obsession with them can be counterproductive. Employees preoccupied with getting good performance reviews will tend to "play" to the evaluation instrument too much. This can, for example, result in behaviors that resist doing necessary jobs that are not in their job description and for which they will not receive "credit." Or they may not want to attempt new tasks or new approaches to their work that will inevitably result in some mistakes that could affect their job performance review.

Social workers as managers need to be aware of the dangers inherent when the promise of employee evaluations become a specter to be feared or the driving force behind doing a good job. Performance reviews *should* exist to help to control and to assist staff in their job performance. Performance standards and employee awareness of them should provide gentle guidance; they should not represent a club poised over an employee's head. The sensitive manager will use performance reviews as a method of control in such a way that they will be perceived as a useful aid to job performance. If reviews become an obsession for staff that overly or inappropriately controls their behavior, a good manager will work to relax their control over staff by reducing the emphasis placed on performance reviews.

Advice and Information

We all are quite generous with our advice and information. Usually gratuitously, we pass on the benefits of our life experiences and knowledge to others. Between peers or persons of comparable power, advice and information are available to be heeded, ignored, or even never heard. But when a person with more power and/or authority than another person gives advice or information, it is often received as *more* than just advice or information. It may be a vehicle of control.

The advice of a parent *may* be only advice, or it may be a tactful, non-humiliating attempt at telling a child what to do. Advice to a 3-year-old is usually synonymous with a directive; it is expected to control behavior. Advice to a teenager is likely to carry little if any expectation of compliance or heeding of the advice. Also, a communication in the form of advice or information may be purely "for your information" in one aspect of a relationship yet may carry the intent of control in another. A professor who tells a student about a job opening generally expects the student to follow up on the information or not, based purely on the student's interest. A "thank you" is about all that the professor expects. But the same professor who tells a student about what is generally regarded to be a major resource for a subject area that the student is researching for a term paper has every expectation that the resource will be cited in the student's paper. The student who ignores the information may discover that the "advice" was much more than just advice.

Relationships between social workers as managers and their subordinates are clearly not equal. Consequently, advice or information offered to a subordinate has much more expectation of and potential for control than advice or information passed between and among peers. This is done with the intention of shaping and controlling the behavior of the staff member. Because the great majority of advice and/or information given by managers is designed to affect the action of subordinates, staff sometimes assume that all of a manager's advice or information is a thinly veiled directive. This can cause problems. If managers intend to step out of their manager's hat long enough to simply share information, peer-to-peer, without wishing to influence the staff member's decisions or behavior in any way, they had better make their intentions very clear. If not, the subordinate may respond to what is perceived to be a directive when none was intended.

Because advice and information can be communicated in a way that controls while not calling attention to a power differential that exists, this is a favorite vehicle of control among both managers and subordinates. Social workers as managers enjoy being able to set necessary limits on the behavior of staff while not having to do it in a way that "puts down" the knowledge and professional competence of a colleague who happens to occupy a lower position on the organizational chart. In turn, subordinates enjoy the face-saving offered by controls in the form of advice and information. Unlike, for example, orders or directives, staff members can at least partially delude themselves into believing that "it's just advice or information." Of course, knowledgeable subordinates know that both advice and information, given the source, are usually meant to control. They know better than to ignore such offerings. They often appreciate not having the presence of a power differential "shoved in their face," however. They are not likely to *feel* as controlled or harassed as when directives are used.

Directives

Sometimes, for one reason or another, staff control through the use of advice and information doesn't work. Some individuals never quite get the message. Some managers never become competent at the subtleties of their use and feel more comfortable saying exactly what they mean. Sometimes there is no time for subtlety for the cost of miscommunication would be too great. Sometimes the manager has a need to remind staff members of the power differential that they have forgotten.

Directives take the form of orders, overt instructions, or other specific demands. They may be aimed at individuals and/or groups and may be used to exert control over a variety of behaviors. They are an especially good choice from the control menu when a conflict situation exists and it has become apparent that consensus cannot be achieved. If, for example, two factions seem unable to work out a compromise over the use of computer hardware, the manager may have to resort to directives. This is a responsibility that the manager cannot shirk. An organization cannot afford the expense of prolonged debate over an issue of relatively low importance to client service, particularly when it becomes apparent that winning the debate is rapidly becoming a higher priority for staff than resolution of the conflict. Someone (the manager) must terminate debate and initiate action. Of course, this only can occur in situations where the manager has the authority to take action.

Not surprisingly, directives are some of the least popular methods of control among those used by social workers in their roles as managers. Subordinates may find directives humiliating. However, though they are often reluctant to admit it, most staff are usually relieved when a directive writes *finis* to an interminable debate among staff.

Directives are generally viewed as a reminder of the locus of power (within the manager) that staff prefer not to see. To most of us, directives reawaken feelings of powerlessness and the figurative slap on the wrist that we thought we left behind when we left our home of origin, turned 21, graduated, left military service, or achieved some other rite of maturity. We naively thought that no one would ever tell us what to do again. Of course, few people ever get to this point in even one sphere of their lives. None of us ever gets to this point in all of life's spheres. But that doesn't mean that we enjoy being reminded of our subordinate position.

Social workers as managers often dislike using directives for control because, on the surface, they seem inappropriate for use between or among helping professionals. We believe that professionals and other dedicated helpers should be able to communicate in ways that don't remind each other of power differentials that exist. Directives may seem antiegalitarian and a bit in conflict with our professional values relating to equal worth among human beings. Shouldn't a suggestion and a smile be sufficient means of control among dedicated persons of goodwill? Perhaps, but as we suggested above, there are many situations when they are not.

One of the most difficult tasks assumed by social workers as managers is learning to use directives comfortably and without guilt. It is helpful to remember that directives are sometimes not only necessary but are also probably the most efficient method of control available to the manager. If used where necessary and appropriate, directives can save a considerable amount of time and effort. Miscommunication can be virtually eliminated.

Most mature professionals and other human service staff recognize the need for directives on occasion. They may even appreciate them as a refreshing change from the approaches of some social work managers whom they regard as overly concerned with possibly insulting or offending subordinates. Employees *expect* to be told what to do by the boss now and then. The judicious use of directives often is perceived as an indication of strength on the part of a manager, of a willingness to take control and to assume that responsibilities of the job. There are many employees who "just want to be told what to do," especially in situations where there is little time for tact and subtlety. This is *not* meant to imply that there is no room for tact in the use of directives. A skillful manager will state a directive in a way that makes the message clear but that a reminder of the power differential is not in evidence any more than absolutely necessary. Among other things, directives given in private or on a one-to-one basis are usually less likely to be resented than those given in the presence of others.

Managers in the business world have long been accustomed to using directives to control. Corporate managers do not seem to exhibit that self-consciousness and apologetic demeanor sometimes seen among social workers. There is no reason to apologize or to feel guilty for using a control method that is efficient and effective. Perhaps, as social workers, we are overly concerned with questioning our motivation for using directives. We may spend too much time asking ourselves, Do we select directives for control because they control well or because we get some sense of gratification (a "power trip") out of using them? Just maybe, the good feeling that sometimes accompanies the use of directives occurs because they seem to work so well!

Obviously, if a social worker as manager relies on directives almost exclusively or in situations where other control vehicles would be preferable, there is likely to be a problem. Morale can be undermined along with initiative of staff. Confidence in and respect for the manager is likely to erode if managers are perceived as enjoying the use of directives just a little too much.

But autocratic managers who relish the use of directives are relatively rare in social work. In our observations, a more common problem is managers who do not make sufficient use of this valuable method of control.

Sanctions

If directives are often underused by social workers as managers, negative sanctions must be on the list of endangered species. Social workers are supposed to reward and be supportive, not to punish or to impose negative sanctions. We talk about appealing to individuals' positive motivation and about building on strengths, not about calling attention to and punishing shortcomings. Our professional values imply a firm belief in the superiority of the carrot over the stick.

Negative sanctions *are* a legitimate control tool of the social worker as manager. They have very limited use, but they can be very effective. Sanctions are designed for use in those situations where certain behaviors simply cannot be tolerated. A sanction spells out both what an employee is forbidden to do and the negative consequences of doing it. The consequences are usually quite drastic. For example, if a manager determines that an organization's programs might be seriously jeopardized by the release of the report of an internal evaluation or audit to the press, the manager might inform all employees that no portion of the report is to be shared with anyone outside the organization. The penalty for violation of the rule would be clearly indicated (for example, immediate dismissal). The threat would not be an idle one; if a violation were proven after due process, the offending employee would be fired. This action would be a deliberate example to others.

Negative sanctions are effective. People will avoid behaviors when they understand that a substantial punishment will be enacted, especially if they see it enacted on another. But sanctions are of very limited use in promoting positive behaviors or desirable activities. They can also have a very damaging effect on morale and on relationships between staff and managers. Consequently, sanctions should be used very sparingly and only in situations where the possibility of absolutely intolerable behaviors exists.

Loyalties

Loyalties can be promoted and fostered by the manager, and they can be powerful vehicles for control. Loyalties, in some form or other, are always present within work situations. Appropriately focused, they contribute to organizational goal attainment. They can also present major obstacles to goal attainment if they are misplaced.

Ideally, employees possess loyalties to the organization and they share and endorse its goals and objectives. Use of training and indoctrination can go a long way toward creating this desirable state. Other loyalties can exist toward peers and subordinates, toward one or more superiors, and, of course, toward one's self. Self-interest is always a major controlling force for staff. The manager may as well acknowledge this truth. A staff member's loyalties toward other persons within the organization can be both positive and negative for the social worker as manager, depending on whether or not the object of the loyalty is a competent, dedicated employee.

Organizational loyalties can be very desirable. When employees feel good about where they work and are proud of an organization's services, the manager is indeed fortunate. Organizational loyalties can serve as powerful inducements to do what is necessary for the good of the organization and for the clients that it serves. An employee who is loyal to the organization will, for example, understand the necessity to work overtime occasionally or to postpone a vacation in order to complete a task such as the timely submission of a grant proposal. Employees are less likely to complain or to insist on extra compensation for doing what is in the best interest of the organization.

Managers should foster the growth of organizational loyalties, but they may also find it useful to appeal to loyalties that already exist. When managers appeal to organizational loyalties, they are saying, in effect, "I'm not asking for me, but for the organization." Genuine, occasional appeals of this sort can elicit desirable behavior among employees who are loyal to the organization. They may result in employees doing something that the manager has no legitimate right to require them to do. Of course, if appeals to organizational loyalties are used too frequently or when no real emergency exists, they can quickly lose their capacity to exert control. Once a manager is perceived as using appeals to organizational loyalty as a means to manipulate or to exploit staff, resentment will be evident. Even appropriate appeals then may meet with resistance. The manager should be careful in the use of organizational loyalties, using them sparingly in only those situations where other more traditional methods of control would not work. They clearly are not suitable for routine requests that must be made of employees.

Staff possess organizational loyalty in various degrees. The sensitive manager learns to identify those employees for whom organizational loyalties represent a powerful source of control, those who are influenced somewhat by them, and those for whom they represent little or no source of leverage. Loyalties also should not be regarded as simply a static characteristic of individual staff. They tend to ebb and flow based on an employee's current attitude toward his or her job. They can be nurtured by the manager so that they are available when needed. This is best done by regular reminders of organizational goals and frequent positive communication to staff about the organization during times when *no* special requests are being made. Employees are most likely to develop good feelings about their association with the organization during those routine but rewarding times when its representatives (managers) are asking no special favors of them except that they do their job as outlined in their job description.

Idealism

Idealism is another available vehicle for control. Like organizational loyalty, idealism tends to exist in people in various degrees. Many people who enter the helping professions possess a strong sense of altruism, perhaps in the form of a felt need to help others. Among some people, the Judeo-Christian ethic, with its emphasis on caring for one's fellow human being, provides individuals with an extra sense of purpose and enhances their dedication to their work. Idealism is certainly appropriate and desirable in fields such as social work. It can be an important source of motivation that, for example, makes it possible for individuals to perform needed services and tasks where conditions are less than favorable and tangible rewards are few. Idealism can also assist the helping professional to see potential for change in situations where other, less idealistic individuals would have given up hope or even would have refused to get involved in the first place.

The manager can and should work to create an organizational climate where individuals' personal ideals can serve as motivators. It generally is in the best interests of all concerned, especially of clients. Ideals should never be ridiculed or allowed to be ridiculed by others. As we suggested in our discussion of organizational loyalties, appeals to an individual's ideals, if employed judiciously, may be used by the manager to elicit behavior that is consistent with organizational goal attainment. As such, they are a source of control, but one that exists within employees themselves, rather than one initiated by the manager. Of course, frequent appeals to an employee's ideals can be quickly perceived as manipulative behavior on the part of the manager. Like loyalties, such appeals are best reserved for occasional use.

Professional Values

Professional values are really a special kind of idealism. They have been acquired a little later in life than have other types of idealism and have been gotten through a process of education and socialization. But professional values control much of our behavior on the job and, to a greater or lesser degree, even off the job. For example, espousal of professional values regarding the primacy of client needs may keep a social worker in the office until 8 P.M. to deal with an emergency despite the fact that workday ends at 5 P.M. Professional values, as we have suggested throughout this book, also govern our behavior as managers. Most of the time they are supportive of good management practice. Now and then, however, professional values seem to run counter to what we, as managers, have to do.

Professional values, because of their capacity to control other employees' behavior, can be a mixed blessing for the manager seeking to promote organizational goal attainment. Usually professional values are consistent with and supportive of the goals of human service organizations. A manager can appeal to them on occasion to promote desired behavior and to constrain undesirable behavior. A good manager should help to promote organizational goals that are consistent with professional values. But sometimes this ideal state is not possible. For example, human service organizations sometimes must function as businesses. They cannot afford to offer services that are inefficient or those that threaten community support for the organization. Consequently, staff members occasionally find that their professional values are in conflict with organizational goals. Lower-level staff spend less time in management activities and more in direct client service. Therefore, they can afford to concern themselves a little less with such matters as agency funding and find it relatively easy to stand on their professional values in the face of agency demands. The point for the manager is this: Professional values consistent with the organization's objectives help to facilitate control. But conflict between professional values and the organization's goals, policies, or procedures provides a rationale for employees to *resist* control. A certain amount of tension between professional values and an organization's objectives is inevitable and also healthy. Professional values help to hold the organization accountable. Fortunately, tension usually remains at a healthy and tolerable level in most human service organizations.

Example

The final control vehicle on our menu is one that we seldom think of as a method for controlling, yet it exerts great influence over the power of staff. It can be a source of support for or resistance to desirable employee behavior, whether we intend it to be or not.

The example set by the manager can affect the behavior of all employees who seek the manager's goodwill, who wish to identify with the manager, and/or who simply wish to advance within the organization. It is less likely to be seen as manipulative on the part of the manager than, for example, appeals to organizational loyalty or to ideals. What the manager says, does, and the attitudes and values that the manager reflects are generally perceived to be norms for the group, the standard to be met. If managers are well respected, their behavior is an especially powerful positive influence on others. For example, the widely admired manager who sometimes puts aside his or her own personal best interests for the good of the organization and its clients will influence others to do the same. If, however, managers communicate that subordinates should make sacrifices but are unwilling to put self-interest aside themselves, their example can provide a negative model.

Social workers as managers cannot choose whether or not they wish to control by example. If they interact at all with staff, even if they are just seen occasionally by them, they *will* set an example that will affect subordinate behavior. The issue is not *whether* they will control by example but *how* their example will influence behavior. Will their example set a desirable role model to emulate? Or will the manager's attitude and behavior have a "do as I say, not as I do" message of hypocrisy? If the latter is the case, even other methods of control that are in place (for example, formal guides, advice and information, or directives) will reflect a weakened capacity to control. Staff may reluctantly allow themselves to be constrained. But they will resent it and be likely to engage in other undesirable, nonproductive behavior when the occasion arises.

In a sense, the manager is always on stage. In the role of manager, the social worker is watched for clues as to how to act, think, and what attitudes are appropriate. When a lower-level staff member engages in a particular behavior, there is less danger that many others will try to emulate it. But when a manager (particularly a higher-level one) does something, a large number of staff are likely to notice and to assume that it represents an example for others to follow. Staff seeking to justify a behavior that they *know* is not desirable within the organization will, of course, use a manager's example as well. For example, lower-level staff members are more likely to call in sick to catch up on their holiday shopping when they see the manager do it. If managers want to support some staff behaviors and constrain others, they are most likely to be successful if their own behavior reflects the desired standards. They may possess the *power* to live by a different set of standards, but their example will only cause resentment and will weaken their overall capacity to control.

THE IDEAL CONTROL PACKAGE

The package of controls that managers select to perform their controlling function will change naturally with conditions, with the changing needs of personnel, and with changes in personnel themselves. Selecting a control package is a rather imprecise science. There is no formula available that can tell us, for example, just what percentage of our controlling should be handled using directives, what percentage by formal guides, etc. One thing *is* certain. If managers find themselves relying very heavily on only one or two control methods from the menu, they should become concerned. The widely diverse control needs of the human service organization and of those employed within it suggest that a varied package is almost always ideal.

Certain broad guidelines are available to help us in development of an effective and efficient control package.[7] They characterize a good package, one that will control as much as is necessary, while not stifling staff initiative.

A Package That Is Comfortable

Perhaps most importantly, the control package selected should "feel right" to social workers as managers. It should not leave them and others with the feeling that they are playing a role or are using methods that are somehow uncomfortable and out of character. Whereas managers may need to use every one of the controls on the menu at some point, in most situations more than one could be selected to do the job. Managers should use most frequently those that fit their personality and style of management. Those who are most comfortable giving advice and information to control and do it effectively should use this method far more often than directives. Of course, when only directives will do the job, they must be able to use them too. Conversely, a manager with a more authoritarian personality may rarely use advice and information to control.

What constitutes a comfortable package of controls for the manager involves more than just the manager and the manager's own personality. It should be tailored to the characteristics of other staff as well. The real emphasis in selection of controls should be on the quality of interaction between controller and controllee that is sought. As much as possible, the interaction should be as natural and comfortable as possible for both. For example, neither participant in the interaction between a relatively young supervisor and a senior subordinate may feel comfortable with the frequent use of directives. Yet directives may be a much more natural way to control if the same supervisor is senior to a subordinate who is a relatively recent graduate.

A Package That Reflects Objectivity

The package selected should be perceived as invulnerable to such influences as whether the manager likes a given employee or not. For example, employee evaluations should emphasize observable standards for assessment that leave no room for subjectivity and emotionalism or for acting out personality conflicts. A manager may have great personal animosity toward an employee, but if the employee is performing well, evaluation instruments and processes should generate a highly favorable evaluation. Other systems of rewards also should reflect a person's job performance. Conversely, a friendship or personal sense of affinity should be precluded from affecting an employee evaluation in any way.

No matter what controls are selected, it should be obvious to all that they are not designed to "get" anyone, but rather to maintain a standard of services that are in the best interest of all. A control attributable to the shortcomings of one individual should be applied to that individual alone. If others don't need it, then it shouldn't be implemented for them. General controls that affect many should not be identifiable as aimed at any one individual. That would only tend to embarrass the individual and cause him or her to be resented by others.

A Package That Has the Potential to Improve Conditions

A good package of controls is not there for its own sake. It is not there only to monitor the activities of others, but to shape them in a way more consistent with organizational goals. Unless staff members see controls as a prelude to change, they are not likely to look favorably on them. If, however, they see them as resulting in improved working conditions and, ultimately, in better client services, they will tolerate them much more easily.

A question that should be asked about a control package is, Will it point up shortcomings *and* will it result in corrective action? It is unfair to burden staff with control packages that do not promise to improve conditions after identifying problems that exist.

A Package That Is Efficient

The control package should be relatively inexpensive to administer and maintain. Specifically, it should result in a net overall saving for the organization. Some controls can cost more than they save in time and resources. For example, half-day staff evaluations every six months can help to exert control, but can they be justified in terms of time away from client service and the ultimate contributions to goal attainment relative to cost?

Some overly rigid control packages control well but at a heavy cost to morale. A manager might maintain tight control over staff activities by not allowing compensatory time for evening work or by denying the request of an employee who commutes 60 miles to work to move to a four-day, 10-hour per day workweek. But the objective of creating a work environment where organizational loyalty is high might be jeopardized in the process. The vigorous use of some controls actually undermines the effectiveness of others. The net gain may be zero or even a minus.

Some behavior problems, sometimes referred to as "corruption" in the literature,[8] are probably best "not seen" by the manager. Once acknowledged, they must be controlled or, if not, they may appear to be tolerated by the manager. Unless the problem is one that threatens goal attainment, it may be best to not call attention to it.

A Package That Focuses on Critical Control Needs

Some poorly managed organizations seem to emphasize control of relatively minor behaviors whereas larger problem behaviors that threaten organizational goal attainment go unchecked. For example, a manager can devote great amounts of control activities to policing the use of the telephone for private business. Does an occasional short personal call to the baby-sitter really represent a dangerous violation of a rule? A one-minute long-distance call of dubious professional content may not be worth the time of the manager or of the staff involved to implement controls aimed at corrective action. The morale of staff and the relationship between manager and the offender may be worth far more to client services than 75 cents added to the phone bill.

What *is* a critical problem suggesting the need for controls? A lack of attention to clients, their rights, and their need for services is critical and is the legitimate focus of a control package. These problems and the staff behaviors that contribute to them *cannot* be ignored. Managers clearly cannot control all staff behaviors of which they do not totally approve. They must maintain a set of priorities that suggests when a package of controls is appropriate and when it is not. Remembering that the client (and not the employees) is the prime beneficiary of a human service organization will go a long way toward helping the manager identify and maintain an appropriate control package that focuses on critical behaviors. Building flexibility into the control package to accommodate changing conditions will also help. Many undesirable behaviors are not all that bad in certain situations. A flexible control package, when appropriate, will allow certain behaviors to be overlooked at some times and corrected at others.

CASE EXAMPLE: A PROBLEM OF INEFFICIENT EFFICIENCY

Mario was the director of an extended-care facility. He prided himself on running a tightly controlled, fiscally sound organization that consistently ended each year in the black. He was regarded as a rising star in the publicly owned corporation of which his facility was a part.

The organization had not always been run as tightly as it had under Mario's leadership. But when he assumed the director's job he immediately set out to convert losses to profits. As a dedicated social work professional, he refused to compromise the quality of patient care. But he also set out to make certain that the maximum number of patients were served whenever possible. His efforts to improve the community image of the facility and his emphasis on adherence to strict rules for making and receiving referrals quickly contributed to an extremely high bed occupancy rate that had not previously existed. As he developed an even tighter package of controls, the facility continued to show an even greater increase in profits.

Before long, Mario began to genuinely enjoy the control that he exerted over the behavior of his staff. This surprised him somewhat, because he had originally dreaded the control responsibilities that went with the job. He soon delegated very few decisions and took special care to monitor and approve carefully the expenditure of funds. He was unaware that his careful fiscal scrutiny was beginning to cause resentment among several of his employees. A few of the professional staff felt insulted by what they saw as Mario's lack of trust of their behavior. But Mario became aware that he had a problem only following the implementation of his new "pen policy."

For several months, Mario had observed what he believed to be unnecessarily high bills for office supplies. He was especially concerned over the great number of pens that staff members were using. It seemed as though every time he looked, a staff member was grabbing another handful of pens. He noticed that several staff members invariably had a pen or two in their pocket when they left work but they never seemed to have one when they reported to work in the morning. He began to wonder whether the organization was not supplying writing supplies for staff, their children, and half the community.

Mario first brought up the pen issue in a staff meeting. He (good-naturedly, he thought) commented on the rising high cost of pens and other supplies. He asked staff to please help conserve the number of pens used. A month later, having noticed little improvement, he shared his observation that staff seemed to be leaving with pens in pockets (hadn't he done the same thing absentmindedly himself!) but rarely bringing them back to work. He wondered aloud if any staff members ever bought school supplies (his effort at a humorous way to address the problem). Several staff members obviously were not amused. (Mario was not known for his sense of humor.) He requested that staff check around home for pens from the organization and that they bring back any that they found. That didn't improve the attitude of his staff very much.

Two more months passed. Only one staff member was seen bringing in pens, but they didn't write. Meanwhile, the amount of pens being taken continued to increase. Unbeknownst to Mario, what was being referred to as his "pen obsession" was becoming a source of amusement and ridicule among staff. One social worker even began slipping pens into Mario's coat pocket before he left work for the day. The occasional amusement provided by the pen issue was short-lived, however. Mario's next effort at control made everyone furious.

Mario decided that staff were challenging his authority by clearly ignoring his request for the return of pens. He was concerned over the continued financial loss to the organization, but he was more concerned over his feelings of powerlessness to do anything about it. He announced and immediately implemented rules and procedures that (in his mind) were certain to solve the pen problem once and for all. The pens were placed in a locked cabinet. A single key was issued to his administrative assistant who was told to make up a roster of secretarial staff who would be in charge of the pen cabinet. The secretary in charge of the cabinet was to sign the key out and sign it back in.

Each staff member was to be issued three new pens. No exceptions were to be made. Following the initial issue, staff members would not be able to receive a new pen unless they turned in an old one to the secretary in charge of the pen cabinet. The secretary was to test the pen to assure that it was no longer usable. If it was, it would be given back to the staff member and no new pen would be issued.

What had been a generally cooperative, congenial work environment quickly deteriorated. Professional staff found Mario's pen solution to be totally demeaning and unacceptable. The secretaries assigned to the pen cabinet and his administrative assistant hated their new assignments. They felt that they had better things to do. They were right. They were regularly taken away from their usual duties in order to get a new pen for a staff member. Relationships between secretarial and professional staffs became more strained.

On a pure dollar cost-benefit basis, Mario's solution was a definite loser. The time spent by staff in implementing it far exceeded the savings in pen costs that were generated. One good secretary quit her job, at least in part over Mario's pen procedure. She was replaced by a new person who required considerable training before he could come "on-line" at the same level of competence as the old employee. The cost in staff morale could not be easily calculated, but it was apparent. Respect for Mario was obviously at a new low. Other new cost-saving controls that he implemented that might ordinarily have been accepted without comment produced ridicule and resentment on the part of staff. They began to resist other rules and policies that had previously gone unchallenged. Finally, most of the staff signed a petition criticizing Mario's controlling and humiliating management style and threatening to resign unless changes were made. They mailed it to the parent corporation.

Mario received a copy of the petition from the chairman of the board along with a request that he address the problem immediately. When he received the letter, Mario finally recognized the problems that his concern over pen costs had caused. He understood how he had mistakenly attempted to over-control an area of behavior that did not represent a critical threat to organizational goal attainment. His options were to continue to try to function as a manager in a hostile work environment, resign, or lose a little face and admit his mistake. He chose the last option. In a staff meeting he acknowledged that his concern with controlling costs had, perhaps, gotten a little out of hand. He cited the pen problem as an example. He announced that, in the future, he would more carefully assess the impact of rules and procedures on costs and on staff morale before implementing them. The pen cabinet would be immediately unlocked and available for whomever needed a pen.

Mario had feared that admitting his mistake and rectifying it would result in a major loss of respect and an inability to control staff behavior in the future. While a few staff members initially gloated over the fact that he had been forced to back down, Mario was surprised to see that many more staff members seemed to have a new respect for him. After a while, the pen issue became an inside joke, and Mario was able to use it on occasion in staff meetings to relieve tension that had become high. He willingly shared his mistake with new managers to illustrate to them how the manager must be careful in selecting those areas where control is indicated. When Mario ultimately left the organization for a higher-level job in the corporation, he was given an appreciative farewell dinner by staff. Among his gifts was an expensive pen, presented along with a collection of humorous remarks appreciated by all.

CONTROLLING FOR THE RIGHT REASONS

The role of manager carries with it a responsibility to control. It also carries with it the *power* to constrain and to control the activities of others. As we all know, the power to control is sometimes quite pleasurable and gratifying. We can easily lose sight of why managers are supposed to control as we get caught up in the gratification that comes with controlling. As we have repeatedly suggested throughout this chapter, the need for control should come from organizational needs (and, of course, the needs of clients) and not solely from the needs of the manager. Control should be viewed as a means to an end, never an end in itself. The potential for a means-end displacement is great. We can easily become obsessed with the process of controlling while losing sight of its purposes.

Complete control cannot be achieved. But a major benefit of control for both the manager and other employees is the reduction of uncertainty within the work environment. Too much uncertainty about what to do or how one will be perceived and evaluated can create anxiety in staff, sometimes to the point of immobilizing them. But a moderate level of uncertainty is both inevitable and desirable. It can be achieved if controls are used appropriately and well.

Excessive control can stifle initiative of staff. The overzealous creation of uniformity and standardization by a manager can quickly communicate to staff that conformity is always desirable. Such a message can cheat the organization of the special and unique talents and expertise of its members. In addition, an overly controlling, heavy-handed approach to management can also promote a type of passive-aggressive response on the part of staff that is not healthy for the organization. Staff members will begin to avoid decision making, passing such matters on to management with an attitude of "You want to control everything, then *you* make the decision." The expertise of staff (to make their own decisions) goes underutilized.

SUMMARY

In this chapter the management function of controlling was presented as closely linked with and sometimes overlapping with other managerial functions, primarily planning and evaluation of staff. We described controlling as the setting of limits and the establishment of standards, the measuring of performance against these standards, and doing whatever is necessary to correct deficiencies. Controlling involves those actions taken by the social worker as manager to influence the behavior of others so that it is more consistent with organizational goals and objectives. We emphasized that, while social workers frequently dread the function of controlling, if done tactfully and well it can provide benefits to both management and other staff, primarily in the form of increased certainty within the work environment.

The various methods for controlling were presented as a menu available to the manager. Control vehicles on the menu included plans, formal guides for action, training, performance review, advice and information, directives, sanctions, loyalties, idealism, professional values, and example. The advantages and disadvantages of each were discussed.

It was emphasized that, whatever package of controls a manager selects, it must remain dynamic and flexible. The package, no matter what its specific composition, should be comfortable for staff involved, perceived as objective, have the potential to improve conditions, should be efficient, and should focus on those areas where control is critical. The dangers of over-control were also noted, especially the way that too much control on the part of the manager can stifle staff initiative and can result in a situation where individual expertise will not be fully utilized.

REFERENCES

1. Bernard Neugeboren, *Organization, Policy and Practice in the Human Services* (New York: Longman, 1985), p. 130.
2. Harold Koontz, Cyril O'Donnell, and Heinz Weihrich, *Essentials of Management*, 4th ed. (New York: McGraw-Hill, 1986), p. 448.
3. Walter Christian and Gerald Hannah, *Effective Management in Human Services* (Englewood Cliffs, NJ: Prentice-Hall, 1983), p. 136.
4. Rex Skidmore, *Social Work Administration* (Englewood Cliffs, NJ: Prentice-Hall, 1983), p. 72.
5. Herbert Simon, *Administrative Behavior* (New York: Macmillan, 1957), p. 16.
6. Myron Weiner, *Human Services Management* (Homewood, IL: Dorsey Press, 1982), p. 277.
7. Koontz, O'Donnell, and Weihrich, *op cit.*, pp. 459–463.
8. Amatai Etzioni, *Capital Corruption: The New Attack on American Democracy* (San Diego: Harcourt Brace Jovanovich, 1984), pp. 76–80.

ADDITIONAL READINGS

Cappelli, P., and McKersie, R. "Management Strategy and the Redesign of Work Rules." *Journal of Management Study*, 24 (1987):441–462.
Edwards, R., Faerman, S., and McGrath, M. "The Competing Values Approach to Organizational Effectiveness: A Tool for Agency Administrators." *Administration in Social Work*, 64 (1985):259–280.
Etzioni, A. "Compliance, Goals and Effectiveness," in *Classics of Organization Theory*, J. Shafritz and J. S. Ott, eds. Chicago: Dorsey Press, 1987.
Goddard, R. "Reshaping Today's Organization for Tomorrow's Needs." *Personnel Journal*, 65 (1986):12.
Graham, C. *Managing the Public Organization*. Washington, DC: C. Q. Press, 1986.
Parker, L. *Developing Control Concepts in the 20th Century*. New York: Garland Publishing, 1986.
Rosengren, W. "Structure, Policy and Style: Strategies of Organizational Control." *Administrative Science Quarterly*, 12 (1967):140–164.
Wilson, E. "What Counts in the Death or Transformation of an Organization?" *Social Forces*, 64 (1985):259–280.

CHAPTER 11

Influencing Through Leadership

The fifth and last major managerial function that we will examine is *leadership*. Leadership is the manager's conscious efforts to influence other persons within the organization to engage willingly in those behaviors that contribute to the attainment of organizational goals. Of course, we could not have gone this far in our discussion of the role of the social worker as manager without already touching on the function of leadership. Managers exert leadership (or they should) when they plan, staff, organize, and control. In a general sense, leadership is what management is about. But it is also a function worthy of individual focus.

We would all agree that good leadership is desirable and that poor leadership or the absence of leadership is undesirable within human service organizations. We probably can give examples of what we perceive to have been good or bad leadership that we have observed. But problems often occur when we are asked to specify *why* leadership was good or bad, or *why* we perceive one individual to be an effective leader and why another person is viewed as ineffective in a leadership role. The difficulty of defining and evaluating leadership is one that has perplexed theorists over the past half century. Researchers and theoreticians have devoted entire careers to the pursuit of a better understanding of leadership. We will begin by summarizing some of the past and current thinking on the subject.

THE ELEMENTS OF LEADERSHIP

A large portion of leadership relates to the concept of influence. Leadership is a little less direct and obvious than control in its efforts to influence (some would say it is less oppressive). But it is no less powerful in shaping the behavior of people within organizations. In fact, it could be argued, managers will be successful in their efforts to control only if they are first perceived as effective leaders. People want to follow the directives and the example of good leaders. They may ignore or circumvent the control efforts of ineffective leaders. Like control, leadership seeks to influence and shape behaviors of staff so that they are supportive of rather than obstructive of organizational goal attainment. Specifically, in human service organizations, managers hope to lead in such a way that they will influence the behavior of subordinates to better contribute to more efficient and more effective client services.

Leadership employs a combination of personal characteristics (of the manager), knowledge, and skills to attempt to influence the behavior of other employees. In this sense, it is closely related to the concept of motivation (see Chapter 8). While we have discussed motivation as a part of staffing, it could just as logically have been considered a component of good leadership.

Ideally, we would like to have our fellow employees willingly do what is in the best interests of the organization and the clients that it serves. With good leadership, this can occur. But those tasks that, by their very nature, are regarded as unpleasant or that are perceived as in conflict with the self-interest of staff may require especially adept leadership. For example, special leadership may be required to elicit any kind of employee enthusiasm for performing cumbersome record keeping, which is required for federal reimbursement in large public welfare agencies and which may leave less time for meeting other job expectations. Yet some managers are able to lead in such a way that employees spend very little time complaining and approach this type of normally unpleasant task in a relatively "upbeat" fashion. Somehow these managers' requests are viewed as reasonable and credible and their motives are not suspect. Clearly, trust is a component of effective leadership. This should come as no surprise to us; it is an important element for success in all of the functions of the social worker as manager.

The specific tasks of leadership tend to vary dependent on the position in the organization occupied by the manager. For example, we expect higher-level administrators to lead through such activities as representing the organization within the community and successfully negotiating with potential funding sources. They can also lead by translating the policies formulated by boards into programs or by formulating standards for the delivery of professional services within the organization. In contrast, mid-level managers such as case supervisors are more likely to lead by assuring that staff do not become so immersed in their work that they lose sight of organizational goals of service, or they may show leadership by allocating resources in ways that promote professional growth and that support lower-level staff in their job performance. For them, leadership may entail such activities as resolving interpersonal conflicts, advocating for better fringe benefits for staff, or promoting pleasant working relationships by scheduling "attitude adjustment" social occasions.

Activities of leadership at any level are designed to exert a positive influence over the daily performance of others. Objectives are achieved in different ways, depending on the manager's position in the organization.

Leadership can and should occur as part of the daily management work of social workers in all positions within the organizational hierarchy. But in the real world of organizations and people, it doesn't always work this way. In human service organizations as in all organizations, it is not uncommon to encounter individuals who, because of the power inherent in their position within the administrative hierarchy, *should* be leaders. They are not. Others occupy a low position on the organizational chart, but are looked to and regarded as leaders. We will examine some of the efforts that have been made to explain why some individuals, regardless of their position, are effective leaders and why others are not.

EFFORTS TO UNDERSTAND LEADERSHIP

Both research and conceptualization about leadership have reflected a number of schools of thought that have risen and then declined in favor. Each has had its vocal advocates and each continues to contribute to our current understandings of leadership.

Trait Theories

Some of the earliest studies of leadership in the United States were based on the assumption that good leadership is synonymous with the possession of certain traits. Research was based in part on studies of persons generally believed to have exhibited good leadership. Attempts were made to identify those "common denominators" possessed by them. One theorist[1] reported a long list of traits that included such widely diverse attributes as social characteristics, intelligence, and even physical appearance. Another theorist presented a list containing such traits as ability to supervise, level of intelligence, initiative, self-assurance, and individualized approaches to work.[2] Such lists continued to appear. Ability to communicate was often mentioned, as was credibility. The lists of traits all appeared logical. Unfortunately, they rarely agreed with each other. A few traits (flexibility, initiative, self-confidence, and intelligence) appeared in virtually every list in some related form. Yet this observation was not, in itself, much of a contribution to our understanding of leadership. True, these four traits probably are associated with good leadership, but they are also traits common to good followers, good friends, and even to preferred pets! They are assets in becoming successful in any arena or at any level in life. Besides, some people who lack one or more of these traits have nevertheless demonstrated themselves to be good leaders. Others seemed to be failures as leaders despite the presence of all four of the traits.

Trait theories of leadership had other problems. They seemed to suggest in a rather undemocratic way that some people are born with what it requires to become leaders and some decidedly are not. This is not a view that sits well with social workers, who believe that individuals *can* change and grow. It also doesn't hold out much hope for leadership training or education. If, for example, a manager were to leave a job, the process of replacing that person would entail identifying someone else with certain desired traits, rather than working with current staff to acquire the knowledge and skills needed. Selection, rather than preparation, is indicated.

Still another shortcoming of the trait theories of leadership relates to the problem of measurement of personal characteristics. Researchers have labored for decades to measure intelligence in ways that do not reflect cultural or ethnic bias. Other traits believed to be common to good leaders have received even less attention and have resulted in measurement instruments that are probably even less likely to exhibit reliability and validity. Often a thin line separates a desirable leadership trait from an undesirable one. Efforts at measurement may miss this fine distinction. For example, can we say with certainty that our measurement can identify the presence of the desirable trait of initiative? Or is it possible that what we believe to be initiative is really an undesirable lack of caution or impetuousness? Similarly, while we may agree that self-confidence is desirable for managers performing leadership functions, arrogance is not. But can we say with certainty that what we observe is the former and not the latter? Can we even be certain that a potential leader has not successfully feigned self-confidence? Measurements of personality characteristics exist, but they are simply not refined to the point where it is possible to make good decisions about the leadership potential of human beings.

The contributions of researchers who advocated the trait theories of leadership seem to lie primarily in the conceptualization of traits that appear to be desirable among leaders. These traits may not be *sufficient* to guarantee good leadership behavior, but they probably help to explain why some people are successful leaders and why others are not. They also may go a long way toward explaining why some managers are able to promote loyalty both to themselves and to the goals that they are attempting to achieve.

Behavioral Theories

The behaviorist school of psychology began to have a major influence on leadership studies during the 1950s and 1960s. The so-called behavioral theories of leadership were also, in part, a reaction to the trait theories, which had emphasized characteristics of the individual rather what leaders do. Behavioral studies of leadership were based on the assumption that good leaders probably *act* differently from weak leaders. If one were to identify how leaders act differently, then others could be taught to behave in a way more consistent with good leadership. Theoretically, at least, behavioral theories of leadership implied a belief that anyone can be helped to become a more effective leader through training and education.

A major advantage of the behavioral approaches to understanding leadership (over the trait theories) is the relative ease with which behavior can be measured. Unlike traits, behaviors can be seen, recorded, and verified. People can be told about behaviors that may be undesirable for leaders and shown how to change them. Leader replacement can be accomplished by retraining those people already within the organization in other roles.

Advocates of the behavioral approaches to leadership shared a problem with trait theory researchers, however. They had difficulty in achieving any real consensus about which behaviors are reflective of good leadership and which are not. Early research sought to classify leader behavior based upon how leaders used the authority granted to them. For example, some leaders tended to be democratic, others authoritarian, and still others seemed to exert little direct influence over subordinates. None of the three types were found to be consistently effective leadership styles or consistently ineffective ones. One type (the autocratic) seemed to be best for productivity in short-term situations, but it seemed to be more injurious to group morale over longer periods of time than was a more democratic style.[3]

The Managerial Grid. Behavioral approaches to the study of leadership have resulted in a focus on leadership style that has persisted into the 1990s. The Managerial Grid, developed in the 1950s and refined in later years by Blake and Mouton,[4] is a commonly used framework for examining the different styles of leadership that exist. The authors suggest that an individual's leadership style can be plotted along the grid based on the person's behavior, specifically the degree to which the person reflects concern for production and the degree to which the individual reflects concern for people within the organization (see Figure 11.1).

Blake and Mouton have identified the characteristics of managers who fall at some of the most common positions on the grid. The 9,1 managers in Figure 11.1 (those who are probably most autocratic) are concerned with tasks, not people. They control and direct their subordinates with little regard for them as human beings. At the opposite extreme (see Figure 11.1), a 1,9 manager (sometimes referred to as one who offers "country club management") offers a very friendly, people-oriented environment, but provides no emphasis on production. A 9,9 management style places heavy emphasis on both, whereas 5,5 style puts a balanced but lesser emphasis on both production and the creation of a supportive work environment (Figure 11.1). A 1,1 manager is not really a manager at all; it is default. Such individuals offer neither concern for production nor concern for people. They are visible as managers, but just barely.

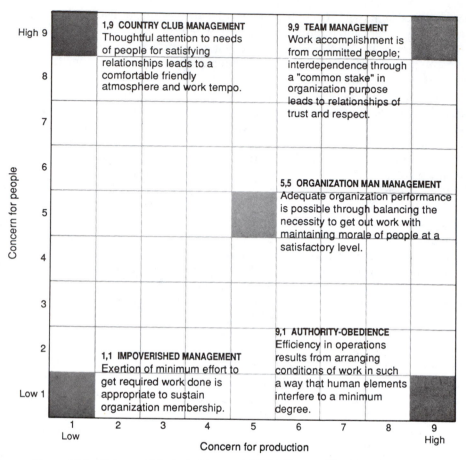

Figure 11.1. Blake and Mouton's Managerial Grid (Source: The Managerial Grid Figure from THE MANAGERIAL GRID III: by Robert R. Blake and Jane Srygley Mouton. Houston: Gulf Publishing Company, Copyright © 1985, page 12. Reproduced by permission.)

The Managerial Grid© is useful for identifying the style of a given manager. It does not, however, suggest which style is best in a given situation (although it seems to suggest that a 9,9 is usually preferable). It also offers no insight into how a particular manager developed his or her style and no prescription as to how an ineffective style can be improved.

Here is one of the most useful ways in which the grid can be employed. It can be very effective as a way for managers to learn how they are perceived by subordinates. It can sometimes be a real revelation to learn that their own perception of their management style differs markedly from the way subordinates view their approach to management. They may also be surprised to see the wide variation in the way two or more subordinates perceive their style as a manager. This can provide valuable feedback and, in some cases, impetus for needed change. Few of us really have an accurate perception of how we "come across." The Managerial Grid, plotted by ourselves (how we perceive our style) and by subordinates (how they perceive our style), can make for some interesting and productive comparisons.

Theory X and Theory Y. Among the other better-known conceptualizations of leadership based upon studies of behavior is Douglas McGregor's Theory X and Theory Y.[5] In his research, McGregor was led to conclude that a leader's management style tends to be heavily influenced by assumptions about the nature of human beings. McGregor saw people as basically "Theory X" or "Theory Y." The assumptions of a Theory X manager tend to reflect a dim view of human nature. A Theory X manager assumes that human beings dislike work and will avoid it whenever possible. They want security, but prefer not to work for it. If they work, it is only because they are threatened with punishment or otherwise coerced or controlled. They really don't want responsibility, lack ambition, and, if they must work, prefer simply to be told what to do.

How would Theory X managers act? Based on the above assumptions about people, they would mistrust their subordinates. They would be inclined to use tangible reward and punishment (or threat of it) to get others to do what needs to be done. They would assume that their authority is resented and would adopt a "we/they" attitude, employing coercion when it might not be needed. They would institute an oppressive, controlling collection of rules and procedures designed to enforce compliance. They would regularly "check up" on subordinates, expecting (perhaps hoping) to catch them in a moment of idleness or in a mistake.

Theory Y managers, in contrast, would hold opposite beliefs about human nature. Their leadership behavior would be based on the assumption that work is not disliked by human beings, but is a natural activity. They would believe that humans if committed to a goal will willingly do what is required to achieve it without threats of punishment or special rewards. People would be assumed to want and to seek responsibility if it is given to them in an appropriate way. Most human beings would be perceived as having an underutilized potential for growth, imagination, and creativity; that is, most are motivated by needs for self-actualization (see Chapter 8).

Not surprisingly, managers who possess a Theory Y orientation toward people would exert a style of leadership designed to capitalize on the assumed inherent capacities of individual subordinates. They would act in a way that communicates trust and a belief in the good intentions of others to work toward organization goal attainment. They probably would reflect less of a sense of "we/they," recognizing that goals are shared. They would work actively to set up and maintain a work environment that enhances growth and creativity and would use no more restrictive controls than would be absolutely necessary.

Of course, Theory X and Theory Y approaches to leadership style are extremes on a continuum. The attitudes of most managers and their accompanying behaviors probably fall somewhere in between. While we, as social workers, probably tend to be more Theory Y in our assumptions about human beings, as realists we must also acknowledge that it is not unusual for persons who act more like Theory X assumptions about human nature to find their way into human service organizations. A Theory Y manager's leadership style might border on the "Pollyanna" and would almost certainly lead to problems and abuses. A Theory X orientation and leadership style would almost certainly lead to a breakdown in group morale.

McGregor did not advocate either a Theory X or a Theory Y position. His contribution to our understanding of leadership lies in the insight that, frequently, how we act as leaders is based largely on our perceptions of people and their preferences regarding work. If we as managers allow our assumptions (lying anywhere along the continuum) to dictate our leadership behaviors without bothering to form an accurate assessment of who our subordinates are and what motivates them, we are destined to have problems. Leading, like other areas of management and other areas of social work practice, is a people skill. It requires a knowledge of human behavior *and* the capacity to recognize individual employee differences. It also requires us as managers to be flexible enough to adapt our leadership style to these differences.

Contingency Theories

The trait approaches to leadership fell short of providing a comprehensive understanding of what makes a good leader. Leadership also is not simply synonymous with acting in certain ways. Contingency theories of motivation evolved from the observed shortcomings of the other two, earlier schools of leadership theory.

Ralph Stogdill conducted leadership studies over several decades. In many ways his conclusions about leadership paralleled the development of theory in the area. As we noted earlier, Stogdill began as an advocate of the trait theories in the 1940s.[6] He later focused more on behaviors, identifying two behaviors, *consideration* and *structure*, as essential to good leadership.[7] (The reader will note that these two behaviors are very similar to the two axes on the managerial grid, concern for people and concern for production.) *Consideration* can be understood as, for example, acting friendly and warm to subordinates and being open to suggestions. *Structure* relates to a regular emphasis on budgets, deadlines, and objectives.

It is often difficult for the social worker as manager to find the appropriate balance between consideration and structure. Subordinates love considera-tion, but one's superiors may view it with suspicion or perceive it as being too "nice." Conversely, use of structure is well received by one's superiors, but can be viewed as oppressive by subordinates. Can a manager really offer both simultaneously, or are the two behaviors really in conflict with each other? Eventually, Stogdill found a way to resolve this theoretical dilemma. He moved in the direction of saying, in effect, that good leadership depends on the situation. Sometimes more structure is needed; sometimes more con-sideration. This line of thinking, the *contingency approach*, takes the position that a leader is good or bad, capable or incompetent, based on the leadership needs of the environment. There are no universal characteristics or behaviors that guarantee a good leader. Characteristics or behaviors that meet the leadership needs of one situation may not be right for another.

We do not have to look far into history to find examples of persons who had traits and behaviors that made them effective leaders in their situations. Yet the same traits and behaviors may have made them unsuccessful leaders at another time and place. Moral and ethical judgments aside, Adolf Hitler was the kind of leader sought by post–WWI Germany. Less malevolent ex-amples can be found in recent American history. John F. Kennedy's relatively young, vigorous, and idealistic leadership was what was desired and needed following the paternal inactivity of the Eisenhower years. Gerald Ford's leadership with its emphasis on integrity and openness was what was needed in the years after Watergate, despite the fact that in other times Ford might have been viewed as an ineffective leader. A nation disillusioned with infla-tion and cynicism welcomed the leadership style of Ronald Reagan and reelected him by an overwhelming margin in 1984. Reagan's characteristic optimism, his belief in traditional values, and his conservative appeals to those who had come to resent high taxes, social programs, and minority advances made him a natural leader for the 1980s. Only late in his second term of office did the "Teflon" begin to wear thin as his laid-back approach to management and misplaced trust of subordinates became increasingly prob-lematic. Reagan's approaches to leadership were no different in 1988 than they were in 1980. But the social environment had changed and they were no longer what was needed and wanted.

Contingency theories of management emphasize that leadership traits and behaviors are more or less desirable, depending on the situation. It has been suggested that there are certain situations in which structure is more im-portant to organizational functioning. For example, when strangers must work together and when time deadlines or other emergency situations exist, it is probably structure that is needed most from the leader. In related research in a social agency, York[8] found that, in times of rapid change, concern for production may be a more valued leadership characteristic than concern for people.

Fred Fiedler, the theoretician most frequently associated with the contingency theories of leadership, sees a leader's capacity to influence subordinates as largely a matter of fit among the leader's style and personality, the characteristics of the work group, and the needs of the work situation.[9] Fiedler observed that the attitudes and needs of individual managers tend to change little; leaders don't adapt well to changing situations. He concluded that it is probably more efficient for organizations to create managerial positions in such a way that they fit the leadership characteristics of existing personnel than to try to change people through training to fit the needs of existing positions. It is interesting to note that, not unlike the trait theories, Fiedler questions the effectiveness of leadership training. As managers, a good portion of our management style may be a "given." But while our personalities may be reasonably "fixed," there are skills that can be learned (for example, listening, delegation, etc.). The basic personality of the manager is definitely an important piece in the leadership puzzle. We have alluded to this elsewhere in this text and will examine it in greater detail in Chapter 12.

LEADERSHIP AND FOLLOWERSHIP

As we have indicated, a great amount of research and study has been conducted on leaders and what constitutes good leadership. However, leadership cannot exist without followers and good leaders require good followers. Social workers as managers, unless they are at the absolute top position in an organization, are both leaders and followers of some other leader. Even executive directors, for example, must follow the leadership of a board of directors, a legislature, or some other body that is superior to them. If social workers as managers are to lead successfully, they must be able to identify the elements of good *followership* and to promote it among staff. As managers, they must also be able to *be* good followers.

The topic of followership has received relatively little attention in our professional literature. Much of the discussion that follows is based on Kuehner's conceptualization.[10]

Every person is both a leader and a follower. One can be a leader in one sphere (for example, a family or a religious congregation) and a follower in another (a community activity or social group). Virtually everyone is also both a leader and a follower within the work sphere. In the same way that leadership skills can be developed, followership skills also can be developed. Generally those characteristics that make good followers are the same characteristics that make good leaders. By developing good followership skills, social workers as managers are also honing skills that will serve them well in their leadership function.

There are many different ways in which one can follow. Each can be more or less suited to the style and demands of the leader. For example, many social workers in public agencies have experienced only authoritarian leadership styles. They learned from experience that good followership entailed primarily doing what their superior told them to do without questioning or thinking much about the request. But suppose a new leader were to be hired who advocates a participatory management approach. The brand of good followership learned by workers would no longer be considered desirable or functional. A new set of expectations for what constitutes good followership must be learned and old expectations and behaviors must be unlearned.

As with leadership, there appears to be some limited consensus as to what characteristics seem to contribute to (but do not guarantee) good followership in all working relationships. Generally, it helps if the follower is dependable, a good team player, possesses solid technical knowledge, exercises sound judgment and decision-making skills, communicates well with leaders, and, perhaps most importantly, understands and supports organizational missions and goals. At another level, good followers must be able to manage themselves, manage their job, and manage their boss.

For the good follower, self-management involves the ability to handle relationships with clients and co-workers and the ability to take responsibility for one's own feelings and behaviors. It also involves maintaining a positive attitude toward one's job and toward the organization.

Job management involves the development of skills to manage time and workload. It entails the acquisition and use of relevant job knowledge and skill in problem-solving and decision-making situations.

Boss management requires that good followers be able to assess both the boss's strengths and weaknesses and their own. The goal is to find ways to complement the boss's functioning and to thereby improve the functioning of the entire work unit. Boss management is closely related to a concept called "managing up" that has been formulated by Austin. He suggests that managing up not only helps the boss but also the follower. If the boss does a better job, the subordinate's job is made easier.[11]

Followers may lack the authority that goes with higher-level positions but have major influence over how well occupants of higher-level positions are able to perform their jobs. They influence both what gets done and how it gets done by their capacity to demonstrate good followership. The followership style of subordinates can also influence the leadership style of the manager who is their superior. For example, immature and overly dependent followers elicit leader behavior such as checking the follower's work, giving detailed instructions, or allowing them and their co-workers to make few decisions. The leader may not fall naturally into this type of management style but may view it as necessary, given the style of followership that exists.

Good followers can exert positive influences on the work environment and on organization goal attainment. Followers often are in closer touch with client services in a human service agency than are leaders. From their perspective, followers are able to identify problems early and to suggest procedures and policies that will promote problem solutions to improve the quality of services. Followers are able to shape the work environment in a positive manner by providing advice and information to influence higher-level decision making.

Much more research on followership is likely to occur in the 1990s and beyond. Undoubtedly it will contribute significantly to our understanding of leadership.

LEADING BY CREATING THE RIGHT CLIMATE

Social workers as managers strive to provide the kind of leadership that will promote effective performance by personnel within the organization. This can be accomplished in part through their one-to-one interaction with colleagues and subordinates, but it also requires the creation and regular nurturing of a work environment in which certain conditions exist. Effective leaders attempt to maintain an organizational climate that is supportive of organizational goal attainment. What would be the characteristics of such a climate?

Respect

A work environment conducive to productivity would reflect mutual respect and confidence. There would be an absence of any unnecessary reminders that a power differential exists. Leaders are charged with certain responsibilities and with making certain decisions from a perspective somewhat different from subordinates. But this does not mean that they are more knowledgeable about everything or that only their perception of a situation is the correct one. They may be no more intelligent, experienced, or creative than those they supervise. They simply occupy a different position, do a different job, and make decisions with access to different information. Failure to remember this can seriously damage morale.

Different is *not* synonymous with superior. It is easy to forget this in one's role as manager and to make erroneous assumptions about the motivation, capacities, and knowledge of people who occupy a lower line on an organizational chart. Individuals treated as inferiors frequently respond as inferiors. There is no reason why managers in performing their leadership function need to treat others in a condescending manner when their inferior status is limited to only one rather narrow sphere of life—their place on the organizational chart. Subtle and less-than-subtle reminders of the relative status of subordinates are only appropriate in matters that relate to this sphere.

Even then, such reminders should be used only as a last resort, when other efforts to influence that convey mutual self-respect have failed. Reminders of subordinate status can quickly injure the mutual respect that is critical to maintaining a healthy work climate.

Mutual confidence can only evolve in a work environment when the leader and other staff have had experience working together. A leader will need to develop a "track record" for competence and skilled leadership under pressure; in turn, subordinates need to show that they too can "deliver" under stress. Confidence also involves feelings of integrity and trustworthiness on the part of all parties involved. There also must be a confidence that both leaders and their subordinates will be judged fairly along objective criteria. We discussed the need for this perception among staff in Chapter 7. But social workers as managers are also sensitive to evaluations of their own performance provided by their subordinates, whether they are regularly scheduled and written (a good idea) or whether they consist of overheard comments made by staff within the organization or reported in the community. Fairness must work both ways. As human beings, we are likely to begin judging others unfairly when we perceive ourselves to be victims of others' unfair evaluations.

Understanding

A climate of mutual fairness requires an understanding of the respective roles of all parties. Do subordinates *really* understand the responsibilities of the leader? If not, they may evaluate the leader's performance unfairly based on mistaken notions of what they think the leader should be doing and how the leader should be doing it. The leader needs to dispel the mystery that often surrounds the role of the manager.

Does the leader *really* understand what a subordinate does and, perhaps more importantly, how it feels to do it? While we would not argue that social workers as managers should always have previously occupied lower-ranking positions in the hierarchy, it helps. If they have not, it is essential that managers get close enough to the jobs of their subordinates to have a real understanding of the rewards and difficulties that go with the job. Even those managers who have come up through the ranks often have a tendency to forget what lower-ranking jobs were like and to lose sight of the pressures that govern day-to-day activities. As leaders, managers should strive to stay in touch with the group norms and value systems of other levels. They should also remain aware of the self-interests that exist at lower levels and that inevitably affect the behavior of staff.

Staff members need to know that, despite assuming the managerial role, their supervisor can empathize with their concerns. This would seem like an easy task for the social worker as manager. Unfortunately, assumption of the role of manager often creates a distance between manager and subordinates that the manager neither sought nor anticipated. This phenomenon probably results in part from the assumptions of staff about all managers' disinterest in subordinates and in part from a natural tendency of managers to forget what it was like before they became managers and to place greatest emphasis on matters of self-interest. For example, an agency manager rewarded for achievements in attracting funding can easily have difficulty understanding why lower-level staff are less euphoric about the acquisition of another grant. If the manager can empathize, however, he or she might be able to understand the staff's attitude. The grant may result in more paperwork for secretarial staff and/or reassignment of professional staff to work in an area not of their choosing. The manager may still feel the need to pursue funding but will be more understanding of the attitudes of others within the organization. The manager may also occasionally reject a funding opportunity that is clearly not in the best interests of or within the interest area of staff. Of course, if this occurs, informing staff about their decision is essential to creating the desired organizational climate.

Advocacy

Managers, in addition to performing other roles, should serve as advocates for staff, sometimes risking their own position of favor with higher-ups to battle for rights and privileges of staff members. It is very easy for leaders to slip quickly into a comfortable stance that entails courting the favor of superiors while showing little regard for the special interests of subordinates. They themselves are evaluated by superiors. The evaluations of subordinates generally represent little more than feedback. Rewards in the form of praise, promotion, and salary increases are given for compliance with the wishes of superiors, not for doing battle with them in an advocacy role. It is also easy to rationalize that, since the goodwill of a board of directors or a chief executive officer is generally desirable for all persons in an organization, avoidance of conflict as an advocate for subordinates is in everyone's best interests. Taken one step further, the best interests of the manager are synonymous with the best interests of subordinates, right? Not always. Managers who do not occasionally take a stand to advocate for staff interests are reneging on their job as a leader. They will eventually pay a price in the form of a loss of respect and confidence. Respect will only begin to be restored when they start advocating for staff interests in situations where they have nothing personally to gain and may even be inviting temporary disfavor of their superiors.

> *CASE EXAMPLE: THE COSTS OF*
> *MISSED LEADERSHIP OPPORTUNITY*
>
> Amber was a supervisor in a large day-care center that employed several social workers. In 1988, one of the social workers that she supervised, Jerome, was accused of sexually abusing a 4-year-old girl who was a client at the center. His

accuser, the child's parent, demanded an investigation. The local child-protection unit of the Department of Social Services thoroughly investigated the complaint, concluded that there was no indication that abuse had occurred, and closed the case for lack of evidence. No criminal charges were filed. Jerome, who had been suspended from work until he was cleared of charges, was reinstated. The director of the agency called him in and expressed her delight that Jerome, who was regarded as an excellent worker, had been found innocent. She asserted her complete confidence in him. She told both him and the rest of her staff that she felt that he was a victim of current hysteria about men in day-care that was occurring as a result of some widely publicized abuse charges in other states. Jerome returned to his job and again demonstrated the competence and dedication that had been reflected in his previous work.

In 1989 Jerome's former wife sued for custody of their 3-year-old daughter. In a deposition, she charged that Jerome had "inappropriately fondled" the child during a recent visit and that she suspected that he had been sexually abusing her in the past. She also initiated criminal charges against him that were reported in a Saturday edition of the local newspaper. A member of the board of directors, who knew about the previous charge, called the center's director at 7 A.M. on Saturday. The director immediately called Amber and demanded that she meet with Jerome at 9 o'clock Monday morning to learn more about the situation. Despite the fact that the newspaper notice gave few details and did not mention Jerome's place of employment, the director was fearful of a telephone call from a parent and wanted to have all available information to be able to respond to inquiries.

Amber was very anxious as she anticipated her meeting with Jerome. The meeting did not go well. Jerome had a ready explanation for his former wife's charges. Her sister had recently been involved in a divorce suit and had gained custody of her children after threatening to charge her husband with sexual abuse. Jerome unequivocally denied any wrongdoing. He explained that his former wife, who had threatened to "get" him anyway, was simply trying a tactic that had worked well for her sister. Amber felt herself getting very annoyed with Jerome's seeming lack of concern about the charges. She didn't seem to be able to get him to understand the potential harm that the allegations might cause the center. The conversation became especially heated when Jerome commented that he felt that Amber was "making a big deal over nothing." Exasperated, Jerome asked, "So, what do you expect me to do?" Amber replied, "Perhaps you should consider resigning. If the director asks for you resignation, I certainly will not support you." Jerome left and slammed the door. Later, the director expressed satisfaction with the way that Amber had handled the matter.

Jerome tendered his resignation. But before he left he gave the other staff his explanation of his wife's charges and also told them that Amber had requested his resignation. Three other professional staff members came to see Amber to request that she ask Jerome to reconsider. She stated simply that the decision was his and that the matter was closed.

On his last day on the job, Jerome came in to see Amber. He told her that he had generally been pleased with his job at the center and with her as his supervisor. But he felt he had not been treated fairly when his wife's charges were made public. In his opinion, Amber should have supported him since "people are considered innocent until proven guilty."

By this time, Amber was no longer angry with Jerome. She told him that she personally believed that he was innocent, as did the director and other staff. But as a manager, she had to consider the best interests of the center, which, she feared, could be destroyed by charges of sexual abuse. Amber spoke honestly and sincerely, but Jerome was not impressed. He left with a look of disgust, shaking his head. Amber was satisfied that the whole messy business was over. It was not.

Within the next three weeks, the other two men on the staff resigned. In their exit interviews, they told Amber that the job just wasn't worth the risk. They knew that, as males, they were particularly vulnerable to reputation-destroying charges of child abuse. But prior to Jerome's problems, they had believed that, if charged, the administration would come to their defense and support. They no longer believed this. They stated that they could not work for a leader who would not serve as their advocate when needed.

The departure of the three men and the general animosity of the remaining staff made Amber's job very difficult. She hired two new social workers (both female; no males applied) but both the two new employees quickly adopted the attitude toward Amber that the others exhibited. She suspected that they had been quickly "oriented" by Megan, the staff member who had been most openly hostile to her.

Amber held a special meeting of her staff to discuss morale problems. She stated that she felt that she owed them an explanation for her actions. She told them that, while she could not reveal the specifics of their conversations, she believed that Jerome's resignation was best for the center. Besides, she emphasized, she had *not* asked for his resignation; it had been his decision. Megan angrily replied that, obviously, Jerome had remembered it differently.

The meeting accomplished little. If anything, the staff were even more angry. When three additional months passed and she began to feel even more isolated from the group, Amber left to take another job. The staff clearly no longer trusted her and she felt that her ability to be an effective supervisor had been irreparably damaged.

Before she began her new job, Amber spent a good deal of time analyzing what had occurred and assuring herself that she would not repeat her mistakes. The director had expressed pleasure with the way that she had handled the problem with Jerome but, obviously, the director's impression of Amber was less important than the attitudes of her former staff members. They had been angry and disappointed because she had not "risked herself" to stand up for a member of her staff. To them, this meant that she could not be depended upon to serve as an advocate for them either. As a manager, she had failed to balance the interests of the center with the interests of her staff. She had suggested to them that she was primarily concerned with taking the "safe" course that was best for the center and for her. She had taken the easier route of antagonizing a subordinate rather than the more difficult one of risking a confrontation with her boss.

Still, as Amber thought about it, the staff's response seemed a little extreme. After a little while they should have "cut her some slack" and gotten over their anger. Then it occurred to Amber that she had not only failed as a manager but she had also failed as a social worker. She had reacted emotionally and judgmentally to Jerome's explanation, deciding that he should be more concerned over his troubles and angrily telling him what to do when direction was inappropriate. In her anger, she had also forgotten that, because she was Jerome's supervisor, her reply that "you should consider resigning" could very easily have been perceived as a demand for his resignation rather than merely the opinion of a colleague as she had intended it to be.

Amber determined that, in her new supervisory position, she would make every effort to balance advocacy for her staff with her perceptions of what was best for the agency, even if occasionally she found herself in disfavor with her boss. She also reminded herself that she was both a social worker and a manager and that her decisions and behavior as a manager should always be consistent with the values and ethics of the profession. If she expected others to adhere to them, she would have to lead by example.

Autonomy

Another characteristic of an organization with a healthy climate is the presence of considerable autonomy. In human service agencies where professional staff and other personnel frequently possess widely diverse knowledge and skills, the leader should seek to create an environment that fosters independence. The optimal level of independence is one in which persons are constrained in the use of their professional judgment no more than is absolutely necessary. The goal is to promote, not to stifle, creative decision making. A leader will need to sort out carefully those activities where creativity is not desirable and to set up appropriate controls (see Chapter 10). But in those circumstances where creativity can and should be employed, support for its exercise should be apparent. Staff will need to feel free to act without always consulting others first. As long as a decision or behavior is within policies and guidelines, staff members should be able to assume that they will be supported, even if things go wrong. The leader can be depended upon.

Communication

The nature and purpose of communication within an organization is a major factor in shaping its climate. Communication will occur in two forms. In its more desirable form, it will consist of information directly related to and supportive of the attainment of the objectives of the organization. For example, it may consist of policy information, advice on how to do a job, and feedback about progress toward desired ends.

A second form of communication that exists within organizations does not relate directly to achievement of objectives, but it most definitely impacts on it. It consists of emotional reactions to what is occurring within the organization and frequently includes negative attitudes that affect group and individual morale.

As a leader, the manager's task is to promote the flow of good, useful, supportive communication while limiting the flow of communication that is destructive of morale and that sidetracks individual and group energies that could be put to more constructive use. This would seem to be a goal that is easily attainable. But why do efforts to promote positive communication so often fail? The most obvious reason for communication failure is a carelessly initiated message sent by a manager. Assumptions on the manager's part are often the problem. Managers may assume that the receiver will understand the jargon that they use or they may assume that the receiver will want to understand. They may assume that staff members will read the bulletin board (they don't) or that a message transmitted verbally to one's immediate subordinate will be transferred without distortion to others down the communication channel. Managers may mistakenly believe that the receiver will read or hear the entire message before concluding what the essence of the communication is, or they may even assume that communication is unnecessary because "everyone already knows."

Communication of even well-constructed and well-initiated messages can break down and cause problems. Anyone who has ever played the childhood game where participants whisper a message from one person to another around a circle will recall that the message finally received back rarely bears much resemblance to the one given. This occurs without any malevolence or self-interest on the part of those doing the communication. Within organizations, "line loss" may be unintentional and a function of the number of times a message is transferred. Or it may result from an intentional selective emphasis, addition, or omission designed to modify the message to meet the needs of the person relaying it.

When formal channels are found to be untrustworthy, informal channels of communication inevitably will develop. Managers then usually have little control over what is transferred. It can become a dangerous combination of half-truths, rumors, and even information that is simply wrong. Worst of all, the manager may not even know what information is being sent along informal channels.

The fact that a power differential exists between a manager and subordinates can also lead to the manager being cut off from information. Managers have authority and power. They can take information and use it to harm those less powerful. Staff may wonder how information will be used by the manager. Will admission of a mistake or a request for help be construed as useful communication or will it be viewed as evidence of incompetence that will be brought up at evaluation time? If the latter is believed to be the case, communication with the manager will not occur.

How much and how accurately subordinates will communicate with a leader is largely dependent on past reactions to subordinates' communication. If subordinates reported bad news, was it responded to with anger and defensiveness as if the manager were being blamed for the problem? Was the messenger "beheaded," or was the messenger shown appreciation for the information? Did communication about a problem that another worker was having result in extra work for the messenger? Were confidences kept as requested, or did the manager reveal the source of information resulting in alienation of the messenger from his or her peers? (The author once registered dissatisfaction with a supervisor about a secretary's breach of confidentiality. The communciation was made with all assurances of anonymity. The next day, the secretary accosted the author with the statement, "I hear you don't like the way I do my job!") Such responses are destructive of trust for the manager and will almost certainly result in future elimination of or distortion of communication in the future. A reaction on the part of the communicator that says "I learned my lesson—next time I'll keep it to myself" only breeds and ever-growing cycle of distrust between managers and others within the organization.

The power differential can also be a deterrent to downward communication. Even a well-stated message can be misconstrued because of who initiated it and the sender's assumed intent. For example, a manager may intend to make a suggestion and may make one, but will the suggestion be perceived as an order? Or the request to be a little more careful about telephone and copy costs may be incorrectly perceived as a warning that a time of austerity and staff reduction is imminent.

Once again, we come back to that critical element for a healthy organizational climate and for effective management—trust. Both trust and distrust come from past experience. Trust that promotes productive and accurate communication must be built over time. Managers must learn to trust the information received from those both above and below them on the organizational chart. Managers must also communicate trust to others. A manager who displays little trust will eventually receive little trust in return. Suspicion, hostility, and resentment promote an in-kind response.

In a healthy work climate, trust fosters desirable communication. The leader communicates a belief that errors and problems will occur, but it is always best if those who must and will eventually know about them find out as soon as possible. Staff should understand that there is reward, not punishment, for good, accurate communication, regardless of the message. It is *failure* to communicate needed information that is undesirable behavior on the part of staff. The manager caught unaware of a problem has more reason to be irate with a subordinate than does the manager who was warned before time in dealing with superiors or a hostile public.

The attitude of a Theory Y manager toward communication is that it is a necessary and desirable vehicle that derives from the demands and expectations of a job. It is used to support the work of other staff and of managers themselves. This is a positive attitude based on the assumption that human beings value their work, want to perform well, and will use communication to help them achieve organization objectives. This attitude results in the use of communication for the mutual benefit of all staff in doing their jobs.

Unfortunately, communication is also used by managers with more of a Theory X orientation. They soon learn that communication can be a powerful vehicle for control and manipulation of staff. It also can be used to remind staff of their subordinate position. Withholding of information can concentrate power (knowledge *is* power) in the hands of the manager. Propaganda and misinformation can be used to change people. A manager can "leak" a possible future change to get a staff reaction before making a final decision or otherwise use communication in a way that is demeaning and manipulative.

A particularly destructive form of communication by some managers involves the use of confidants. Believing that staff are easily manipulated, managers have been known to confide in several different staff members, implying to each one that he or she is somehow special and uniquely worthy of trust. Managers may criticize and even ridicule other staff, or otherwise reveal confidences about other staff that are inappropriately shared. In the short run, this behavior can co-opt staff members who may be impressed and pleased with their "special" status. But before long, intelligent human beings notice that they are only one of several participants in the game. They conclude (correctly) that if the manager is critical of others to them, he or she is probably also critical of them to others. They feel manipulated and perceive that their intelligence has been insulted. They become resentful, and trust is eroded.

The prescription for the social worker as manager should be obvious. Avoid communicating information about problems of staff performance to persons other than the individuals themselves. If others must be consulted, it should be the manager's peers, or better yet, one's own supervisor. *Never* communicate to subordinates that they are any more "special" than any other staff person and avoid any overtures on the part of staff members to form a relationship that sets them apart from their peers. The temptation to use communication as power is tempting, but it should be avoided by the social worker as manager.

One type of communication essential to a healthy work climate is feedback, which tells managers, among other things, how well they are doing their job. It is definitely more pleasant to receive (and to give) good feedback than bad feedback, but both types of communication are essential. In their role as managers and functioning as leaders, social workers can easily slip into a pattern of weighing more heavily the information received from those who present a more positive, flattering picture of their leadership than information from those who are more critical. While we all state that we value feedback, we like the positive "strokes" and the messenger who delivers them more than the critical message and its messenger. But we may *need* to hear the voice of the outspoken critic even more.

There is a tendency on the part of some managers to surround themselves with people who think like they do and who clearly admire them and their work. The admiration may be genuine or it may be the flattery of a sycophant who hopes to profit by meeting the needs of the manager for flattery. Regardless of the case, a person who thinks and/or states that a manager is the most brilliant and skillful individual whom they have ever had the pleasure of knowing is really not a very useful source of information. Consciously or unconsciously, such people are likely to screen and shield the manager from needed criticism. They may also tend to impugn the motives of others who offer well-intended, unsolicited criticism to the manager. Social work managers must depend on subordinates as sources of information and feedback. If managers perceive that they are receiving many more compliments than critical questions, subordinates may not be doing their job. If managers find themselves listening primarily to those who think that they "hung the moon" and distancing themselves ever further from those who occasionally take the time and risk themselves to be critical, they should view this as a warning. Perhaps their need for compliments has become more important than the need for valid feedback. Social workers as managers need to know what they have done well so that they can do it again, but they also need to know when they make mistakes (and we all make them) so that they can avoid repeating them. They must make a constant effort to keep open all lines of communication, not just the ones that bring information that they like to hear.

SUMMARY

In our discussion of the fifth major function of the social worker as manager, leadership was described as the manager's conscious efforts to influence other persons within the organization to engage willingly in those behaviors that contribute to the attainment of organizational goals. We acknowledged that leadership overlaps with the other management functions and that, for many people, leadership and management are virtually synonymous.

Chapter 11 examined efforts to understand what makes some people good leaders while others are less successful in their leadership efforts. The contributions and shortcomings of the trait, behavioral, and contingency theories of leadership were summarized. The concept of followership was introduced and its relationship to leadership was discussed.

It was suggested that, in any situation, good leadership requires the creation and maintenance of an organizational climate that is conducive to goal attainment. The elements of that climate were proposed. They include respect, understanding, advocacy, autonomy, and positive communication.

REFERENCES

1. Ralph Stogdill, "Personal Factors Associated with Leadership," *Journal of Psychology*, 25 (1948):35–71.
2. E. E. Ghiselli, "Managerial Talent," *American Psychologist*, XVI (1963):632–641.
3. Fremont Kast and James Rosenzweig, *Organization and Management: A Systems Approach*, 2nd ed. (New York: McGraw-Hill, 1974), p. 349.
4. Robert Blake and Jane Mouton, *The Managerial Grid III: The Key to Leadership Excellence* (Houston, TX: Gulf Publishing Co., 1985).
5. Douglas McGregor, *The Human Side of Enterprise* (New York: McGraw-Hill, 1960).
6. Stogdill, "Personal Factors," op. cit.
7. Ralph Stogdill, *Handbook of Leadership: A Survey of Theory and Research* (New York: Free Press, 1974).
8. Reginald York, "Can Change Be Effectively Managed?" *Administration in Social Work*, I(2), (Summary 1977):196.
9. Fred Fiedler, *A Theory of Leadership Effectiveness* (New York: McGraw-Hill, 1967).
10. Karen Kuehner, "Followership." Presentation at the National Eligibility Workers Association Annual Training Conference, New York, August 18, 1987.
11. Michael Austin, "Managing Up: Relationship Building Between Middle Management and Top Management." Presentation at the National Association of Social Workers Annual Conference. New Orleans, September 12, 1987.

ADDITIONAL READINGS

Brilliant, E. "Social Work Leadership: A Missing Ingredient?" *Social Work*, 31 (1986):325–331.

Fiedler, F. *A Theory of Leadership Effectiveness*. New York: McGraw-Hill, 1967.

Fiedler, F. *New Approaches to Effective Leadership*. New York: Wiley, 1987.

Hunt, J., and Larson, L., eds. *Leadership Frontiers*. Kent, OH: Kent State University Press, 1975.

Hunt, J. *Managing People at Work*, 2nd. New York: McGraw-Hill, 1986.

Kleinschrod, W. "The Mystique of Leadership." *Administrative Management*, 48 (1987):41.

Mintzberg, H. *Power In and Around Organizations*. Englewood Cliffs, NJ: Prentice-Hall, 1983.

Perlmutter, F., and Slavin, S. *Leadership In Social Administration*. Philadelphia: Temple University Press, 1980.

Tannenbaum, R. *Leadership and Organization*. New York: Garland Publishing, 1987.

Wolf, M., Keyser, D., and Aurner, R. *Effective Communication In Business*. Cincinnati: South-Western Publishing Company, 1979.

York, R., and Hastings, T. "Worker Maturity and Supervisory Leadership Behavior." *Administration in Social Work*, 9 (1985/86):37–47.

Yukl, G. *Leadership in Organizations*. Englewood Cliffs, NJ: Prentice-Hall, 1981.

PART III

Other Variables That Influence Management

Our understanding of the role of manager would not be complete without a recognition that certain other influences outside the control of the manager can greatly affect one's ability to manage. Chapter 12 looks at human factors that frequently enter in. Managers and the staff with whom they work are people. As such, they are subject to the phenomena that affect all kinds of human interaction. Women or ethnic minority managers are especially likely to encounter problems of discrimination that can become an obstacle to their ability to manage. But all of us are potential victims of stereotypes and prejudice. Other human factors in management (management style, management stress, and social interaction issues) are also discussed in Chapter 12.

Chapter 13 looks at some situations that occur frequently in human service agencies and that greatly affect the role of the social worker as manager. The need for rapid or major change, an inevitable part of life in social work practice, receives special attention. In earlier chapters, the importance of a manager developing a reputation for objectivity and for being trustworthy were emphasized. These characteristics take on even greater importance in the situations discussed in Chapter 13.

CHAPTER 12

Human Factors

In our discussion to this point of the management functions of the social worker we have focused upon the knowledge, values, and skills that are conducive to good management. We have also suggested that the identity of managers themselves, as unique human beings, influences how successfully or unsuccessfully they are able to plan, staff, organize, control, and lead. A manager's identity is strongly influenced by both demographic characteristics and by the life experiences that have shaped the manager's personality. In this chapter we will examine how these factors can be both supportive of and a hindrance to a social worker's capacity to manage.

THE IMPORTANCE OF DIFFERENCES
FOR MANAGEMENT

An individual's demographic characteristics as well as his or her life experiences must be regarded as a given. As social workers, we also recognize that significant personality change is possible, but very difficult. So why bother to examine the influence of variables that are essentially "set"? For one thing, recognition of who we are and how we are likely to be perceived by others within an organization allows us to understand and to anticipate some of the problems that may arise. It helps to explain why people react the way they do to us as managers. It can help us to understand how sometimes success comes so easily in our role as manager and why, on other occasions, staff respond with resistance, suspicion, resentment, and other less-than-desirable responses to perfectly appropriate management behaviors. Understanding of human variables that affect management may also provide social workers as managers with hints as to how they might overcome some of the personal animosity that invariably exists within organizations where human beings must interact.

Demographic characteristics of the manager undoubtedly influence a person's capacity to manage. In our society, as in any society, it *does* make a difference whether an individual is male or female, younger or older. It matters whether others are members of an ethnic minority group or not or whether they have physical or other characteristics that may make them appear to be different or similar to other staff. Social workers are well aware of the fact that a person's perceived membership in a subgroup affects the ways in which others react to that person. In our professional education, we devote a considerable amount of course time to examining discrimination and its effects on the social functioning of human beings. We seek better ways to help clients who are victims of discrimination.

A manager's ability to function (to manage) is likely to be affected by discrimination. For example, a manager's identity as a woman or a man or as white, black, Latino, native American, or a member of some other group can affect the way staff members relate to that person. It can be either a plus or a minus for the social worker as manager. Managers can either benefit or suffer from staff discrimination, dependent in part on whether they are perceived as similar to or different from other staff members.

Discrimination is basically a neutral word. It simply means that it is possible to notice difference. As practitioners, as managers, and as staff relating to higher-level managers, social workers need to recognize differences in people and to relate appropriately to these differences. Recognition of difference is essential for good practice and for good management, a point that we stressed in earlier chapters. As managers, it allows us to appreciate the special attributes of staff and to use them most effectively. It also is essential that staff discriminate in their relationships with managers; that is, that they be able to recognize the characteristics of managers that make them unique as human beings and learn how best to relate to them (part of good followership). However, as we know, discrimination is more likely to have negative consequences than positive ones. There is a big difference between recognizing differences and *appreciating* them (the positive) and recognizing differences and, based on them, making erroneous stereotypes and treating people in *less desirable* ways (negative discrimination). This latter form of discrimination is the one that social workers see most often and the one that they endeavor to confront and eliminate.

The social worker as manager cannot afford to engage in negative discriminatory behavior toward staff. We emphasized this in our discussion of staffing issues. It is professionally unethical and puts the organization at risk for legal action. It is also just poor management that will inevitably destroy trust and the social worker's effectiveness in performing management functions.

Are social workers as managers victimized by negative forms of discrimination directed against them? Definitely. Articles and entire books are devoted to the problems of women and minority managers,[1] topics that we will only briefly address in this text. To better understand the negative forms of discrimination that affect managers, it is useful to examine carefully two related terms, *prejudice* and *stereotype*. Prejudice has been defined as "interpersonal hostility that is directed against individuals based on their membership in a minority group."[2] It relates to a negative feeling or attitude about people based on their group membership—for example, because they are old, black, female, handicapped, etc. A stereotype is closely related but slightly different. It results from a *cognitive* (rather than emotional) function. It is really a cognitive breakdown. A stereotype can be viewed as a standardized, overgeneralized mental picture representing an uncritical judgment based on group membership. A stereotype denies or fails to recognize individual difference; it suggests an inability to individualize in one's perception of another person.

Traditionally, we have tended to believe that the negative forms of discrimination (treating others in a less desirable way based on their perceived membership in a minority group) have occurred because people hold prejudices that cause them to engage in stereotyping. Levin and Levin dispute this notion, suggesting instead that negative discrimination provides its own rewards (economic, social, intrapersonal), and that we use stereotypes and prejudices to justify practices of negative discrimination.[3] Their position has a certain compelling logic within our study of management. Hasn't it been profitable for white males to treat women and minorities as second-class citizens within organizations? Are such stereotypes as "women don't make good managers" or "a black person can't supervise a white person" only a rationalization for discriminatory practices that benefit white males? Perhaps. Whether discrimination results from or results in prejudice and discrimination is an interesting philosophical question, but one that is not critical to the social worker as manager. What *is* important is an understanding that who one is can affect how well one is able to perform the functions of manager. As managers, we need to be able to recognize the prejudices, stereotypes, and, most importantly, the behaviors of other staff (discrimination) that can impinge on our ability to manage and to be able to minimize their effects.

Forms and Consequences of Discrimination

Historically and to this day, managers have been hindered by several types of undesirable treatment if they were female or a member of certain ethnic groups or held some other form of minority group status. Both subordinates and superiors have treated them in ways that have hindered their ability to manage. Being a woman or a minority (and, sometimes, being a man) can present certain problems for the social worker as manager. Being a member of more than one group (who isn't?) can result in even greater jeopardy. We will examine some different forms that discrimination based on a manager's demographic characteristics can take.

Forms of Discrimination That Affect Managers

Usually when we think of discrimination we think of a type of behavior that excludes or denies an individual access to something to which he or she is entitled. The obvious forms of denial such as discriminatory pay scales and limited access to promotions have especially affected women and minorities in both human services and in all other sectors of the job market.[4] Social workers' ability to manage is undoubtedly affected by the rewards that they receive (or don't receive) and their perception of their potential for upward mobility. But the denial of access that can most directly affect people's capacity to perform their management functions is the denial of needed *information*. If, for example, superiors or subordinates do not provide to a woman manager the details of a particularly messy situation that exists within an organization, they can be hindering her ability to make good management decisions that relate to it. The shut off or limiting of information may be deliberate and designed to hinder her ability to function as a manager. It may also be paternalistic, seeking to "spare" her based on stereotypes about her "sensitivity" or "tendency toward emotionality." Or it may result from her lack of membership in the "old boys' network" where valuable information is exchanged over a golf game or at informal males-only social hours after work on Friday afternoons.

The lack of informal social contacts with manager-peers and other staff can be particularly problematic for the woman or minority manager. Of course, male social workers in an organization where they feel socially cut off by a predominantly female staff can experience the same type of information shortage. Managers need good information (and a lot of it) to do their job. Formal communication by way of memos and other such vehicles are not enough to be "on top of" situations and to be able to engage in sound decision making. Managers need both formal and informal information; social isolation tends to deny them access to the latter.

Another problem often faced by social workers as managers relates to perceptions of their management behaviors based on their demographic characteristics. They may be doing or saying exactly what other managers are doing or saying, but will it be perceived in the same way? For example, because of the persistent negative stereotypes of women as disorganized, inefficient, and emotional, interpretations of the same behavior may be much

Impressions From An Office

The family picture is on HIS desk:	The family picture is on HER desk:
Ah, a solid, responsible family man.	Umm, her family will come before her career.
HIS desk is cluttered:	**HER desk is cluttered:**
He's obviously a hard worker and a busy man.	She's obviously a disorganized scatterbrain.
HE is talking with his co-workers:	**SHE is talking with her co-workers:**
He must be discussing the latest deal.	She must be gossiping.
HE's not at his desk:	**SHE's not at her desk:**
He must be at a meeting.	She must be in the ladies' room.
HE's not in the office:	**SHE's not in the office:**
He's meeting customers.	She must be out shopping.
HE's having lunch with the boss:	**SHE's having lunch with the boss:**
He's on his way up.	They must be having an affair.
The boss criticized HIM:	**The boss criticized HER:**
He'll improve his performance.	She'll be very upset.
HE got an unfair deal:	**SHE got an unfair deal:**
Did he get angry?	Did she cry?
HE's getting married:	**SHE's getting married:**
He'll get more settled.	She'll get pregnant and leave.
HE's having a baby:	**SHE's having a baby:**
He'll need a raise.	She'll cost the company money in maternity benefits.
HE's going on a business trip:	**SHE's going on a business trip:**
It's good for his career.	What does her husband say?
HE's leaving for a better job:	**SHE's leaving for a better job:**
He knows how to recognize a good opportunity.	Women are undependable.

Figure 12.1. Perceptions of Behavior: Male and Female Managers (Source: Natasha Josefowitz, *Paths to Power*, © 1980, Addison-Wesley Publishing Co., Inc., Reading, Massachusetts. Fig. on page 60. Reprinted with permission.)

How to tell a Businessman
from a Businesswoman

A businessman is aggressive;
a businesswoman is pushy.
He is careful about details;
she is picky.
He loses his temper because
he's so involved in his job;
she's bitchy.
He's depressed (or hung over),
so everyone tiptoes past his office;
she's moody, so it must be
her time of the month.
He follows through;
she doesn't know when to quit.
He's firm;
she's stubborn.
He makes wise judgements;
she reveals her prejudices.
He is a man of the world;
she's been around.
He isn't afraid to say what he thinks;
she's opinionated.
He exercises authority;
she's tyrannical.
He's discreet;
she's sensitive.
He's a stern taskmaster;
she's difficult to work for.

Figure 12.2. CB/ZAK Enterprizes, San Francisco, CA (Poster).

more negative for women than for men. (See Figures 12.1 and 12.2.) Similarly, older managers who become angry at staff incompetence may have their warranted and appropriate reprimand of a staff member dismissed as simply another sign that they are getting "old and irritable." Black managers may have their appropriate enforcement of rules and procedures interpreted as indicating that they are meeting some intrapersonal need to exert control over white staff. White male managers' concerned efforts to orient a new female staff member to her job responsibilities may be perceived as paternalistic or condescending or, even worse, as an effort to become overly familiar with her.

Staff will inevitably engage in some stereotyping based on the characteristics of the manager, whatever those characteristics are. Unfortunately, the stereotypes are almost always accompanied by negative types of discrimination. They may result in the manager being taken less seriously than he or she should be or in certain erroneous assumptions about the manager that can only result in problems in interaction with staff. Whenever superiors, peers, and subordinates relate to the social work manager as a member of a group and fail to individualize the person who is that manager, trouble is waiting to happen. Some other examples of dangerous and erroneous stereotypes based on a manager's group membership that staff may have might include:

1. The manager (female) doesn't really need the job and will probably leave soon anyway.
2. The manager (physical handicap) probably got the job to meet affirmative action requirements.
3. The manager (white male) was probably not the best-qualified for promotion to supervisor and got the job through unfair advantage.
4. The manager (older employee) will not be able to handle the pressure when the workload gets heavy.
5. The manager (younger employee) will not be able to command the respect of senior subordinates.
6. The manager (Latino) was hired to placate the community and probably knows nothing about management.
7. The manager (a former beauty pageant winner) is probably not very bright and was hired for her appearance.
8. The manager (a supervisor for 15 years) has probably reached his or her level of incompetence.
9. The manager (a retired military officer) will excessively dominate and control the staff.
10. The manager (Jewish) will probably show favoritism to staff who are also Jewish.

The message to the social worker as manager should be clear. No matter what demographic characteristics managers possess, staff will inevitably hold some stereotypes about them, especially when they first assume the role of manager. Stereotypes can encourage behavior that can harm one's capacity to manage and have the potential to erode the trust that we have emphasized as so important to good management. Managers *should* be able to fulfill their role expectations as managers without having the motivation for their behavior erroneously interpreted by staff with reference to their demographic characteristics. But if stereotypes about the manager exist, the management functions of the social worker are likely to be misunderstood and even resented.

All of our examples of stereotyping have been negative because any time our behaviors as managers are misread, we are likely to have problems. Of course, on rare occasions, erroneous stereotypes based on the characteristics of the manager can be positive. For example, the older manager initially may be assumed to be very knowledgeable and experienced; the retired military officer may be assumed to be a good leader; the woman or ethnic minority manager may be assumed to be especially competent to have "beaten the odds" against moving up in the organization, or the white male may be assumed to be well qualified to supervise the all-female staff. The younger manager may be assumed to possess a high energy level; the supervisor with 15 years' experience must really know his or her job, etc., etc. These stereotypes can work to the manager's advantage, at least in the short run. But what if the manager doesn't live up to the stereotype based on demographic characteristics? For example, individuals may not possess the attributes that they were assumed to have; their strengths as managers may lie elsewhere. Stereotypes (even the positive ones) can result in disappointment and disillusionment when they are found to have little basis in reality.

Social workers as managers must help staff members see beyond the demographic characteristics of themselves as managers. This is *not* to suggest that good management necessarily involves baring one's soul to staff or revealing more than the manager wishes of his or her personal self. It does suggest, however, that managers should be open about themselves *as managers*, their philosophies of management, their style, and even, on occasion, what they perceive to be their weaknesses and strengths. Staff seek an environment of management certainty in which to do their jobs. They want to know what they can expect from the manager in the way of behavior; they should not have to rely on assumptions that may be based on stereotypes about the manager's demographic characteristics.

Letting staff see and recognize the uniqueness of the social worker as manager will reduce some of the liabilities faced by managers who tend to be victims of stereotyping, prejudice, and discrimination. The social work manager of the 1990s and into the early twenty-first century must assume that, for example, being a manager and a woman or a manager and a member of an ethnic minority group will continue to create special problems. Fortunately, a large amount of empirical research is being conducted that should provide both insight and assistance in dealing with these problems. The literature (some of which is noted at the end of this chapter) can be of help.

MANAGEMENT STYLE

As social workers, managers are aware of the importance of life experiences and their shaping effects on the personality of human beings. As managers, our management style cannot help but be an extension of our personalities. How we plan, staff, organize, control, and lead will generally reflect a close resemblance to our approach to the other tasks of life. Management style and behavior should reflect a comfortable compromise between the manager's personality and the specific management requirements of the situation.

The reader will recall that we described different approaches to planning (Chapter 4) and controlling (Chapter 10) as menus. The implication of this way of conceptualizing management activities is that there are a variety of ways to get a job done. For example, the manager can select between rules and policies to perform a given task of planning. The situation may well dictate the better choice. But another important variable to consider in the selection process is the personality of the manager. Managers who select a type of plan from the planning menu (Chapter 4) that is clearly out of character will not be likely to use it well and run a high risk of failure. They also may jeopardize their credibility and trust among staff as they appear to be trying to be someone whom they are not.

The prescription for the social worker as manager is the same as for any successful social work practitioner—"know thyself." In earlier chapters we emphasized the importance of selecting approaches to management tasks that are logical extensions of the social worker's personality. But how can we zero in on just who we are as persons and as managers? Several theorists have attempted to identify management "types" that occur in organizations. (We alluded to one such polarization in the previous chapter when we discussed Theory X and Theory Y.) The various typologies tend to present extreme forms of management style. We can see elements of ourselves in them, but they really may not describe where many of us fall (in the middle) with occasional digressions into either extreme, based largely on the management needs of the situation. A hint of our managerial style can be identified in response to our preferences to questions that we might ask ourselves. For example:

1. In response to a hostile task environment, do we find it more natural to buffer it out or to attempt to "win it over"?
2. Are we most sympathetic to and do we see the most logic in scientific management, administrative management, or bureaucratic management theories? How comfortable are we with participative management approaches that allow others to share in decision making?
3. When we plan, do we prefer plans such as rules that allow for little discretion in staff decision making or do we choose plans that maximize staff use of autonomy and professional discretion?
4. Do we prefer to work with staff with similar professional credentials, or are we comfortable with a variety of types of staff and the unique contributions and potential problems that they bring? Where do we stand on "professionalizing" the organization?
5. How supportive of professional growth are we? Do we see the professional career development of staff members as our responsibility, even if it results in their sometimes moving beyond us or outside the organization? Do we place more value on locals or cosmopolitans?

6. What is our attitude toward staff evaluation and personnel actions? Do we welcome them as opportunities to promote growth and to influence the quality of services offered or do we approach them with dread, fearing resentment and anger from staff?

7. Can we accept and appreciate staff who appear to be motivated by factors different from our own sources of motivation, or do we wish for and work to shape our staff into people who are more like us?

8. Do we welcome and support group cohesiveness? Do we recognize the existence and value of an informal organization and of occasional conflict with staff or do these make us feel uncomfortable? Do we see communication as a means to promote effective work or a way to control staff?

9. Do we prefer to rely almost exclusively on line authority or are we comfortable in use of staff and functional authority whenever they seem possible?

10. Do we prefer to exercise a considerable amount of direct control through use of such methods as orders and rules or do we prefer to exercise the minimum control necessary and to appear less controlling by using methods such as advice and information and policies?

11. How do we perceive the relative importance of support and structure for good leadership?

Our personality and its reflection in our management style rest somewhere along a continuum between controlling and untrusting on one extreme and laid-back and trusting on the other. Kotin and Sharaf referred to those who are "tight" administrators and those who are "loose" as being the two extreme types.[5] They noted that tight administrators use formal reminders of their status differential, clear-cut delegation of authority and responsibility, reliance on rules and traditions, adherence to the hierarchical chain of command, and formal communication through regular meetings, memos, reports, and forms. On the opposite end of the continuum, loose administrators use primarily informal reminders of status differential, rarely fall back on rules and traditions to influence, bypass the chain of command when desirable, prefer informal communication methods, and show a capacity to tolerate some role ambiguity related to a lack of clearly designated roles, responsibility, and authority.

While the social worker's overall management style is largely a product of personality, it should also be emphasized that both growth and flexibility in the social worker's approaches to management are desirable. The manager who can comfortably be tough and authoritarian when needed and who also can be tolerant and supportive when required has some definite advantages over other managers who have a more limited repertoire. The observation that, as a person, we may naturally tend to prefer a more controlling or a more laid-back approach to management does not absolve us from working toward the successful use of opposite approaches. The truly skilled manager has become comfortable with the entire menu of approaches and can use them as the situation indicates. In Chapter 13 we will examine a few situations that strongly suggest the need for specific management approaches. They are the *best* way to address a situation, regardless of the natural predilections of the manager's personality.

STRESSES INHERENT IN MANAGEMENT

In their roles as managers, social workers will necessarily experience a certain amount of stress that "goes with the territory." Even direct practitioners who devote relatively little of their day to the functions of management (as opposed to, for example, executive directors engaged in management functions most of every day) experience these stresses from time to time.

What type of stresses occur with management activities? For one thing, social workers as managers cannot assume the comfortable position of "we" (the practitioner) and "they" (the administrator) that frequently is available to the social worker who is delivering services to clients. As managers, they will experience some of the resentment generally reserved for those higher up in the administration. Both staff and clients are likely to vent frustration on the manager, particularly within highly bureaucratized organizations. The manager can easily feel caught in the middle of conflicts that inevitably occur between lower-level staff and upper-level administrators. It sometimes can be troubling for social workers as managers to know that, in their role, they *are* part of the establishment that they may have complained about so often. This can leave managers in a state of conflicting loyalties (to peers? to the organization?). The role of manager forces one to assume a new perspective and to think and act like "management."

Many social workers enter the profession because they seek the rewards that come from helping individual clients and client groups directly. The functions of management can be time-consuming and can cause managers to be frustrated in their desire to work with clients. They may resent the work behind the desk that denies them client access. As managers, they may have to spend sizable parts of their day in completing paperwork or in seeing only other professionals. They also may be keenly aware of the limited resources available to assist both staff and clients and may feel frustrated that they cannot offer more help.

Managers make many decisions each day. This can be stressful. As managers, social workers may feel very alone in their decision making and in taking responsibility for its consequences. They may not have a supervisor to take on the ultimate responsibility for the consequences of their decisions. Some of the decisions (for example, staff evaluations) that are made autonomously may carry major impact on the lives and careers of staff, a realization that can result in stress. When social workers assume authority for such decisions in their roles as managers, they are likely to be placed in interpersonal conflict with staff members, a situation that may be especially stressful for them. They may dislike the use of certain types of authority but may feel compelled to exercise them anyway in the interest of good management practice.

Many of the stresses that accompany the role of manager can be summed up in one word—isolation. As a manager, a basically gregarious individual may feel cut off from friends and co-workers. This person may feel the need to establish and maintain a certain professional distance from staff. Staff may naturally distance themselves from the manager as the manager begins to be perceived by staff in a different way. It is possible to be an effective manager and a beloved co-worker, but it doesn't happen very often. A degree of isolation cannot be avoided. For many social workers, this is the greatest source of stress in their role as manager.

SOCIALIZING WITH STAFF

Inevitably, social workers as managers must reconcile their need to work in a cordial and mutually supportive environment with their need as managers to be perceived as fair, objective, and trustworthy people. As a co-worker, both informal interaction and socializing (fraternization) done during working hours and outside of them are natural, pleasurable, and generally innocuous behaviors. In the role of manager, however, the issue of how much to be personally involved with staff is a difficult one. Intimate personal relationships between managers and those that, for example, they supervise and evaluate are almost universally discouraged. Many organizations have rules or at least policies that seem to recognize the potential role conflicts that exist when intense personal relationships and professional relationships exist simultaneously. But is all socializing with staff to be discouraged? Can a manager be both friend to a staff member and an effective manager? There are no simple answers.

All of a manager's functions are facilitated if the manager is perceived as objective and worthy of trust. Friendships with staff that go beyond job requirements have the potential to lead to staff members questioning these characteristics of the manager. On the other hand, aloofness and deliberate efforts to keep a social distance from staff can also erode feelings of trust in the manager. People that we don't know at all are likely to be perceived as untrustworthy and unpredictable. These are not impressions that are conducive to good management. So, what is an appropriate mix of friendship and distance between manager and staff? The answer is, as in most management issues, it depends. Some managers are able to maintain close personal relationships with staff, yet their objectivity when it comes to, for example, staff evaluations remains unquestioned. For other managers, even a little socializing can lead to a challenging of their objectivity. As social workers, we know that the different capacities of people involved in any human interaction affect its meaning to them and how it is perceived by others. Socialization between managers and other staff is no different.

The manager seeking to establish the ideal balance in regard to socializing with staff that promotes a staff perception of objectivity and trust must give serious thought to three questions and their most likely answers:

1. To what degree can *I* be involved in friendship relationships with staff without it compromising my ability to be objective?
2. To what degree can the other person (each person must be considered individually) be involved in a friendship relationship with me without that person relating differently (inappropriately) in some way to me in my role as manager?
3. To what degree will others' perception of my objectivity and trustworthiness be affected because of my friendship relationship with a staff member, regardless of how well the two of us are able to handle it?

The first question can be addressed primarily through self-analysis. Managers must determine whether they can make the necessary role shifts as required. For example, can they have dinner at the home of a staff member on Sunday and evaluate or, if necessary, reprimand that same person on Monday? Few of us could do this without compromising our ability to be objective and to manage effectively. But some people *could* attend a staff party and have little trouble in shifting to the managerial role. Others could not even do this. Some managers choose to have no outside-the-office contact with staff because they recognize that socializing would be likely to limit their ability to manage. They deliberately avoid any outside friendships with those with whom they work. Any of these behaviors can be appropriate, based on managers' knowledge of themselves and their capacities.

Even if the manager is perfectly capable of making necessary role switches, the other individual involved may not be, or may attempt to use a friendship to manipulate the manager's behavior. Some staff will easily recognize the different roles that must be played and will make the shift accordingly. Others may inadvertently or intentionally let the roles blur a little. They may attempt to use a friendship or a shared social occasion to their advantage, either by applying pressure to the supervisor ("I thought we were friends!'') or by implying that a "special" relationship exists to other staff. Any socializing or implication of a personal friendship should probably be avoided with this type of individual. Letting down of barriers may be perceived as an opportunity for exploitation and manipulation.

Managers may be able to "switch hats" with total assurance that their objectivity in relating to staff will not be compromised. The staff member with whom they have a social relationship may likewise recognize the need for strict role differentiation and be able to accomplish it. In fact, the social relationship with one or more staff members may be totally independent from and in no way impinge on manager-staff relationships. But other staff may not *perceive* this to be the case. Their perception may be reason enough to avoid the friendship with a subordinate. After all, what is perceived to be true might as well be true in terms of its consequences.

Many reasons exist why other staff members might perceive that a friendship with a subordinate is a problem, even when the two parties involved in the friendship have completely worked through their respective relationships. There is a natural tendency of staff to assume that managers have favorites and give preferential treatment. Unfortunately, they are often correct. Speculation on who is the favorite (office gossip) is interesting grist for dull days. Those who are not receiving good evaluations or are being passed over for promotion may have a special need to rationalize to themselves and to others why they are not receiving more positive feedback. ("Maybe I should start getting together socially with them. I might get better evaluations!")

Even the staff member/friend can suffer when these perceptions exist among staff. Rewards and kudos that are legitimately earned and objectively awarded by the manager will tend to be discounted by other staff members, especially those who are jealous and/or not happy with their own rewards. They may be looking for excuses to criticize the manager anyway. ("I guess we know why they got it, don't we!")

The friend's relationships with other staff can be affected in one of two ways. Some staff members may become inordinately friendly to the person, hoping to become more friendly with the manager themselves or to get the staff member/friend to speak well of them to the manager. Others may resent and shun the person for no legitimate reason. Good communication and collegial working relationships can be damaged or can be prevented from developing.

Managers must be certain that they, the other individual, and all other staff members can tolerate a social relationship with a subordinate. Can they establish the relationship without damaging their reputation for objectivity and trust, so essential for good management practice? If not, socializing much beyond attendance at mandatory staff functions is probably a dangerous practice. But then so can refusal to socialize, which appears to be a pompous reminder of a status differential!

The decision as to how much socializing (both on the job and off) is good and healthy for organizational goal achievement is a difficult one. It will depend in large part on the individual personalities of those involved. For every manager in every work situation, there is a socializing threshold that, if crossed, can hinder the manager's capacity to manage. Finding just where that threshold is (and it changes over time and situations) and not crossing it requires extreme sensitivity on the part of managers. They need to know and understand both themselves and other employees. The special insights into human behavior possessed by the social worker are a real asset in this endeavor.

SUMMARY

In our overview of some of the "people" variables that influence a social worker's capacity to perform the function of management, we have emphasized that, no matter what the demographic characteristics of managers, they are subject to problems of stereotyping, prejudice, and discrimination. Problems of women and minority managers are particularly prevalent. Social workers as managers may need to help staff look beyond outward characteristics and to recognize their individual characteristics as managers.

Management style was described as a logical extension of the manager's life experiences and personality. It should be comfortable, but also dynamic and open to growth. Questions were asked that would assist managers to better identify their place on the management style continuum. The continuum was seen as ranging between controlling and untrusting on one end and laid-back and trusting on the other.

The major stresses inherent in the functions of management were identified. Discussion of a particularly troublesome one, isolation from other staff, led to an in-depth look at the issue of the advisability of maintaining both social and professional relationships with staff. Questions were proposed to assist the manager in determining when socializing is and is not recommended.

In the next and final chapter we will look at one more piece in the complicated puzzle that is management. Several situational variables that influence the management functions of the social worker will be examined.

REFERENCES

1. Roslyn Chernesky and Marcia Bombyk, "Women's Ways and Effective Management," *Affilia*, III (1988):48–61; B. A. Stead, ed., *Women in Management* (Englewood Cliffs, NJ: Prentice-Hall, 1985); A. Herbert, "The Minority Administrator: Problems, Prospects and Challenges," in *Social Administration: The*

Management of the Social Services, Vol. 1, Simon Slavin, ed. (New York: The Haworth Press, 1985), pp. 212–224.

2. Jack Levin and William Levin, *The Functions of Discrimination and Prejudice* (New York: Harper & Row, 1982), p. 65.

3. Ibid., pp. 81–89.

4. Jacqueline Sutton, "Sex Discrimination Among Social Workers," *Social Work*, *XXVII*(3), (May 1982):211–217.

5. Joel Kotin and Myron Sharaf, "Management Succession and Administrative Style," *Psychiatry*, XXX (1967):237–248.

ADDITIONAL READINGS

Benokraitis, N., and Feagin, J. *Modern Sexism*. Englewood Cliffs, NJ: Prentice-Hall, 1986.

Braiker, B. "The Secret of Psychological Stamina." *Working Woman*, September 1986, pp. 129–132, 155.

Carr-Ruffino, N. "How Do You Rate as a Manager?" *Executive Female*, 10, 1987, pp. 47–50.

Chernesky, R. "The Sex Dimension of Organizational Processes: Its Impact on Women Managers. In *Social Administration: The Management of the Social Services*, Vol. 1. S. Slavin, ed. New York: The Haworth Press, 1985, pp. 225–236.

Dobbins, G., and Platz, S. "Sex Differences in Leadership: How Real Are They?" *Academy of Management Review*, 29 (1986):118–125.

Harvey, S., and Raider, M. "Administrator Burnout." *Administration in Social Work*, 8 (1984):81–90.

Levin, J., and Levin, W. *The Functions of Discrimination and Prejudice*. New York: Harper & Row, 1982.

Moore, L. L., ed. *Not as Far as You Think: The Realities of Working Women*. Lexington, MA: Lexington Books, 1986.

Purcell, J. "Mapping Management Styles in Employee Relations." *Journal of Management Study*, 24 (1987):533–548.

Rincon, E. L., and Keys, C. "The Latino Social Service Administrator: Development Tasks and Management Concerns." In *Social Administration: The Management of the Social Services*, Vol. 1. S. Slavin, ed. New York: Haworth Press, 1985, pp. 237–250.

Stead, B. A. *Women in Management*. Englewood Cliffs, NJ: Prentice-Hall, 1985.

Wright, R., King, S., and Berg, W. "Job Satisfaction in the Workplace: A Study of Black Females in Management Positions." *Journal of Social Service Research*, 8 (1985): 65–79.

York, R., Henley, H., and Gamble, D. "Barriers to the Advancement of Women in Social Work Administration." *Journal of Social Service Research*, 9 (1985):1–15.

CHAPTER 13

Situational Factors

In the last chapter we examined how the characteristics and personalities of managers and staff can influence the functions of management. The "people" variables in management are extremely important for social workers as managers to identify and to take into account. But a second group of factors, the specialized situations that exist in human service organizations, are of at least equal importance. Managers must be able to recognize them, consider alternatives, and adapt their management behaviors accordingly. In this chapter we will look at a small sampling of situations commonly faced by social workers as managers that influence the activities of planning, staffing, organizing, controlling, and leading.

ECONOMIC AUSTERITY

In many human service organizations, tight funding seems to be more the rule than the exception. People who have worked more than a few years in our profession have heard on many occasions references to "hard times ahead" and impending funding and staff cutbacks. They may sometimes wonder if such warnings are not little more than alarmist utterings by manipulative administrators seeking to justify their tightfisted style of management and to strike fear in the hearts of staff who are not performing up to standard. Undoubtedly, administrators have occasionally used scenarios of economic austerity as means to threaten and control. But frequently (and unfortunately) the threat of doing as much or even more with fewer resources is real. Both the nature of social work practice and attitudes frequently held by the general public virtually guarantee that economic austerity is an ever-impending threat if not a current reality. Historically, social workers like to point to the high priorities put on social services during the Lyndon Johnson administration as "the good old days." Programs and staff were rapidly expanding along with generous allocation of government funds. While emphasis on accountability and federal cutbacks in financial support for human services did not impact as heavily on some areas as others in the years that followed, conditions have never been as good. The Reagan years in particular provided managers with plenty of experience in managing under conditions of economic austerity.

Is managing during a time of real and threatened reduction of funding really that different from managing during better times? Yes and no. The tasks and principles of management remain the same, but during economic austerity the need for good management is even greater and the margin for error is even smaller. Efficiency becomes critical; waste in the use of limited resources (personnel, funds, facilities, supplies, etc.) cannot be permitted. Challenges to the identity of the client as the prime beneficiary are likely to be more frequent and more persistent. This is especially true for those organizations whose clients are not among society's favorites; for example, the poor or the mentally ill. A more watchful and a more threatening task environment may loom over the organization. It must be dealt with repeatedly and with tact.

Which changes in emphasis in the planning tasks of management are likely to occur during a time when an organization faces economic austerity? Selections from the planning menu may reflect a reduction in the use of professional judgment and discretion by lower-level staff. Rules may replace policies; procedures may gain wider usage. A general tightening designed to standardize staff behaviors and to minimize the risk of potential embarrassment within the task environment may be required on the part of the social worker as manager. Contingency planning takes on greater importance. Crises must be anticipated and plans made. For example, what if the manager is not authorized to replace staff members who leave or must delete a current service? Decisions that must be made are critical and cannot be made without considerable forethought.

Austerity also has the potential to affect greatly a manager's staffing functions. Hiring of new staff may cease to be a managerial task or, if a few staff members can be hired, they must be carefully selected to maximize their potential value to the organization. Increased reliance on nonprofessionals and on volunteers must be considered for their cost-saving benefits, but their implications for the quality of sevices must also be given careful thought. Staff dissatisfaction and turnover and the inability of the manager to rehire can result in loss of a critical balance between locals and cosmopolitans among employees. The manager must be prepared to react to unhealthy shifts in the makeup of staff groups.

The structure and nature of supervision may also require change. Some supervisory personnel may need to assume more responsibility for direct services to clients. Reduction in grade (RIFTS) with resultant pay decreases can cause serious morale problems that must be addressed. Those persons who remain in supervisory roles may need to expand the number of staff whom they supervise. Individuals must be identified who can function with greater autonomy, thereby freeing up precious supervisory time for those who really need it.

Managers, if they perceive a high level of staff capacity for autonomous functioning, may resort to greater use of functional authority to maximize use of supervisory resources. If they don't and they fear the consequences of the errors of subordinates, they may pull back and use more staff authority or even rely almost entirely on line authority. Overall, they may feel the need to reorganize the activities under their influence in order to create a more efficient operation.

Training (as we have defined it), while costly, cannot be ignored. It is critical as continuing staff must quickly learn to function in new roles, under new conditions, and with minimal errors. Other forms of continuing education (staff development and education) may need to be put on hold for a while because of limited funding.

Evaluation and elimination of less competent and less productive staff becomes an inevitable necessity. The survival of the organization may not allow for special considerations to staff who are not productive. For example, it may not be possible to allow a secretary who makes good coffee but does little else well to remain on the payroll until retirement. Of course, in many organizations, unionization or tenure, which places heavy value on seniority, may seriously limit the manager's capacity to eliminate incompetent personnel. This is a special source of frustration when personnel funding is limited and staff cutbacks must be made, especially if more competent but less senior staff have to go. Staff evaluations that carefully document performance become more important than ever for the manager in a time of economic austerity, as does the staff perception that a manager's decisions will be fair.

Whether staff will pull together to survive times of economic austerity or whether they will become acutely dissatisfied and even resign their jobs will depend heavily on the degree of trust that the manager is able to generate. Group cohesiveness, promoted by the manager, can increase the likelihood that staff will help each other to survive through difficult times. If the social worker as manager can provide recognition of an awareness of the problems that exist as well as appreciation for staff efforts under stress, this will help. Of course, if managers can also honestly describe the situation as only temporary, the chances of a positive response will be increased. As sacrifices by staff are inevitably required, it also helps if managers are perceived as making their own sacrifices and concessions for the good of the organization and its clients.

Austerity may require that fewer custom services to clients be offered. A consolidation of vehicles used to market services may also need to occur. Publicity and outreach, two desirable but costly activities, may have to be suspended.

In times of difficulty, people naturally seek good leadership. Social workers as managers may need to adapt their leadership style to accommodate more than the usual amount of consideration. If staff are being asked to perform tasks that are new to them, additional structure may also need to be provided. Staff input into decision making may be helpful to staff morale, but only if input is likely to be used. Participatory management may have to be used very sparingly. It suggests the presence of alternatives that may not exist during a time of austerity and is a costly use of staff and management time.

In short, during times of economic austerity the social worker as manager must be attuned to the special needs of the situation. Good managers must be even better and the tasks of management may require more time and effort than usual.

TIME PRESSURES

Human services managers, not unlike their business counterparts, often find themselves facing nearly impossible deadlines. For example, insensitive bureaucracies may impose deadlines for procedural changes that leave little time to prepare and to learn new methods of performing tasks. Or, little warning may precede the submission deadline for a grant proposal that, if funded, can assure the financial survival of the organization or at least the continued employment of staff. The social worker as manager who must plan, staff, organize, control, and lead work group activities so objectives are not just met but met by a certain date must provide a specialized form of management. As in times of austerity, good management practices and a reputation for fairness will go a long way toward successful management under time pressures.

While some adaptation in the manager's approaches to all the functions of management may be indicated, leadership deserves special focus. The kind of leadership needed by the work group operating under time pressures may be quite different from that which is otherwise effective. Specifically, an authoritarian style of leadership may be preferable and is more likely to be tolerated when staff are working against time. A "tell me what to do and I'll do it" attitude is likely to exist. Of course, acceptance of authoritarian leadership is dependent on staff acceptance of the value of successful meeting of deadlines, of the completion of the task itself and of its potential rewards. A work group that, for example, really doesn't want the work that would result from the awarding of a grant or contract cannot be expected to respond well to authoritarian leadership by the manager seeking to meet the deadline for its submission. There must be a common, desired goal. Authoritarian leadership is also more readily tolerated and even sought when the manager is successful in communicating why discussion, debate, and staff input into decision making are not desirable. If time constraints are viewed by staff as the reason for authoritarian leadership, it will be more likely accepted than if staff believe that they are simply perceived as having little knowledge and insight to contribute to decision making.

Confidence in the manager's ability to help the group to succeed in meeting the time deadline is critical. Reasonable people will work toward a desired goal if they perceive a high likelihood of success. They will not if they seriously doubt the manager's leadership abilities and his or her capacity to "pull it off." Past successes in meeting time deadlines and in producing quality results will help to ensure confidence in the manager's leadership. As always, trust is critical to successful management under conditions of time pressure. Especially important are trust in the motives of the manager in committing resources to the task and trust that work expectations for individual staff will not be excessive.

CHANGE

Change, like economic austerity, is a condition so common within human service organizations that it almost doesn't seem like a special situation. Certainly the nature of social work practice and those people that we serve guarantees that some level of change is almost always in the works. Some changes within organizations are greater than others. Changes range all the way from minor changes in policies or procedures to changes in the organization's services and clients served. *Any* change can represent a severe threat to service delivery if not addressed well by the social worker as manager.

Many different areas of change can affect the work environment in human service organizations. Historically, major changes in personnel have been common (a high rate of staff turnover). Dramatic changes in funding sources and amounts also have been frequent. Changes in technology (for example, strategies and methods of psychiatric treatment, approaches to rehabilitation of those in correctional facilities, community versus institution-based work with the mentally retarded) can require rapid and comprehensive change within organizations. The identification of new client groups (for example, AIDS patients and their families, battered husbands, the homeless, or the abused elderly) can lead to the creation of new structures and programs. Both rapid organizational growth and, more frequently, dramatic cutbacks in services created the need for changes within human service organizations during the 1980s.

Management during a time of rapid change requires an understanding of change itself, how people are likely to react to it, and how it is best facilitated by the manager. In recent years, most changes have not resulted from enlightened concern for improved service delivery. Funding cutbacks, threatened and curtailed programs, and conservative attacks on many fronts have compounded the need for change within organizations and accelerated it. Changes have occurred in services, structure, role, and personnel. Bewildered clients and staff have required the help of the social worker as manager to try to sort through changes resulting from growth in practice knowledge, administrative necessity, and/or governmental dictates and to assess their ultimate impact on services.[1]

Change and its implementation occupy an increasingly large percentage of managers' time. Managers require the theoretical preparation related to organizational change that Granvold has proposed; for example, "a comprehensive knowledge of organizational theory, administration, management and supervision."[2] Much of the discussion in earlier chapters of this text should be of help to managers who must deal with organizational change. Certain other specific insights, drawn from studies of organizations, seem particularly useful for the managers seeking to implement change successfully.

Writers in organizational theory stress the importance during times of change of organizational continuity and of preservation of the integrity of the organization as a system. This would seem to be especially critical for work in the human services. A manufacturing plant can close down to retool for the next year's model; a service delivery system cannot stop service delivery to prepare for change. Change must be absorbed while services continue. The basic character of the agency, and both its public and its internal identity, must not be altered to the point where critical relationships and linkages to other organizations and systems are jeopardized.

Times of change may shake the staff's usually solid commitment to the organization and its goals. As one observer noted, "It is at this juncture that conflict between the worker and the organization become most clearly manifest."[3] The relationship between superiors and subordinates may undergo unusual stress during times of change, and managers are natural targets for resentment and frustration that cannot easily be directed at the more esoteric "organization." Managers can anticipate this reaction, try to understand it, and put it into perspective. It helps to remember that managers constitute a "buffer zone which contains heretical confrontations between the individual and the social organizations."[4]

Managers need to communicate both stability and certainty[5] at the same time that they are working to implement change. Staff and clients must be helped to recognize that the objectives and essential characteristics of the agency, in most instances, will remain largely unchanged. If chaos and trauma are to be avoided, the manager must also assure that change is incremental and implemented in tolerable amounts.

The change strategies of the manager are more likely to succeed if the complete cycle of change is accomplished; that is, unfreezing, change, and refreezing.[6] This theory suggests that each step is a prerequisite to the next. Failure to achieve the ultimate change objective, where new behaviors or attitudes finally become comfortable and natural, is usually explained by inadequate attention to earlier stages, particularly to the first stage, unfreezing. In the unfreezing stage, the individual (staff member for our purposes) must become sufficiently uncomfortable with the old way of doing things to want to change as required. Unfreezing by the manager can be brought about through any combination of presentation of data, appeals to professional values and ethics, logic, bargaining, or even threats. Of course, the specific strategy or combination of strategies used will be a function of personality and style of the manager and of the worker. It also is a function of the time available for change, the scope and nature of the change desired, and the amount of flexibility inherent in the requirement for change. The second step, the change itself, will occur only after unfreezing has occurred.

The final stage of change (refreezing) can occur only if the manager provides adequate reinforcement of learning. The methods employed to accomplish this must be individualized to both manager and staff. They can take the form of a variety of rewards, compliments, and encouragement. Whenever possible, staff members should be encouraged to adopt a response to change based upon their own preferences from among possible alternatives to change implementation. In the ideal world, the new way of doing things will become so comfortable that it is no longer even identifiable as someone else's idea, suggestion, or directive. If this ideal can be achieved, resistance to the change will dissipate. The new way will appear to be only logical and natural to the worker.

Some changes occur largely as a response to problems identified by the manager. This happens naturally for social workers as managers because of the perspective on the organization that they possess.[7] Quite often, changes also will result from administrative pressures, fiscal expediency, or some other force not related to problems or needs identified by the manager. Managers may face differing levels of resistance and even outright hostility to changes that are not of their doing. The decision to use participative management approaches to change implementation, adversary approaches that assume that resistance will occur, or any other approach between these two extremes must be made based upon an accurate assessment of personnel. Specifically, managers must assess the staff's capacity, readiness, and motivation to change. Of course, they must also apply self-awareness (see Chapter 12) in selecting an approach that is within the range of their management style and their personality.

An error sometimes made by managers is the use of democratic decision making when the nature of the change or the time constraints required for its implementation do not allow for such a process. Most reasonable professionals can understand that some changes, particularly those that evolve from federal mandate or from some other higher power, leave little or no room for negotiation or creative input at the local level. What is infuriating to most staff is a request for input into how to implement change followed by no indication that suggestions were even considered. Real participation in decision making is appreciated. It can result in a more cooperative approach to change on the part of staff. But the manager who gives only the pretense of participation will quickly be found out and will be resented for wasting the time and honest efforts of staff. The transparency of the manager's manipulation will result in what workers perceive as an insult to their intelligence. Trust can be irreparably damaged. The likelihood of future resistance to participation, even that which is genuinely sought, will be increased.

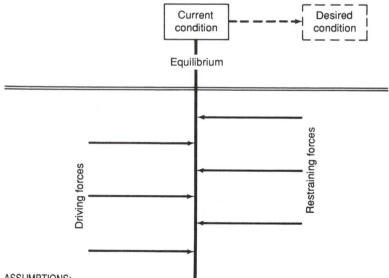

ASSUMPTIONS:
1. Most problems or situations have multiple causes.
2. Most problems or situations are held in equilibrium between driving and restraining forces.
3. We are more likely to accomplish changes if we identify these forces.
4. It is frequently easier to make changes by reducing restraining forces.

Figure 13.1. Force Field Analysis (Source: *Organization and Management: A Systems Approach*, by Fremont E. Kast and James E. Rosenzweig, 1974. By permission, McGraw-Hill Book Company [p. 590].)

The social worker as manager will need to select a supportive role appropriate for each individual staff member's needs. Close monitoring of staff behavior may be welcomed by one individual but resented by another. Some individuals may require frequent reassurance that they are meeting expectations while others may prefer to receive initial orientation and then be left alone while only occasionally "touching base" with the manager.

Resistance to Change

Change is almost certain to be resisted to some degree by at least some staff members. It is helpful to conceptualize the presence of both driving forces (for change) and resisting forces (against change) in all situations where change is attempted (see Figure 13.1). Change will be able to occur if either driving forces for change can be increased so as to overwhelm restraining forces, or if restraining forces are reduced. These are the two options available to the manager. The first is the far less desirable method, as increasing driving forces often only tends to increase resistance. A vicious circle and, frequently, a power struggle will result.[8] The supervisor who wishes to promote change will need to identify resistances that constitute restraining forces and to select some of the more promising ones as targets for reduction.

The literature suggests many reasons why staff might resist change.[9] The reasons overlap slightly, but taken individually or as a group, they represent formidable obstacles for the manager whose job is to facilitate change. The literature is also helpful in suggesting at least some strategies for successful presentation of change. It stresses the importance of a managerial climate supportive of change, an idea to which we will return after presentation of reasons for resistance. They include:

1. *Changes can appear to violate professional values.* Professionals can be expected to (and should) resist a change if they perceive it as a violation of client rights or professional ethics. (Managers should probably question their own position regarding the change if workers' concerns are found to have validity.)

2. *Inertia.* The laws of physics suggest that, unless challenged, we tend not to change. To do anything differently requires a conscious effort. For example, people, when not assigned seats, will almost always sit in the same place in classrooms or meetings. We drive the same route to work, even though other, equally good routes are available. Routines are comfortable and conserve energy; we resist change that might upset these routines.

3. *Change results in uncertainty.* People may know from experience that they can succeed in the old way of doing things; but there is no such assurance after change. Successful and competent staff are some-

times those most likely to resist changes that threaten to remove them from the favorable known and into the unknown. Less competent staff may be less resistive because they have less to lose from the journey into the unknown.

4. *Misunderstanding of the change.* Rumors can spread quickly and exaggerations often occur before changes are fully understood. Sometimes one or two possible but very unlikely effects of a proposed change are widely discussed as if they were a virtual certainty, creating resistance among even the most level-headed of staff. A "worst case scenario" is a frequent occurrence in staff discussions about a proposed change.

5. *Fear of loss.* Changes may result in obsolescence of many types. Feared loss of job is the most dramatic source of resistance, particularly among staff with little seniority. But loss of prestige (or fear of losing it) as the rules are changed can cause senior employees, currently valued for their knowledge and skills, to resist changes as vigorously as if their jobs were threatened.

6. *Antagonism toward the personnel proposing the change.* Even changes that would benefit staff are sometimes resisted because of a combination of distrust and dislike based upon previous interaction with the proposer. The person who proposes a change can pre-doom it to resistance, especially if staff do not trust the person.

7. *Lack of confidence in the manager.* A staff member may like the change and the proposer of change but resist change because of a lack of confidence in the manager's ability to implement it successfully. Does the manager have a history of reversing himself or herself or of being unable to troubleshoot when problems arise? If so, why waste the necessary effort to engage in the change? (This source of resistance was discussed earlier as a potential problem of the manager when time pressures are present.)

8. *Lack of participation.* Occasionally staff members may believe that they should have been involved in planning for change because of certain expertise or insights. Resentment at noninvolvement can result in resistance to change that might otherwise have been supported. Staff members may be seeking to save face among peers who may question, if the idea has merit, why weren't they involved in suggesting it?

9. *Failure to see the need.* A staff member may be genuinely unconvinced as to why the change represents a preferable alternative to present approaches. Old methods or procedures may have brought little criticism, so why change? Inability to perceive the need for different behaviors can be a major source of resistance.

10. *Timing.* Some changes, normally acceptable, may be resisted in time

of overwork, interpersonal conflict, or when they come too soon after other changes. The tolerance for change of individuals (as well as organizations) has its limits.

11. *Social relationships.* A staff member may resist change if it threatens existing social interaction, of great importance to individuals in organizations. If the change requires that the staff member no longer eat lunch with a friend or walk to the parking lot with a co-worker, great resistance to a perfectly rational change may be observed.

12. *Change can upset power balances.* Factions and cliques almost inevitably exist. Some very dismayed managers have observed that everyone may resist a good change suggestion if individuals on both sides believe that the other side may stand to benefit more than their group.

13. *Informal organizational pressure.* In order to maintain friendships, staff members may resist a change that they might otherwise support. Disapproval of the manager is probably preferable to peer ostracism or other sanctions for most staff.

14. *Belief that change equals criticism.* If not tactfully presented, change may be perceived as a message that staff haven't been doing well enough in the past. It may be seen as an effort to correct some deficiency in an individual's job performance.

15. *Change resistance itself has benefits.* Poor workers have found that by organizing change resistance they can (a) make new friends among co-workers of varying competencies and (b) divert attention away from their work performance.

16. *Resistance because of one's basic personality.* Some staff members are just negative and pessimistic by nature. They have taken on the role of resident foot-dragger and will resist any change because they think it is expected of them.

Many of the sources of resistance to change have one thing in common—they result from an individual's recognition or belief that change may depreciate one's value, particularly the value of one's experience. As we suggested in item 3 above, those individuals upon whom a supervisor usually depends may become leaders in resistance unless they can be convinced that their skills and knowledge will continue to be valued in the future. It is true that change is somewhat of an equalizer among staff members. All must start new and prove themselves competent again.

It may be some consolation for the social worker as manager to remember that a massive, undifferentiated resistance to change rarely occurs in any but its earliest stages.[10] After a while there exist advocates for nearly any change among staff, as long as the change is rationally conceived and well-intentioned.

Implementing Change

Social workers as managers cannot delegate the responsibility for explaining about changes and working with staff to help them adjust to them. It is not enough simply to announce changes and wait for them to occur. When changes are announced, staff may listen politely but they may not feel comfortable in asking about areas of their concern. They will not have had the time and opportunity to talk to others about the changes or to think through how their job might be affected.

Both the preparation for and the implementation of change are ongoing processes for the manager. In discussing the role of the supervisor, Kadushin suggests conditions under which successful change is most likely to occur:

> Change is best accomplished if supervisees participate from the start in planning the change, if they are informed early of the nature of the planned change, if the change is introduced slowly, preferably with some initial trial effort, if expectations are made clear and understandable, if the change is in line with perceived agency norms and objectives, if there is some assurance that the change will have the effect predicted, if the administration, including supervisors, communicate strong conviction in the desirability of the change, if there is some appreciation of, and empathy with the difficulties that change generates for the staff, and if provision is made to reduce the costs of change to the staff.[11]

Tact is imperative in all areas of interpersonal management behavior, but especially in presentation of change. Change should be presented in such a way that it does not suggest a criticism of staff. Ideally, change should be viewed as a process worked out together by intelligent and dedicated professionals. The social worker as manager will need to explain the need for change and its most likely ramifications in an honest, straightforward manner. If possible, the limits of threat to job security and possible loss of status should be discussed. Assurances of training and support should be given only if they can be offered. If new role expectations are to result, specific criteria for job performance must be developed in such a way that accusations of arbitrariness and favoritism can be avoided.[12] Changes can be viewed by staff as an opportunity to reward and to punish; it must be clear that the manager has no intention of engaging in either behavior.

The manager should also review with staff what the profession has learned about clients and their likely reactions to change. This will help to reinforce the perception that the needs of clients remain the number-one priority. Staff should be reminded that clients, particularly those in the public sector, may be operating at the security-need level. Clients live with almost daily threats to mental health care, food stamps, Social Security, and other services as reflected and reported in the media. Clients may perceive any change as a first step in some master plan for withdrawal of assistance and/or services. Feelings of clients may surface in the form of distrust or anger with the slightest provocation if the change appears to represent a threat to security.[13] The manager may need to help staff to anticipate, understand, and handle these reactions so that they will not become just an additional source of frustration and conflict during the time of transition.

What if managers themselves are doubtful regarding the merits of the change? Kadushin suggests that "responsibility of acting in defense of agency policy can be a source of considerable dissatisfaction."[14] Defending any agency policy to staff can be difficult; if the manager does not agree with it, the job can be made worse. As we have emphasized repeatedly, attempts at duplicity are useless and ill-advised. Staff members who have worked any length of time with the manager should know the manager well and would certainly know if he or she was trying to sell a change that they themselves opposed. Honesty in the form of healthy skepticism in presenting a change to a worker may be acceptable in presenting changes to mature professionals. Skepticism communicates doubt about the value of a change but withholds judgment pending time and an honest effort. It says, "I have some questions about the change myself, but I will give it a 100 percent effort and evaluate its viability at some later date. I expect you to do the same."

Skepticism can be healthy and appropriate. It is *not* the same as cynicism. Cynicism tends to ridicule the change, exaggerate its shortcomings, and downplay its virtues. It implies a hope for failure. It says, "I think the change is ridiculous, don't think it will work, and it is probably in your best interest to agree with me. I will not work hard toward its achievement and really wish that you would join me in sabotaging it, or at least in hoping that my prediction will be fulfilled."

Skepticism is normal among thinking, concerned managers. If held within check, it provides the potential for a valid assessment of change. Cynicism is never helpful during times of change. It pre-dooms the best of ideas and innovations by helping to reinforce staff negativism. It can help to achieve a self-fulfilling prophecy.

Problems relating to change, including resistance, can be avoided or at least lessened through prevention. The difficulties inherent in the task of change implementation can be greatly reduced if the manager has been successful in creating and maintaining a managerial climate conducive to change. To do this, the social worker as manager must constantly stress the inevitability of change. This message should be communicated at the time that a staff member is hired and reinforced regularly thereafter. Change must be portrayed as inevitable and desirable, given the nature of social work services and the changing service needs of members of our society. Presented this way, it is less likely to be perceived as criticism of past staff performance when it occurs.

Changes should be discussed freely, as soon as they are perceived as very likely to occur. Staff should not be allowed to become embarrassed by learning of changes from media or clients. Information regarding changes should not be withheld or used by managers to manipulate behavior. A manager with a reputation for open, equal-access presentation of change plans is more likely to be trusted when changes occur than one who "plays it close to the vest." A manager's credibility is important for effective communication about the change to occur. What is said must be heard accurately, without second-guessing or reading between the lines by staff. The motives and sincerity of the manager should be unquestioned. A manager with a policy and a reputation for fair treatment of people during change will be trusted in subsequent times of change.

Support during times of change is also important, and several questions must be addressed. Is adequate support offered? Are tooling-up and training-time allowances for staff adequate and reasonable? Are mistakes, unavoidable whenever new learning is occurring, handled with consideration? Are they examined for their learning potential, or used as ammunition to punish staff? Will evaluations reflect an understanding of the difficulty of first-time efforts? During times of change, the manager should be known to adhere to an evaluation policy that rates workers on effort put forward and on growth. Specifically, the evaluation of the individual should be at least partially independent of the success or failure of the change itself while new behaviors are being learned.

The social worker as manager must maintain an optimistic stance toward change and should communicate a belief that most changes ultimately have positive results. Fearful, anxious discussions regarding change with staff can be harmful to morale; it is better if they never occur. During times of change, the manager can and should be a role model for other staff, maintaining an attitude that change is essential for growth and ever-improving services to clients.

The existence of a sense of humor regarding change is essential. In our society, changes within human service organizations sometimes occur so rapidly that all of us will feel overwhelmed at times. Sound insights regarding change, tempered with a sense of humor, will help the manager to promote an organizational climate where change is viewed as both tolerable and challenging.[15]

STAGNATION

Change is good and necessary for social systems. Ideally, the manager can help to maintain a condition similar to the biological state of homeostasis in which the basic identity of the organization and its units is maintained while the organization changes over time to accommodate a changing environment. As long as change occurs in reasonable dosages and not too rapidly, its presence makes for a stimulating and a growth-promoting work environment.

Insufficient change (stagnation) is a problem encountered by managers less frequently than too much or too rapid change, but it can be just as harmful to group morale and staff functioning. Some types of organizations are particularly vulnerable to the problem of not enough change. They may offer services that, because of their nature, have changed little over time. They may offer desirable employment with excellent employee benefits and job security that result in little employee turnover or replacement. They may be neither growing nor in danger of cutting back, just there doing what society expects of them.

In a basically static organization, the manager faces the challenge of keeping staff stimulated by their work and continuing to invest large amounts of energy into it. This may not be easy. Staff may know their job and perform it well. There may be more than enough technical competence, but a shortage of inspiration, creativity, and enthusiasm. For the social worker as manager in such situations, appropriate use of continuing education is indicated. Staff should be encouraged to grow and to seek new and different types of work activities. A reward system that values new behaviors (for example, a senior staff person who begins to write for publication or to present papers at conferences) will communicate to others that new approaches to one's job and the incorporation of new ideas are important. Professional growth and the obligation to share knowledge with others should be portrayed as career-long activities.

Occasionally, job changes within the organization should be considered if staff are agreeable. A helping person with less experience in a given practice method but with the enthusiasm of discovery can sometimes offer clients more than a seasoned veteran for whom effective performance of a service has become second nature.

The organization may appear to be static on the outside: solid, well established, and accepted by the community. But it does not have to be undynamic within. The manager who makes a practice of rewarding innovation and positive change and who is constantly seeking to bring new ideas and innovations into the organization can help to fight stagnation. If new and challenging ideas cannot enter the organization through the presence of new staff, old staff can be renewed by providing for contact with the outside.

MANAGEMENT SUCCESSION

Few social workers assume their management responsibilities within a brand-new organization. They take over from another person whose past management style, personality, and behaviors have left an "act to follow." Inevitably, the influence of a manager's predecessor will continue to be felt for a period of time after that person has moved on to other responsibilities. Depending on how his or her predecessor was perceived by staff, the new manager will face certain potential difficulties that will impact on the manager's ability to perform the functions of management.

Following the Beloved Previous Manager

In assuming management duties previously performed by another individual who was highly liked and respected, the social worker may face an uphill battle. Comparisons, usually negative ones, are inevitable, at least in the beginning. Even if the previous manager had a few faults, they are likely to be forgotten or glossed over by a loyal staff. The Rebecca Myth,[16] or the tendency to idealize a former leader and to regard the new one with suspicion and resentment, is a common problem. When the new manager makes mistakes, as he or she most certainly will while functioning in a new role, staff may tend openly to express feelings of disgust and longing for the return of the manager's predecessor. If the previous manager is still employed within the organization, the problem can be exacerbated as staff members continue to hope for that individual's return.

The difficulties inherent in succeeding a beloved manager logically would seem to dissipate with time. But they may not. Especially if differences in management style are very obvious, problems can get worse rather than better. In most circumstances it is advisable for the manager to state the obvious to staff, and the sooner the better. As soon as it is apparent that negative comparisons, previous loyalties, and unrealistic antagonisms toward the new manager are beginning to interfere with productive interaction between the manager and one or more staff, the problem should be addressed. Staff may need to be reminded as clearly and directly as possible that the manager is indeed a different person with a different style and a different way of doing things. This point may have to be made repeatedly. If staff expect to be treated fairly and objectively by the manager (and this is a reasonable expectation), they will need also to treat the manager as a unique individual. They should be told this. The previous manager should *not* be disparaged in any way; this would only increase staff resentment. But every effort should be made to discourage comparisons of managers by staff.

As we discussed in the previous chapter, a social worker's management style should not be a carefully kept secret. It should be communicated regularly to staff members, allowing his or her behavior to become predictable over time. It is, therefore, not enough for new managers simply to state that they are different from a previous, beloved manager. Examples of their management behaviors and philosophies should be stated and practiced. The sooner that their differences from the previous manager are known and (it is hoped) appreciated, the quicker the shadow of the previous manager will fade. Managers, like any other professionals, have a right to be judged fairly on their own performance without reference to others. This is a principle that is consistent with social work practice values. It is usually well received and accepted by staff within the helping professions.

Following the Despised Previous Manager

The social worker who succeeds another manager who was generally disliked and resented would seem to be in store for an easy time. Assuming that most staff are dedicated and competent and that the cause of resentment was primarily the manager's shortcomings, the new manager cannot help but look good. Indeed, a "honeymoon period" is likely to occur. Flattery will abound. Compliments on the new manager's approach to his or her work (usually accompanied by comparisons with the previous manager's approaches) are likely to be common. Compliments can be very nice to hear, can be quite seductive, and can give the new manager a false sense of security and of how simple good management really is. But the honeymoon period may not last for long.

When the new manager makes his or her first mistake, a tolerant attitude may prevail as staff remind themselves and each other that "it used to be much worse." But as the new manager continues to make demands and occasionally to offend (an inevitable part of the job of managing), harsh judgment may follow and resentment may quickly build. Similarities between the old and new managers will be pointed out with expressions of disgust and disappointment. Some similarities *will* exist, in part because the previous manager performed some tasks according to sound management principles. Left unchecked, generalizations about the new manager may begin to occur as the person is erroneously perceived by staff as "really no different" from the old manager.

A tendency to become quickly disillusioned with and to turn against the new manager should come as no great surprise to the social worker as manager. As practitioners, we know that people develop patterns of behavior. Among other things, they tend to place the blame for difficulties and discomforts that occur either on themselves or on others. If their tendency was to blame the previous manager for problems on the job, they can easily fall back into this old pattern in their relationship with the new manager. They will tend to fault the new manager whether justified or not.

Addressing the potential problems inherent in succeeding a despised manager involves a process very similar to that used in situations where one must succeed a manager who was very well liked. In both instances, comparison and an inability of staff to recognize and respond to differences are the enemies that must be confronted and neutralized. Shortly after assuming the functions of manager, it may be necessary to remind staff that the new manager is different, but not *totally* different, from the previous occupant of the job. Defense of the predecessor's practices (those that were good) should be open and frequent, and complaints, criticism, and, especially, ridicule of the former manager's work should be discouraged. It is tempting and easy to listen to "war stories" about the previous manager's blunders. A shortcut to acceptance by staff can be achieved by joining in the derogation of their work. But this is a bad practice that will eventually cost the new manager more than it will gain. Not only is such behavior unprofessional but it also sets a poor example for staff by saying that it is okay to disparage other members of the team. Besides, neither the new manager nor other staff members are in a position to really know or understand the reasoning behind the previous manager's decisions and behaviors.

Whether the previous manager was beloved, despised, or somewhere in between, the message to staff should be clear. It should be expressed quickly after assuming a management role and reinforced verbally and by the new manager's behavior. The message is this:

> The previous manager's actions are history. They made their contribution to organizational goal achievement and I plan to make mine. I am a different individual with a different style, but I will sometimes act the same as my predecessor and differently at other times because I believe it to be the best way to get the job done. I want you [staff] to get to know me and how I work and to ask questions to help you—and me—to better understand what I do and why I do it. I will evaluate you and appreciate you each as individuals and I expect you to do the same for me.

Promotion into a Managerial Role

The social worker assuming management functions is not always new to the work environment and to continuing staff. In fact, a more likely situation in human service organizations involves the movement of employees into a role that requires them to spend more of their time managing (promotion). In the new role, they may have administrative authority over those who previously occupied the same or comparable position as themselves on the administrative chart. In short, the new manager's subordinates were peers last week. This situation has its special problems that can interfere with the manager's capacity to perform a job effectively.

In all situations, as human beings we tend to develop patterns of relating to each other. We establish levels of intimacy and familiarity that are appropriate for the respective roles that we occupy. Close friendships, intense rivalries, good-natured ridicule, and even flirtation are not unusual among peers in a work environment. As long as they exist by mutual consent and do not interfere with the productivity of the persons involved (conditions *not* present in situations such as sexual harassment on the job), these relationships between peers can be productive and can make the job a little more enjoyable.

When an individual assumes greater management responsibility and acquires administrative authority over former peers, the previous relationships necessarily will change. As a social worker assumes new responsibilities and functions as a manager, new patterns of relationship will have to be developed. It is often difficult for the social worker as manager to make the transition. It can also be difficult for the former peers who are now subordinates. The isolation that we described in Chapter 12 as a stress of management may be especially felt during the time of transition.

In order to make necessary changes in relationships (depending on the situation and the people involved, they are not always that dramatic), managers must be sure themselves and communicate clearly to staff that it is the needs of the organization and not their own intrapersonal needs that dictate the changes. Managers must not allow staff to conclude that they are now "too good for their old friends" or impressed with themselves and their new status. On the other hand, reality dictates that managers probably cannot remain "one of the gang," and efforts to do so may result in staff resentment.

Sensitive professional staff members generally recognize the need for establishing new relationships when one of their peers assumes more management responsibilities. While some might occasionally use old friendships to manipulate the manager or to seek special favors, there is usually a greater tendency among former peers to create a greater social distance than is necessary. This is a time of experimentation for all parties involved as staff and manager renegotiate their relationships with each other. Staff will not, for example, express complaints about "the administration" as freely around the manager as they previously did. In turn, some topics (such as the work of other staff) that the manager previously discussed are no longer suitable for even casual discussion between manager and staff.

Some initial overreaction to the assumption of new roles is likely on the part of both the manager and former peers. This is probably desirable in the long run. It tends to underline the reality that managers and those over whom they have authority are not and cannot be peers. Reassurances that mutual respect and friendships with the manager need not end will come a little later as relationships gradually become reestablished under new guidelines.

Bitterness among some staff over the loss of a "special" friendship with the new manager can usually be expected. If both individuals sought the manager's job, it is likely to be even more intense. Even if the former close friend remains a confidant for a while after the manager assumes his or her new responsibilities, this cannot be allowed to continue. The importance of the manager being perceived as objective and trustworthy in dealing with staff precludes the existence of any staff member who has greater access to or who appears to be treated in a special way by the manager.

Inevitably, a former peer and close friend will be critical of the manager's style or behavior. Cut off from the manager's perspective on events within the organization, such individuals will disagree about a decision or the way that the manager performs some aspect of the job. Their critical response to the manager *may* result at least in part from their sense of alienation. But their criticism and disagreement, if expressed openly and logically, may also be an indication that the difficult interpersonal transition has been accomplished and that the manager is now open to the second-guessing and critique by staff that comes with the job of manager. A good manager will usually assume the latter, will objectively evaluate the criticism of the other individual, and will value the person's opinion. Managers will resist the temptation to dismiss the criticism as bitterness over a lost interpersonal closeness and turn instead to those individuals who are all too ready with praise. Such people are present within virtually every work environment and will sometimes seek to achieve personal gain from the role transitions that are required when a peer assumes greater management responsibility.

Managers who possess the values, knowledge, and skills of the social worker will be ideally suited to handle the interpersonal problems that can occur when they find themselves with administrative authority over those who were previously their peers. They should be able to assess and to understand the motivation behind staff reactions and behaviors. But this does not guarantee that the transition will be an easy one.

Becoming a Manager

Regardless of the line that they occupy on an organizational chart, the social worker who is a successful manager learns to think like a manager and to take on the personal identity of a manager. Unless an individual makes a conscious effort to become a manager, he or she can easily "slip in and out" of the manager's hat, perform the functions of the manager, but never really perform them comfortably or particularly well.

How can social workers *become* managers? For one thing, they can read and remain current on new theory and developments within the field of management. They can subscribe to and read one or more journals (within social work and/or in related fields such as business) and can even make their own contributions to knowledge by writing articles for professional journals.

Association with other managers also helps the social worker to think and feel like a manager. This can occur informally in semi-social situations. It can also take place at seminars and symposia that provide knowledge and skills to new and experienced managers. Some managers have chosen to set up groups consisting of other managers and themselves who regularly get together to discuss topics of management relevance over lunch or at other times. The group members (frequently from a variety of organizations) learn from each other as they form valuable managers' networks.

As we have indicated throughout this book, successful management, just like other areas of social work practice, involves the application of knowledge, skills, and appropriate values. The social worker who approaches management with determination and commitment and who is willing to make the necessary effort to become a competent manager as well as a competent social worker will have a high likelihood for success as he or she performs the functions of management.

SUMMARY

In Chapter 13 we added still another dimension to our understanding of management, namely situational factors that sometimes influence social workers as they attempt to perform the functions of management. Examples of situational variables included some of those that are very familiar to workers in the helping professions: economic austerity, time pressures, change, and stagnation. As in earlier chapters, both trust in the manager and in the manager's objectivity and fairness were emphasized as absolutely essential to successful management under these conditions.

Two special problems of management succession, namely following the beloved manager and succeeding the despised manager, were discussed. Managers were advised to emphasize their own identity and style of management to staff in order to minimize problems of succession that are likely to occur. Interpersonal barriers to good management that sometimes arise when an individual is given authority over former peers were noted. The importance of renegotiation of roles in such circumstances was emphasized. Hints for helping the social worker to think and feel like a manager were provided.

In Chapter 13 and throughout this text, we have emphasized the importance of managers understanding and using their knowledge of human behavior. Words and phrases that have occurred regularly in our discussion are trust, objectivity, focus on goal attainment, and the client as the prime beneficiary. These terms, which have been proposed as synonymous with good management, should be familiar to social workers. Good management and good social work practice are much more similar than dissimilar. The knowledge, values, and skills of our profession will help to provide what is needed for the social worker to become an effective manager. It is hoped that this text will also make a contribution.

REFERENCES

1. Robert W. Weinbach, "Implementing Change: Insights and Strategies for the Supervisor, *Social Work*, 29 (1984):282–286.
2. Donald K. Granvold, "Training Social Work Supervisors to Meet Organizational and Worker Objectives," *Journal of Education for Social Work*, 14 (1978):44.
3. Alfred Kadushin, *Supervision in Social Work* (New York: Columbia University Press, 1976), p. 68.
4. Dwight Harshbarger, "The Individual and the Social Order: Notes on the Management of Heresy and Deviance in Complex Organizations," *Human Relations*, 26(2) (1973):264.
5. James D. Thompson, *Organizations in Action* (New York: McGraw-Hill, 1967), pp. 148–149.
6. Kurt Lewin, *Field Theory in Social Science* (New York: Harper & Row, 1951).
7. Harleigh B. Trecker, *Social Work Administration* (New York: Association Press, 1971), pp. 172–173.
8. Fremont E. Kast and James E. Rosenzweig, *Organization and Management: A Systems Approach* (New York: McGraw-Hill, 1974), pp. 590–591.
9. Steven Kerr and Elaine B. Kerr, "Why Your Employees Resist Perfectly Rational Changes," *Hospital Financial Management*, 26 (January 1972):4–6; Bernard Neugeboren, *Organization, Policy and Practice in the Human Services*, (New York: Longman, 1985), pp. 182–188.
10. Herman Resnick, "Tasks in Changing the Organization from Within (COFW)." *Administration in Social Work*, 2 (1978):36–37.
11. Kadushin, *Supervision in Social Work,* op. cit., p. 70.
12. Edward Lowenstein et al., "The Management of Organizational Change: Some Findings and Suggestions," *Public Welfare, 31*(1) (Winter 1973):56–57.
13. Arthur Pierson, "Social Work Techniques with the Poor, *Social Casework, 51*(8) (October 1970):481–485.
14. Kadushin, *Supervision in Social Work,* op. cit., p. 69.
15. The preceding discussion of "Change" (pp. 297–306) is from *Social Work.* Copyright 1984, National Association of Social Workers, Inc. Portions of this article have appeared in *Social Work*, 29, 3 (March 1984), pp. 282–286.
16. Alvin M. Gouldner, *Patterns of Industrial Bureaucracy* (Glencoe, IL: The Free Press, 1954), p. 79.

ADDITIONAL READINGS

Gortner, H., Mahler, J., and Nicholson, J. *Organization Theory: A Public Perspective*. Chicago: Dorsey Press, 1987.
Kotin, J., and Sharaf, M. "Management Succession Revisited." In *Social Administration*, Simon Slavin, ed. New York: Haworth Press, 1978, pp. 165–169.
Munson, C. *An Introduction to Clinical Social Work Supervision*. New York: Haworth Press, 1983, pp. 191–208.

Neugeboren, B. *Organization, Policy and Practice in the Human Services*. New York: Longman, 1985, pp. 179–210.

Resnick, H., and Patti, R., eds. *Change from Within: Humanizing Social Welfare Organizations*. Philadelphia: Temple University Press, 1980.

White, S. *Managing Health and Human Services Programs*. New York: Free Press, 1981, pp. 1–13.

Worchel, P. "Trust and Distrust." In *The Social Psychology of Intergroup Relations*, W. Austin and S. Worchel, eds. Belmont, CA: Wadsworth, 1979, pp. 174–187.

Epilogue

Early in this book we described good management as those activities that help to create a work environment conducive to productivity and that result in attainment of organizational goals. We attempted, little by little, to piece together the characteristics of that ideal work environment. Years ago, other authors described the characteristics of the ideal, healthy organization and its antithesis, the unhealthy organization. This description presented verbatim serves as an excellent summary of many of the points made in this book:

SOME CHARACTERISTICS OF
UNHEALTHY AND HEALTHY ORGANIZATIONS[1]

Unhealthy
1. Little personal investment in organizational objectives except at top levels.

2. People in the organization see things going wrong and do nothing about it. Nobody volunteers. Mistakes and problems are habitually hidden or shelved. People talk about office troubles at home or in the halls, not with those involved.

Healthy
1. Objectives are widely shared by the members and there is a strong and consistent flow of energy toward those objectives.

2. People feel free to signal their awareness of difficulties because they expect the problems to be dealt with and they are optimistic that they can be solved.

Unhealthy

3. Extraneous factors complicate problem-solving. Status and boxes on the organization chart are more important than solving the problem. There is an excessive concern with management as a customer, instead of the real customer. People treat each other in a formal and polite manner that masks issues—especially with the boss. Nonconformity is frowned upon.

4. People at the top try to control as many decisions as possible. They become bottlenecks, and make decisions with inadequate information and advice. People complain about managers' irrational decisions.

5. Managers feel alone in trying to get things done. Somehow orders, policies, and procedures don't get carried out as intended.

6. The judgment of people lower down in the organization is not respected outside the narrow limits of their jobs.

7. Personal needs and feelings are side issues.

8. People compete when they need to collaborate. They are very jealous of their area of responsibility. Seeking or accepting help is felt to be a sign of weakness. Offering help is unthought of. They distrust each other's motives and speak poorly of one another; the manager tolerates this.

Healthy

3. Problem-solving is highly pragmatic. In attacking problems, people work informally and are not preoccupied with status, territory, or second-guessing "what higher management will think." The boss is frequently challenged. A great deal of nonconforming behavior is tolerated.

4. The points of decision-making are determined by such factors as ability, sense of responsibility, availability of information, work load, timing, and requirements for professional and management development. Organizational level as such is not considered a factor.

5. There is a noticeable sense of team play in planning, in performance, and in discipline—in short, a sharing of responsibility.

6. The judgment of people lower down in the organization is respected.

7. The range of problems tackled includes personal needs and human relationships.

8. Collaboration is freely entered into. People readily request the help of others and are willing to give in turn. Ways of helping one another are highly developed. Individuals and groups compete with one another, but they do so fairly and in the direction of a shared goal.

Unhealthy	*Healthy*
9. When there is a crisis, people withdraw or start blaming one another.	9. When there is a crisis, the people quickly band together in work until the crisis departs.
10. Conflict is mostly covert and managed by office politics and other games, or there are interminable and irreconcilable arguments.	10. Conflicts are considered important to decision-making and personal growth. They are dealt with effectively, in the open. People say what they want and expect others to do the same.
11. Learning is difficult. People don't approach their peers to learn from them, but have to learn by their own mistakes; they reject the experience of others. They get little feedback on performance, and much of that is not helpful.	11. There is a great deal of on-the-job learning based on a willingness to give, seek, and use feedback and advice. People see themselves and others as capable of significant personal development and growth.
12. Feedback is avoided.	12. Joint critique of progress is routine.
13. Relationships are contaminated by maskmanship and image building. People feel alone and lack concern for one another. There is an undercurrent of fear.	13. Relationships are honest. People do care about one another and do not feel alone.
14. People feel locked into their jobs. They feel stale and bored but constrained by the need for security. Their behavior, for example in staff meetings, is listless and docile. It's not much fun. They get their kicks elsewhere.	14. People are "turned on" and highly involved by choice. They are optimistic. The workplace is important and fun (why not?).
15. The manager is a prescribing father to the organization.	15. Leadership is flexible, shifting in style and person to suit the situation.
16. The manager tightly controls small expenditures and demands excessive justification. He allows little freedom for making mistakes.	16. There is a high degree of trust among people and a sense of freedom and mutual responsibility. People generally know what is important to the organization and what isn't.
17. Minimizing risk has a very high value.	17. Risk is accepted as a condition of growth and change.

Unhealthy	*Healthy*
18. "One mistake and you're out."	18. "What can we learn from each mistake?"
19. Poor perfomance is glossed over or handled arbitrarily.	19. Poor performance is confronted, and a joint resolution sought.
20. Organization structure, policies, and procedures encumber the organization. People take refuge in policies and procedures, and play games with organization structure.	20. Organization structure, procedures, and policies are fashioned to help people get the job done and to protect the long-term health of the organization, not to give each bureaucrat his due. They are also readily changed.
21. Tradition!	21. There is a sense of order, and yet a high rate of innovation. Old methods are questioned and often give way.
22. Innovation is not widespread but in the hands of a few.	22. The organization itself adapts swiftly to opportunities or other changes in its marketplace because every pair of eyes is watching and every head is anticipating the future.
23. People swallow their frustrations: "I can do nothing. It's *their* responsibility to save the ship."	23. Frustrations are the call to action. "It's my/our responsibility to save the ship."

REFERENCE

1. J. Fordyce and R. Weil, *Managing with People*, © 1979, Addison-Wesley Publishing Co., Inc., Reading, Massachusetts. Pages 11–14. Reprinted with permission.

Index